REAL WORLD

MACRO

TWENTY-EIGHTH EDITION

EDITED BY AMY GLUCKMAN, JOHN MILLER, BRYAN SNYDER,

CHRIS STURR, AND THE *DOLLARS & SENSE* COLLECTIVE

REAL WORLD MACRO, 28th edition

ISBN: 978-1-878585-86-8

Published by:
Economic Affairs Bureau, Inc. d/b/a *Dollars & Sense*
29 Winter Street, Boston, MA 02108
617-447-2177; dollars@dollarsandsense.org.
For order information, contact Economic Affairs Bureau or visit: www.dollarsandsense.org.

Real World Macro is edited by the *Dollars & Sense* Collective, which also publishes *Dollars & Sense* magazine and the classroom books *Real World Micro, The Economic Crisis Reader, Current Economic Issues, Real World Globalization, Real World Latin America, Real World Labor, Real World Banking and Finance, The Wealth Inequality Reader, The Environment in Crisis, Introduction to Political Economy, Unlevel Playing Fields: Understanding Wage Inequality and Discrimination, Striking a Balance: Work, Family, Life,* and *Grassroots Journalism.*

The 2011 *Dollars & Sense* Collective:
Arpita Banerjee, Ben Collins, Katharine Davies, Amy Gluckman, Ben Greenberg, Vera Kelsey-Watts, James McBride, John Miller, Larry Peterson, Linda Pinkow, Paul Piwko, Smriti Rao, Alejandro Reuss, Bryan Snyder, Chris Sturr, and Jeanne Winner.

Co-editors of this volume: Amy Gluckman, John Miller, Bryan Snyder, and Chris Sturr
Editorial assistant: Maureen Kellett
Production assistant: Maureen Kellett
Design and layout: Chris Sturr, Katharine Davies

Printed in U.S.A.

CONTENTS

CHAPTER 4 • FISCAL POLICY, DEFICITS, AND DEBT

CHAPTER 5 • MONETARY POLICY AND FINANCIAL MARKETS

CHAPTER 6 • UNEMPLOYMENT AND INFLATION

CHAPTER 7 • PERSPECTIVES ON MACROECONOMIC POLICY

CHAPTER 8 • INTERNATIONAL TRADE AND FINANCE

INTRODUCTION:
THE TWO ECONOMIES

It sometimes seems that the United States has not one, but two economies. The first economy exists in economics textbooks and in the minds of many elected officials. It is an economy in which no one is unemployed for long, families are rewarded with an ever-improving standard of living, and anyone who works hard can live the American Dream. In this economy, people are free and roughly equal, and each individual carefully looks after him- or herself, making voluntary choices to advance their own economic interests. Government has some limited roles in this world, but it is increasingly marginal, since the macroeconomy is a self-regulating system of wealth generation.

The second economy is described in the writings of progressives, environmentalists, union supporters, and consumer advocates—as well as honest business writers who recognize that the real world does not always conform to textbook models. This second economy features vast disparities of income, wealth, and power. It is an economy where economic instability and downward mobility are facts of life. Jobs disappear, workers suffer long spells of unemployment, and new jobs seldom afford the same standard of living as those lost. And, periodically, market economies unravel, much like today. As for the government, it sometimes adopts policies that ameliorate the abuses of capitalism, and other times does just the opposite, but it is always an active and essential participant in economic life.

If you are reading this introduction, you are probably a student in an introductory college course in macroeconomics. Your textbook will introduce you to the first economy, the harmonious world of self-regulating stability. *Real World Macro* will introduce you to the second.

Why "Real World" Macro?

A standard economics textbook is full of powerful concepts. It is also, by its nature, a limited window on the economy. What is taught in most introductory macroeconomics courses today is a relatively narrow set of concepts. Inspired by classical economic theory, most textbooks depict an inherently stable economy in little need of government intervention. But fifty years ago, textbooks were very different. Keynesian economic theory, which holds that government action can and must stabilize

1

modern monetized economies, occupied a central place in introductory textbooks. Even Marxist economics, with its piercing analysis of class structure and instability in capitalism, appeared regularly on the pages of those textbooks. The contraction of economics education has turned some introductory courses into little more than celebrations of today's economy as "the best of all possible worlds."

Real World Macro, designed as a supplement to a standard macroeconomics textbook, is dedicated to widening the scope of economic inquiry. Its articles rub mainstream theory up against reality by providing vivid, real-world illustrations of economic concepts. And where most texts uncritically present the key assumptions and propositions of traditional macroeconomic theory, *Real World Macro* asks provocative questions: What are alternative propositions about how the economy operates and who it serves? What difference do such propositions make? What might actually constitute the best of all possible macroeconomic worlds?

For instance, *Real World Macro* questions the conventional wisdom that economic growth lifts all boats or benefits all of us. While mainstream textbooks readily allow that economic growth has not benefited us all to the same degree, we go further and ask, "Who benefits from economic growth and by how much?" "Who has been left behind by the economic growth of the last two decades?" The answers are quite disturbing. Today, economic growth, when it occurs, benefits far fewer of us than it did just a few decades ago. Economic growth in the last decade did more to boost profits and less to lift wages than any economic upswing since World War II. The truth is that spreading the benefits of economic growth more widely, through public policy intended to improve the lot of most people in the work-a-day world, would not only make our economy more equitable, but would start to resolve today's economic crisis.

Today's economy is emerging from what is widely recognized to be the worst crisis since the Great Depression. But you might not know that the day-to-day operation of the market economy, left to its own devices, brought on that crisis. Unregulated financial markets, the concentration of political and social power in the hands of powerful business interests, and gaping inequality pushed most people into debt at the same time that it fueled speculative excesses sparking the crisis. Explaining how and why that happened and what to do about it is every responsible economist's job.

Today, with unemployment still at its highest levels in seven decades, government needs to step up and become the economy's employer of last resort. Similarly, with the financial system having been shaken to the core, the government needs to step in and properly regulate financial markets and institutions. Those two steps will go a long way toward improving the lot of those who have fallen on hard times and will reduce the likelihood of future crises. Finally, genuine and sustained full employment, with unemployment rates as low as 2%, will lead to "a major reduction in the incidence of poverty, homelessness, sickness, and crime," as William Vickery, the Nobel-prize winning economist, once argued. We think that policies like this, and the alternative propositions that lie behind them, are worth debating—and that requires hearing a range of views.

What's in This Book

Real World Macro is organized to follow the outline of a standard economics text. Each chapter leads off with a brief introduction, including study questions for the chapter, and then provides several short articles from *Dollars & Sense* magazine that illustrate the chapter's key concepts—77 articles in all. In many cases, the articles have been updated or otherwise edited to heighten their relevance.

Here is a quick walk through the chapters.

Chapter 1, Measuring Economic Performance, starts off the volume by taking a critical look at the standard measures of economic activity. What do those measures actually tell us about the quality of life in today's economy, and what crucial aspects of economic life do they leave uncounted? This chapter also looks at why the latest ups and downs of the business cycle, the current crisis and the anemic economic expansion that preceded it, and the feeble current recovery have left so many in dire straits.

Chapter 2, Wealth, Inequality, and Poverty, examines these three end products of economic growth. *Dollars & Sense* authors show who is accumulating wealth and who isn't, and argue that inequality is not a prerequisite to economic growth, but rather a major contributor to today's economic crisis.

Chapter 3, Savings and Investment, peers inside the pump house of economic growth and comes up with some probing questions. How are stock prices determined? Who owns them; who doesn't? What caused the mortgage crisis and what can be done about it? Finally, what public policies have proven track records of encouraging investment and promoting stable and functional housing and financial markets.

Chapter 4, Fiscal Policy, Deficits, and Debt, assesses current government spending and tax policy. The chapter's authors examine the Obama stimulus package, arguing that more needs to be done and that unprecedented "peacetime" deficits should not be an impediment to government action. But more pro-rich tax cuts and yet another military buildup, policies that helped get us into this fiscal and economic mess, will not get us out of it. Nor will privatizing Social Security. Rather what is needed, according to our authors, are stronger social programs, expanded and greener infrastructure investment, taxes designed to dampen speculation, and the government's commitment to be the economy's employer of last resort.

Chapter 5, Monetary Policy and Financial Markets, explains how the Federal Reserve Board (aka "the Fed") conducts monetary policy and how its actions contributed to today's financial crisis. It details the Fed's efforts to bail out investment banks and other financial institutions brought down in the crisis and how those institutions have been transformed in the process, becoming yet larger and more powerful. The chapter asks whose interests the Fed serves: those who hold financial assets, or the rest of us? The authors also address how the Fed and financial institutions can be transformed to better serve our needs.

Chapter 6, Unemployment and Inflation, reveals how macroeconomic policy that prioritizes price stability over full employment puts the interests of business owners and bondholders ahead of the interests of workers. The chapter begins with a critique of the "natural rate" of unemployment concept. It then looks at the causes of the persistent and long-term unemployment that is the hallmark of today's economy. The chapter also discusses the effects of unemployment, inflation, productivity growth, and the spread of offshore outsourcing on workers' bargaining power and living standards and what might be done to improve their position.

Chapter 7, Perspectives on Macroeconomic Policy, introduces alternatives to classical-inspired macroeconomic theory. It begins with a critical analysis of the New Classical economists' claim that the macroeconomy is inherently stable, and then discusses what Keynes actually said about the practice of fiscal policy in an economic crisis. The chapter also develops Marxist and feminist perspectives on macroeconomic theory and policy, and on neoliberal economic policymaking. Finally, the chapter explains in everyday language how the economy fell into crisis during 2008 and 2009, uncovering the causes of the crisis and its roots in the inequalities of the real economy and the unregulated excesses of the housing and financial markets.

Chapter 8, International Trade and Finance, critically assesses the prevailing neoliberal policy prescriptions for the global economy. The articles criticize globalization based on "free trade" and financial liberalization, looking closely at its effects on economic growth, global inequality and poverty, and "economic freedom." They consider the role of the U.S. dollar in the global economy. They also look at the recent uprising of Chinese workers and the China's role in the world economy. Finally, the articles report on the pervasive inequality of the global economy and the effects of global trade agreements on workers in the developing world and assess proposals to improve international labor standards and to eliminate sweatshop conditions.

Chapter 1

MEASURING ECONOMIC PERFORMANCE

INTRODUCTION

Most macroeconomics textbooks begin with a snapshot of today's economy as seen through the lens of the standard measures of economic performance. This chapter provides a different view of today's economy, one far more critical of current economic policy and performance, one that asks what the standard measures of economic performance really tell us.

In "When is a Recession Over?" economist John Miller explains how the National Bureau of Economic Research identifies the waves of business activity that constitute the business cycle. Miller traces the course of this decade's business cycle from a feeble expansion, which did little to improve the standard of living of most people, to the Great Recession, which has left millions of people in dire straits. He asks when the disastrous downturn will end in the real world, not just in the record book of economists (Article 1.1). Not for quite a while, according to economist Fred Moseley. He points out that high unemployment is likely to be with us for quite a while, if job creation in the recovery from the Great Recession mirrors that in the two most recent recoveries, those following the 1991 and 2001 recessions (Article 1.4). And that makes today a dismal time to graduate from college, as recent college graduate and *Dollars & Sense* intern Katherine Faherty reports (Article 1.6). Finally economist Alejandro Reuss demonstrates that the U.S economy today is producing as much output per person as it had back in 2005, before the crisis hit, yet employing fewer workers for fewer hours. Ironically this increase in labor productivity has done little to boost the standard of living of most workers and left many without jobs (Article 1.2).

Miller's next article shows how the official unemployment rate understates the extent of unemployment. Correcting the official rate for underemployed workers and discouraged job-seekers, the unemployment rate reaches a 68-year high (Article 1.3). Job losses in the Great Recession hit male-dominated jobs especially hard, as economist Heather Boushey documents. She calls for more support for female workers who increasingly find themselves in the role of family breadwinners (Article 1.5).

Economists' measures of inflation also suffer from serious deficiencies. Joshua Holland documents how recent changes in the Consumer Price Index, the best-known inflation measure, dramatically reduced the "official" rate of inflation. Those changes spruced up reported economic performance and reduced the cost-of-living adjustments received by seniors on Social Security and others (Article 1.9).

Real GDP, or Gross Domestic Product adjusted for inflation, is the economist's measure of the value of economic output. Increases in real GDP define economic growth, and for economists, rising real GDP per capita shows that a nation's standard of living is improving. Our authors are not convinced. Jonathan Rowe argues that GDP actually counts environmental destruction, worsening health, and ruinous overconsumption as contributions to economic growth and national well-being (Article 1.7). While Rowe worries that GDP includes the wrong things, Lena Graber and John Miller discuss what it excludes: work in the home that is essential to economic well-being. They report that counting home-based work—from cleaning to child care—would add 33% to 112% to the GDP of industrialized economies and even more to the GDP of developing economies (Article 1.8).

Discussion Questions

1. (Articles 1.1, 1.4) How does the National Bureau of Economic Research determine when a recession has begun and when it is over? Under what conditions would you declare the Great Recession over?

2. (Article 1.1) How does the expansion of last decade's business cycle compare to the typical expansion since World War II? How does the recent contraction compare to the typical postwar recession?

3. (Article 1.2) How is it that real GDP per capita in the United States could have returned its levels in 2005 before the crisis and so many be seemingly worse off than six years ago?

4. (Article 1.3) What are the shortcomings of the official (U-3) unemployment rate? Using the data in the table, calculate the more comprehensive U-6 unemployment rate for February 2010. Be sure to show each step of the conversion from the U-3 unemployment rate to the U-6 rate.

5. (Articles 1.4 and 1.6) How do the job prospects of recent college graduates and others looking for work in the current economic recovery compare with the job prospects of those who were looking for work in previous economic recoveries?

6. (Article 1.5) Why did men's unemployment increase more quickly than women's unemployment in the recent economic contraction? What are some possible policy responses that could address this gender disparity in unemployment levels? Is it important or desirable to do so?

7. (Article 1.7) How is GDP measured, and what does it represent? What are Rowe's criticisms of GDP? Do you find them convincing?

8. (Article 1.7) Rowe discusses the Genuine Progress Indicator (GPI) as an alternative measure of economic progress. What are the differences between GDP per capita and the GPI? Which do you think provides a better measure of economic progress and why?

9. (Article 1.8) Wages for housework might sound outlandish, but there are several economic justifications for valuing work in the home. What are they? In your opinion, should this work be paid? If so, by whom?

10. (Article 1.8) Suppose we decided that home-based work should be included in macroeconomic measures. How should it be counted?

11. (Article 1.9) How did the changes in the Consumer Price Index in the 1990s lower the reported rate of inflation? In your opinion, which of those changes, if any, were justified? Why?

Article 1.1

WHEN IS A RECESSION OVER?

BY JOHN MILLER
April 2010

Yogi Berra, the Yankee great, once said about a baseball game, "It ain't over until it's over." If Yogi had been talking about the Great Recession, he would have said, "It ain't over even when it's over."

As far back as September 2009, when the economy was first showing signs of a return to economic growth, Federal Reserve Board chair Ben Bernanke called the Great Recession of 2008 and 2009 "likely over" and declared that the U.S. economy had begun a recovery. He quickly added that the economy would continue to lose jobs. And it did—with the unemployment rate climbing to double digits later in the fall.

When economists at the National Bureau of Economic Research (NBER), a private research organization designated by the Commerce Department as the nation's arbiter of the business cycle, officially declare the Great Recession over, they will likely identify September 2009 as its end date and the beginning of the economic recovery. But people surely will not believe the recession is over, despite the NBER's pronouncement, until jobs return and their economic well-being improves. And that could be quite a while.

Let's look at what economists mean when they declare that a recession is over and a recovery is underway, and why that announcement is unlikely to mean that happy days are here again for most people in the work-a-day economy, let alone those looking for work.

A Date with a Business Cycle

The NBER tracks the ebb and flow of economic activity , from the trough of a recession to the peak of an expansion and back down into a trough. In the first phase of the cycle—the expansion—the economy grows as companies produce more goods and services and hire more workers. In the second phase, companies produce fewer goods and throw workers out of their jobs, and the economy contracts. The NBER has identified nine complete business cycles in the U.S. economy since World War II (see table).

The NBER's Dating Committee, currently a group of seven economists, admits that the dating process is "fuzzy." The committee has no rigid rules for determining the start or end of a business cycle. The members reach a consensus after studying a broad array of macroeconomic indicators. In short, they eyeball the data. The committee's founders worked with 46 indicators. Today the NBER's Business Conditions Digest lists around 1,000 measures. Members study the GDP, industrial production, employment, real income, trade, several interest rates, and personal income, as well as several composite indices, including the index of coincident indicators, which measures employment, income, output, and sales.

The Great Recession shows how hard it is to date business cycles. Economists define a recession as two consecutive quarters of negative real growth, or declining output, as measured by GDP. But applying even this shorthand definition is not easy. It takes time for the federal government to publish official GDP figures. And the committee looks for several indicators to show that a decline in activity has spread across the economy before it feels comfortable declaring a recession.

In December 2008, the economy had not yet suffered two consecutive quarters of negative economic growth. Nonetheless, mounting monthly job losses convinced the NBER to declare that a recession had begun a whole year earlier, in December 2007. The economy had lost jobs every month from December 2007 on—the longest period of job-loss since the Great Depression.

If dating the onset of a recession is difficult, dating its end is even harder. Economists agree even less on how to determine when a recession finishes and an expansion begins. They generally divide expansions into two phases. In the first phase, the economy recovers the ground it lost—in terms of jobs, output, and other measures—during the recession. When the economy grows beyond its pre-recession levels, the expansion enters its second phase. Economists declare a recession over only when they know a recovery has reached this second phase. They then date the expansion back to when the economy began recouping the lost output. Should the

U.S. BUSINESS CYCLES, 1949-2010

Trough	Peak	Trough	Expansion (months)	Contraction (months)	Full Cycle (months)
Oct 1949	July 1953	Aug 1954	45	13	58
Aug 1954	July 1957	Apr 1958	35	9	44
Apr 1958	May 1960	Feb 1961	25	9	34
Feb 1961	Nov 1969	Nov 1970	105	12	117
Nov 1970	Dec 1973	Mar 1975	37	16	53
Mar 1975	Jan 1980	July 1980	57	6	63
July 1980	July 1981	Nov 1982	12	16	28
Nov 1982	July 1990	Mar 1991	93	8	101
Mar 1991	Mar 2001	Nov 2001	120	8	128
Nov 2001	Dec 2007	??	73	?	?

Source: Economic Cycle Research Institute, National Bureau of Economic Research.

recovery falter and the economy start to contract again before it reaches that second phase, economists consider the recession to have continued.

As of April 2010, the NBER had yet to declare the Great Recession officially over. At this point, economic growth had already returned to the U.S. economy. Beginning in the third quarter of 2009, the economy stopped contracting and then grew substantially in the last three months of 2009, boosted by businesses restocking their depleted inventories. By that measure the Great Recession seemed to have ended. But job losses continued until March 2010, when a surge of temporary hiring, mostly of government census workers, along with the stanching of job losses across the private sector and modest job growth in some sectors, produced the first non-trivial monthly net job gains since November 2007. The official unemployment rate still hovered near double-digit levels. If the NBER, in the name of consistency, uses employment to date the end of the recession as it did to date its onset, then the recession surely continued into 2010.

The Business Cycle and the Zero Decade

Beyond that, the NBER measures the ups and downs of a business cycle, not how the economy affects people's economic well-being. Over the last decade, a lengthy economic expansion did less to improve the economic well-being of most people and the ensuing contraction did more to decimate the economic well-being of most people than any business cycle since the Great Depression of the 1930s.

Economic expansions are supposed to improve our life-chances, not just swell the economy. But not this decade's.

Beginning in November 2001, the economy grew for 73 months or just over six years, reaching a peak in December 2007. That is longer than the 57-month average duration of other postwar expansions. But GDP grew at an anemic annual rate of 2.5% in the 2001-07 expansion, far below the 4.3% average for post-World War II expansions.

Job creation was even more dismal than output growth during the expansion. From 2001 to the end of 2007 the economy added jobs more slowly than during any other postwar expansion—only at about one-third the rate posted by the average postwar expansion. With sluggish economic growth and few new jobs, economic expansion did little to lift incomes, alleviate poverty, or improve the economic well-being of all but the best-off.

• For the first time in the postwar period, median household income (corrected for inflation) at the peak of this expansion was still below its level at the previous peak in 2000.

• For the first time in a postwar expansion, the poverty rate failed to decline.

• After correcting for inflation, wages and salaries grew at just half the rate of the average postwar expansion.

As these figures make clear, the combination of sluggish economic growth, few new jobs, and stagnant wages and incomes had left many people behind long before the economy collapsed in 2008 and intensified their hardship.

And the Great Recession did make things worse, far worse. A frightening financial panic, a virulent housing bust, and plummeting economic output left export-driven economies and financial centers across the globe in crisis. Japan and Eurozone major exporters suffered steep declines in output, as did Asian tigers such as Singapore. Even the red-hot Chinese economy hit the pause button in the first half of 2009. U.S. autoworkers, European and U.S. finance workers, Japanese electronics workers, Chinese garment workers, and Indian software workers lost their jobs as world export markets dried up.

In the United States, by March 2010, the recession had wiped out 8.4 million jobs. Construction, manufacturing of all sorts, and the financial industry, all male-dominated sectors, were especially hard hit. Retail sales, typically more recession-proof, were decimated as well. Electronics giant Circuit City closed its doors, and the venerable Filene's Basement laid off scores of workers.

After reviewing the feeble expansion and devastating recession that followed, economist and *New York Times* columnist Paul Krugman suggested that we call the first decade of this century "the zero decade." Job creation for the decade was basically zero. Zero economic gains for the typical family. Zero gains for homeowners. And zero gains on the stock market, even before taking inflation into account.

Dim Prospects for a Genuine Recovery

Even though the economy has begun growing again, the prospects of lower unemployment rates anytime soon remain bleak. Following the last downturn, in 2001, the U.S. economy took more than three years to replace the jobs lost in the recession. If the current sluggish recovery creates jobs at the same pace as the last one, it would take 86 months, or until December 2016, to replace all of the jobs lost in this downturn.

In that case, many people will endure great economic suffering long after the date the NBER declares the official end of the recession.

Sources: "Determination of the December 2007 Peak in Economic Activity," National Bureau of Economic Research, Dec. 11, 2008, www.nber.org/cycles/dec2008.html; Sara Murray and Ann Zimmerman, "Bernanke: Recession Likely Over—Fed Chief Doesn't Expect Many New Jobs to Appear Soon: Retail Sales Climb 2.7%," *Wall Street Journal*, Sept. 16, 2009; Paul Krugman, "The Big Zero," *New York Times*, Dec. 28, 2009; Josh Bivens and John Irons, "A Feeble Recovery," Economic Policy Institute Briefing Paper #214; Aviva Aron-Dine, Chad Stone, and Richard Kogan, "How Robust Is the Current Economic Expansion?," Center on Budget and Policy Priorities, Jan. 14, 2008.

Article 1.2

SAME OUTPUT + FEWER HOURS = ECONOMIC CRISIS?

Today's economic crisis is less about the quantity of output than the distribution of income and leisure.

BY ALEJANDRO REUSS
September/October 2010

During the current crisis, real (inflation-adjusted) GDP per capita for the U.S. economy declined for six consecutive quarters. It has since increased for four consecutive quarters, though the figure for the second quarter of this year remains well below the pre-crisis peak. This might seem like an indication that real GDP per capita is a good measure of economic well-being. We're in a severe crisis, everyone thinks things are bad, and GDP is down. Even though GDP has been growing again recently, we're still not back to the level of prosperity before the crisis.

Consider, however, that real GDP per capita for the second quarter of 2010 was higher than it was in the second quarter of 2005—and in fact for every previous quarter in U.S. history. Now, hardly anyone thinks that things are better in the United States today, economically, than they were in 2005—or that, excepting about three years between 2005 and 2008, things are better economically now than they have ever been before. It can't be that our only problem is having fewer goods and services (as measured by real GDP per capita), since similar levels back in 2005 were not considered a disaster.

One alternative explanation is that the level of GDP does not matter as much as the change in GDP. Maybe we've gotten used to higher levels of affluence, and now miss the extra goods and services. At first blush, that doesn't seem like the issue

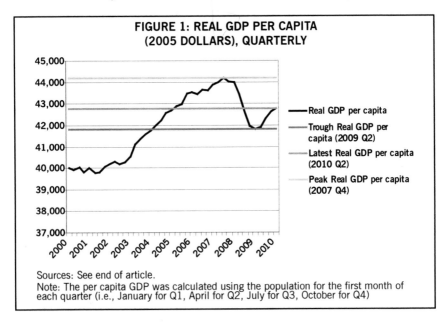

FIGURE 1: REAL GDP PER CAPITA (2005 DOLLARS), QUARTERLY

— Real GDP per capita

⋯ Trough Real GDP per capita (2009 Q2)

⋯ Latest Real GDP per capita (2010 Q2)

⋯ Peak Real GDP per capita (2007 Q4)

Sources: See end of article.
Note: The per capita GDP was calculated using the population for the first month of each quarter (i.e., January for Q1, April for Q2, July for Q3, October for Q4)

either. The difference between the pre-crisis peak in real per capita GDP and even the trough of the recession is surprisingly small, less than 6%. Many people, counting on their incomes not only to remain at the higher (pre-crisis) level but to keep increasing, however, undoubtedly made spending decisions that are now difficult to reverse—like buying a house of a certain size and location or sending one's children to a certain college. Even if the decline in incomes were spread evenly across the population, for those living close to the limits of their means, it might be difficult to "scale back."

Of course, the impact of the recession has not fallen equally on everyone, and that is much closer to the crux of the problem. The unemployed have borne the brunt of the recession. The official number of unemployed people in the U.S. labor force dipped below 6.5 million just before the recession, in the first half of 2007. Today, it stands at nearly 15 million. For the unemployed themselves, this means not only a loss of income but also of an important source of personal identity and self-esteem, of a major part of their social lives, and of future career prospects. For millions of others, mass unemployment means increased insecurity and anxiety about their own futures.

Real U.S. GDP in 2009 was nearly the same as for 2006—just under $13 trillion. (The Bureau of Economic Analysis reports figures of $12.8806 trillion (in 2005 dollars) for 2009 and $12.9762 trillion for 2006). While these measures of total output produced are nearly identical, the figures for the number of workers employed and the number of work hours required to produce that output are strikingly different. In 2006, about 138.7 million workers (16 years and over) were employed, compared to only about 134.4 million in 2009. The total time spent at work, by all workers 16 and over, was about 18 billion hours less in 2009 than in 2006.

Producing the same quantity of output in fewer hours means that labor productivity has increased. There are several possible causes: increased intensity or pace of work (or "speed up"), increased worker skill, improved production methods, or greater quantity or quality of tools used. During the current crisis, multiple factors may have been involved. High unemployment itself reduces workers' bar

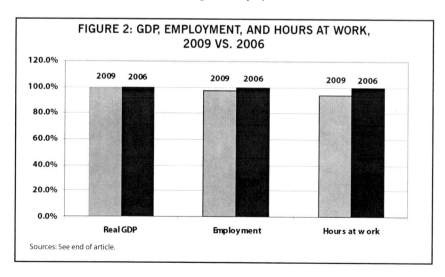

FIGURE 2: GDP, EMPLOYMENT, AND HOURS AT WORK, 2009 VS. 2006

Sources: See end of article.

gaining power. Employers know that there are plenty of unemployed workers who are desperate for a job. Meanwhile, workers who do have jobs are desperate to keep them. This makes it relatively easy for employers to push down wages or demand a faster pace of work. It may also be that workers' average skill level has increased, if for no other reason than that less-skilled workers are disproportionately represented among those laid off. There may also have been innovation in production methods and technology that explain part of this productivity increase.

Increased productivity is not intrinsically a bad thing. It can mean being able to produce more goods—and a higher "standard of living"—without additional work hours. Increases in productivity have been a major source of economic growth in capitalist economies. As long as demand for goods and services keeps pace with rising productive capacity, productivity increases generally fuel rising real output. In principle, increased productivity can also mean being able to produce the same amount of goods in fewer work hours. Fewer work hours can mean more leisure time and a higher quality of life.

The increase in productivity over the last few years, however, has not been matched by an increase in demand for goods. Overall demand now stands around the same level as a few years ago and at a significantly lower level than at the peak of the last boom, even as overall productive capacity has increased. The managers of capitalist enterprises do not set workers to produce goods just because they can, but because they (the managers) believe that this output can be sold at a profit. The decline in demand, then, means that some productive resources go unused—in the form of shuttered factories and idle machinery, and a dramatic decrease in employment and work hours.

This decline in work hours has not been distributed sensibly or equitably among all members of the population—in the form of a shorter regular working week, more vacation time, or an earlier retirement. Therefore, we have the strange paradox that today the U.S. economy produces about as much output (real goods and services) as it did in 2006, and requires billions fewer work hours to do so, which sounds like a good thing. And yet, as a result, we find ourselves in a disastrous crisis—millions have lost their jobs and main sources of income, while uncounted millions live in fear of a similar fate.

Karl Marx and Friedrich Engels wrote, over 150 years ago, that capitalist economies, in which goods are produced only if they can be sold, and will not be produced at all if they cannot be sold for a profit, had created a new kind of economic crisis: "an epidemic that, in all earlier epochs, would have seemed an absurdity—the epidemic of over-production." Economic crises in previous societies, Marx and Engels understood, had been caused by an inadequate supply of goods, the results of drought, flood, war, and the like. In capitalist societies, for the first time in human history, there appeared crises as a result not of too little productive capacity, but of too much—"too much civilization, too much means of subsistence, too much industry, too much commerce."

Marx and Engels spoke of "too much means of subsistence, too much industry" with a sort of grim irony. They did not mean that there was really too much productive power compared to peoples' needs or wants, but compared to their buying power (what later economists termed "effective demand"). It is certainly questionable whether endlessly producing more goods and services is really the key to making us better off—as opposed to enjoying greater leisure time, a more pleasant environment, greater economic security, less economic inequality, greater autonomy at work, etc. However, there's no reason that the development of greater productive power must exact the enormous toll of human suffering that it can—and, very often, does—in a capitalist economy.

Sources: Bureau of Labor Statistics, Labor Force Statistics (CPS), Table A-1, "Employment status of the civilian population by sex and age," www.bls.gov/webapps/legacy/cpsatab1.htm; Bureau of Labor Statistics, "Persons at work in agriculture and related and in nonagricultural industries by hours of work," 2006, ftp.bls.gov/pub/special.requests/lf/aa2006/aat19.txt; Bureau of Labor Statistics, "Persons at work in agriculture and related and in nonagricultural industries by hours of work," 2009, ftp.bls.gov/pub/special.requests/lf/aat19.txt; Bureau of Economic Analysis, Table 1.1.6. Real Gross Domestic Product, Chained Dollars (A) (Q), bea.gov/national/nipaweb/SelectTable.asp; Census Bureau, Table 1. "Monthly Population Estimates for the United States, April 1, 2000, to July 1, 2010," www.census.gov/popest/national/NA-EST2009-01.html; Karl Marx and Friedrich Engels, *The Communist Manifesto.*

Article 1.3

THE *REAL* UNEMPLOYMENT RATE HITS A 68-YEAR HIGH

BY JOHN MILLER

July/August 2009; updated April 2010

Although you have to dig into the statistics to know it, unemployment in the United States over the last year has been worse than at any time since the end of the Great Depression.

From December 2007, when the recession began, to February 2010, 8.4 million U.S. workers lost their jobs. The big three U.S. automakers closed plants and let white-collar workers go too. Heavy equipment manufacturer Caterpillar and giant banking conglomerate Citigroup both laid off thousands of workers. Alcoa, the aluminum maker, let workers go. Computer maker Dell and express shipper DHL both canned many of their workers. Circuit City, the leading electronics retailer, went out of business, costing its 40,000 workers their jobs. Lawyers in large national firms got the ax. Even on Sesame Street, workers lost their jobs.

The official unemployment rate peaked at 10.1% in October 2009—higher than in all but the 1982 recession, the worst since World War II. The current downturn pushed up unemployment rates more than any other postwar recession, even including the double dip recessions of the early 1980s (see figure, next page).

Some groups of workers faced even higher official unemployment rates. As of February 2010, unemployment rates for black, Hispanic, and teenage workers were 15.8%, 12.4% and 25.0% respectively. Workers without a high-school diploma confronted a 15.6% unemployment rate, while the unemployment rate for workers with just a high-school diploma was 10.5%. More than one in four (26.5%) construction workers were unemployed. In Michigan, the hardest hit state, unemployment was at 14.1% in February 2010. Unemployment rates in fifteen other states and the District of Columbia were at double-digit levels as well.

As bad as they are, these figures dramatically understate the true extent of unemployment. First, they exclude anyone without a job who is ready to work but has not actively looked for a job in the previous four weeks. The Bureau of Labor Statistics classifies such workers as "marginally at-

THE FEBRUARY 2010 UNEMPLOYMENT PICTURE (DATA IN THOUSANDS, NOT SEASONALLY ADJUSTED)	
Civilian Labor Force	153,194
Employed	137,203
Unemployed	15,991
Marginally Attached Workers	2,527
Discouraged workers	1,204
Reasons other than discouragement	1,323
Part-time for Economic Reasons	9,282
Slack work or business conditions	6,708
Could only find part-time work	2,252

Sources: Bureau of Labor Statistics, Tables A-1, A-8. A-15, A-16. Data are not seasonally adjusted because seasonally adjusted data for marginally attached workers are not available.

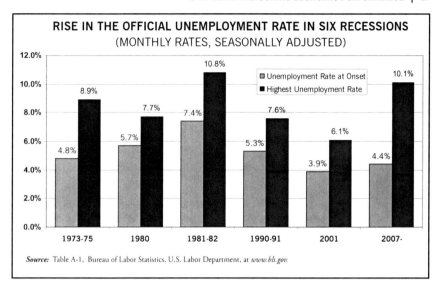

RISE IN THE OFFICIAL UNEMPLOYMENT RATE IN SIX RECESSIONS
(MONTHLY RATES, SEASONALLY ADJUSTED)

Source: Table A-1, Bureau of Labor Statistics, U.S. Labor Department, at *www.bls.gov.*

tached to the labor force" so long as they have looked for work within the last year. Marginally attached workers include so-called discouraged workers who have given up looking for job-related reasons, plus others who have given up for reasons such as school and family responsibilities, ill health, or transportation problems.

Second, the official unemployment rate leaves out part-time workers looking for full-time work: part-time workers are "employed" even if they work as little as one hour a week. The vast majority of people working part-time involuntarily have had their hours cut due to slack or unfavorable business conditions. The rest could only find part-time work.

To its credit, the BLS has developed alternative unemployment measures that go a long way toward correcting the shortcomings of the official rate. The broadest alternative measure, called U-6, counts as unemployed "marginally attached workers" as well as those employed "part time for economic reasons."

When those adjustments are taken into account for February 2010, the unemployment rate soars to 16.8%. While below its peak of 17.4% back in October 2009, the February 2010 adjusted unemployment rate still represents a historic high. Leaving aside the current downturn, it is higher than at any time back to 1994, when the BLS introduced the U-6 measure. It is also higher than the BLS's earlier and yet broader adjusted unemployment rate, the U-7, ever was. The BLS began calculating the U-7 rate in 1976 but discontinued it in 1994 in favor of the U-6 rate. In the 1982 recession the U-7 reached 15.3%, its highest level. In fact, no bout of unemployment since the last year of the Great Depression in 1941 would have produced an adjusted unemployment rate as high as what workers in the United States have suffered over the last year.

Why is the real unemployment rate so much higher than the official, or U-3, rate? First, forced part-time work in the last year reached higher levels than any all the way back to 1956 and including the 1982 recession. In February 2010, 8.8 million workers were forced to work part time for economic reasons. Forced part-timers are concentrated in retail, food services, and construction; about a quarter of them

---

Calculating the Real Unemployment Rate

The BLS calculates the official unemployment rate, U-3, as the number of unemployed as a percentage of the civilian labor force. The civilian labor force consists of employed workers plus the officially unemployed, those without jobs who are available to work and have looked for a job in the last four weeks. Applying the data found in the table yields an official unemployment rate of 10.4%, or a seasonally adjusted rate of 9.7%, for February 2010.

The comprehensive U-6 unemployment rate adjusts the official rate by adding marginally attached workers and workers forced to work part time for economic reasons to the officially unemployed. To find the U-6 rate the BLS takes that higher unemployment count and divides it by the official civilian labor force plus the number of marginally attached workers. (No adjustment is necessary for forced part-time workers since they are already counted in the official labor force as employed workers.)

Accounting for the large number of marginally attached workers and those working part-time for economic reasons raises the count of unemployed to 27.8 million workers for February 2010. Those numbers push up the U-6 unemployment rate to 17.9%, or a seasonally adjusted rate of 16.8%.

---

are young workers between 16 and 24. The number of discouraged workers is high today as well. In February 2010, the BLS counted 2.5 million "marginally attached" workers. That is the highest number since 1994, when the agency introduced this measure (although it was matched by the January 2010 number).

While the economy may be escaping the throes of a catastrophic downturn, unemployment, no matter how it's measured, will continue to impose devastating costs on society and on those without a job or unable to find full-time work.

Sources: U.S. Dept. of Labor, "The Unemployment Rate and Beyond: Alternative Measures of Labor Underutilization," *Issues in Labor Statistics,* June 2008; John E. Bregger and Steven E. Haugen, "BLS introduces new range of alternative unemployment measures," *Monthly Labor Review,* October 1995.

Article 1.4

UNEMPLOYMENT: HOW BAD FOR HOW LONG?

The outlook is grim unless there is serious government intervention.

BY FRED MOSELEY
March/April 2010

How bad will unemployment be in the months and years ahead? One way to answer that question is to look at how long it took the U.S. economy to regain jobs in previous post-war recessions. By this measure, the employment outlook is quite grim.

Since the recession began in December 2007, the U.S. economy has lost 8.4 million jobs, or 6.2% of employment, over 25 months. This is the biggest decline in the postwar period, and the recession is not yet over.

In none of the other recessions since World War II has the economy lost such a large percentage of its employment base. None of the other recessions in the figure below show such a high cumulative percent decline of employment. (The vertical axis shows the percentage cumulative decline from the beginning of the recession, i.e., the month employment peaks; the horizontal axis shows the number of months from the peak of employment.)

The 1981-82 recession gives us some hint of what would happen if the U.S. economy falls into "double-dip" recession in the years ahead, which many economists consider a distinct possibility. The total decline of employment in the recession of 1981-82 was only 3% and the jobs lost in recession were recovered in just 11 months. Nonetheless, the rate of unemployment reached a peak of 10.8%, the highest of the postwar period. That was because the 1981-82 recession followed close on the heels of a recession in 1980. In this "double-dip" recession, the two declines of employment were smaller than the current decline and yet the combined effect was a rate of unemployment of almost 11%.

The two most recent recessions, 1990 and 2001, look distinctly different from the 1981-82 recession. These were mild recessions and the declines of employment were only 1.5% and 2% respectively. But for both of these recessions, the recoveries were disturbingly slow and it took much longer to replace the jobs lost in the recession than after previous recessions. It took 30 months in the early 1990s and 47 months in the early 2000s to return to the previous peak in employment. In these "jobless recoveries," the rate of unemployment continued to increase for months after the recovery of employment began.

The main causes of the slow growth of employment in these recent jobless recoveries were the slow growth of output, or Gross Domestic Product (GDP), and business emphasis on cost-cutting, especially labor costs. The latter factor led companies to force existing employees to work harder and produce more output rather than hire more workers as demand picked up. The emphasis on cost-cutting also led companies to outsource operations to low-wage areas of the world.

These factors are still very much present in the U.S. economy today. It is widely forecast that GDP growth in the years ahead will be very slow by historical comparisons (perhaps even slower than in the previous two jobless recoveries) and business seems as eager as ever to cut labor costs. In addition, as demand picks up, companies will first increase the hours of the large number of existing part-time workers before they start hiring new workers. So this is shaping up to be the mother of all jobless recoveries, which will result in high rates of unemployment for years to come.

How long will it take for employment in the U.S. economy to return to its previous peak? The graph suggests that it will take at least 48 months. Of course, returning to the previous peak would not guarantee that the rate of unemployment would decline because of the growth of the labor force. But increasing employment at least makes it possible that the rate of unemployment might start to decline.

How many months will it take to recover the 8.4 million jobs that have been lost? That depends on the average monthly increase of employment in the months and years ahead. If the average monthly increase of employment turns out to be 200,000 per month—which would be more than twice as fast as in the last recovery—then it would take 42 more months to return to the previous peak employment.

Even if the average monthly increase turns out to be 300,000—and this is surely over-optimistic—it would take 28 more months, or until mid-2012, to return to the previous peak employment. In this scenario, what would the rate of unemployment likely be in mid-2012? Employment would be the same as in December 2007. At that time, the official rate of unemployment was 5%. Assuming that the labor force increases 1% per year, it will have increased at least 4% between December 2007 and mid-2012. So the rate of unemployment in mid-2012 would be about 4% higher than in December 2007, or around 9%.

And this is the optimistic scenario. If there is a "double-dip" recession, then the official rate of unemployment will still be over 10% for years to come. This means that the true rate of unemployment—including involuntary part-time workers and marginally attached or discouraged workers who have stopped looking for jobs—would likely top 15%.

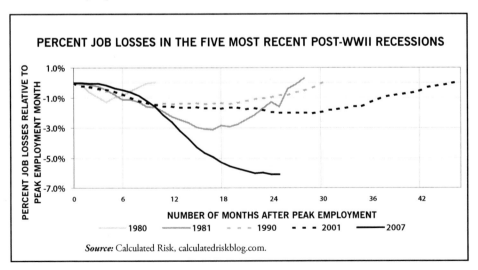

PERCENT JOB LOSSES IN THE FIVE MOST RECENT POST-WWII RECESSIONS

Source: Calculated Risk, calculatedriskblog.com.

In other words, U.S. workers will be facing a long period of very high unemployment. Already, 40% of the officially unemployed have been unemployed for six months or more—the highest since records have been kept starting in 1948—and the percentage of total unemployed (including "discouraged workers") is much higher. And these percentages will go even higher in the months ahead.

Long-term unemployment like this has very serious negative effects on workers—it makes it much harder to return to employment and it has hidden costs on families, children, and communities.

To avoid this economic disaster for working people, we should demand that Congress pass a Full Employment Law, committing the federal government to provide jobs for all workers willing and able to work any time there are not enough private sector jobs. Such a law would be based on the principle that a job with a decent income is a basic economic right.

Could we afford a full-employment law? Contrary to what the deficit hawks claim, the answer is yes. A full-employment jobs program could be paid for by higher taxes on the rich and by a significant reduction in military spending. It's not about a lack of funds—it's about priorities. If the government abandoned its current priorities of keeping tax rates on the rich low and giving the military a blank check for foreign wars, it could instead help workers cope with the long-term after-effects of recession.

Thanks to the website Calculated Risk (calculatedriskblog.com) for the idea for the graph accompanying this article and for sharing the data.

Article 1.5

WOMEN BREADWINNERS, MEN UNEMPLOYED

BY HEATHER BOUSHEY
July 2009

The employment situation over the past 19 months has dramatically changed for millions of American families. Since the Great Recession began in December 2007, there has been a sharp rise in the number of married couples where a woman is left to bring home the bacon because her husband is unemployed. What is striking is not only how many more families are experiencing unemployment among husbands, but also how this loss of the traditional breadwinner has occurred across a variety of demographic groups.

The reason that more married couples now boast women as the primary breadwinners is because men have experienced greater job losses than women over the course of this recession, losing three out of every four jobs lost. This puts a real strain on family budgets since women typically earn only 78 cents for every dollar men earn. In the typical married-couple family where both spouses work, the wife brings home just over a third—35.6%—of the family's income.

What's equally worrisome is that most families receive health insurance through the employers of their husbands. So when husbands lose their jobs, families are left struggling to find ways to pay for health insurance at the same time they are living on just a third of their prior income. These new health insurance costs can be crushing if families have to turn to the individual insurance market, where coverage is limited and expensive, or pay for continued coverage through their husbands' old insurance policies, which is possible because of federal law but is also expensive—though the American Recovery and Reinvestment Act subsidized that cost for many workers. Still, many families with an unemployed worker simply have to go without health insurance.

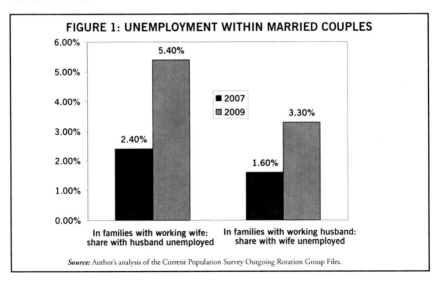

FIGURE 1: UNEMPLOYMENT WITHIN MARRIED COUPLES

Source: Author's analysis of the Current Population Survey Outgoing Rotation Group Files.

FIGURE 2: NON-EMPLOYMENT WITHIN MARRIED COUPLES

Source: Author's analysis of the Current Population Survey Outgoing Rotation Group Files.

The job losses mounting among husbands are acute this year. Figure 1 shows that the share of families where women hold down a job while men are unemployed jumped sharply in 2009 compared to 2007 at the peak of the last economic cycle. In the first five months of 2009, 5.4% of working wives had an unemployed husband at home—that is, a husband who was actively searching for work, but could not find a job—compared to an average of 2.4% over the first five months of 2007. This means that there are about 2 million working wives today with an unemployed husband.

In contrast, working husbands continue to be less likely to have an unemployed wife. In the first five months of 2009, an average of only 3.3% of husbands had an unemployed wife at home, up from 1.6%. Importantly, the difference in the shares of unemployed husbands and wives is not due to women telling the surveyor that they are "out of the labor force" rather than report they are out of a job, willing to work, and actively seeking employment. Figure 2 examines non-working spouses and shows not only a sharp rise in the share of working wives who have a non-working husband but also the share of both husbands and wives who are either unavailable to work or are not looking for a job.

So far this year, 15.6% of working wives have a husband who is not working, up a stunning 3.5 percentage points from early 2007, when 12.1% of working wives had a husband who did not work. But working husbands did not see a similarly large increase in their chances of having a non-working wife. In 2007, 29.4% of husbands had a non-working wife, up only 0.8 percentage points to 30.2% in 2009.

Families with children have been hit especially hard hit by unemployment. Among working wives in families with a small child—under age six—at home, 5.9% have an unemployed husband. This is higher than among families with a working wife but with no child under age six at home, where 5.3% have an unemployed husband.

Among families with a working wife and a child under age 18, the share with an unemployed husband is 5.7%, compared to 5.0% among those with no children. This means that there are 1 million working wives with children at home, but an unemployed husband. The numbers are smaller for families with a working husband and an unemployed wife. The share with a child under age 18 is 3.2%—compared to 3.4% among those with no children.

The share of workers with an unemployed spouse is lower than the overall unemployment rate of 9.5%. Typically, married workers have lower unemployment rates compared to single workers and they stay unemployed for shorter periods of time. There are many reasons why this is the case, but one is that married workers may have more of an incentive to find work as quickly as possible—if possible—because there are more people relying on their earnings, compared to single workers—at least single workers without children. Of course, single mothers, who typically have higher unemployment than other workers, do have children relying on their earnings and are under similar pressures to find employment.

Especially striking in the recently released data is the sharp increase in breadwinner wives and unemployed husbands across demographic groups. The table below shows, for example, that among young (ages 18 to 24) families with a working wife, one in ten married women (9.9%) has an unemployed husband, up 5.5 percentage points from early 2007. Among working women without a high school

UNEMPLOYMENT AMONG FAMILIES WITH A WORKING SPOUSE					
	In families with working wife: Share with husband unemployed			In families with working husband: Share with wife unemployed	
	January - May 2007	January - May 2009	Percentage point change	January - May 2007	January - May 2009	Percentage point change
All families	2.4	5.4	3	1.6	3.3	1.7
Ages 18 to 24	4.4	9.9	5.5	4.8	6	1.2
Ages 25 to 54	2.4	5.5	3.1	1.6	3.3	1.7
Ages 55 to 64	1.9	4.1	2.2	1.4	3	1.6
Less than highschool	4.3	8.3	4	2.7	5.8	3.1
High school	2.7	6.8	4.1	2	3.9	1.9
Some college	2.6	5.5	2.9	1.4	2.8	1.4
College	1.7	3.9	2.2	1.2	2.4	1.2
White, non-Hispanic	2.1	4.7	2.6	1.4	2.8	1.4
Black, non-Hispanic	4.1	7.8	3.7	2.9	3.9	1
Hispanic, any race	3.4	7.7	4.3	2.2	5.1	2.9
Other race, non-Hispanic	2.5	6.3	3.8	1.9	3.2	1.3
No children under age 18	2.3	5	2.7	1.6	3.4	1.8
Children under age 18	2.4	5.7	3.3	1.7	3.2	1.5
No children under age six	2.3	5.3	3	1.6	3.4	1.8
Children under age six	2.5	5.9	3.4	1.7	3	1.3

Source: Author's analysis of the Current Population Survey Outgoing Rotation Group Files.

degree, slightly less than one in ten (8.3%) have an unemployed husband, up four percentage points since 2007. This share of women with unemployed husbands has increased 2.2 percentage points among wives with a college degree.

There has also been a sharp rise in the share of families where both the husband and wife are unemployed. Between the first five months of 2007 and of 2009, the share of married-couple families with both spouses unemployed rose to 0.5% from 0.1%, meaning that one in 500 families is struggling with dual unemployment. The share of families with a child under age 18 with both parents unemployed is 0.6%, meaning that one in 165 families with children have both parents looking for work.

Among some demographic groups dual unemployment rises to one in 100: young couples (with a spouse between 18 and 24), less-educated couples (where either spouse has no more than a high-school degree), and African-American families (0.9% of African-American wives in the labor force are unemployed and have an unemployed husband, while 0.8% of African-American husbands in the labor force are unemployed with an unemployed wife).

The Great Recession that began in December 2007 has now lasted 19 months. The unemployment picture remains tough: Unemployment rose to 9.5% in June and 29.0% of unemployed workers have been out of work for at least six months—a shocking fact given that 3.4 million of the 6.5 million people who have lost their jobs since the recession began were laid off only within the past six months. There are now more than five unemployed workers available for every job opening and the employment prospects for men seem especially challenging given the continued layoffs in manufacturing and construction. Families will continue to rely on the earnings of a working woman for a long time to come.

As families need the earnings of wives more than ever, policymakers should focus their attention on ensuring that women—including mothers—have access to good jobs with benefits that will support their families. There could not be a more important moment to pass legislation ensuring pay equity for all workers. Nor could there be a more important time to ensure that caregivers are not discriminated against by employers.

The Paycheck Fairness Act, which passed the House in January, would go a long way toward eradicating pay inequalities, but it is languishing in the Senate. The Equal Employment Opportunity Commission issued new guidelines in 2007 to help employers avoid caregiver discrimination, but more could be done to use develop this guidance to ensure that every caregiver has the same access to good jobs as other workers. These and other policy solutions to the crisis facing women breadwinners need to be acted upon swiftly.

Source: Bureau of Labor Statistics, "Women in the Labor Force: A Databook," (Washington, DC: U.S. Department of Labor, 2008), Table 24.

The data analysis for this report was conducted by Jeff Chapman. The analysis compares the experiences of married couples from the first five months of 2007 to the first five months of 2009. Note that data are only for married heterosexual couples and do not include cohabitating heterosexual couples or lesbian or gay couples, married or otherwise.

Article 1.6

A DISMAL TIME TO GRADUATE

What the recession means to the class of 2009, including me.

BY KATHERINE FAHERTY
January/February 2010

The current state of the economy is hitting recent graduates hard. As a 2009 college graduate, I speak from experience. Seven months after graduating I have secured an unpaid internship and a part-time job, which puts me in the same boat as many of my classmates. Last spring one of my professors kindly reminded our assembly of scared and excited seniors that it was a dismal time to graduate. He was right. Unemployment for my age group (20-24) reached a staggering 16% in November, compared to 11.1% in November 2008.

My roommate, who has a master's degree in art history, has only been able to find an unpaid internship at an auction house plus a part-time receptionist job. Even without the part-time job, the Bureau of Labor Statistics would count her as employed because she goes to "work" at the auction house every day. She is among the hordes of recent graduates holding unpaid internships that were once the sole province of college students—a viable route only for grads with family resources to fall back on.

Another friend has been on a constant job search since March. She moved back into her parents' house and returned to her old summer job as a bank teller. Then she took a job at the local mall so she could make her student-loan payments. She gets a great discount at her store, but she's not putting her double degree in economics and psychology to use. Like almost 32% of workers under 25, she is "underemployed." Along with those who want full-time jobs but can find only part-time ones, underemployed workers are counted as employed. So

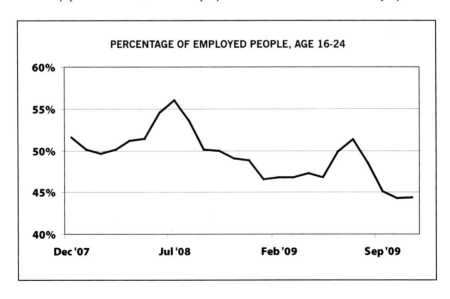

neither group shows up in the most widely reported unemployment rate (the BLS's "U-3" measure).

A few of my friends were lucky enough to find jobs in their desired fields. One deploys her dual majors at a Massachusetts economic and environmental consulting firm. She is in the minority of last year's college graduates; just 48% were employed in September, including all of those underemployed receptionists and cashiers.

While I don't personally know anyone who hasn't found something to do, New York City's Covenant House does; the organization, which serves young people facing homelessness, has seen a 25% increase in residents. Around the country, there are some 4,088,000 unemployed people ages 16 to 24 looking for work. It's a pretty dismal state, especially since there are 6.3 people vying for every available job as of October 2009, again not including all the interns, the underemployed, and the involuntary part-timers still vying for those jobs.

In October, *BusinessWeek* labeled us "the lost generation." I disagree. We're not lost, just confused and frustrated. No one wants to get stuck in a rut. According to Yale economist Lisa Kahn, recession graduates never fully recover. Early-1980s recession graduates earned 8% less than comparable graduates in non-recession years in their first year out of college and are still earning less almost 20 years later. Kahn characterized the consequences of graduating during a recession as "large, negative, and persistent."

It's clear that we need more jobs with career ladders available to entry-level candidates. But until more jobs become available, I, like my classmates, will try to move forward, hoping my internship and part-time job build character (or at least enhance my résumé) and looking for the light at the end of the tunnel. ❑

Sources: The Class of 09 Curse," *Wall Street Journal*, May 9, 2009; "The Employment Situation –November 2009," Bureau of Labor Statistics; "The Lost Generation," *BusinessWeek*, October 8, 2009; "Who's Paying for the Recession Most of All? Young Workers," alternet.org, November 9, 2009; Tony Pugh, "Recession's Toll: Most Recent College Grads Working Low-Skill Jobs," McClatchy, June 25, 2009.

Article 1.7

THE GROWTH CONSENSUS UNRAVELS

BY JONATHAN ROWE

September/October 2002

Economics has been called the dismal science, but beneath its gray exterior is a system of belief worthy of Pollyanna.

Yes, economists manage to see a dark cloud in every silver lining. Downturn follows uptick, and inflation rears its ugly head. But there's a story within that story—a gauzy romance, a lyric ode to Stuff. It's built into the language. A thing produced is called a "good," for example, no questions asked. The word is more than just a term of art. It suggests the automatic benediction which economics bestows upon commodities of any kind.

By the same token, an activity for sale is called a "service." In conventional economics there are no "dis-services," no actions that might be better left undone. The bank that gouges you with ATM fees, the lawyer who runs up the bill—such things are "services" so long as someone pays. If a friend or neighbor fixes your plumbing for free, it's not a "service" and so it doesn't count.

The sum total of these products and activities is called the Gross Domestic Product, or GDP. If the GDP is greater this year than last, then the result is called "growth." There is no bad GDP and no bad growth; economics does not even have a word for such a thing. It does have a word for less growth. In such a case, economists say growth is "sluggish" and the economy is in "recession." No matter what is growing—more payments to doctors because of worsening health, more toxic cleanup—so long as there is more of it, then the economic mind declares it "good."

This purports to be "objective science." In reality it is a rhetorical construct with the value judgments built in, and this rhetoric has been the basis of economic debate in the United States for the last half century at least. True, people have disagreed over how best to promote a rising GDP. Liberals generally wanted to use government more, conservatives less. But regarding the beneficence of a rising GDP, there has been little debate at all.

If anything, the Left traditionally has believed in growth with even greater fervor than the Right. It was John Maynard Keynes, after all, who devised the growth-boosting mechanisms of macroeconomic policy to combat the Depression of the 1930s; it was Keynesians who embraced these strategies after the War and turned the GDP into a totem. There's no point in seeking a bigger pie to redistribute to the poor, if you don't believe the expanding pie is desirable in the first place.

Today, however, the growth consensus is starting to unravel across the political spectrum and in ways that are both obvious and subtle. The issue is no longer just the impact of growth upon the environment—the toxic impacts of industry and the like. It now goes deeper, to what growth actually consists of and what it means in people's lives. The things economists call "goods" and "services" increasingly don't strike people as such. There is a growing disconnect between the way people experience growth and the way the policy establishment talks about it, and this gap is becoming an unspoken subtext to much of American political life.

The group most commonly associated with an antigrowth stance is environmentalists, of course. To be sure, one faction, the environmental economists, is trying to put green new wine into the old bottles of economic thought. If we would just make people pay the "true" cost of, say, the gasoline they burn, through the tax system for example, then the market would do the rest. We'd have benign, less-polluting growth, they say, perhaps even more than now. But the core of the environmental movement remains deeply suspicious of the growth ethos, and probably would be even if the environmental impacts somehow could be lessened.

In the middle are suburbanites who applaud growth in the abstract, but oppose the particular manifestations they see around them—the traffic, sprawl and crowded schools. On the Right, meanwhile, an anti-growth politics is arising practically unnoticed. When social conservatives denounce gambling, pornography, or sex and violence in the media, they are talking about specific instances of the growth that their political leaders rhapsodize on other days.

Environmentalists have been like social conservatives in one key respect. They have been moralistic regarding growth, often scolding people for enjoying themselves at the expense of future generations and the earth. Their concern is valid, up to a point—the consumer culture does promote the time horizon of a five year old. But politically it is not the most promising line of attack, and conceptually it concedes too much ground. To moralize about consumption as they do is to accept the conventional premise that it really is something chosen—an enjoyable form of self-indulgence that has unfortunate consequences for the earth.

That's "consumption" in the common parlance—the sport utility vehicle loading up at Wal-Mart, the stuff piling up in the basement and garage. But increasingly that's not what people actually experience, nor is it what the term really means. In economics, consumption means everything people spend money on, pleasurable or not. Wal-Mart is just one dimension of a much larger and increasingly unpleasant whole. The lawyers' fees for the house settlement or divorce; the repair work on the car after it was rear-ended; the cancer treatments for the uncle who was a three-pack-a-day smoker; the stress medications and weight loss regimens—all these and more are "consumption." They all go into the GDP.

Cancer treatments and lawyer's fees are not what come to mind when environmentalists lament the nation's excess consumption, or for that matter when economists applaud America's "consumers" for keeping the world economy afloat. Yet increasingly such things are what consumption actually consists of in the economy today. More and more, it consists not of pleasurable things that people choose, but rather of things that most people would gladly do without.

Much consumption today is addictive, for example. Millions of Americans are engaged in a grim daily struggle with themselves to do less of it. They want to eat less, drink less, smoke less, gamble less, talk less on the telephone—do less buying, period. Yet economic reasoning declares as growth and progress, that which people themselves regard as a tyrannical affliction.

Economists resist this reality of a divided self, because it would complicate their models beyond repair. They cling instead to an 18th century model of human psychology—the "rational" and self-interested man—which assumes those complexities away. As David McClelland, the Harvard psychologist, once put it, economists "haven't even discovered Freud, let alone Abraham Maslow." (They also haven't discovered the Apostle Paul, who lamented that "the good that I would I do not, but the evil that I would not, that I do.")

Then too there's the mounting expenditure that sellers foist upon people through machination and deceit. People don't choose to pay for the corrupt campaign finance system or for bloated executive pay packages. The cost of these is hidden in the prices that we pay at the store. As I write this, the *Washington Post* is reporting that Microsoft has hired Ralph Reed, former head of the Christian Coalition, and Grover Norquist, a right-wing polemicist, as lobbyists in Washington. When I bought this computer with Windows 95, Bill Gates never asked me whether I wanted to help support a bunch of Beltway operators like these.

This is compulsory consumption, not choice, and the economy is rife with it today. People don't choose to pay some $40 billion a year in telemarketing fraud. They don't choose to pay 32% more for prescription drugs than do people in Canada. ("Free trade" means that corporations are free to buy their labor and materials in other countries, but ordinary Americans aren't equally free to do their shopping there.) For that matter, people don't choose to spend $25 and up for inkjet printer cartridges. The manufacturers design the printers to make money on the cartridges because, as the *Wall Street Journal* put it, that's "where the big profit margins are."

Yet another category of consumption that most people would gladly do without arises from the need to deal with the offshoots and implications of growth. Bottled water has become a multibillion dollar business in the United States because people don't trust what comes from the tap. There's a growing market for sound insulation and double-pane windows because the economy produces so much noise. A wide array of physical and social stresses arise from the activities that get lumped into the euphemistic term "growth."

The economy in such cases doesn't solve problems so much as create new problems that require more expenditure to solve. Food is supposed to sustain people, for example. But today the dis-economies of eating sustain the GDP instead. The food industry spends some $21 billion a year on advertising to entice people to eat food they don't need. Not coincidentally there's now a $32 billion diet and weight loss industry to help people take off the pounds that inevitably result. When that doesn't work, which is often, there is always the vacuum pump or knife. There were some 110,000 liposuctions in the United States last year; at five pounds each that's some 275 tons of flab up the tube.

It is a grueling cycle of indulgence and repentance, binge and purge. Yet each stage of this miserable experience, viewed through the pollyanic lens of economics, becomes growth and therefore good. The problem here goes far beyond the old critique of how the consumer culture cultivates feelings of inadequacy, lack and need so people will buy and buy again. Now this culture actually makes life worse, in order to sell solutions that purport to make it better.

Traffic shows this syndrome in a finely developed form. First we build sprawling suburbs so people need a car to go almost anywhere. The resulting long commutes are daily torture but help build up the GDP. Americans spend some $5 billion a year in gasoline alone while they sit in traffic and go nowhere. As the price of gas increases this growth sector will expand.

Commerce deplores a vacuum, and the exasperating hours in the car have spawned a booming subeconomy of relaxation tapes, cell phones, even special bibs. Billboards have 1-800 numbers so commuters can shop while they stew. Talk radio thrives on traffic-bound commuters, which accounts for some of the contentious, get-out-of-my-face tone. The traffic also helps sustain a $130 billion a year car wreck industry; and if Gates succeeds in getting computers into cars, that sector should get a major boost.

The health implications also are good for growth. Los Angeles, which has the worst traffic in the nation, also leads—if that's the word—in hospital admissions due to respiratory ailments. The resulting medical bills go into the GDP. And while Americans sit in traffic they aren't walking or getting exercise. More likely they are entertaining themselves orally with a glazed donut or a Big Mac, which helps explain why the portion of middle-aged Americans who are clinically obese has doubled since the 1960s.

C. Everett Koop, the former Surgeon General, estimates that some 70% of the nation's medical expenses are lifestyle induced. Yet the same lifestyle that promotes disease also produces a rising GDP. (Keynes observed that traditional virtues like thrift are bad for growth; now it appears that health is bad for growth too.) We literally are growing ourselves sick, and this puts a grim new twist on the economic doctrine of "complementary goods," which describes the way new products tend to spawn a host of others. The automobile gave rise to car wash franchises, drive-in restaurants, fuzz busters, tire dumps, and so forth. Television produced an antenna industry, VCRs, soap magazines, ad infinitum. The texts present this phenomenon as the wondrous perpetual motion machine of the market—goods beget more goods. But now the machine is producing complementary ills and collateral damages instead.

Suggestive of this new dynamic is a pesticide plant in Richmond, California, which is owned by a transnational corporation that also makes the breast cancer drug tamoxifen. Many researchers believe that pesticides, and the toxins created in the production of them, play a role in breast cancer. "It's a pretty good deal," a local physician told the *East Bay Express*, a Bay Area weekly. "First you cause the cancer, then you profit from curing it." Both the alleged cause and cure make the GDP go up, and this syndrome has become a central dynamic of growth in the U.S. today.

Mainstream economists would argue that this is all beside the point. If people didn't have to spend money on such things as commuting or medical costs, they'd simply spend it on something else, they say. Growth would be the same or even greater, so the actual content of growth should be of little concern to those who promote it. That view holds sway in the nation's policy councils; as a result we try continually to grow our way out of problems, when increasingly we are growing our way in.

To the extent conventional economics has raised an eyebrow at growth, it has done so mainly through the concept of "externalities". These are negative side effects suffered by those not party to a transaction between a buyer and a seller. Man buys car, car pollutes air, others suffer that "externality." As the language implies, anything outside the original transaction is deemed secondary, a subordinate reality, and therefore easily overlooked. More, the effects upon buyer and seller—the "internalities" one might say—are assumed to be good.

Today, however, that mental schema is collapsing. Externalities are starting to overwhelm internalities. A single jet ski can cause more misery for the people who reside by a lake, than it gives pleasure to the person riding it.

More importantly, and as just discussed, internalities themselves are coming into question, and with them the assumption of choice, which is the moral linchpin of market thought.

If people choose what they buy, as market theory posits, then—externalities aside—the sum total of all their buying must be the greatest good of all. That's the ideology behind the GDP. But if people don't always choose, then the model starts to fall apart, which is what is happening today. The practical implications are obvious. If growth consists increasingly of problems rather than solutions, then scolding people for consuming too much is barking up the wrong tree. It is possible to talk instead about ridding our lives of what we don't want as well as forsaking what we do want—or think we want.

Politically this is a more promising path. But to where? The economy may be turning into a kind of round robin of difficulty and affliction, but we are all tied to the game. The sickness industry employs a lot of people, as do ad agencies and trash haulers. The fastest-growing occupations in the country include debt collectors and prison guards. What would we do without our problems and dysfunctions?

The problem is especially acute for those at the bottom of the income scale who have not shared much in the apparent prosperity. For them, a bigger piece of a bad pie might be better than none.

This is the economic conundrum of our age. No one has more than pieces of an answer, but it helps to see that much growth today is really an optical illusion created by accounting tricks. The official tally ignores totally the cost side of the growth ledger—the toll of traffic upon our time and health for example. In fact, it actually counts such costs as growth and gain. By the same token, the official tally ignores the economic contributions of the natural environment and the social structure; so that the more the economy destroys these, and puts commoditized substitutes in their places, the more the experts say the economy has "grown." Pollute the lakes and oceans so that people have to join private swim clubs and the economy grows. Erode the social infrastructure of community so people have to buy services from the market instead of getting help from their neighbors, and it grows some more. The real economy—the one that sustains us—has diminished. All that has grown is the need to buy commoditized substitutes for things we used to have for free.

So one might rephrase the question thus: how do we achieve real growth, as opposed to the statistical illusion that passes for growth today? Four decades ago, John Kenneth Galbraith argued in *The Affluent Society* that conventional economic reasoning is rapidly becoming obsolete. An economics based upon scarcity simply doesn't work in an economy of hyper-abundance, he said. If it takes a $200 billion (today) advertising industry to maintain what economists quaintly call "demand," then perhaps that demand isn't as urgent as conventional theory posits. Perhaps it's not even demand in any sane meaning of the word.

Galbraith argued that genuine economy called for shifting some resources from consumption that needs to be prodded, to needs which are indisputably great: schools, parks, older people, the inner cities and the like. For this he was skewered as a proto-socialist. Yet today the case is even stronger, as advertisers worm into virtually every waking moment in a desperate effort to keep the growth machine on track.

Galbraith was arguing for a larger public sector. But that brings dysfunctions of its own, such as bureaucracy; and it depends upon an enlarging private sector as a fiscal base to begin with. Today we need to go further, and establish new ground rules for the economy, so that it produces more genuine growth on its own. We also need to find ways to revive the nonmarket economy of informal community exchange, so that people do not need money to meet every single life need.

In the first category, environmental fiscal policy can help. While the corporate world has flogged workers to be more productive, resources such as petroleum have been in effect loafing on the job. If we used these more efficiently the result could be jobs and growth, even in conventional terms, with less environmental pollution. If we used land more efficiently—that is, reduced urban sprawl—the social and environmental gains would be great.

Another ground rule is the corporate charter laws. We need to restore these to their original purpose: to keep large business organizations within the compass of the common good. But such shifts can do only so much. More efficient cars might simply encourage more traffic, for example. Cheap renewable power for electronic devices could encourage more noise. In other words, the answer won't just be a more efficient version of what we do now. Sooner or later we'll need different ways of thinking about work and growth and how we allocate the means of life.

This is where the social economy comes in, the informal exchange between neighbors and friends. There are some promising trends. One is the return to the traditional village model in housing. Structure does affect content. When houses are close together, and people can walk to stores and work, it encourages the spontaneous social interaction that nurtures real community. New local currencies, such as Time Dollars, provide a kind of lattice work upon which informal nonmarket exchange can take root and grow.

Changes like these are off the grid of economics as conventionally defined. It took centuries for the market to emerge from the stagnation of feudalism. The next organizing principle, whatever it is, most likely will emerge slowly as well. This much we can say with certainty. As the market hurdles towards multiple implosions, social and environmental as well as financial, it is just possible that the economics profession is going to have to do what it constantly lectures the rest of us to do: adjust to new realities and show a willingness to change.

Article 1.8

WAGES FOR HOUSEWORK: THE MOVEMENT & THE NUMBERS

BY LENA GRABER AND JOHN MILLER

July/August 2002

The International Wages for Housework Campaign (WFH), a network of women in Third World and industrialized countries, began organizing in the early 1970s. WFH's demands are ambitious—"for the unwaged work that women do to be recognized as work in official government statistics, and for this work to be paid."

Housewives paid wages? By the government? That may seem outlandish to some, but consider the staggering amount of unpaid work carried out by women. In 1990, the International Labor Organization (ILO) estimated that women do two-thirds of the world's work for 5% of the income. In 1995, the UN Development Programme's (UNDP) Human Development Report announced that women's unpaid and underpaid labor was worth $11 trillion worldwide, and $1.4 trillion in the United States alone. Paying women the wages they "are owed" for unwaged work, as WFN puts it, would go a long way toward undoing these inequities and reducing women's economic dependence on men.

Publicizing information like this, WFH—whose International Women Count Network now includes more than 2,000 non-governmental organizations (NGOs) from the North and South—and other groups have been remarkably successful in persuading governments to count unwaged work. In 1995, the UN Fourth World Conference on Women, held in Beijing, developed a Platform for Action that called on governments to calculate the value of women's unpaid work and include it in conventional measures of national output, such as Gross Domestic Product (GDP).

So far, only Trinidad & Tobago and Spain have passed legislation mandating the new accounting, but other countries—including numerous European countries, Australia, Canada, Japan, and New Zealand in the industrialized world, and Bangladesh, the Dominican Republic, India, Nepal, Tanzania, and Venezuela in the developing world—have undertaken extensive surveys to determine how much time is spent on unpaid household work.

The Value of Housework

Producing credible numbers for the value of women's work in the home is no easy task. Calculating how many hours women spend performing housework—from cleaning to childcare to cooking to shopping—is just the first step. The hours are considerable in both developing and industrialized economies. (See Table 1.)

What value to place on that work, and what would constitute fair remuneration—or wages for housework—is even more difficult to assess. Feminist economists dedicated to making the value of housework visible have taken different approaches to answering the question. One approach, favored by the UN's International Research and Training Institute for the Advancement of Women (INSTRAW), bases the market value of work done at home on the price of market goods and services that are similar to those produced in the home (such as meals served in restaurants or cleaning done by professional firms). These output-based evaluations estimate that counting unpaid household production would add 30-60% to the GDP of industrialized countries, and far more for developing countries. (See Table 2.)

A second approach evaluates the inputs of household production—principally the labor that goes into cooking, cleaning, childcare, and other services performed in the home, overwhelmingly by women. Advocates of this approach use one of three methods. Some base their calculations on what economists call opportunity cost—the wages women might have earned if they had worked a similar number of hours in the market economy. Others ask what it would cost to hire someone to do the work—either a general laborer such as a domestic servant (the generalist-replacement method) or a specialist such as a chef (the specialist-replacement method)—and then assign those wages to household labor. Ann Chadeau, a researcher with the Organization for Economic Cooperation and Development, has found the specialist-replacement method to be "the most plausible and at the same time feasible approach" for valuing unpaid household labor.

These techniques produce quite different results, all of which are substantial in relation to GDP. With that in mind, let's look at how some countries calculated the monetary value of unpaid work.

Unpaid Work in Canada, Great Britain, and Japan

In Canada, a government survey documented the time men and women spent on unpaid work in 1992. Canadian women performed 65% of all unpaid work, shouldering an especially large share of household labor devoted to preparing meals, maintaining clothing, and caring for children. (Men's unpaid hours exceeded women's only for outdoor cleaning.)

	Childcare Time	Cleaning Time	Food Prep Time	Shopping Time	Water/Fuel Collection	Total Time[a]
TABLE 1 WOMEN'S TIME SPENT PER DAY PERFORMING HOUSEHOLD LABOR, BY ACTIVITY, IN HOURS:MINUTES						
Australia (1997[b])	2:27	1:17	1:29	0:58	n.a.	3:39
Japan (1999)	0:24	2:37	n.a.	0:33	n.a.	3:34
Norway (2000)	0:42	1:16	0:49	0:26	0:01	3:56
U.K. (2000)	1:26	1:35	1:08	0:33	n.a.	4:55
Nepal (1996)	1:28	2:00	5:30	0:13	1:10	11:58

Note: Some activities, especially child care, may overlap with other tasks

[a] Totals may include activities other than those listed.

[b] Only some percentage of the population recorded doing these activities. Averages are for that portion of the population. Generally, figures represent a greater number of women than men involved. *Sources:* Australia: <www.abs.gov.au/ausstats>; Japan: <www.unescap.org/stat>; Norway: <www.ssb.no/tidsbruk_en>; United Kingdom: <www.statistics.gov.uk/themes/social_finances/TimeUseSurvey>; Nepal: INSTRAW, *Valuation of Household Production and the Satellite Accounts* (Santo Domingo: 1996), 34-35; <www.cbs.nl/isi/iass>.

The value of unpaid labor varied substantially, depending on the method used to estimate its appropriate wage. (See Table 3.) The opportunity-cost method, which uses the average market wage (weighted for the greater proportion of unpaid work done by women), assigned the highest value to unpaid labor, 54.2% of Canadian GDP. The two replacement methods produced lower estimates, because the wages they assigned fell below those of other jobs. The specialist-replacement method, which paired unpaid activities with the average wages of corresponding occupations—such as cooking with junior chefs, and childcare with kindergarten teachers—put the value of Canadian unpaid labor at 43% of GDP. The generalist-replacement method, by assigning the wages of household servants to unpaid labor, produced the lowest estimate of the value of unpaid work: 34% of Canadian GDP. INSTRAW's output-based measure, which matched hours of unpaid labor to a household's average expenditures on the same activities, calculated the value of Canada's unpaid work as 47.4% of GDP.

In Great Britain, where unpaid labor hours are high for an industrialized country (see Table 1), the value of unpaid labor was far greater relative to GDP. The British Office for National Statistics found that, when valued using the opportunity cost method, unpaid work was 112% of Britain's GDP in 1995! With the specialist-replacement method, British unpaid labor was still 56% of GDP—greater than the output of the United Kingdom's entire manufacturing sector for the year.

In Japan—where unpaid labor hours are more limited (see Table 1), paid workers put in longer hours, and women perform over 80% of unpaid work—the value of unpaid labor is significantly smaller relative to GDP. The Japanese Economic

TABLE 2
VALUE OF UNPAID HOUSEHOLD LABOR AS % OF GDP, USING OUTPUT-BASED EVALUATION METHOD

Country	% of GDP
Canada (1992)	47.4%
Finland (1990)	49.1%
Nepal (1991)	170.7%

Source: INSTRAW, *Valuation of Household Production and the Satellite Accounts* (Santo Domingo, 1996), 62, 229.

TABLE 3
VALUE OF UNPAID HOUSEHOLD LABOR IN CANADA AS % OF GDP, 1992

Evaluation Method	% of GDP
Opportunity Cost (before taxes)	54.2 %
Specialist-Replacement	43.0%
Generalist-Replacement	34.0%
Output-Based	47.4%

Source: INSTRAW, *Valuation of Household Production and the Satellite Accounts* (Santo Domingo: 1996), 229.

Planning Agency calculated that counting unpaid work in 1996 would add between 15.2% (generalist-replacement method) and 23% (opportunity-cost method) to GDP. Even at those levels, the value of unpaid labor still equaled at least half of Japanese women's market wages.

Housework Not Bombs

While estimates vary by country and evaluation method, all of these calculations make clear that recognizing the value of unpaid household labor profoundly alters our perception of economic activity and women's contributions to production. "Had household production been included in the system of macro-economic accounts," notes Ann Chadeau, "governments may well have implemented quite different economic and social policies."

For example, according to the UNDP, "The inescapable implication [of recognizing women's unpaid labor] is that the fruits of society's total labor should be shared more equally." For the UNDP, this would mean radically altering property and inheritance rights; access to credit; entitlement to social security benefits, tax incentives, and child care; and terms of divorce settlements.

For WFH advocates, the implications are inescapable as well: women's unpaid labor should be paid—and "the money," WFH insists, "must come first of all from military spending."

Here in the United States, an unneeded and dangerous military buildup begun [in 2002] has already pushed up military spending from 3% to 4% of GDP. Devoting just the additional 1% of GDP gobbled up by the military budget to wages for housework—far from being outlandish—would be an important first step toward fairly remunerating women who perform necessary and life-sustaining household work.

Sources: Ann Chadeau, "What is Households' Non-Market Production Worth?" *OECD Economic Studies* No. 18 (Spring 1992); Economic Planning Unit, Department of National Accounts, Japan, "Monetary Valuation of Unpaid Work in 1996" <unstats.un.org/unsd/methods/timeuse/ tusresource_papers/japanunpaid.htm>; INSTRAW, *Measurement and Valuation of Unpaid Contribution: Accounting Through Time and Output* (Santo Domingo: 1995); INSTRAW, *Valuation of Household Production and the Satellite Accounts* (Santo Domingo: 1996); Office of National Statistics, United Kingdom, "A Household Satellite Account for the UK," by Linda Murgatroyd and Henry Neuberger, *Economic Trends* (October 1997) <www.statistics.gov.uk/hhsa/hhsa/Index. html>; Hilkka Pietilä, "The Triangle of the Human Ecology: Household-Cultivation-Industrial Production," *Ecological Economics Journal* 20 (1997); UN Development Programme, Human Development Report (New York: Oxford University Press, 1995).

Article 1.9

CPI BLUES

Changes to the Consumer Price Index dramatically reduced the "official" rate of inflation.

BY JOSHUA HOLLAND
November/December 2008

Think about economic conditions in the 1970s, and you're likely to have visions of gas lines snaking around corners, a weary Jimmy Carter looking droopy and forlorn in the Oval Office, and the general sense of "malaise" (Carter's word) that Ronald Reagan exploited so adroitly to give rise to the new conservative movement. You're also likely to think of high rates of inflation.

Over the last few years, even as the prices of food, energy, and other goods have soared, the mainstream media have maintained that today's inflation does not compare to those unhappy years. This past July [2008], *Newsweek* reassuringly noted that "the Consumer Price Index is rising at a 3% annual rate, compared with 13% in 1979." (More recently, in the wake of the global economic turmoil, some commentators are even talking about the danger of *de*flation.) But talk of inflation rarely mentions that the measures of inflation commonly discussed today bear little resemblance to the stats used in the 1970s.

In large part, that's because the Consumer Price Index (CPI)—the measure most frequently cited in media reports—is used to determine government benefits like Social Security, federal and state pensions, and Medicare payments. Recalculating inflation downward was a back-door way of keeping the growth of these entitlements in check without pissing off veterans' groups or the AARP.

The CPI was historically based on a relatively simple formula. Officials took a theoretical "basket of goods" that "typical" consumers required and averaged their current prices. Beginning in the early 1990s, however, conservative economists were unhappy that increases in the CPI kept increasing entitlement payments to government employees, vets, and the elderly—whiners and greedy gray-hairs. Through some impressive intellectual contortions, they came up with a number of proposals for adjusting how inflation is measured.

They began by weighting items in the basket differently. Federal Reserve Chair Alan Greenspan argued that it was wrong to compare the price of a pound of steak one year to the price of a pound of steak the next because when steak gets too expensive, people start eating hamburger—they lead more frugal lives when prices rise, and the measure of inflation should reflect their decisions. But as economist John Williams, author of the *Shadow Government Statistics* newsletter, notes:

> Replacing hamburger for steak in the calculations would reduce the inflation rate, but it represented the rate of inflation in terms of *maintaining a declining standard of living*. Cost of living was being replaced by the cost of survival. The old system told you how much you had to increase your income in order to keep

buying steak. The new system promised you hamburger, and then dog food, perhaps, after that. [emphasis mine]

In the same vein, conservative economists argued that the CPI wasn't taking into account the increased enjoyment people got from buying shiny new consumer goods. That new toaster may have cost you 60% more than the one you bought just five years ago, but the new one has a computer chip that monitors the internal temperature, and that makes it harder to burn the toast. Therefore, they argued, your happiness at having perfect toast every morning should be factored into the CPI.

In 1995, under Bill Clinton, the Boskin Commission—led by a former economic adviser to the first President Bush—was formed to "fix" the way we measure the CPI by applying these economists' views. Changes were quietly made, with little Congressional oversight. Ostensibly designed to improve accuracy, their net result was a dramatic reduction of the official rate of inflation.

While the mainstream media tout our 3% annual rate of inflation (5% since this spring), the reality is that inflation, using the CPI as it was calculated before the Clinton-era changes went into effect, was more than 8% in July. And that's not including a whole other set of methodological changes made in 1983.

Until 1983, the CPI included the cost of owning a house—it factored in home prices, mortgage rates, and real estate taxes. But then the Bureau of Labor Statistics—the agency that crunches all these numbers—decided to replace the cost of home ownership with rents (actually, a rental equivalent) as the key housing component in the CPI. But while home prices increased dramatically between 1995 and 2005, the "owners' equivalent rent" used to calculate inflation actually declined by a few points. As a result, the rising housing costs many U.S. families have faced over the past decade have not been reflected in the CPI. (That rents did not rise along with home prices, argued economists like Dean Baker, was evidence that the housing boom was in fact a "bubble," untethered from the basic laws of supply and demand.)

The average rate of inflation during the 1970s was just over 7% (and 9.75% during the Carter years). Williams estimates that today's CPI understates the inflation rate as it was calculated before the Reagan era by about seven percentage points. The figure above shows the CPI from 1980 to August 2008 as it is measured today compared with Williams' calculation of the inflation rate using the earlier methodologies.

It's a controversial claim, but if Williams is right, inflation in the first eight years of the 21st century has averaged around 9.5%—or two percentage points *higher* than it averaged during the 1970s. Compare that with the official inflation rate, which averaged 2.4% over that period.

Even more misleading is the "core" inflation rate, used by the Federal Reserve. The "core" rate simply excludes certain "volatile" goods from the basket —little things like energy and food. In recent years it's become increasingly popular among pundits to cite the core rate, but with energy and food costs making up about a quarter of most household expenses (and significantly more for low-income households), it's a poor measure of the economic pain most Americans have been feeling.

In just the last year (ending in June), food prices increased by more than 5%, and energy costs skyrocketed by almost 25%.

To gauge what most of us are really experiencing on a day-to-day basis, one might imagine economic reporters relying on a monthly "pizza index" instead of the Consumer Price Index. According to a February report by Al Olson of MSNBC, "Pizza makers have seen their cheese costs soar this year from $1.30 a pound to $1.76 a pound. Even worse, the flour used to make the dough has gone from $3 to $7 a bushel to $25 a bushel in less than a year." Between the second quarters of 2007 and 2008, even the cost of the paperboard used to make pizza boxes increased by 8%. (Several years of rising tomato prices—for the sauce—were blunted by the salmonella scare.)

The same is true for a host of items that working America buys every day. According to Olson, "If you're looking for a sure sign the U.S. economy is headed in the wrong direction, all you need to do is look at the skyrocketing price of 'recession-proof' foods: pizza, hot dogs, bagels and beer." But those items, and other costs that have a significant impact on ordinary people, are under-counted in the Consumer Price Index.

Sources: Daniel Gross, "Why Its Worse Than You Think," *Newsweek.* June 16, 2008; John Williams, "Consumer Price Index," *Government Economic Reports: Things You've Suspected But Were Afraid To Ask,* October 1, 2006; Al Olson, "Pizza and Beer Now Cost an Arm and a Leg," *MSNB,* Feb 29, 2008; Bureau of Labor Statistics, "Consumer Price Index Summary," July 2008 (www.bls. gov); Dean Baker, "Bush's House of Cards," *The Nation,* August 9, 2004.

WEALTH, INEQUALITY, AND POVERTY

INTRODUCTION

Wealth and inequality are both end products of today's economic growth. But while all macroeconomics textbooks investigate wealth accumulation, most give less attention to wealth disparities. The authors in this chapter fill in the gap by looking at who makes out, and who doesn't, with the accumulation of wealth.

"Slicing Up at the Long Barbeque" (Article 2.1) starts the discussion by providing hard numbers on today's income and wealth gaps. Economist Jim Cypher documents the alarming increase in U.S. inequality, which has reached levels not seen since the Great Depression. This holds for both income (how much you or your family makes in a year) and wealth (the assets you or your family owns minus your debts). Today, the top 1% of households own nearly two-fifths of the nation's wealth and the richest 20% get nearly three-fifths of our national income. Median household income (after adjusting for inflation) is declining. For Cypher, these numbers define who gorged, who served, and who got roasted during the last thirty years. And as economist Arthur MacEwan points out, those measures, which capture the huge bonuses of upper-level executives, give a better picture of the extent of today's inequality than the shares of total national income that are represented by wages versus non-wage forms of income such as corporate profits, net interest income, and rental income (Article 2.5).

Along with those gaping inequalities has come an even greater concentration of income even within the top 1%, with much of the income gains in recent years going to the top tenth and hundredth of that 1%. These oligarchs, not the college graduates who populate the top fifth of the income distribution, are, according to economist Paul Krugman, the drivers of today's inequality (Article 2.2). What is more, economic growth has not facilitated social mobility. As Krugman reports in a second article, it is not just left-wing critics who say so, but the business press as well. The number of people who go from rags to riches—while always so few as to be near-mythical—has decreased since 1980 (Article 2.4). In addition, low-wage workers are five times less likely to have sick days at their job than workers at the top of the wage scale (Article 2.3). On top of that, poverty rates, which according to most experts badly underestimate the extent of poverty in the United States, continued to rise during the 2001-2007 economic expansion (Article 2.6). In addition, because its inflation adjustment badly underestimates the importance of rapidly rising child-care and health-care costs in the budgets of poor families, the traditional measure understates the extent of poverty by yet a larger margin with each passing year (Article 2.7).

It doesn't have to be this way. Economist Chris Tilly debunks the myth that inequality is necessary for economic growth, showing that among both developing and industrial economies and across regions within countries, there is no correlation between higher inequality and faster economic growth. He argues that greater equality actually supports economic growth by bolstering spending, promoting agricultural and industrial productivity, and reducing social conflict (Article 2.5). Finally, social scientists Gar Alperovitz and Lew Daly document that the source of the technological innovation that has driven economic growth in the U.S. economy over the last 140 years has been the collective and historical accumulation of knowledge. Their point? Economic growth does not depend on the concentration of wealth in the hands of a few captains of industry or financial barrons (Article 2.4).

Discussion Questions

1. (General) The authors in this chapter believe that the distribution of wealth is as important as wealth itself, and consider greater economic equality an important macroeconomic goal. What are some arguments for and against this position? Where do you come down in the debate?

2. (Articles 2.1, 2.2, 2.3, 2.4, 2.5) Who benefited from the wealth accumulation of the last two decades? How did stockholders fare versus wage earners? How did the distribution of wealth by income group and by race change during the decade?

3. (Articles 2.1, 2.2, 2.3, 2.4, 2.5) "A rising tide lifts all boats," proclaimed John F. Kennedy as he lobbied for pro-business tax cuts in the early 1960s. Did the 1990s boom and the current economic recovery lift all boats? What do the changes in income, wealth, and poverty suggest?

4. (Article 2.6, 2.7) What are the shortcomings of the federal poverty threshold? How could the United States change the way it calculates the poverty threshold to get a more accurate measure of the incidence of poverty? And how have the Labor Department's adjustments of the poverty threshold for inflation affected its accuracy as a measure of the incidence of poverty?

5. (Article 2.2) Why does economist Krugman disagree with the Congressional testimony of of Fed chair Bernanke about the sources of today's inequality?

6. (Article 2.3) The myth of the "New Economy" bolstered the illusion that anyone can get rich quick in this country, but Paul Krugman says it just ain't so. What

evidence does he present to argue that social mobility is declining? Do you find his evidence compelling?

7. (Article 2.4) What has been the chief driver of economic growth in the United States over the last 140 years and who has earned the wealth and income created by that economic growth?

8. (Article 2.5) How does U.S. national income get divided among those who work for wages and those who don't? And why, according to MacEwan, does this division fail to identify the source of today's worsening inequality?

9. (Article 2.9) Why do conservatives argue that inequality is good for economic growth? What counterarguments does Tilly use to challenge this traditional view of the tradeoff between inequality and growth? What evidence convinces Tilly that equality is good for economic growth? Does that evidence convince you?

SLICING UP AT THE LONG BARBEQUE
Who gorges, who serves, and who gets roasted?

BY JAMES M. CYPHER
January/February 2007

Economic inequality has been on the rise in the United States for 30-odd years. Not since the Gilded Age of the late 19th century—during what Mark Twain referred to as "the Great Barbeque"—has the country witnessed such a rapid shift in the distribution of economic resources.

Still, most mainstream economists do not pay too much attention to the distribution of income and wealth—that is, how the value of current production (income) and past accumulated assets (wealth) is divided up among U.S. households. Some economists focus their attention on theory for theory's sake and do not work much with empirical data of any kind. Others who *are* interested in these on-the-ground data simply assume that each   individual or group gets what it deserves from a capitalist economy. In their view, if the share of income going to wage earners goes up, that must mean that wage earners are more pro-ductive and thus deserve a larger slice of the nation's total income—and vice versa if that share goes down.

Heterodox economists, however, frequently look upon the distribution of income and wealth as among the most important shorthand guides to the overall state of a society and its economy. Some are interested in economic justice; others may or may not be, but nonetheless are convinced that changes in income distribution signal underlying societal trends and perhaps important points of political tension. And the general public appears to be paying increasing attention to income and wealth inequality. Consider the strong support voters have given to recent ballot questions raising state minimum wages and the ex-tensive coverage of economic inequality that has suddenly begun to appear in mainstream news outlets like the *New York Times*, the *Los Angeles Times*, and the *Wall Street Journal*, all of which published lengthy article series on the topic in the past few years. Just last month, news outlets around the country spotlighted the extravagant bonuses paid out by investment firm Goldman Sachs, including a $53.4 million bonus to the firm's CEO.

By now, economists and others who do pay attention to the issue are aware that income and wealth inequality in the United States rose steadily during the last three decades of the 20th century. But now that we are several years into the 21st, what do we know about income and wealth distribution today? Has the trend toward inequality continued, or are there signs of a reversal? And what can an understanding of the entire post-World War II era tell us about how to move again toward greater economic equality?

The short answers are: (1) Income distribution is even more unequal that we thought; (2) The newest data suggest the trend toward greater inequality continues, with no signs of a reversal; (3) We all do better when we all do better. During the 30 or so years after World War II the economy boomed and every stratum of society did better—pretty much at the same rate. When the era of shared growth ended, so too did much of the growth: the U.S. economy slowed down and recessions were deeper, more frequent, and harder to overcome. Growth spurts that did occur left most people out: the bottom 60% of U.S. households earned only 95 cents in 2004 for every dollar they made in 1979. A quarter century of falling incomes for the vast majority, even though average household income rose by 27% in real terms. Whew!

The Classless Society?

Throughout the 1950s, 1960s, and 1970s, sociologists preached that the United States was an essentially "classless" society in which everyone belonged to the middle class. A new "mass market" society with an essentially affluent, economically homogeneous population, they claimed, had emerged. Exaggerated as these claims were in the 1950s, there was some reason for their popular acceptance. Union membership reached its peak share of the private-sector labor force in the early 1950s; unions were able to force corporations of the day to share the benefits of strong economic growth. The union wage created a target for non-union workers as well, pulling up all but the lowest of wages as workers sought to match the union wage and employers often granted it as a tactic for keeping unions out. Under these circumstances, millions of families en-tered the lower middle class and saw their standard of living rise markedly. All of this made the distribution of income more equal for decades until the late 1970s. Of course there were outliers—some millions of poor, disproportionately blacks, and the rich family here and there.

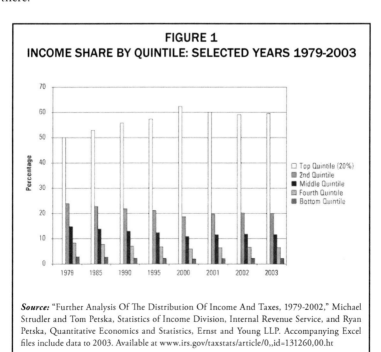

FIGURE 1
INCOME SHARE BY QUINTILE: SELECTED YEARS 1979-2003

Source: "Further Analysis Of The Distribution Of Income And Taxes, 1979-2002," Michael Strudler and Tom Petska, Statistics of Income Division, Internal Revenue Service, and Ryan Petska, Quantitative Economics and Statistics, Ernst and Young LLP. Accompanying Excel files include data to 2003. Available at www.irs.gov/taxstats/article/0,,id=131260,00.ht

Something serious must have happened in the 1970s as the trend toward greater economic equality rapidly reversed. Here are the numbers. The share of income received by the bottom 90% of the population was a modest 67% in 1970, but by 2000 this had shrunk to a mere 52%, according to a detailed study of U.S. income distribution conducted by Thomas Piketty and Emmanuel Saez, published by the prestigious National Bureau of Economic Research in 2002. Put another way, the top 10% increased their overall share of the nation's total income by 15 percentage points from 1970 to 2000. This is a rather astonishing jump—the *gain* of the top 10% in these years was equivalent to more than the *total income received annually* by the bottom 40% of households.

To get on the bottom rung of the top 10% of households in 2000, it would have been necessary to have an adjusted gross income of $104,000 a year. The real money, though, starts on the 99th rung of the income ladder—the top 1% received an unbelievable 21.7% of all income in 2000. To get a handhold on the very bottom of this top rung took more than $384,000.

The Piketty-Saez study (and subsequent updates), which included in its measure of annual household income some data, such as income from capital gains, that generally are not factored in, verified a rising *trend* in income inequality which had been widely noted by others, and a *degree* of inequality which was far beyond most current estimates.

The Internal Revenue Service has essentially duplicated the Piketty-Saez study. They find that in 2003, the share of total income going to the "bottom" four-fifths of households (that's 80% of the population!) was only slightly above 40%. (See Figure 1.) Both of these studies show much higher levels of inequality than were previously thought to exist based on widely referenced Census Bureau studies. The Census studies still attribute 50% of total income to the top fifth for 2003, but this number appears to understate what the top fifth now receives—nearly 60%, according to the IRS.

A Brave New (Globalized) World For Workers

Why the big change from 1970 to 2000? That is too long a story to tell here in full. But briefly, we can say that beginning in the early 1970s, U.S. corporations and the wealthy individuals who largely own them had the means, the motive, and the opportunity to garner a larger share of the nation's income—and they did so.

Let's start with the motive. The 1970s saw a significant slowdown in U.S. economic growth, which made corporations and stockholders anxious to stop sharing the benefits of growth to the degree they had in the immediate postwar era.

Opportunity appeared in the form of an accelerating globalization of economic activity. Beginning in the 1970s, more and more U.S.-based corporations began to set up production operations overseas. The trend has only accelerated since, in part because international communication and transportation costs have fallen dramatically. Until the 1970s, it was very difficult—essentially unprofitable—for giants like General Electric or General Motors to operate plants offshore and then import their foreign-made products into the United States. So from the 1940s to the 1970s, U.S. workers had a geographic lever, one they have now almost entirely lost. This erosion in workers' bargaining power has undermined the middle class and decimated the unions that once managed to assure the working class a generally comfortable economic existence. And today, of course, the tendency to send jobs offshore is affecting many highly trained professionals such as engineers. So this process of gutting the middle class has not run its course.

Given the opportunity presented by globalization, companies took a two-pronged approach to strengthening their hand vis-à-vis workers: (1) a frontal assault on unions, with decertification elections and get-tough tactics during unionization attempts, and (2) a debilitating war of nerves whereby corporations threatened to move offshore unless workers scaled back their demands or agreed to givebacks of prior gains in wage and benefit levels or working conditions.

A succession of U.S. governments that pursued conservative, pro-corporate economic policies provided the means. Since the 1970s, both Republican and Democratic administrations have tailored their economic policies to benefit corporations and shareholders over workers. The laundry list of such policies includes

- new trade agreements, such as NAFTA, that allow companies to cement favorable deals to move offshore to host nations such as Mexico;
- tax cuts for corporations and for the wealthiest households, along with hikes in the payroll taxes that represent the largest share of the tax burden on the working and middle classes;
- lax enforcement of labor laws that are supposed to protect the right to organize unions and bargain collectively.

Exploding Millionairism

Given these shifts in the political economy of the United States, it is not surprising that economic inequality in 2000 was higher than in 1970. But at this point, careful readers may well ask whether it is misleading to use data for the year 2000, as the studies reported above do, to demonstrate rising inequality. After all, wasn't 2000 the year the NASDAQ peaked, the year the dot-com bubble reached its maximum volume? So if the wealthiest households received an especially large slice of the nation's total income that year, doesn't that just reflect a bubble about to burst rather than an underlying trend?

To begin to answer this question, we need to look at the trends in income and wealth distribution *since* 2000. And it turns out that after a slight pause in 2000-2001, inequality has continued to rise. Look at household income, for example. According to the standard indicators, the U.S. economy saw a brief recession in 2000-2001 and has been in a recovery ever since. But the median household income has failed to recover. In 2000 the median household had an annual income of $49,133; by 2005, after adjusting for inflation, the figure stood at $46,242. This 6% drop in median household income occurred while the inflation-adjusted Gross Domestic Product *expanded* by 14.4%.

When the Census Bureau released these data, it noted that median household income had gone up slightly between 2004 and 2005. This point was seized upon by Bush administration officials to bolster their claim that times are good for American workers. A closer look at the data, however, revealed a rather astounding fact: Only 23 million households moved ahead in 2005, most headed by someone aged 65 or above. In other words, subtracting out the cost-of-living increase in Social Security benefits and increases in investment income (such as profits, dividends, interest, capital gains, and rents) to the over-65 group, workers again suffered a *decline* in income in 2005.

Another bit of evidence is the number of millionaire households—those with net worth of $1 million or more excluding the value of a primary residence and any IRAs. In 1999, just before the bubbles burst, there were 7.1 million millionaire households in the United States. In 2005, there were 8.9 million, a record number. Ordinary workers may not have recovered from the 2000–2001 rough patch yet, but evidently the wealthiest households have!

Many economists pay scant attention to income distribution patterns on the assumption that those shifts merely reflect trends in the productivity of labor or the return to risk-taking. But worker productivity *rose* in the 2000-2005 period, by 27.1% (see Figure 2). At the same time, from 2003 to 2005 average hourly pay *fell* by 1.2%. (Total compensation, including all forms of benefits, rose by 7.2% between 2000 and 2005. Most of the higher compensation spending merely reflects rapid increases in the health insurance premiums that employers have to pay just to maintain the same levels of coverage. But even if benefits are counted as part of workers'

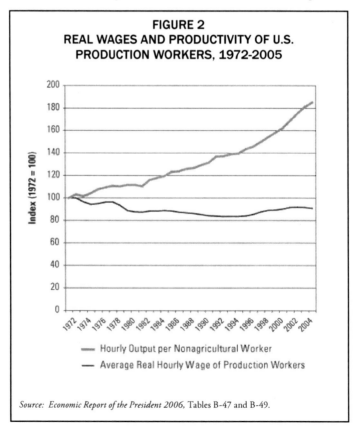

FIGURE 2
REAL WAGES AND PRODUCTIVITY OF U.S.
PRODUCTION WORKERS, 1972-2005

Index (1972 = 100)

—— Hourly Output per Nonagricultural Worker
—— Average Real Hourly Wage of Production Workers

Source: Economic Report of the President 2006, Tables B-47 and B-49.

pay—a common and questionable practice—productivity growth outpaced this elastic definition of "pay" by 50% between 1972 and 2005.)

And at the macro level, recent data released by the Commerce Department demonstrate that the share of the country's GDP going to wages and salaries sank to its lowest postwar level, 45.4%, in the third quarter of 2006 (see Figure 3). And this figure actually overstates how well ordinary workers are doing. The "Wage & Salary" share includes *all* income of this type, not just production workers' pay. Corporate executives' increasingly munificent salaries are included as well. Workers got roughly 65% of total wage and salary income in 2005, according to survey data from the U.S. Department of Labor; the other 35% went to salaried professionals—medical doctors and technicians, managers, and lawyers—who comprised only 15.6% of the sample.

Moreover, the "Wage & Salary" share shown in the National Income and Product Accounts includes bonuses, overtime, and other forms of payment not included in the Labor Department survey. If this income were factored in, the share going to nonprofessional, nonmanagerial workers would be even smaller. Bonuses and other forms of income to top employees can be many times base pay in important areas such as law and banking. Goldman Sachs's notorious 2006 bonuses are a case in point; the typical managing director on Wall Street garnered a bonus ranging between $1 million and $3 million.

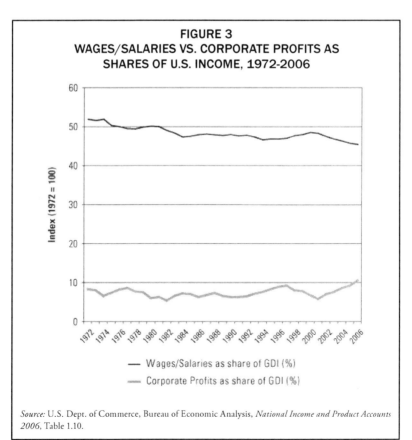

FIGURE 3
WAGES/SALARIES VS. CORPORATE PROFITS AS SHARES OF U.S. INCOME, 1972-2006

— Wages/Salaries as share of GDI (%)
— Corporate Profits as share of GDI (%)

Source: U.S. Dept. of Commerce, Bureau of Economic Analysis, *National Income and Product Accounts 2006*, Table 1.10.

So, labor's share of the nation's income is falling, as Figure 3 shows, but it is actually falling much faster than these data suggest. Profits, meanwhile, are at their highest level as a share of GDP since the booming 1960s.

These numbers should come as no surprise to anyone who reads the news: story after story illustrates how corporations are continuing to squeeze workers. For instance, workers at the giant auto parts manufacturer Delphi have been told to prepare for a drop in wages from $27.50 an hour in 2006 to $16.50 an hour in 2007. In order to keep some of Caterpillar's manufacturing work in the United States, the union was cornered into accepting a contract in 2006 that limits new workers to a maximum salary of $27,000 a year—no matter how long they work there—compared to the $38,000 or more that long-time Caterpillar workers make today. More generally, for young women with a high school diploma, average entry-level pay fell to only $9.08 an hour in 2005, down by 4.9% just since 2001. For male college graduates, starter-job pay fell by 7.3% over the same period.

Aiding and Abetting

And the federal government is continuing to play its part, facilitating the transfer of an ever-larger share of the nation's income to its wealthiest households. George W. Bush once joked that his constituency was "the haves and the have-mores"—this may have been one of the few instances in which he was actually leveling with his audience. Consider aspects of the four tax cuts for individuals that Bush has implemented since taking office. The first two cut the top *nominal* tax rate from 39.6% to 35%. Then, in 2003, the third cut benefited solely those who hold wealth, reducing taxes on dividends from 39.6% to 15% and on capital gains from 20% to 15%. (Bush's fourth tax cut—in 2006—is expected to drop taxes by 4.8% percent for the top one tenth of one percent of all households, while the median household will luxuriate with an extra nickel per day.)

So, if you make your money by the sweat of your brow and you earned $200,000 in 2003, you paid an *effective* tax rate of 21%. If you earned a bit more, say another $60,500, you paid an effective tax rate of 35% on the additional income. But if, with a flick of the wrist on your laptop, you flipped some stock you had held for six months and cleared $60,500 on the transaction, you paid the IRS an effective tax rate of only 15%. What difference does it make? Well, in 2003 the 6,126 households with incomes over $10 million saw their taxes go down by an average of $521,905 from this one tax cut alone.

These tax cuts represent only one of the many Bush administration policies that have abetted the ongoing shift of income away from most households and toward the wealthiest ones. And what do these top-tier households do with all this newfound money? For one thing, they save. This is in sharp contrast to most households. While the top fifth of households by income has a savings rate of 23%, the bottom 80% as a group dissave—in other words, they go into debt, spending more than they earn. Households headed by a person under 35 currently show a negative savings rate of 16% of income. Today *overall* savings—the savings of the top fifth minus the dis-savings of the bottom four-fifths—are slightly negative, for the first time since the Great Depression.

Here we find the crucial link between income and wealth accumulation. Able to save nearly a quarter of their income, the rich search out financial assets (and sometimes real assets such as houses and businesses) to pour their vast funds into. In many instances, sometimes with inside information, they are able to generate considerable future income from their invested savings. Like a snowball rolling downhill, savings for the rich can have a turbo effect—more savings generates more income, which then accumulates as wealth.

Lifestyles of the Rich

Make the rich even richer and the creative forces of market capitalism will be unleashed, resulting in more savings and consequently more capital investment, raising productivity and creating abundance for all. At any rate, that's the supply-side/neoliberal theory. However—and reminiscent of the false boom that defined the Japanese economy in the late 1980s—the big money has not gone into productive investments in the United States. Stripping out the money pumped into the residential real estate bubble, inflation-adjusted investment in machinery, equipment, technology, and structures increased only 1.4% from 1999 through 2005—an average of 0.23% per year. Essentially, productive investment has stagnated since the close of the dot-com boom.

Instead, the money has poured into high-risk hedge funds. These are vast pools of unregulated funds that are now generating 40% to 50% of the trades in the New York Stock Exchange and account for very large portions of trading in many U.S. and foreign credit and debt markets.

And where is the income from these investments going? Last fall media mogul David Geffen sold two paintings at record prices, a Jasper Johns ($80 million) and a Willem de Kooning ($63.5 million), to two of "today's crop of hedge-fund billionaires" whose cash is making the art market "red-hot," according to the *New York Times*.

Other forms of conspicuous consumption have their allure as well. Boeing and Lufthansa are expecting brisk business for the newly introduced 787 airplane. The commercial version of the new Boeing jet will seat 330, but the VIP version offered by Lufthansa Technik (for a mere $240 million) will have seating for 35 or fewer, leaving room for master bedrooms, a bar, and the transport of racehorses or Rolls Royces. And if you lose your auto assembly job? It should be easy to find work as a dog walker: High-end pet care services are booming, with sales more than doubling between 2000 and 2004. Opened in 2001, Just Dogs Gourmet expects to have 45 franchises in place by the end of 2006 selling hand-decorated doggie treats. And then there is Camp Bow Wow, which offers piped-in classical music for the dogs (oops, "guests") and a live Camper Cam for their owners. Started only three years ago, the company already has 140 franchises up and running.

According to David Butler, the manager of a premiere auto dealership outside of Detroit, sales of Bentleys, at $180,000 a pop, are brisk. But not many $300,000 Rolls Royces are selling. "It's not that they can't afford it," Butler told the *New York Times*, "it's because of the image it would give." Just what is the image problem in Detroit? Well, maybe it has something to do with those Delphi workers facing a 40% pay cut. Michigan's economy is one of the hardest-hit in the nation. GM, long a symbol of U.S. manufacturing prowess, is staggering, with rumors of possible bankruptcy rife. The best union in terms of delivering the goods for the U.S. working class, the United Auto Workers, is facing an implosion. Thousands of Michigan workers at Delphi, GM, and Ford will be out on the streets very soon. (The top three domestic car makers are determined to permanently lay off three-quarters of their U.S. assembly-line workers—nearly 200,000 hourly employees. If they do, then the number of auto-workers employed by the Big Three—Ford, Chrysler, and GM—will have shrunk by a staggering 900,000 since 1978.) So, this might not be the time to buy a Rolls. But a mere $180,000 Bentley—why not?

Had Enough of the "Haves"?

In the era Twain decried as the "great barbeque," the outrageous concentration of income and wealth eventually sparked a reaction and a vast reform movement. But it was not until the onset of the Great Depression, decades later, that massive labor/social unrest and economic collapse forced the country's political elite to check the growing concentration of income and wealth.

Today, it does not appear that there are, as yet, any viable forces at work to put the brakes on the current runaway process of rising inequality. Nor does it appear that this era's power elite is ready to accept any new social compact. In a recent report on the "new king of Wall Street" (a co-founder of the hedge fund/private-equity buyout corporation Blackstone Group) that seemed to typify elite perspectives on today's inequality, the *New York Times* gushed that "a crashing wave of capital is minting new billionaires each year." Naturally, the *Times* was too discreet to mention is that those same "crashing waves" have flattened the middle class. And their backwash has turned the working class every-which-way while pulling it down, down, down.

But perhaps those who decry the trend can find at least symbolic hope in the new boom in yet another luxury good. Private mausoleums, in vogue during that earlier Gilded Age, are back. For $650,000, one was recently constructed at Daytona Memorial Park in Florida—with matching $4,000 Medjool date palms for shade. Another, complete with granite patio, meditation room, and doors of hand cast bronze, went up in the same cemetery. Business is booming, apparently, with 2,000 private mausoleums sold in 2005, up from a single-year peak of 65 in the 1980s. Some cost "well into the millions," according to one of the nation's largest makers of cemetery monuments. Who knows: maybe the mausoleum boom portends the ultimate (dead) end for the neo-Gilded Age.

Sources: Jenny Anderson, "As Lenders, Hedge Funds Draw Insider Scrutiny," *NY Times* 10/16/06; Steven Greenhouse, "Many Entry-Level Workers Feel Pinch of Rough Market," *NY Times* 9/4/06; Greenhouse and David Leonhardt, "Real Wages Fail to Match a Rise in Productivity," *NY Times* 8/28/06; Paul Krugman, "Feeling No Pain," *NY Times* 3/6/06; Krugman, "Graduates vs. Oligarchs," *NY Times* 2/27/06; David Cay Johnston, *Perfectly Legal* (Penguin Books, 2003); Johnston, "Big Gain for Rich Seen in Tax Cuts for Investments," *NY Times* 4/5/06; Johnston, "New Rise in Number of Millionaire Families," *NY Times* 3/28/06; Johnston, "'04 Income in US was Below 2000 Level," *NY Times* 11/28/06; Leonhardt, "The Economics of Henry Ford May Be

Passé," *NY Times* 4/5/06; Rick Lyman, "Census Reports Slight Increase in '05 Incomes," *NY Times* 8/30/06; Micheline Maynard and Nick Bunkley, "Ford is Offering 75,000 Employees Buyout Packages," *NY Times* 9/15/06; Jeremy W. Peters, "Delphi Is Said to Offer Union a One-Time Sweetener," *NY Times* 3/28/06; Joe Sharky, "For the Super-Rich, It's Time to Upgrade the Old Jumbo Jet," *NY Times* 10/17/06; Guy Trebay, "For a Price, Final Resting Place that Tut Would Find Pleasant" *NY Times* 4/17/06.

Article 2.2

GRADUATES VERSUS OLIGARCHS

BY PAUL KRUGMAN
February 2006

Ben Bernanke's maiden Congressional testimony as chairman of the Federal Reserve was, everyone agrees, superb. He didn't put a foot wrong on monetary or fiscal policy.

But Mr. Bernanke did stumble at one point. Responding to a question from Representative Barney Frank about income inequality, he declared that "the most important factor" in rising inequality "is the rising skill premium, the increased return to education."

That's a fundamental misreading of what's happening to American society. What we're seeing isn't the rise of a fairly broad class of knowledge workers. Instead, we're seeing the rise of a narrow oligarchy: income and wealth are becoming increasingly concentrated in the hands of a small, privileged elite.

I think of Mr. Bernanke's position, which one hears all the time, as the 80-20 fallacy. It's the notion that the winners in our increasingly unequal society are a fairly large group—that the 20% or so of American workers who have the skills to take advantage of new technology and globalization are pulling away from the 80% who don't have these skills.

The truth is quite different. Highly educated workers have done better than those with less education, but a college degree has hardly been a ticket to big income gains. The 2006 Economic Report of the President tells us that the real earnings of college graduates actually fell more than 5% between 2000 and 2004. Over the longer stretch from 1975 to 2004 the average earnings of college graduates rose, but by less than 1% per year.

So who are the winners from rising inequality? It's not the top 20%, or even the top 10%. The big gains have gone to a much smaller, much richer group than that.

A new research paper by Ian Dew-Becker and Robert Gordon of Northwestern University, "Where Did the Productivity Growth Go?," gives the details. Between 1972 and 2001 the wage and salary income of Americans at the 90th percentile of the income distribution rose only 34%, or about 1% per year. So being in the top 10% of the income distribution, like being a college graduate, wasn't a ticket to big income gains.

But income at the 99th percentile rose 87%; income at the 99.9th percentile rose 181%; and income at the 99.99th percentile rose 497%. No, that's not a misprint.

Just to give you a sense of who we're talking about: the nonpartisan Tax Policy Center estimates that this year the 99th percentile will correspond to an income of $402,306, and the 99.9th percentile to an income of $1,672,726. The center doesn't give a number for the 99.99th percentile, but it's probably well over $6 million a year.

Why would someone as smart and well informed as Mr. Bernanke get the nature of growing inequality wrong? Because the fallacy he fell into tends to dominate polite discussion about income trends, not because it's true, but because it's comforting. The notion that it's all about returns to education suggests that nobody is to blame for rising inequality, that it's just a case of supply and demand at work. And it also suggests that the way to mitigate inequality is to improve our educational system—and better education is a value to which just about every politician in America pays at least lip service.

The idea that we have a rising oligarchy is much more disturbing. It suggests that the growth of inequality may have as much to do with power relations as it does with market forces. Unfortunately, that's the real story.

Should we be worried about the increasingly oligarchic nature of American society? Yes, and not just because a rising economic tide has failed to lift most boats. Both history and modern experience tell us that highly unequal societies also tend to be highly corrupt. There's an arrow of causation that runs from diverging income trends to Jack Abramoff and the K Street project.

And I'm with Alan Greenspan, who—surprisingly, given his libertarian roots—has repeatedly warned that growing inequality poses a threat to "democratic society." It may take some time before we muster the political will to counter that threat. But the first step toward doing something about inequality is to abandon the 80-20 fallacy. It's time to face up to the fact that rising inequality is driven by the giant income gains of a tiny elite, not the modest gains of college graduates.

Reprinted with permission from the *New York Times*, February 27, 2006.

Article 2.3

THE DEATH OF HORATIO ALGER

BY PAUL KRUGMAN
January 2004

The other day I found myself reading a leftist rag that made outrageous claims about America. It said that we are becoming a society in which the poor tend to stay poor, no matter how hard they work; in which sons are much more likely to inherit the socioeconomic status of their fathers than they were a generation ago.

The name of the leftist rag? *Business Week*, which published an article titled "Waking Up From the American Dream." The article summarizes recent research showing that social mobility in the United States (which was never as high as legend had it) has declined considerably over the past few decades. If you put that research together with other research that shows a drastic increase in income and wealth inequality, you reach an uncomfortable conclusion: America looks more and more like a class-ridden society.

And guess what? Our political leaders are doing everything they can to fortify class inequality, while denouncing anyone who complains—or even points out what is happening—as a practitioner of "class warfare."

Let's talk first about the facts on income distribution. Thirty years ago we were a relatively middle-class nation. It had not always been thus: Gilded Age America was a highly unequal society, and it stayed that way through the 1920s. During the 1930s and '40s, however, America experienced what the economic historians Claudia Goldin and Robert Margo have dubbed the Great Compression: a drastic narrowing of income gaps, probably as a result of New Deal policies. And the new economic order persisted for more than a generation. Strong unions, taxes on inherited wealth, corporate profits and high incomes, and close public scrutiny of corporate management all helped to keep income gaps relatively small. The economy was hardly egalitarian, but a generation ago the gross inequalities of the 1920s seemed very distant.

Now they're back. According to estimates by the economists Thomas Piketty and Emmanuel Saez—confirmed by data from the Congressional Budget Office—between 1973 and 2000 the average real income of the bottom 90% of American taxpayers actually fell by 7%. Meanwhile, the income of the top 1% rose by 148%, the income of the top 0.1% rose by 343% and the income of the top 0.01% rose 599%. (Those numbers exclude capital gains, so they're not an artifact of the stock-market bubble.) The distribution of income in the United States has gone right back to Gilded Age levels of inequality.

Never mind, say the apologists, who churn out papers with titles like that of a 2001 Heritage Foundation piece, "Income Mobility and the Fallacy of Class-Warfare Arguments." America, they say, isn't a caste society—people with high incomes this year may have low incomes next year and vice versa, and the route to wealth is open to all. That's where those commies at *Business Week* come in. As they point out (and as economists and sociologists have been pointing out for some time), America actually is more of a caste society than we like to think. And the caste lines have lately become a lot more rigid.

The myth of income mobility has always exceeded the reality. As a general rule, once they've reached their 30s, people don't move up and down the income ladder very much. Conservatives often cite studies like a 1992 report by Glenn Hubbard, a Treasury official under the elder Bush who later became chief economic adviser to the younger Bush, that purport to show large numbers of Americans moving from low-wage to high-wage jobs during their working lives. But what these studies measure, as the economist Kevin Murphy put it, is mainly "the guy who works in the college bookstore and has a real job by his early 30s." Serious studies that exclude this sort of pseudo-mobility show that inequality in average incomes over long periods isn't much smaller than inequality in annual incomes.

It is true, however, that America was once a place of substantial intergenerational mobility—sons often did much better than their fathers. A classic 1978 survey found that among adult men whose fathers were in the bottom 25% of the population as ranked by social and economic status, 23% had made it into the top 25%. In other words, during the first thirty years or so after World War II, the American dream of upward mobility was a real experience for many people.

Now for the shocker: The *Business Week* piece cites a new survey of today's adult men, which finds that this number has dropped to only 10%. That is, over the past generation upward mobility has fallen drastically. Very few children of the lower class are making their way to even moderate affluence. This goes along with other studies indicating that rags-to-riches stories have become vanishingly rare, and that the correlation between fathers' and sons' incomes has risen in recent decades. In modern America, it seems, you're quite likely to stay in the social and economic class into which you were born.

Business Week attributes this to the "Wal-Martization" of the economy, the proliferation of dead-end, low-wage jobs and the disappearance of jobs that provide entry to the middle class. That's surely part of the explanation. But public policy plays a role—and will, if present trends continue, play an even bigger role in the future.

Put it this way: Suppose that you actually liked a caste society, and you were seeking ways to use your control of the government to further entrench the advantages of the haves against the have-nots. What would you do?

One thing you would definitely do is get rid of the estate tax, so that large fortunes can be passed on to the next generation. More broadly, you would seek to reduce tax rates both on corporate profits and on unearned income such as dividends and capital gains, so that those with large accumulated or inherited wealth could more easily accumulate even more. You'd also try to create tax shelters mainly useful for the rich. And more broadly still, you'd try to reduce tax rates on people with high incomes, shifting the burden to the payroll tax and other revenue sources that bear most heavily on people with lower incomes.

Meanwhile, on the spending side, you'd cut back on healthcare for the poor, on the quality of public education and on state aid for higher education. This would make it more difficult for people with low incomes to climb out of their difficulties and acquire the education essential to upward mobility in the modern economy.

And just to close off as many routes to upward mobility as possible, you'd do everything possible to break the power of unions, and you'd privatize government functions so that well-paid civil servants could be replaced with poorly paid private employees.

It all sounds sort of familiar, doesn't it?

Where is this taking us? Thomas Piketty, whose work with Saez has transformed our understanding of income distribution, warns that current policies will eventually create "a class of rentiers in the U.S., whereby a small group of wealthy but untalented children controls vast segments of the US economy and penniless, talented children simply can't compete." If he's right—and I fear that he is—we will end up suffering not only from injustice, but from a vast waste of human potential.

Goodbye, Horatio Alger. And goodbye, American Dream.

Article 2.4

THE UNDESERVING RICH

Collectively produced and inherited knowledge and the (re)distribution of income and wealth.

BY GAR ALPEROVITZ AND LEW DALY
March/April 2010

Warren Buffett, one of the wealthiest men in the nation, is worth nearly $50 billion. Does he "deserve" all this money? Why? Did he work so much harder than everyone else? Did he create something so extraordinary that no one else could have created it? Ask Buffett himself and he will tell you that he thinks "society is responsible for a very significant percentage of what I've earned." But if that's true, doesn't society deserve a very significant share of what he has earned?

When asked why he is so successful, Buffett commonly replies that this is the wrong question. The more important question, he stresses, is why he has *so much to work with* compared to other people in the world, or compared to previous generations of Americans. How much money would I have "if I were born in Bangladesh," or "if I was born here in 1700," he asks.

Buffett may or may not deserve something more than another person working with what a given historical or collective context provides. As he observes, however, it is simply not possible to argue in any serious way that he deserves *all* of the benefits that are clearly attributable to living in a highly developed society.

Buffett has put his finger on one of the most explosive issues developing just beneath the surface of public awareness. Over the last several decades, economic research has done a great deal of solid work pinpointing much more precisely than in the past what share of what we call "wealth" society creates versus what share any individual can be said to have earned and thus deserved. This research raises profound moral—and ultimately political—questions.

Recent estimates suggest that U.S. economic output per capita has increased more than twenty-fold since 1800. Output per hour worked has increased an estimated fifteen-fold since 1870 alone. Yet the average modern person likely works with no greater commitment, risk, or intelligence than his or her counterpart from the past. What is the primary cause of such vast gains if individuals do not really "improve"? Clearly, it is largely that the scientific, technical, and cultural knowledge available to us, and the efficiency of our means of storing and retrieving this knowledge, have grown at a scale and pace that far outstrip any other factor in the nation's economic development.

A half century ago, in 1957, economist Robert Solow calculated that nearly 90% of productivity growth in the first half of the 20th century (from 1909 to 1949) could only be attributed to "technical change in the broadest sense." The supply of labor and capital—what workers and employers contribute—appeared almost incidental to this massive technological "residual." Subsequent research inspired by Solow and others continued to point to "advances in knowledge" as the main source of growth. Economist William Baumol calculates that "nearly 90 percent . . . of current GDP was contributed by innovation carried out since 1870." Baumol judges that his estimate, in fact, understates the cumulative influence of past advances: Even "the steam engine, the railroad, and many other inventions of an earlier era, still add to today's GDP."

Related research on the sources of invention bolsters the new view, posing a powerful challenge to conventional, heroic views of technology that characterize progress as a sequence of extraordinary contributions by "Great Men" (occasionally "Great Women") and their "Great Inventions." In contrast to this popular view, historians of technology have carefully delineated the incremental and cumulative way most technologies actually develop. In general, a specific field of knowledge builds up slowly through diverse contributions over time until—at a particular moment when enough has been established—the next so-called "breakthrough" becomes all but inevitable.

Often many people reach the same point at virtually the same time, for the simple reason that they all are working from the same developing information and research base. The next step commonly becomes obvious (or if not obvious, very likely to be taken within a few months or years). We tend to give credit to the person who gets there first—or rather, who gets the first public attention, since often the real originator is not as good at public relations as the one who jumps to the front of the line and claims credit. Thus, we remember Alexander Graham Bell as the inventor of the telephone even though, among others, Elisha Gray and Antonio Meucci got there at the same time or even before him. Newton and Leibniz hit upon the calculus at roughly the same time in the 1670s; Darwin and Alfred Russel Wallace produced essentially the same theory of evolution at roughly the same time in the late 1850s.

Less important than who gets the credit is the simple fact that most breakthroughs occur not so much thanks to one "genius," but because of the longer historical unfolding of knowledge. All of this knowledge—the overwhelming source of all modern wealth—comes to us today *through no effort of our own*. It is the generous and unearned gift of the past. In the words of Northwestern economist Joel Mokyr, it is a "free lunch."

Collective knowledge is often created by formal public efforts as well, a point progressives often stress. Many of the advances which propelled our high-tech economy in the early 1990s grew directly out of research programs and technical systems financed and often collaboratively developed by the federal government. The Internet, to take the most obvious example, began as a government defense project, the ARPANET, in the early 1960s. Up through the 1980s there was little private investment or interest in developing computer networks. Today's vast software industry also rests on a foundation of computer language and operating hardware developed in large part with public support. The Bill Gateses of the world—the heroes of the "New Economy"—might still be working with vacuum tubes and punch cards were it not for critical research and technology programs created or financed by the federal government after World War II. Other illustrations range from jet airplanes and radar to the basic life science research undergirding many pharmaceutical industry advances. Yet the truth is that the role of collectively inherited knowledge is far, far greater than just the contributions made by direct public support, important as they are.

A straightforward but rarely confronted question arises from these facts: If most of what we have today is attributable to advances we inherit in common, then why should this gift of our collective history not more generously benefit all members of society?

The top 1% of U.S. households now receives more income than the bottom 120 million Americans combined. The richest 1% of households owns nearly half of all investment assets (stocks and mutual funds, financial securities, business equity, trusts, non-home real estate). The bottom 90% of the population owns less than 15%; the bottom half—150 million Americans—owns less than 1%. If America's vast wealth is mainly a gift of our common past, what justifies such disparities?

Robert Dahl, one of America's leading political scientists—and one of the few to have confronted these facts—put it this way after reading economist Edward Denison's pioneering work on growth accounting: "It is immediately obvious that little growth in the American economy can be attributed to the actions of particular individuals." He concluded straightforwardly that, accordingly, "the control and ownership of the economy rightfully belongs to 'society.'"

Contrast Dahl's view with that of Joe the Plumber, who famously inserted himself into the 2008 presidential campaign with his repeated claim that he has "earned" everything he gets and so any attempt to tax his earnings is totally unjustified. Likewise, "we didn't rely on somebody else to build what we built," banking titan Sanford Weill tells us in a *New York Times* front-page story on the "New Gilded Age." "I think there are people," another executive tells the *Times*, "who because of their uniqueness warrant whatever the market will bear."

A direct confrontation with the role of knowledge—and especially inherited knowledge—goes to the root of a profound challenge to such arguments. One way to think about all this is by focusing on the concept of "earned" versus "unearned" income. Today this distinction can be found in conservative attacks on welfare "cheats" who refuse to work to earn their keep, as well as in calls even by some Republican senators to tax the windfall oil-company profits occasioned by the Iraq war and Hurricane Katrina.

The concept of unearned income first came into clear focus during the era of rapidly rising land values caused by grain shortages in early 19th-century England. Wealth derived *simply* from owning land whose price was escalating appeared illegitimate because no individual truly "earned" such wealth. Land values—and especially explosively high values—were largely the product of factors such as fertility, location, and population pressures. The huge profits (unearned "rents," in the technical language of economics) landowners reaped when there were food shortages were viewed as particularly egregious. David Ricardo's influential theory of "differential rent"—i.e., that land values are determined by differences in fertility and location between different plots of land—along with religious perspectives reaching back to the Book of Genesis played a central role in sharpening this critical moral distinction.

John Stuart Mill, among others, developed the distinction between "earned" and "unearned" in the middle decades of the 19th century and applied it to other forms of "external wealth," or what he called "wealth created by circumstances." Mill's approach fed into a growing sense of the importance of societal inputs which produce economic gains beyond what can be ascribed to one person working alone in nature without benefit of civilization's many contributions. Here a second element of what appears, historically, as a slowly evolving understanding also becomes clear: If contribution is important in determining rewards, then, Mill and others urged, since society at large makes major contributions to economic achievement, it too has "earned" and deserves a share of what has been created. Mill believed strongly in personal contribution and individual reward, but he held that in principle wealth "created by circumstances" should be reclaimed for social purposes. Karl Marx, of course, tapped the distinction between earned and unearned in his much broader attack on capitalism and its exploitation of workers' labor.

The American republican writer Thomas Paine was among the first to articulate a societal theory of wealth based directly on the earned\unearned distinction. Paine argued that everything "beyond what a man's own hands produce" was a gift which came to him simply by living in society, and hence "he owes on every principle of justice, of gratitude, and of civilization, a part of that accumulation back again to society from whence the whole came." A later American reformer, Henry George, focused on urban land rather than the agricultural land at the heart of Ricardo's concern. George challenged what he called "the unearned increment" which is created when population growth and other societal factors increase land values. In Britain, J. A. Hobson argued that the unearned value created by the industrial system in general was much larger than just the part which accrued to landowners, and that it should be treated in a similar (if not more radical and comprehensive) fashion. In a similar vein, Hobson's early 20th-century contemporary Leonard Trelawny Hobhouse declared that the "prosperous business man" should consider "what single step he could have taken" without the "sum of intelligence which civilization has placed at his disposal." More recently, the famed American social scientist Herbert Simon judged that if "we are very generous with ourselves, I suppose we might claim that we 'earned' as much as one fifth of [our income]."

The distinction between earned and unearned gains is central to most of these thinkers, as is the notion that societal contributions—including everything an industrial economy requires, from the creation of laws, police, and courts to the development of schools, trade restrictions, and patents—must be recognized and rewarded. The understanding that such societal contributions are both contemporary and have made a huge and cumulative contribution over all of history is also widely accepted. Much of the income they permit and confer now appears broadly analogous to the unearned rent a landlord claims. What is new and significant here is the further clarification that by far the most important element in all this is the accumulated *knowledge* which society contributes over time.

All of this, as sociologist Daniel Bell has suggested, requires a new "knowledge theory of value"—especially as we move deeper into the high-tech era through computerization, the Internet, cybernetics, and cutting-edge fields such as gene therapy and nanotechnology. One way to grasp what is at stake is the following: A person today working the same number of hours as a similar person in 1870—working just as hard but no harder—will produce perhaps 15 times as much economic output. It is clear that the contemporary person can hardly be said to have "earned" his much greater productivity.

Consider further that if we project forward the past century's rate of growth, a person working a century from now would be able to produce—and potentially receive as "income"—up to seven times today's average income. By far the greatest part of this gain will also come to this person as a free gift of the past—the gift of the new knowledge created, passed on, and inherited from our own time forward.

She and her descendents, in fact, will inevitably contribute less, relative to the huge and now expanded contribution of the past, than we do today. The obvious question, again, is simply this: to what degree is it meaningful to say that this person will have "earned" all that may come her way? These and other realities suggest that the quiet revolution in our understanding of how wealth is created has ramifications for a much more profound and far-reaching challenge to today's untenable distribution of income and wealth.

Article 2.5

WHO GETS THE VALUE WE ALL PRODUCE?

BY ARTHUR MacEWAN
March/April 2011

> Dear Dr. Dollar:
> *I found government statistics that seem to show that workers' share of gross domestic product (GDP) is just 55% and that the other 45% goes to people who didn't work for it. Can this be true?*
> —Doug Marshall, United Steelworkers Local 8957, Bell, Calif.

Usually, when I look at some economic phenomenon, I find myself thinking, "It's always worse than we think it is!" However, this is one of those rare instances where maybe it's not as bad as we think it is. *Maybe*. While the figure of 55% of GDP going to wages (and benefits) is correct, not everything else goes to "people who didn't work for it."

First of all, not all of GDP goes to people as income. So let's look at a different measure known as National Income. The table below gives the breakdown for 2008 (not an unusual year for these figures).

The income categories here that fall clearly under the rubric of "people who didn't work for it" are corporate profits, net interest income, and rental income—which together account for less than 20% of the total. Many "proprietors" are people who work for their income—doctors and other professionals, shopkeepers, farmers, etc.

The trouble is that these data don't tell us what we really want to know. Included in the "wages, salaries, and benefits" category are the huge salaries and bonuses

---

NATIONAL INCOME BY CATEGORY, 2008

	$ in billions	Percent*
Wages, salaries, and benefits	8,037.4	63.6
Corporate profits	1,360.4	10.8
Net interest income	815.1	6.5
Rental income	210.4	1.7
Proprietors' income	1,106.3	8.8
Tax adjustments	1,047.3	8.3
Other adjustments	58.4	.5

*Does not add up to 100% due to rounding

Notes: All data are before income taxes. "Tax adjustments" are indirect taxes, e.g., sales and property taxes. "Net interest" is the interest paid by private enterprises less the interest received by private enterprises, plus the interest paid by the rest of the world less the interest received by the rest of the world. Interest payments on mortgage and home equity loans are included in interest paid by private enterprises because home ownership is treated in the national accounts as a private enterprise.

Source: *Economic Report of the President 2010*, TABLE B–28. National income by type of income, 1960–2009.

that go to high-level executives, incomes that really should be in the profits category. Also, with the rapid rise in health care costs, "benefits" represent a growing share of workers' total compensation. Take out the "benefits," and in 2008 "wages and salaries" accounted for only 51.8% of National Income; in the 1970s, this figure averaged 56.8%.

Then there is depreciation. Approximately 12% of GDP in 2008 was classified as depreciation of capital equipment and resources, and is not included as part of National Income. This money goes to firms, but it doesn't count in the calculation of their profits. Not only does this give firms a distinct tax advantage, but it also involves a very unequal treatment of firms and real people. We real people spend a lot on depreciation of our homes, cars, and everything else that needs repairing or replacing over time; but we can't take those costs as a tax deduction. If we could deduct depreciation from our incomes before paying our taxes, our incomes—like firms' incomes—would appear smaller (and our taxes would be less).

These sorts of data showing shares of National Income or GDP do tell us some interesting things, but they don't really tell us how the value we all produce gets divided up. Perhaps the best way to see that is by looking directly at what's called the "size distribution of income"—that is, what percentage of income goes to each percentage group of the population, from the top to the bottom. In 2007, on the eve of the implosion of the economy, the 1% at the very top was getting almost 25% of all income, and the top 10% was getting almost 50% of all income. In 1928, with the Great Depression about to descend on the country, the figures were just about the same. But things have been better. In the 1970s, these figures were about 9% of income for the top 1% and about 33% of income for the top 10%.

So maybe it's at least as bad as we think it is after all.

Article 2.6

MEASURES OF POVERTY

BY ELLEN FRANK
January/February 2006, updated May 2009

> Dear Dr. Dollar:
> *Can you explain how poverty is defined in government statistics? Is this a realistic definition?*
> —Susan Balok, Savannah, Ga.

Each February, the Census Bureau publishes the federal poverty thresholds—the income levels for different sized households below which a household is defined as living "in poverty." Each August, the bureau reports how many families, children, adults, and senior citizens fell below the poverty threshold in the prior year. The table below lists the federal poverty thresholds as of 2008.

Using these income levels, the Census Bureau reported that 12.5% percent of U.S. residents and 18.0% of U.S. children lived in poverty in 2007. Black Americans experience poverty at nearly double these rates: 24.5% of all Blacks and 34.5% of Black children live in households with incomes below the poverty line.

The poverty threshold concept was originally devised by Social Security analyst Mollie Orshansky in 1963. Orshansky estimated the cost of an "economy food plan" designed by the Department of Agriculture for "emergency use when funds are low." Working from 1955 data showing that families of three or more spent one-third of their income on food, Orshansky multiplied the food budget by three to calculate the poverty line. Since the early 1960s, the Census Bureau has simply recalculated Orshansky's original figures to account for inflation.

The poverty line is widely regarded as far too low for a household to survive on in most parts of the United States. For one thing, as antipoverty advocates point out, since 1955 the proportion of family budgets devoted to food has fallen from one-third to one-fifth. Families expend far more on non-food necessities such as child care, health care, transportation, and utilities today than they did 50 years ago, for obvious reasons: mothers entering the work force, suburbanization and greater dependence on

Household Size	Federal Poverty Threshold
1 person	$11,201
2 people	14,417
3 people	17,330
4 people	21,834
5 people	25,694

the auto, and soaring health care costs, for example. Were Orshansky formulating a poverty threshold more recently, then, she would likely have multiplied a basic food budget by five rather than by three.

Furthermore, costs—particularly for housing and energy—vary widely across the country, so that an income that might be barely adequate in Mississippi is wholly inadequate in Massachusetts. Yet federal poverty figures make no adjustment for regional differences in costs.

A number of state-level organizations now publish their own estimates of what it takes to support a family in their area, in conjunction with the national training and advocacy group Wider Opportunities for Women. Using local data on housing costs, health care premiums, taxes, and child care costs as well as food, transportation and other necessities, these "self-sufficiency standards" estimate that a two-parent two-child family needs between $40,000 and $70,000 a year, depending on the region, to cover basic needs.

State and federal officials often implicitly recognize that official poverty thresholds are unrealistically low by setting income eligibility criteria for antipoverty programs higher than the poverty level. Households with incomes of 125%, 150%, or even 185% of the federal poverty line are eligible for a number of federal and state programs. In addition, the Census Bureau publishes figures on the number of households with incomes below 200% of the federal poverty line—a level many social scientists call "near poor" or "working poor."

Poverty calculations also have critics on the right. Conservative critics contend that the official poverty rate overstates poverty in the United States. While the Census Bureau's poverty-rate calculations include Social Security benefits, public assistance, unemployment and workers' compensation, SSI (disability) payments, and other forms of cash income, they exclude noncash benefits from state and federal antipoverty programs like Food Stamps, Medicaid, and housing subsidies. If the market value of these benefits were counted in family income, fewer families would count as "poor." On the other hand, by not counting such benefits, policy makers have a better grasp of the numbers of Americans in need of such transfer programs.

Resources: For background information on poverty thresholds and poverty rate calculations, see aspe.hhs.gov/poverty/papers/hptgssiv.htm. Self-sufficiency standards for different states can be found at www.sixstrategies.org/states/states.cfm. In addition, the Economic Policy Institute has calculated family budgets for the 435 metropolitan areas: www.epi.org/content/budget_calculator.

Article 2.7

LIES, DAMNED LIES, AND POVERTY STATISTICS

The Census Bureau is right to reconsider the official poverty line.

BY JEANNETTE WICKS-LIM
July/August 2010

S tatistics matter. Take the newly popularized statistic, the "underemployment rate," that the media began to report during the Great Recession. This rate adds part-time workers who can't find the full-time work they want and people who have given up looking for work altogether to the officially unemployed. In April the underemployment rate reached 17%, indicating that workers are feeling the economic downturn more severely than suggested by the 9.9% official unemployment rate.

The official poverty line similarly misses the mark in measuring economic suffering in the United States. Poverty experts have long recognized that the poverty income threshold published by the Census Bureau marks an excessively severe level of economic deprivation. But the problem isn't just that the poverty line is too low. Anyone can multiply the poverty line by two and use that to define poverty; that's how eligibility for subsidy programs like reduced-price school lunches is determined. The official poverty line, however, actually represents a living standard that deteriorates year after year.

The problem is that the Census Bureau adjusts the poverty line every year for overall inflation with the "Consumer Price Index for All Urban Consumers" (CPI-U). To calculate the CPI-U, a team of Census Bureau surveyors asks consumers about their purchases and determine the cost of the typical "basket" of goods and services purchased. The change in the price tag of this basket from one year to the next is the overall inflation rate. The flaw in using the CPI-U to adjust the poverty line is that the budget of a low-income household is different from that of a middle-income household. We can see this by comparing the Basic Family Budget produced by the Economic Policy Institute (EPI) and average consumer basket used by the DOL to track inflation (see pie charts).

Two expenses—health care and child care—take up greater proportions of EPI's Basic Family Budget than in the DOL's av-

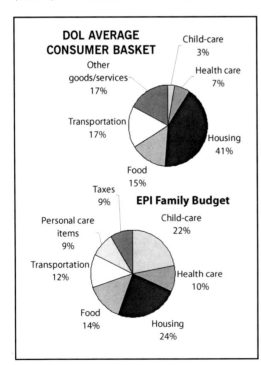

erage consumer basket. This is because the DOL's basket reflects spending by the average household, not specifically households with children. The Basic Family Budget also assumes, reasonably, that all adults in the household need to hold jobs (thus the high child care expenses). Moreover, non-essential items such as recreation activities and extra clothing that an average consumer may buy do not fit into a budget restricted to basic needs.

These differences between the budgets are crucial. Child-care and health-care costs have been rising dramatically faster than overall inflation. According to the DOL, between 1999 and 2009 the cost of child care rose by 57% and the cost of health care rose by 50%. This compares to a general rise in prices of 29%.

Here's a simple exercise to demonstrate what this means. The 1999 official poverty line was $16,895 for a family of four. Double this number is a more reasonable poverty line of $33,790. The Census Bureau raised the poverty line by 29% between 1999 and 2009--the amount of inflation measured by the CPI-U. Twice the 2009 poverty line therefore is $43,590. The income required to support the same *standard of living* in 2009 as in 1999, however, requires a bigger, 39% adjustment up to $46,970 to reflect the rapidly rising costs of child-care and health care. In other words, in 2009, a low-income four-person household would need to bring in another $3,400 over and above the inflation-adjusted $43,590 to maintain the same standard of living in 2009 as in 1999. This $3,400 deficit in the CPI-adjusted figure is equal to over 2/3 of this family's medical care budget.

This past March, the Census Bureau announced that it is undertaking a major project to reconsider how it measures poverty. This is a welcome development. Without revising the official poverty line to reflect the actual costs of families' basic needs, the key statistic we use to understand economic deprivation in the United States will not only undercount the poor, but it will do so by a larger margin every passing year. As the saying goes, "Statistics can be made to prove anything—even the truth."

Sources: "Observations from the Interagency Technical Working Group on Developing a Supplemental Poverty Measure," U.S. Census Bureau, March 2010, census.gov; Economic Policy Institute, "Basic Family Budget Calculator," 2010, epi.org.

Article 2.8

ACCESS TO PAID SICK DAYS VASTLY UNEQUAL

BY ELISE GOULD
April 2011

More than one-third of all workers--38%--have no paid sick days. When these workers get sick, they are either forced to go to work, or stay home without pay and risk losing their job. Access to sick days is also vastly unequal: As shown in the figure, workers at the top of the scale are more than four times more likely to have sick days than workers at the bottom of the wage scale. Only 19% of low-wage workers have paid sick days, compared with 86% of high-wage workers. These low-income workers are the ones who can least afford to lose pay when they are sick.

A 2010 study found that the vast majority of nations (163 in total, almost all of them much poorer than the United States) guarantee paid sick days for workers. A law giving American workers that same benefit could increase productivity in the workforce through heightened worker loyalty, reduced turnover, and reduced workplace illness.

Note: This article originally appeared as an Economic Snapshot at the website of the Economic Policy Institute (www.epi.org/economic_snapshots).

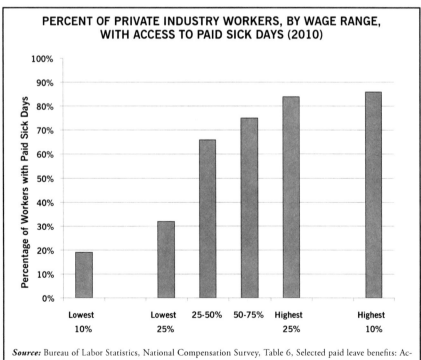

PERCENT OF PRIVATE INDUSTRY WORKERS, BY WAGE RANGE, WITH ACCESS TO PAID SICK DAYS (2010)

Source: Bureau of Labor Statistics, National Compensation Survey, Table 6, Selected paid leave benefits: Access, March 2010.

Article 2.9

GEESE, GOLDEN EGGS, AND TRAPS
Why inequality is bad for the economy.

BY CHRIS TILLY
July/August 2004

Whenever progressives propose ways to redistribute wealth from the rich to those with low and moderate incomes, conservative politicians and economists accuse them of trying to kill the goose that lays the golden egg. The advocates of unfettered capitalism proclaim that inequality is good for the economy because it promotes economic growth. Unequal incomes, they say, provide the incentives necessary to guide productive economic decisions by businesses and individuals. Try to reduce inequality, and you'll sap growth. Furthermore, the conservatives argue, growth actually promotes equality by boosting the have-nots more than the haves. So instead of fiddling with who gets how much, the best way to help those at the bottom is to pump up growth.

But these conservative prescriptions are absolutely, dangerously wrong. Instead of the goose-killer, equality turns out to be the goose. Inequality stifles growth; equality gooses it up. Moreover, economic expansion does not necessarily promote equality—instead, it is the types of jobs and the rules of the economic game that matter most.

Inequality: Goose or Goose-Killer?

The conservative argument may be wrong, but it's straightforward. Inequality is good for the economy, conservatives say, because it provides the right incentives for innovation and economic growth. First of all, people will only have the motivation to work hard, innovate, and invest wisely if the economic system rewards them for good economic choices and penalizes bad ones. Robin Hood-style policies that collect from the wealthy and help those who are worse off violate this principle. They reduce the payoff to smart decisions and lessen the sting of dumb ones. The result: people and companies are bound to make less efficient decisions. "We must allow [individuals] to fail, as well as succeed, and we must replace the nanny state with a regime of self-reliance and self-respect," writes conservative lawyer Stephen Kinsella in *The Freeman: Ideas on Liberty* (not clear how the free woman fits in). To prove their point, conservatives point to the former state socialist countries, whose economies had become stagnant and inefficient by the time they fell at the end of the 1980s.

If you don't buy this incentive story, there's always the well-worn trickle-down theory. To grow, the economy needs productive investments: new offices, factories, computers, and machines. To finance such investments takes a pool of savings. The rich save a larger fraction of their incomes than those less well-off. So to spur growth, give more to the well-heeled (or at least take less away from them in the form of taxes), and give less to the down-and-out. The rich will save their money and then invest it, promoting growth that's good for everyone.

Unfortunately for trickle-down, the brilliant economist John Maynard Keynes debunked the theory in his *General Theory of Employment, Interest, and Money* in 1936. Keynes, whose precepts guided liberal U.S. economic policy from the 1940s through the 1970s, agreed that investments must be financed out of savings. But he showed that most often it's changes in investment that drive savings, rather than the other way around. When businesses are optimistic about the future and invest in building and retooling, the economy booms, all of us make more money, and we put some of it in banks, 401(k)s, stocks, and so on. That is, saving grows to match investment. When companies are glum, the process runs in reverse, and savings shrink to equal investment. This leads to the "paradox of thrift": if people try to save too much, businesses will see less consumer spending, will invest less, and total savings will end up diminishing rather than growing as the economy spirals downward. A number of Keynes's followers added the next logical step: shifting money from the high-saving rich to the high-spending rest of us, and not the other way around, will spur investment and growth.

Of the two conservative arguments in favor of in-equality, the incentive argument is a little weightier. Keynes himself agreed that people needed financial consequences to steer their actions, but questioned whether the differences in payoffs needed to be so huge. Certainly state socialist countries' attempts to replace material incentives with moral exhortation have often fallen short. In 1970, the Cuban government launched the Gran Zafra (Great Harvest), an attempt to reap 10 million tons of sugar cane with (strongly encouraged) volunteer labor. Originally inspired by Che Guevara's ideal of the New Socialist Man (not clear how the New Socialist Woman fit in), the effort ended with Fidel Castro tearfully apologizing to the Cuban people in a nationally broadcast speech for letting wishful thinking guide economic policy.

But before conceding this point to the conservatives, let's look at the evidence about the connection between equality and growth. Economists William Easterly of New York University and Gary Fields of Cornell University have recently summarized this evidence:

- Countries, and regions within countries, with more equal incomes grow faster. (These growth figures do not include environmental destruction or improvement. If they knocked off points for environmental destruction and added points for environmental improvement, the correlation between equality and growth would be even stronger, since desperation drives poor people to adopt environmentally destructive practices such as rapid deforestation.)
- Countries with more equally distributed land grow faster.
- Somewhat disturbingly, more ethnically homogeneous countries and regions grow faster—presumably because there are fewer ethnically based inequalities.
- In addition, more worker rights are associated with higher rates of economic growth, according to Josh Bivens and Christian Weller, economists at two Washington think tanks, the Economic Policy Institute and the Center for American Progress.

These patterns recommend a second look at the incentive question. In fact, more equality can actually strengthen incentives and opportunities to produce.

Equality as the Goose

Equality can boost growth in several ways. Perhaps the simplest is that study after study has shown that farmland is more productive when cultivated in small plots. So organizations promoting more equal distribution of land, like Brazil's Landless Workers' Movement, are not just helping the landless poor—they're contributing to agricultural productivity!

Another reason for the link between equality and growth is what Easterly calls "match effects," which have been highlighted in research by Stanford's Paul Romer and others in recent years. One example of a match effect is the fact that well-educated people are most productive when working with others who have lots of schooling. Likewise, people working with computers are more productive when many others have computers (so that, for example, e-mail communication is widespread, and know-how about computer repair and software is easy to come by). In very unequal societies, highly educated, computer-using elites are surrounded by majorities with little education and no computer access, dragging down their productivity. This decreases young people's incentive to get more education and businesses' incentive to invest in computers, since the payoff will be smaller.

Match effects can even matter at the level of a metropolitan area. Urban economist Larry Ledebur looked at income and employment growth in 85 U.S. cities and their neighboring suburbs. He found that where the income gap between those in the suburbs and those in the city was largest, income and job growth was slower for everyone.

"Pressure effects" also help explain why equality sparks growth. Policies that close off the low-road strategy of exploiting poor and working people create pressure effects, driving economic elites to search for investment opportunities that pay off by boosting productivity rather than squeezing the have-nots harder. For example, where workers have more rights, they will place greater demands on businesses. Business owners will respond by trying to increase productivity, both to remain profitable even after paying higher wages, and to find ways to produce with fewer workers. The CIO union drives in U.S. mass production industries in the 1930s and 1940s provide much of the explanation for the superb productivity growth of the 1950s and 1960s. (The absence of pressure effects may help explain why many past and present state socialist countries have seen slow growth, since they tend to offer numerous protections for workers but no right to organize independent unions.) Similarly, if a government buys out large land-holdings in order to break them up, wealthy families who simply kept their fortunes tied up in land for generations will look for new, productive investments. Industrialization in Asian "tigers" South Korea and Taiwan took off in the 1950s on the wings of funds freed up in exactly this way.

Inequality, Conflict, and Growth

Inequality hinders growth in another important way: it fuels social conflict. Stark inequality in countries such as Bolivia and Haiti has led to chronic conflict that hobbles economic growth. Moreover, inequality ties up resources in unproductive uses such as paying for large numbers of police and security guards—attempts to prevent individuals from redistributing resources through theft.

Ethnic variety is connected to slower growth because, on the average, more ethnically diverse countries are also more likely to be ethnically divided. In other words, the problem isn't ethnic variety itself, but racism and ethnic conflict that can exist among diverse populations. In nations like Guatemala, Congo, and Nigeria, ethnic strife has crippled growth—a problem alien to ethnically uniform Japan and South Korea. The reasons are similar to some of the reasons that large class divides hurt growth. Where ethnic divisions (which can take tribal, language, religious, racial, or regional forms) loom large, dominant ethnic groups seek to use government power to better themselves at the expense of other groups, rather than making broad-based investments in education and infrastructure. This can involve keeping down the underdogs—slower growth in the U.S. South for much of the country's history was linked to the Southern system of white supremacy. Or it can involve seizing the surplus of ethnic groups perceived as better off—in the extreme, Nazi Germany's expropriation and genocide of the Jews, who often held professional and commercial jobs.

Of course, the solution to such divisions is not "ethnic cleansing" so that each country has only one ethnic group—in addition to being morally abhorrent, this is simply impossible in a world with 191 countries and 5,000 ethnic groups. Rather, the solution is to diminish ethnic inequalities. Once the 1964 Civil Rights Act forced the South to drop racist laws, the New South's economic growth spurt began. Easterly reports that in countries with strong rule of law, professional bureaucracies, protection of contracts, and freedom from expropriation—all rules that make it harder for one ethnic group to economically oppress another—ethnic diversity has no negative impact on growth.

If more equality leads to faster growth so everybody benefits, why do the rich typically resist redistribution? Looking at the ways that equity seeds growth helps us understand why. The importance of pressure effects tells us that the wealthy often don't think about more productive ways to invest or reorganize their businesses until they are forced to. But also, if a country becomes very unequal, it can get stuck in an "inequality trap." Any redistribution involves a tradeoff for the rich. They lose by giving up part of their wealth, but they gain a share in increased economic growth. The bigger the disparity between the rich and the rest, the more the rich have to lose, and the less likely that the equal share of boosted growth they'll get will make up for their loss. Once the gap goes beyond a certain point, the wealthy have a strong incentive to restrict democracy, and to block spending on education which might lead the poor to challenge economic injustice—making reform that much harder.

Does Economic Growth Reduce Inequality?

If inequality isn't actually good for the economy, what about the second part of the conservatives' argument—that growth itself promotes equality? According to the conservatives, those who care about equality should simply pursue growth and wait for equality to follow.

"A rising tide lifts all boats," President John F. Kennedy famously declared. But he said nothing about which boats will rise fastest when the economic tide comes in.

Growth does typically reduce poverty, according to studies reviewed by economist Gary Fields, though some "boats"—especially families with strong barriers to participating in the labor force—stay "stuck in the mud." But inequality can increase at the same time that poverty falls, if the rich gain even faster than the poor do. True, sustained periods of low unemployment, like that in the late 1990s United States, do tend to raise wages at the bottom even faster than salaries at the top. But growth after the recessions of 1991 and 2001 began with years of "jobless recoveries"—growth with inequality.

For decades the prevailing view about growth and inequality within countries was that expressed by Simon Kuznets in his 1955 presidential address to the American Economic Association. Kuznets argued that as countries grew, inequality would first increase, then decrease. The reason is that people will gradually move from the low-income agricultural sector to higher-income industrial jobs—with inequality peaking when the workforce is equally divided between low- and high-income sectors. For mature industrial economies, Kuznets's proposition counsels focusing on growth, assuming that it will bring equity. In developing countries, it calls for enduring current inequality for the sake of future equity and prosperity.

But economic growth doesn't automatically fuel equality. In 1998, economists Klaus Deininger and Lyn Squire traced inequality and growth over time in 48 countries. Five followed the Kuznets pattern, four followed the reverse pattern (decreasing inequality followed by an increase), and the rest showed no systematic pattern. In the United States, for example:

- incomes became more equal during the 1930s through 1940s New Deal period (a time that included economic decline followed by growth);
- from the 1950s through the 1970s, income gaps lessened during booms and expanded during slumps;
- from the late 1970s forward, income inequality worsened fairly consistently, whether the economy was stagnating or growing.

The reasons are not hard to guess. The New Deal intro-duced widespread unionization, a minimum wage, social security, unemployment insurance, and welfare. Since the late 1970s, unions have declined, the inflation-adjusted value of the minimum wage has fallen, and the social safety net has been shredded. In the United States, as elsewhere, growth only promotes equality if policies and institutions to support equity are in place.

Trapped?

Let's revisit the idea of an inequality trap. The notion is that as the gap between the rich and everybody else grows wider, the wealthy become more willing to give up overall growth in return for the larger share they're getting for themselves. The "haves" back policies to control the "have-nots," instead of devoting social resources to educating the poor so they'll be more productive.

Sound familiar? It should. After two decades of widening inequality, the last few years have brought us massive tax cuts that primarily benefit the wealthiest, at the expense of investment in infrastructure and the education, child care, and income supports that would help raise less well-off kids to be productive adults. Federal and state governments have cranked up expenditures on prisons, police, and "homeland security," and Republican campaign organizations have devoted major resources to keeping blacks and the poor away from the polls. If the economic patterns of the past are any indication, we're going to pay for these policies in slower growth and stagnation unless we can find our way out of this inequality trap.

Chapter 3

SAVINGS AND INVESTMENT

INTRODUCTION

Never a slip from the savings cup to the investment lip. That is the orderly world of classical macroeconomics, where every cent of household savings is neatly transferred to corporate investment. In the classical world, savings markets—governed by all-powerful interest rates—work seamlessly to assure that savings are matched by investments, fueling growth in the private economy, which in turn guarantees full employment. Should the flow of savings exceed the uptake of corporate investment, falling interest rates automatically solve the problem.

In the real world, macroeconomies are far messier than classical macroeconomists suggest—a proposition no one doubts today. Keynes argued that there is no neat connection, or nexus, between savings and investment in a modern financial economy. Savings often sit, hoarded and uninvested. And interest rates, no matter how low, seldom coax balky investors to lay out their money in a weak economy. In the Keynesian world, economies regularly suffer from investment shortfalls that lead to recessions and cost workers their jobs.

In this chapter, Gretchen McClain and Randy Albelda report on one critical test of the classical and Keynesian visions, conducted by economist Steven Fazzari. In a massive study of 5,000 manufacturing firms, Fazzari rated the influence of interest rates, business cycle conditions, and firms' financial conditions on their investment in plant and equipment. He concluded that the influence of interest rates is overrated, putting him squarely in the Keynesian camp (Article 3.1).

According to conventional wisdom, the stock market boom of the last decade should have benefited most people in the United States who own corporate stock either directly or indirectly through mutual funds or retirement accounts. But, as Sylvia Allegretto shows, the share of households that own stock has been falling in recent years, and the wealthiest Americans own the great bulk of stock by value (Article 3.2). Also, as economist Ellen Frank explains, there is no logical connection between rising stock prices and rising investment. Stock prices are based on traders' guesses about which stocks are likely to catch the eye of other traders—guesses that can have little to do with actual economic conditions (Article 3.3).

But it was residential investment, a housing boom followed by a mortgage crisis and housing bust, that triggered the instability and uncertainty of today's economic crisis. The housing crisis hit the subprime mortgage market and low-income homeowners first. Amy Gluckman and Howard Karger report on the confusing and risky mortgage options used to get low-income borrowers into trouble (Article 3.5).

The housing crisis then spread to engulf the entire mortgage market and the new financial instruments derived from mortgages, eventually threatening the entire financial system. Economist Gerald Friedman provides a succinct history of financial bubbles in the U.S. economy that demonstrates why financial markets need to be regulated (Article 3.4). And economist Heidi Garrett-Peltier makes the case for a national infrastructure bank. She's convinced that such a bank could upgrade the badly deteriorated bridges, roads, levees, and power systems on which the U.S. economy depends, boost private investment, and counteract economic downturns, even those as severe as the one that followed the financial crisis of 2008 (Article 3.6).

Finally, economist Ramaa Vasudevan provides a primer on the increased importance of financial markets, financial institutions, and financial elites in today's economy and its governing institutions. That failed financial corporations have received massive bailouts, for Vasudevan, only underlines the power they wield in the era of financialization (Article 3.7).

Discussion Questions

1. (Article 3.1) Keynes argued that savings and investment were not balanced by the interest rate but by changes in the level of aggregate output. How does the essay by McClain and Albelda support this claim?

2. (Article 3.1) According to McClain and Albelda, how did Fazzari rate the influence of interest rates, business cycle conditions, and firms' financial conditions on corporate investment? What do his findings suggest about Keynesian and classical theories of investment? Based on his findings, what stabilization policies might be appropriate to promote investment?

3. (Article 3.2) If nearly half of U.S. households own stock either directly or indirectly, how could a rise in the Dow index be inconsequential for most of them?

4. (Article 3.3) During the 1930s, Keynes compared the stock market to a newspaper beauty contest that asked readers to pick the photo of the contestant that other readers would pick as the prettiest. Frank suggests that Keynes' analogy still holds for today's stock market. How does Frank's explanation of stock prices compare with the one in your textbook? Do you find it convincing?

5. (Article 3.4) What aspects of financial assets make them subject to speculative manias and panics? And what does this pattern suggest about the proper public policy for overseeing financial markets?

6. (Article 3.5) What are some of the creative new mortgage products that proliferated in the sub-prime mortgage market, where the financial crisis first emerged. Are Gluckman and Karger right that we should read "creative" as confusing and risky?

7. (Article 3.6) What evidence does Garrett-Peltier rely upon to make the case for a U.S. national infrastructure bank? And exactly how would infrastructure spending boost private investment?

8. (Article 3.7) What is financialization? How does it manifest itself in today's economy? How did it contribute to the recent financial crisis?

Article 3.1

BOOSTING INVESTMENT
The overrated influence of interest rates

BY GRETCHEN McCLAIN AND RANDY ALBELDA
July 1993, revised April 2001

Few economists or politicians would disagree that an economy's prospects for long-term growth depend on the productive capacity of its people and its physical equipment. But what to invest in—and how to get the appropriate economic actors to invest—is a matter of much debate.

All economies face a choice between using their productive resources to produce goods and services to be consumed now, and forsaking today's consumption to produce more goods for the future. While catering to consumption today may be more satisfying for wealthier countries and absolutely vital for poor countries, it fails to provide for future growth.

Investing in new plant and equipment can stimulate growth over time, as it provides the physical capacity for new production. Moreover, new plant and equipment tend to be better designed than the existing capital stock, and the improvement usually helps to boost output per worker. If this new productivity translates into higher wages, investment can also increase a country's standard of living and improve employment possibilities. In turn, improving human productive capacity—through training and education—can lead to growth and increased productivity in the long run.

Investment, and the consequent increase in productivity, is critical for international economic success. The more efficiently a country can produce a product, the more competitive that country will be in the world market. Since international markets provide an avenue of demand for our goods, the more domestically produced products and services we can sell abroad, the more jobs we can support here.

Investment can also help stimulate the economy in the short run. During an economic downturn, increased investment will yield more jobs and income for workers who would otherwise be unemployed. They will then return their income to the market when they purchase goods and services, which will boost demand for those products. Economists call this the "multiplier effect." The increase in demand in turn encourages firms to invest more so that they can meet that demand—known to economists as the "accelerator effect." All in all, such a cycle creates more jobs, income, and spending.

While few economists dispute the importance of investment, many disagree on what type is needed, which sectors of the economy are best able to provide it, and what are the best ways to encourage investment. Typically, these debates have revolved around the government's role in encouraging private investment in new plant and equipment. But the role that public investment in infrastructure and education plays in promoting not only our economic well-being and growth, but also in encouraging private investment, could and should widen the terms of the debate.

The Backdrop

The traditional economic argument about investment—and the prevailing conservative line espoused by elected officials at the federal and state levels—has been that the most important fiscal policies to encourage privately owned firms to invest are those which boost profits. If the government helps provide the conditions for profitability, the argument goes, firms will be encouraged to make the right types of investment.

Government tax-and-spend policies during the 1980s and 1990s have often tried to promote investment by reducing corporate taxes, in order to boost profits and stimulate savings. Such measures were supposed to leave firms with a bigger bottom line, in the hope that they would turn profits into new plant and equipment. Cuts in personal income tax rates—especially for the wealthiest—were intended to leave people with more after-tax income that they could save. Higher savings, according to this logic, translates into lower interest rates which in turn lead to more investment. While such policies have been very effective in redistributing money from the poor to the wealthy, they did not do much for investment. For example, the amount of new fixed investment (i.e., new plant and equipment) relative to the total amount of plant and equipment actually sank to its lowest post-World War II mark between 1989 and 1991.

Merely providing the conditions for profit-making does not mean that private firms will plow those profits back into new plant and equipment. Speculation on real-estate markets, the value of foreign currencies, or the price of silver and gold could easily eat up new profits. Much of the money generated for investment in the 1980s financed mergers and acquisitions, which generally resulted in less employment and little new physical productive capacity. And, perhaps even more important, new investment by U.S. firms may not take place in the United States. Investing abroad has been the trend since the 1970s. Finally, even if there is domestic investment and it increases productivity, unless workers share in those gains it may not promote robust growth or increase the standard of living of the country as a whole.

In the face of the failure of the 1980s policies to promote investment, conservatives came up with a new explanation of why the economy was so sluggish: the deficit. Ironically, the conservative policies mentioned above were largely responsible for the public debt, but nonetheless Republicans, along with many Democrats galvanized by billionaire Ross Perot, latched onto deficit reduction as the most important fiscal policy of the 1990s.

The deficit, they argued, kept long-term interest rates high because it created competition for precious funds. The result was that federal borrowing, necessitated by debt-financed government spending and tax cuts, "crowded out" private investment. The best solution, they said, was to reduce the deficit and bring down long-term interest rates so that private investment would thrive.

Identifying Influence

Economist Steven Fazzari tackled these assumptions in a study of the influence of the federal government's taxing and spending policies on private investment. Using a large data base from Standard and Poor on over 5,000 manufacturing firms from 1971 to 1990, Fazzari tested three different factors for their effects on levels of investment in plant and equipment: interest rates, the business cycle, and the financial conditions of the firms.

According to Fazzari, these three "channels of influence" shape patterns of investment. First, he takes on the traditionalists, by addressing the costs associated with investment: the price of borrowing money (i.e., interest rates), depreciation (how fast the new piece of equipment or building will lose its value), and taxes affecting both corporate profits and dividends. To measure this channel, Fazzari employs the interest rate on one type of corporate bond.

Next, he considers the influence of the business cycle by looking at sales growth. Traditional economic theory tends to assume a ready market, but Fazzari suggests instead that firms make investment decisions based on their perception of their ability to sell their products. The more robust current sales are and are expected to be, the more likely firms will be willing to risk new investment—regardless of the interest rate. Since the general condition of the economy influences sales levels, it also has an impact on investment.

In Fazzari's examination of the third channel of influence—the financial condition of firms—he again questions conventional wisdom, this time about the supply and demand for loans. Most economists assume that if the expected return on an investment exceeds the interest rate, then the project is profitable and will be undertaken. This is most likely to be true when the firm in question has enough cash on hand from prior profits to make the investment without asking a bank for a loan. Many firms, though, need to borrow money, and some are unable to persuade banks to loan it to them. Banks often refuse loan applications from new businesses with few assets, or charge them prohibitively high interest rates. Even if a young firm finds a potentially profitable investment, severe constraints on raising capital may prevent the firm from pursuing it. A firm's financial condition—not the projected rate of return on the new investment—can thus end up determining whether or not investment takes place.

Perfecting Policy

After looking at the importance of interest rates, the business cycle, and the financial conditions of firms in determining investment, Fazzari found that interest rates exert the weakest influence of the three factors. He concludes that there is no evidence that interest rates significantly affect investment for the fastest growing firms in his sample. Based on these findings, Fazzari claims that "it would be speculative to base policy on the assumption that interest rates drive investment to an important extent, especially for growing firms."

So, what kinds of fiscal policies should we adopt? If we believe Fazzari's results, we should be looking for those that attend to the financial conditions of firms and stimulate demand for products.

A tax cut targeted not at the very rich but at the "middle class" would probably give investment at least a temporary boost by generating increased consumption. Increased sales from a temporary tax cut create the illusion of a permanent increase in demand, and the multiplier and accelerator effects discussed earlier come into play. In order to meet what firms believe is a permanent increase in demand for their goods, they make investments in more equipment, more factories, and more employees.

Another means of encouraging investment that Fazzari evaluates is cutting corporate income taxes. Such cuts increase firms' after-tax profits, leaving them with a larger pool of funds to invest if they so choose. Since there is no guarantee that they will invest the savings from reduced taxes, though, Fazzari prefers investment tax credits (ITCs) to cuts in taxes for all firms. Only if firms invested would they be able to reduce their corporate tax bills. In Fazzari's view, ITCs will effectively encourage investment whether it is sensitive to interest rates or not.

The most important lesson from Fazzari's analysis is that concerns about investment should not stand in the way of policy initiatives that are important for society, such as spending on education and job training, simply because they may increase the federal budget deficit and cause interest rates to rise. Government investments in public works and education will likely increase productivity in the long run, and this can only be good for investment. Moreover, if investment is not sensitive to interest rates, then the much-discussed "crowding out" effect of deficit spending on private business is bound to be very small. And as Fazzari points out, when unemployment is high, the stimulative effects of deficit spending on sales may far outweigh the impacts of increased interest rates.

The focus on balanced budgets should be tempered by a thorough analysis of what this policy implies for society's immediate and long-term welfare. When we underinvest in the economy during a recession by eliminating educational and social investments, the foregone technical innovation resulting from this underinvestment may lead to less efficient workers, and lower productivity, for many years.

Fazzari's results not only repudiate the traditional answer to lagging investment—tax cuts for the wealthy and the lowering of interest rates. Instead, the government should be trying to stimulate the economy through improved physical and social infrastructure, which will boost not only sales but investment and incomes.

Article 3.2

DOW'S REBOUND AFTER THE GREAT RECESSION INCONSEQUENTIAL FOR MOST AMERICANS

BY SYLVIA A. ALLEGRETTO
October 2010

The Dow has rebounded nicely following the bursting of the housing bubble in 2008 and the Great Recession that followed. As of October 2010, the Dow was just above 11,000—a significant improvement over its recent low of 6,630 in March 2009. The Dow has surpassed the 10,000 mark for the greater part of 2010 even as there has not been much improvement in the overall economy. It is clear that there is a disconnect between the stock market and the broader economy, as measured in terms of job growth or the unemployment rate. Thus, it is important to put stock market gains into perspective for average working families. Fostered by the constant focus and widespread attention given to the performance of the stock market, conventional wisdom has it that everyone in the United States is heavily invested in the stock market. However, the data tell a different story.

The most recent triennial data from the Survey of Consumer Finances show that the historically increasing trend in the shares of all households owning any stock was reversed after 2001, when just over half (51.9%) were in the stock market in some form. In 2004 the share fell to just under half (48.6%), which was the first such decline on record (Figure 1), and there was little improvement in 2007when the share was about the same (49.1%).

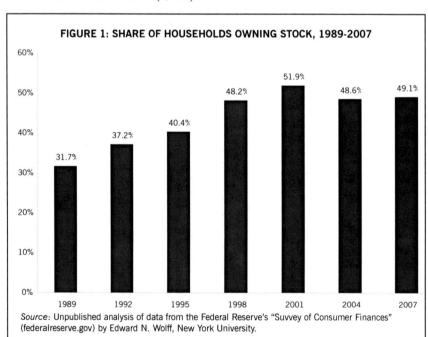

FIGURE 1: SHARE OF HOUSEHOLDS OWNING STOCK, 1989-2007

Source: Unpublished analysis of data from the Federal Reserve's "Suvvey of Consumer Finances" (federalreserve.gov) by Edward N. Wolff, New York University.

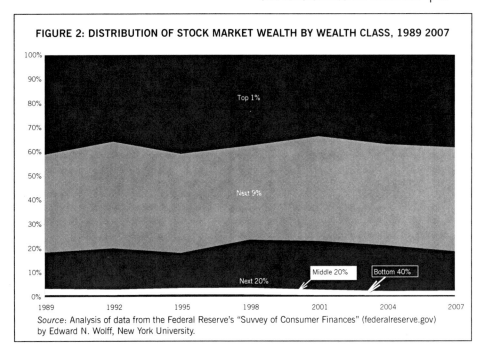

FIGURE 2: DISTRIBUTION OF STOCK MARKET WEALTH BY WEALTH CLASS, 1989 2007

Source: Analysis of data from the Federal Reserve's "Suvvey of Consumer Finances" (federalreserve.gov) by Edward N. Wolff, New York University.

The distribution of stocks by value is highly tilted to the wealthiest Americans, as shown in Figure 2. In 2007, the wealthiest one percent owned 38.2% of all stocks, while the next 9% owned 43.0%. Hence, the wealthiest 10% controlled about 80% of all stocks while the bottom 90% owned just over 20%. Given the starkness and persistence of inequality in stock holdings, there is no reason to think those in the bottom 90% are doing any better in 2010.

For the most part, lower-, middle-, and even upper-middle-income working-age households depend on their paychecks, not stock portfolios, to meet their everyday needs. Typical working families that own stock do so in retirement plans that are costly to turn into cash. Therefore, increasing stock value does little to help them make ends meet at a time when wages for most workers have been stagnant for decades.

Sources: The figures are unpublished updates of Figure 5F and Table 5.7 from *The State of Working America 2006/2007* by Lawrence Mishel, Jared Bernstein, and Sylvia Allegretto, an Economic Policy Institute Book (Ithaca, N.Y.: ILR Press, an imprint of Cornell University Press, 2007).

Article 3.3

WHO DECIDES STOCK PRICES?

BY ELLEN FRANK
May/June 2002

> Dear Dr. Dollar:
>
> *During the course of a single day, a stock can go up and down frequently. These changes supposedly reflect the changing demand for that stock (and its potential resale value) or changing expectations of a company's profitability. But this seems too vague to me. How can these factors be so volatile? Who actually decides, or what is the mechanism for deciding, when a stock price should go up or down and by how much?*
>
> —Joseph Balszak, Muskegon, Mich.

Let's start with your last question first—how are stock prices determined? Shares in most large established corporations are listed on organized exchanges like the New York or American Stock Exchanges. Shares in most smaller or newer firms are listed on the NASDAQ—an electronic system that tracks stock prices.

Every time a stock is sold, the exchange records the price at which it changes hands. If, a few seconds or minutes later, another trade takes place, the price at which that trade is made becomes the new market price, and so on. Organized exchanges like the New York Stock Exchange will occasionally suspend trading in a stock if the price is excessively volatile, if there is a severe mismatch between supply and demand (many people wanting to sell, no one wanting to buy) or if they suspect that insiders are deliberately manipulating a stock's price. But in normal circumstances, there is no official arbiter of stock prices, no person or institution that "decides" a price. The market price of a stock is simply the price at which a willing buyer and seller agree to trade.

Why then do prices fluctuate so much? The vast bulk of stock trades are made by professional traders who buy and sell shares all day long, hoping to profit from small changes in share prices. Since these traders do not hold stocks over the long haul, they are not terribly interested in such long-term considerations as a company's profitability or the value of its assets. Or rather, they are interested in such factors mostly insofar as news that would affect a company's long-term prospects might cause *other traders* to buy the stock, causing its price to rise. If a trader believes that others will buy shares (in the expectation that prices will rise), then she will buy as well, hoping to sell when the price rises. If others believe the same thing, then the wave of buying pressure will, in fact, *cause* the price to rise.

Back in the 1930s, economist John Maynard Keynes compared the stock market to a contest then popular in British tabloids, in which contestants had to look at photos and choose the faces that *other contestants* would pick as the prettiest. Each contestant had to look for photos "likeliest to catch the fancy of the other competitors, all of whom are looking at the problem from the same point of view." Similarly, stock traders try to guess which stocks other traders will buy. The successful trader is the one who anticipates and outfoxes the market, buying before a stock's price rises and selling before it falls.

Financial firms employ thousands of market strategists and technical analysts who spend hours poring over historical stock data, trying to divine the logic behind these price changes. If they could unlock the secret of stock prices, they could arm their traders with the ability to always buy low and sell high. So far, no one has found this particular holy grail. And by continuing to guess and gamble, traders send prices gyrating.

For small investors, who do hold stock for the long term and will need to cash in their stocks at some point to finance their retirements, the volatility of the market can be a source of constant anxiety. Every time a share in, say, General Electric is traded, the new price is used to revalue *all* outstanding shares—just as the value of your home appreciates when the house down the block sells for more than a similar house sold last week. But the value of your home wouldn't be so high if every house on your block were suddenly put up for sale. Similarly, if all ten billion outstanding shares of General Electric—or even a small fraction of them—were put up for sale, they wouldn't fetch anywhere near the current market price. Small investors need to keep in mind that the gains and losses on their 401(k) statements are just hypothetical paper gains and losses. You won't know the true value of your stocks until you actually try to sell them.

Article 3.4

FROM TULIPS TO MORTGAGE-BACKED SECURITIES

BY GERALD FRIEDMAN
January/February 2008

Thirty years ago, economist Charles Kindleberger published a little book, *Manias, Panics, and Crashes,* describing the normal tendency of capitalist financial markets to fluctuate between speculative excess (or "irrational exuberance" in the words of a recent central banker) and panic. Kindleberger describes about 40 of these panics over the nearly 260 years from 1720–1975, or one every seven years. Following Kindleberger's arithmetic, we were due for a panic because it had been seven years since the high-tech bubble burst and the stock market panic of 2000-01. And the panic came, bringing in its wake a tsunami of economic woe, liquidity shortages, cancelled investments, rising unemployment, and economic distress.

Of course, more than mechanics and arithmetic are involved in the current financial panic. But there is a sense of inevitability about the manias and panics of capitalist financial markets, a sense described by writers from Karl Marx to John Maynard Keynes, Hyman Minsky, John Kenneth Galbraith, and Robert Shiller. The problem is that financial markets trade in unknown and unknowable future returns. Lacking real information, they are inevitably driven by the madness of crowds.

Unlike tangible commodities whose price should reflect its real value and real cost of production, financial assets are not priced according to any real returns, nor even according to some expected return, but rather according to expectations of what others will pay in the future, or, even worse, expectations of future expectations that others will have of assets' future return. Whether it is Dutch tulips in 1637, the South Sea Bubble of 1720, Florida real estate in the 1920s, or mortgage-backed securities today, it is always the same story of financial markets floating like a manic-depressive from euphoria to panic to bust. When unregulated, this process is made still worse by market manipulation, and simple fraud. Speculative markets like these can make some rich, and can even be exciting to watch, like a good game of poker; but this is a dangerous and irresponsible way to manage an economy.

There was a time when governments understood. Learning from past financial disasters, the United States established rules to limit the scope of financial euphoria and panic by strictly segregating different types of banks, by limiting financial speculation, and by requiring clear accounting of financial transactions. While they were regulated, financial markets contributed to the best period of growth in American history, the "glorious thirty" after World War II. To be sure, restrictions on speculative behavior and strict regulations made this a boring time to be a banker, and they limited earnings in the financial services sector. But, limited to a secondary role, finance served a greater good by providing liquidity for a long period of steady and relatively egalitarian economic growth.

Of course, over time we forgot why we had regulated financial markets, memory loss helped along by the combined efforts of free-market economists and self-interested bankers and others on Wall Street. To promote "competition," we lowered the barriers between different types of financial institutions, widening the scope of financial markets. We moved activities such as home mortgage lending onto national markets and allowed a rash of bank mergers to create huge financial institutions too large to be allowed to fail, but never too large to operate irresponsibly. Despite the growing scope and centralization of financial activity, the government accepted arguments that we could trust financial firms to self-regulate because it was in their interest to maintain credible accounting.

So we reap the whirlwind with a market collapse building to Great Depression levels. Once again, we learn history's lesson from direct experience: capitalist financial markets cannot be trusted. It is time to either re-regulate or move beyond.

Article 3.5

THE NEW WORLD OF HOME LOANS

BY AMY GLUCKMAN AND HOWARD KARGER
September/October 2007

Buying a home is the largest purchase most families will make in their lifetimes, the largest expenditure in a family budget, and the single largest asset for two-thirds of homeowners. It's also the most fraught with danger—in large part thanks to the growing chasm between ever-higher home prices and stagnant lower- and middle-class incomes. The last decade has seen an unprecedented surge in home prices to levels that current incomes simply do not support. For example, only 18% of Californians can afford the median house in the state using traditional loan-affordability calculations.

This disparity might have put a dent in the mortgage finance business. But no: in 2005, Americans owed $5.7 trillion in mortgages, a 50% increase in just four years. Over the past decade the mortgage finance industry has developed creative schemes designed to squeeze potential homebuyers, albeit often temporarily, into houses they cannot afford.

Most of the new mortgage products fall into the category of subprime mortgages—those offered to people whose problematic credit drops them into a lower lending category. They are generally adjustable-rate mortgages (ARMs) with some kind of a twist. Here are a few of these "creative" (read: confusing and risky) mortgage options.

Option ARM: With this loan, borrowers choose each month which of three or four different—and fluctuating—payments to make:

• full (principal+interest) payment based on a 30-year or 15-year repayment schedule.

• interest-only payment—does not reduce the loan principal or build homeowner equity. Borrowers who pay only interest for a period of time then face a big jump in the size of monthly payments or else are forced to refinance.

• minimum payment—may be lower than one month's interest; if so, the shortfall is added to the loan balance. The result is "negative amortization": over time, the principal goes up, not down. Eventually the borrower may have an "upside down" mortgage where the debt is greater than the market value of the home.

According to the credit rating firm Fitch Ratings, up to 80% of all option ARM borrowers choose the minimum monthly payment option. So it's no surprise that in 2005, 20% of option ARMs were "upside down." When a negative amortization limit is reached, the minimum payment jumps up to fully amortize the loan for the remaining loan term. In other words, borrowers suddenly have to start paying the real bill.

Even borrowers who pay more than the monthly minimums can face payment shocks. Option ARMs often start with a temporary super-low teaser interest rate (and correspondingly low monthly payments) that allows borrowers to qualify for "more house." The catch? Since the low initial monthly payment, based on interest rates as low as 1.25%, is not enough to cover the real interest rate, the borrower eventually faces a sudden increase in monthly payments.

Balloon Loan: This loan is written for a short 5- to 7-year term during which the borrower pays either interest and principal each month or, in a more predatory form, interest only. At the end of the loan term, the borrower must pay off the entire loan in a lump sum—the "balloon payment." At that point, buyers must either refinance or lose their homes. Balloon loans are known to real estate pros as "bullet loans," since if the loan comes due—forcing the owner to refinance—during a period of high interest rates, it's like getting a bullet in the heart. According to the national organizing and advocacy group ACORN, about 10% of all subprime loans are balloons.

Balloon loans are sometimes structured with monthly payments that fail to cover the interest, much less pay down the principal. Although the borrower makes regular payments, her loan balance increases each month: negative amortization. Many borrowers are unaware that they have a negative amortization loan until they have to refinance.

Shared Appreciation Mortgage (SAM): These are fixed-rate loans for up to 30 years that have easier credit qualifications and lower monthly payments than conventional mortgages. In exchange for a lower interest rate, the borrower relinquishes part of the future value of the home to the lender. Interest rate reductions are based on how much appreciation the borrower is willing to give up. SAMs discourage "sweat equity" since the homeowner receives only some fraction of the appreciation resulting from any improvements. Not surprisingly, these loans have been likened to sharecropping.

Stated-Income Loan: Aimed at borrowers who do not draw regular wages from an employer but live on tips, casual jobs that pay under the table, commissions, or investments, this loan does not require W-2 forms or other standard wage documentation. The trade-off: higher interest rates.

No-Ratio Loan: The debt-income ratio (the borrower's monthly payments on debt, including the planned mortgage, divided by her monthly income) is a standard benchmark that lenders use to determine how large a mortgage they will write. In return for a higher interest rate, the no-ratio loan abandons this benchmark; it is aimed at borrowers with complex financial lives or those who are experiencing divorce, the death of a spouse, or a career change.

Article 3.6

THE CASE FOR A NATIONAL INFRASTRUCTURE BANK

A bank could be a recession-proof source of jobs.

BY HEIDI GARRETT-PELTIER
November/December 2010

Tragic events in recent years, such as the Minnesota bridge collapse or New Orleans' failed levees, combined with the daily aggravations of pot holes and power failures, underscore the need for improved infrastructure across the United States. The American Society of Civil Engineers gave the United States a "D" on its most recent *Report Card for America's Infrastructure*; the organization estimates that it will cost $2.2 trillion over the next five years to bring our infrastructure up to "good" condition.

Besides helping prevent disasters, infrastructure improvements create jobs. Maintenance, repair, and new construction of roads, buildings, water, and energy systems create jobs for engineers, construction crews, machinery manufacturers, and bookkeepers, among others.

Infrastructure improvements also have so-called positive externalities: their social benefits are greater than the financial gains earned by the parties who fund them. Improving roads, bridges, and transit systems can increase productivity, lower the cost of maintaining cars and buses, and reduce carbon emissions. Energy investments can increase productivity, and if directed toward energy efficiency and renewables, can also promote environmental sustainability. Investments in water systems lead to better health and lower health care costs.

Private companies cannot reap financial rewards from all of these indirect benefits. For instance, a private rail company could not feasibly charge a fee to everyone who enjoys less-congested roads or cleaner air thanks to a new rail line. So infrastructure projects have traditionally been publicly funded, primarily at the local level with some state and federal assistance.

Public infrastructure funding often falls short, however. In a recession, state and local tax revenues fall, making it harder to fund infrastructure projects precisely at a time when they could help the economy recover. Another problem is that during downturns and recoveries alike, higher-income localities are better able to fund their own roads or water systems than poorer ones. So available funds do not necessarily go to the projects providing the greatest benefits.

Today the United States invests in infrastructure at only half the level the ASCE recommends. One proposal for an innovative method to finance infrastructure is currently garnering bipartisan interest—a national infrastructure bank (NIB). An NIB would be a quasi-public agency whose function would be to use some federal funds to leverage a much larger amount of state, local, and private money which it would then provide to infrastructure projects.

An NIB could use various tools to finance infrastructure. It could sell bonds to private investors. It could be set up as a revolving loan fund, whereby an initial pool of funds is lent, and future loans made only once the earlier ones are repaid. It could even make grants for certain projects.

There are merits and drawbacks to any of these financing models. Some would make the NIB entirely self-sustaining, and so compel it to prioritize projects with a revenue stream, for instance from tolls, that would go to paying back the loan. Such a model would limit the bank's ability to choose projects with greater social benefits but less ability to repay funds quickly: it might fund construction of a toll road to a wealthy suburb rather than an upgrade to a municipal water system despite the latter's greater benefit. Other models would require more federal spending, but would give the bank greater flexibility to fund projects with less revenue potential.

In any case, a national infrastructure bank would make an important contribution to upgrading and expanding the country's infrastructure. It would boost the overall level of infrastructure spending. By leveraging private investment, it could continue to fund infrastructure projects even during recessions. Plus, it would make infrastructure spending more equitable since it would raise funds from a geographically distributed population, then target those funds toward the areas of greatest need.

Article 3.7

FINANCIALIZATION: A PRIMER

BY RAMAA VASUDEVAN
November/December 2008

You don't have to be an investor dabbling in the stock market to feel the power of finance. Finance pervades the lives of ordinary people in many ways, from student loans and credit card debt to mortgages and pension plans.

And its size and impact are only getting bigger. Consider a few measures:

• U.S. credit market debt—all debt of private households, businesses, and government combined—rose from about 1.6 times the nation's GDP in 1973 to over 3.5 times GDP by 2007.

• The profits of the financial sector represented 14% of total corporate profits in 1981; by 2001-02 this figure had risen to nearly 50%.

These are only a few of the indicators of what many commentators have labeled the "financialization" of the economy—a process University of Massachusetts economist Gerald Epstein succinctly defines as "the increasing importance of financial markets, financial motives, financial institutions, and financial elites in the operation of the economy and its governing institutions."

In recent years, this phenomenon has drawn increasing attention. In his latest book, pundit Kevin Phillips writes about the growing divergence between the real (productive) and financial economies, describing how the explosion of trading in myriad new financial instruments played a role in polarizing the U.S. economy. On the left, political economists Harry Magdoff and Paul Sweezy had over many years pointed to the growing role of finance in the operations of capitalism; they viewed the trend as a reflection of the rising economic and political power of "rentiers"—those whose earnings come from financial activities and from forms of income arising from ownership claims (such as interest, rent, dividends, or capital gains) rather than from actual production.

From Finance to Financialization

The financial system is supposed to serve a range of functions in the broader economy. Banks and other financial institutions mop up savings, then allocate that capital, according to mainstream theory, to where it can most productively be used. For households and corporations, the credit markets facilitate greatly increased borrowing, which should foster investment in capital goods like buildings and machinery, in turn leading to expanded production. Finance, in other words, is supposed to facilitate the growth of the "real" economy—the part that produces useful goods (like bicycles) and services (like medical care).

In recent decades, finance has undergone massive changes in both size and shape. The basic mechanism of financialization is the transformation of future streams of income (from profits, dividends, or interest payments) into a tradable asset like a stock or a bond. For example, the future earnings of corporations are transmuted into equity stocks that are bought and sold in the capital market. Likewise, a loan, which involves certain fixed interest payments over its duration, gets a new life when it is converted into marketable bonds. And multiple loans, bundled together then "sliced and diced" into novel kinds of bonds ("collateralized debt obligations"), take on a new existence as investment vehicles that bear an extremely complex and opaque relationship to the original loans.

The process of financialization has not made finance more effective at fulfilling what conventional economic theory views as its core function. Corporations are not turning to the stock market as a source of finance for their investments, and their borrowing in the bond markets is often not for the purpose of productive investment either. Since the 1980s, corporations have actually spent more money buying back their own stock than they have taken in by selling newly issued stock. The granting of stock options to top executives gives them a direct incentive to have the corporation buy back its own shares—often using borrowed money to do so—in order to hike up the share price and allow them to turn a profit on the sale of their personal shares. More broadly, instead of fostering investment, financialization reorients managerial incentives toward chasing short-term returns through financial trading and speculation so as to generate ballooning earnings, lest their companies face falling stock prices and the threat of hostile takeover.

What is more, the workings of these markets tend to act like an upper during booms, when euphoric investors chase the promise of quick bucks. During downturns these same mechanisms work like downers, turning euphoria into panic as investors flee. Financial innovations like collateralized debt obligations were supposed to "lubricate" the economy by spreading risk, but instead they tend to heighten volatility, leading to amplified cycles of boom and bust. In the current crisis, the innovation of mortgage-backed securities fueled the housing bubble and encouraged enormous risk-taking, creating the conditions for the chain reaction of bank (and other financial institution) failures that may be far from over.

Financialization and Power

The arena of finance can at times appear to be merely a casino—albeit a huge one—where everyone gets to place her bets and ride her luck. But the financial system carries a far deeper significance for people's lives. Financial assets and liabilities represent claims on ownership and property; they embody the social relations of an economy at a particular time in history. In this sense, the recent process of financialization implies the increasing political and economic power of a particular segment of the capitalist class: rentiers. Accelerating financial transactions and the profusion of financial techniques have fuelled an extraordinary enrichment of this elite.

This enrichment arises in different ways. Financial transactions facilitate the reallocation of capital to high-return ventures. In the ensuing shake-up, some sectors of capital profit at the expense of other sectors. More important, the capitalist class as a whole is able to force a persistent redistribution in its favor, deploying its newly expanded wealth to bring about changes in the political-economy that channel even more wealth its way.

The structural changes that paved the way for financialization involved the squashing of working-class aspirations during the Reagan-Thatcher years; the defeats of the miners' strike in England and of the air traffic controllers' (PATCO) strike in the United States were perhaps the most symbolic instances of this process. At the same time, these and other governments increasingly embraced the twin policy mantras of fighting inflation and deregulating markets in place of creating full employment and raising wages. Corporations pushed through legislation to dismantle the financial regulations that inhibited their profitmaking strategies.

Financialization has gathered momentum amid greater inequality. In the United States, the top 1% of the population received 14.0% of the national after-tax income in 2004, nearly double its 7.5% share in 1979. In the same period the share of the bottom fifth fell from 6.8% to 4.9%.

And yet U.S. consumption demand has been sustained despite rising inequality and a squeeze on real wages for the majority of households. Here is the other side of the financialization coin: a massive expansion of consumer credit has played an important role in easing the constraints on consumer spending by filling the gap created by stagnant or declining real wages. The credit card debt of the average U.S. family increased by 53% through the 1990s. About 67% of low-income families with incomes less than $10,000 faced credit card debt, and the debt of this group saw the largest increase—a 184% rise, compared to a 28% increase for families with incomes above $100,000. Offered more and more credit as a privatized means of addressing wage stagnation, then, eventually, burdened by debt and on the edge of insolvency, the working poor and the middle class are less likely to organize as a political force to challenge the dominance of finance. In this sense, financialization becomes a means of social coercion that erodes working-class solidarity.

As the structures created by financial engineering unravel, the current economic crisis is revealing the cracks in this edifice. But even as a growing number of U.S. families are losing their homes and jobs in the wake of the subprime meltdown, the financial companies at the heart of the crisis have been handed massive bailouts and their top executives have pocketed huge pay-outs despite their role in abetting the meltdown—a stark sign of the power structures and interests at stake in this era of financialization.

Sources: Robin Blackburn, "Finance and the Fourth Dimension," *New Left Review* 39 May-June 2006; Robert Brenner, "New Boom or Bubble," *New Left Review* 25 Jan-Feb 2004; Tamara Draut and Javier Silva, "Borrowing to make ends meet," *Demos*, Sept 2003; Gerald Epstein, "Introduction" in G. Epstein, ed., *Financialization and the World Economy*, 2006; John Bellamy Foster, "The Financialization of Capitalism," *Monthly Review*, April 2007; Gretta Krippner, "The financialization of the US economy," *Socio-Economic Review* 3, Feb. 2005; Thomas Palley, "Financialization : What it is and why it matters," Political Economy Research Institute Working Paper #153, November 2007; A. Sherman and Arin Dine, "New CBO data shows inequality continues to widen," Center for Budget Priorities, Jan. 23, 2007; Kevin Phillips, *Bad Money: Reckless Finance, Failed Politics, and the Global Crisis of American Capitalism*, 2008.

Chapter 4

FISCAL POLICY, DEFICITS, AND DEBT

INTRODUCTION

Most textbooks depict a macroeconomy stabilized by government intervention. Reflecting the influence of Keynes, they look at ways the government can use fiscal policy—government spending and taxation—to bolster a flagging economy. Today's economy, mired in the worst economic crisis since the Great Depression, is surely flagging. Worse yet, that crisis comes on the heels of a feeble economic expansion that created fewer jobs and did less to raise wages than any other economic expansion since World War II.

What is the role of fiscal policy in this context? As the crisis worsened in the fall of 2008, the federal government dramatically increased spending. First Congress passed the Troubled Asset Recovery Program (TARP), which bailed out giant investment banks and insurance companies. It then passed the Obama stimulus package and budget, which provided some much-needed domestic spending but also boosted military spending. At the same time, the Federal Reserve and the Federal Deposit Insurance Corporation (which insures bank deposits) issued loans, lines of credit, and loan guarantees and pledged an emergency fund to clean up losses on Wall Street. All told, the federal government, the Fed, and the FDIC sunk nearly the value of a year's total U.S. national output into propping up the failed financial sector and rescuing the economy. (See Chapter 5 for more on the financial bailout.)

That spending, along with the Bush administration's 2001 and 2003 tax cuts and military spending to prosecute wars in Iraq and Afghanistan pushed the federal budget far into the red, ringing up an estimated deficit of $1.5 trillion, or 9.8% of GDP, in 2011. That record "peacetime" deficit and those in the next few years will swell federal government debt to 77% of GDP by 2021, according to the latest estimates.

Our coverage begins with economist John Miller's provocative article "How I Learned to Stop Worrying and Love the Deficit" (Article 4.3). Miller maintains that deficit-financed stimulus spending was what stood between us and a complete economic collapse. He calls for yet more domestic spending and yet larger deficits to alleviate the economic suffering that continues unabated. In Article 4.4, economist Marty Wolfson tackles two persistent myths about budget deficits: that the government should never spend more than it takes in, and that doing so creates a burden on future generations. Deficit spending that puts unemployed people to work and boosts productivity, he argues, is the right policy during a recession and need not burden our grandchildren. In Article 4.5, economist Arthur MacEwan spells out why the private spending that would counteract an economic downturn is unlikely to be forthcoming, rendering government action in the form of deficit spending necessary to get a stalled economy going again. State governments are facing massive revenue shortfalls as well, reports economist Marianne Hill (Article 4.6). Federal support and budget slashing will not close those gaps in a sustained way, she argues, so state governments must expand their tax base beyond regressive sales taxes and stop multi-state corporations from avoiding state taxes (Article 4.4).

Economist Ryan Dodd makes the case for the government acting as the economy's employer of last resort, arguing that direct job creation is the ultimate cure to catastrophic economic slumps (Article 4.1). Economist Gerald Friedman debunks the claim that direct job creation and other government spending failed to pull the economy out of the Great Depression. Friedman shows that the U.S. economy slumped in the late 1930s precisely because the federal government cut back on its stimulus spending and direct job creation (Article 4.2). Heidi Garrett-Peltier, an economist at the Political Economy Research Institute, makes the case that dollar per dollar, government spending on clean energy, health care, and education creates more jobs than military spending (Article 4.8). Economist Jeannette Wicks-Lim, also at the Political Economy Research Institute, argues that a clean-energy program would produce more jobs, dollar for dollar, than fossil fuel related activities. She adds the while a clean-energy program would generate jobs for workers at all levels of education, many of those jobs would be accessible to workers without a college education, who have been the hardest hit in the Great Recession (Article 4.7).

Economist Paul Krugman's essay explains that the 2001–2003 tax cuts can only be sustained by shredding the social safety net, the kind of spending that adds far more to economic growth than the Bush tax cuts. Unfortunately, as he shows, that was exactly the point (Article 4.9). Miller takes on the related claim that yet another round of pro-rich tax cuts, much like the Reagan tax cuts of the early 1980s, would invigorate the current sluggish recovery. He shows that the Reagan recovery was lackluster and, moreover, benefited little from those tax cuts (Article 4.10). In another article, Miller makes the case for a transaction tax on stock and other securities trades as a way to reduce speculation in financial markets and to restore a focus on longer-term planning and job creation in the economy (Article 4.11).

With record budget deficits, attention has turned to the long-term solvency of Social Security, and conservatives are once again issuing calls for privatization. Economist Doug Orr examines the merits of their proposals and finds them wanting. Orr shows that, left alone, Social Security is unlikely to suffer a shortfall in revenues, let alone a crisis (Article 4.12).

Discussion Questions

1. (Article 4.1) What is the case for making the federal government the "employer of last resort"? Why is Dodd convinced a modern WPA program will work?

2. (Article 4.2) What evidence does Friedman marshall to make the case that federal spending, especially if it had been applied in larger and continuing doses, could have brought the Great Depression to an end by 1940?

3. (Article 4.3) Are today's record-setting "peacetime" federal government budget deficits a problem? Why or why not? Should we aim to balance the budget over the next few years as the economy emerges from its financial crisis? If so, how should this be accomplished?

4. (Article 4.4) According to Wolfson, what factors are important in determining whether the government debt is affordable? Why does he claim that such debt does not necessarily impose a burden on future generations; under what circumstances does he argue it can be a burden?

6. (Article 4.5) According to MacEwan, why is a shortfall in private spending unlikely to be self-correcting?

5. (Article 4.6) How large are the budget gaps faced by state governments and how might they go about durably closing those gaps?

7. (Article 4.7, 4.8) What factors make government spending on clean energy an effective economic stimulus and jobs program? And how does clean energy compare with military spending or fossil-fuel spending as an economic stimulus and jobs program?

8. (Article 4.9) What does Krugman think is the hidden agenda of those currently pushing for tax cuts? Do you agree with his analysis? Explain why or why not.

9. (Article 4.10) What exactly was the track record of the Reagan recovery? Why is Miller unconvinced that another application of Reagan-like pro-rich tax cuts will boost today's sluggish economic recovery?

10. (Article 4.11) What evidence does Miller present to make the case that U.S. financial markets are inefficient and that a financial transaction tax would improve their efficiency?

11. (Article 4.12) What convinces Orr that the Social Security system is not suffering a crisis? What is the looming bond market crisis that Orr says is the real concern of those who want to privatize Social Security?

Article 4.1

A NEW WPA?

National governments, by serving as "employers of last resort," could guarantee full employment by providing a job for anyone ready, willing and able to work.

BY RYAN A. DODD
March/April 2008

Dark clouds are now looming over America's economic future. As first the stock market boom and then the housing boom have come to an end, along with the fountains of cheap credit that were their mainspring, the perennial gale of unemployment is blowing in. The president and Congress have addressed the downturn with tax rebates and talk of "debt relief." Meanwhile, public infrastructure is crumbling. Workers' wages are stagnating while their work hours are rising. Health insurance is becoming less and less affordable for the typical family. And as U.S. military spending escalates, government spending on essential services is drastically reduced.

All of these facts serve to remind us that capitalist economies are inherently unstable and structurally incapable of creating full employment at decent wages and benefits. While tax rebates and debt relief may provide some minor protection from the coming economic storm, these measures are temporary—and inadequate—responses to a perpetual problem. As an alternative to these ad hoc policies or, worse yet, the free-market fundamentalism still widely preached in Washington, some economists and policymakers, in the United States and abroad, are touting a policy that seeks to end unemployment via a government promise to provide a job to anyone ready, willing, and able to work.

Argentina's Experiment in Direct Job Creation

In early December 2001, following nearly two decades of neoliberal restructuring, the Argentine economy collapsed. Apparently, two decades of privatization, liberalization, and government austerity, ushered in by Argentina's brutal military junta (in power from 1976 to 1983), were not enough to sate the appetites of global financial capital: earlier that year the International Monetary Fund had withheld $1.3 billion in loans the country needed to service its $142 billion external debt. In response to the IMF's action, the government froze all bank accounts (although many wealthy Argentines managed to relocate their funds abroad before the freeze) and drastically cut government spending. As a consequence, the economy experienced a severe depression as incomes and expenditures fell through the floor. The unemployment rate shot up to a record 21.5% by May 2002, with over 50% of the population living in poverty.

The popular response to the crisis was massive. Protests and demonstrations erupted throughout the country. The government went through five presidents in the course of a month. Workers eventually reclaimed dozens of abandoned factories and created democratically run cooperative enterprises, many of which are still in operation today and are part of a growing coop movement.

Reclaiming factories was a lengthy and difficult process, however, and the immediate problem of unemployment remained. In response, in April 2002 the Argentine government put into place a direct job creation program known as *Plan Jefes de Hogar* ("Heads-of-Household Plan"), which promised a job to all heads of households satisfying certain requirements. In order to qualify, a household had to include a child under the age of 18, a person with a disability, or a pregnant woman; the household head had to be unemployed; and each household was generally limited to only one participant in the program. The program provided households with 150 pesos a month for four hours of work a day, five days a week. Program participants mainly engaged in the provision of community services and/or participated in worker training programs administered by local nonprofits.

While limited in scope and viewed by many in the government as an emergency measure, the program was incredibly successful and popular with its workers. It provided jobs and incomes to roughly two million workers, or 13% of Argentina's labor force, as well as bringing desperately needed goods and services—from community gardens to small construction projects—to severely depressed neighborhoods. The entry of many women into the program, while their husbands continued to look for jobs in the private sector, had a liberating effect on traditional family structures. And by some accounts, the program helped facilitate the cooperative movement that subsequently emerged with the takeover of abandoned factories. Not surprisingly, as Argentina's economy has recovered from the depths of the crisis, the government has recently made moves to discontinue this critical experiment in direct job creation.

"Employer of Last Resort"

The Argentine experience with direct job creation represents a real-world example of what is often referred to as the *employer of last resort* (ELR) proposal by a number of left academics and public policy advocates. Developed over the course of the past two decades, the ELR proposal is based on a rather simple idea. In a capitalist economy, with most people dependent on private employment for their livelihoods, the government has a unique responsibility to guarantee full employment. This responsibility has been affirmed in the U.N. Universal Declaration of Human Rights, which includes a right to employment. A commitment to full employment is also official U.S. government policy as codified in the Employment Act of 1946 and the Humphrey-Hawkins Act of 1976.

Although many versions of the ELR proposal have been put forward, they all revolve around the idea that national governments could guarantee full employment by providing a job to anyone ready, willing, and able to work. The various proposals differ mainly on the wage and benefit packages they would provide to participants. The most common proposal calls for paying all participants a universal basic wage and benefit package, regardless of skills, work experience, or prior earnings. This wage and benefit package would then form the effective minimum for both the public and private sectors of the economy. After fixing a wage and benefit package, the government would allow the quantity of workers in the program to float, rising and falling in response to cyclical fluctuations in private-sector employment.

As with Argentina's program, ELR proposals typically call for participants to work in projects to improve their local communities—everything from basic infrastructure projects to a Green Jobs Corps. Most ELR proponents also advocate a decentralized approach similar to Argentina's, with local public or nonprofit institutions planning and administering the projects, though it is essential that the program be funded at the national level.

This raises an important question: How will governments pay for such a large-scale program? Wouldn't an ELR program require significantly raising taxes or else result in exploding budget deficits? Can governments really afford to employ everyone who wants a job but cannot find one in the private economy? Advocates of ELR address the issue of affordability in different ways, but all agree that the benefits to society vastly outweigh the expense. Many ELR advocates go even further, arguing that any talk of "costs" to society misrepresents the nature of the problem of unemployment. The existence of unemployed workers represents a net cost to society, in terms of lost income and production as well as the psychological and social stresses that result from long spells of unemployment. Employing them represents a net benefit, in terms of increased incomes *and* enhanced individual and social wellbeing. The real burden of an ELR program, from the perspective of society, is thus effectively zero.

Most estimates of the direct cost of an ELR program are in the range of less than 1% of GDP per year. For the United States, this was less than $132 billion in 2006, or about 5% of the federal budget. (By way of comparison, in 2006 the U.S. government spent over $120 billion on the wars in Iraq and Afghanistan—and that figure does not include the cost of lives lost or ruined or the future costs incurred, for example, for veterans' health care.) Furthermore, an ELR program provides benefits to society in the form of worker retraining, enhanced public infrastructure, and increased social output (e.g., cleaner parks and cities, free child care, public performances, etc.). By increasing the productivity of those participants who attend education or training programs, an ELR program would also decrease real costs throughout the economy. Estimates of program costs take into account a reduction in other forms of social assistance such as food stamps, cash assistance, and unemployment insurance, which would instead be provided to ELR participants in the form of a wage and benefit package. Of course, those who cannot work would still be eligible for these and other forms of assistance.

Today, the ELR idea is mostly confined to academic journals and conferences. Still, proponents can point to a number of little known real-world examples their discussions have helped to shape. For example, the Argentine government explicitly based its *Jefes de Hogar* program on the work of economists associated with the Center for Full Employment and Price Stability (CFEPS) at the University of Missouri-Kansas City. Daniel Kostzer, an economist at the Argentine Ministry of Labor and one of the main architects of the program, had become familiar with the CFEPS proposal and was attempting to create such a program in Argentina a few years before the collapse provided him with the necessary political support. Similar experiments are being considered or are currently underway in India, France, and Bolivia. Advocates of ELR proposals can also be found at the Levy Economics Institute (U.S.), the Center for Full Employment and Equity (Australia), and the National Jobs for All Coalition (U.S.).

The Case for Direct Job Creation

Involuntary unemployment is a fundamental and inherent feature of a capitalist economy left to its own devices. In a society where most people depend on employment in the private sector for their livelihood, the inability of a capitalist economy to consistently create enough jobs for all who seek work is deeply troubling, pointing to the need for intervention from outside of the private sector. ELR advocates view national governments—with their unique spending abilities, and with their role as, in principle, democratically accountable social institutions—as the most logical institutions for collective action to bring about full employment. In addition, government job creation is viewed as the simplest and most direct means for overcoming the problem of involuntary unemployment in a capitalist economy.

The standard mainstream response to the problem of unemployment is to blame the victims of capitalism for lacking the necessary talents, skills, and effort to get and keep a job. Hence, the mainstream prescription is to promote policies aimed at enhancing the "human capital" of workers in order to make them more "competitive" in a rapidly globalizing economy. The response of ELR advocates is that such policies, if they accomplish anything at all, simply redistribute unemployment and poverty more equitably. For example, according to the Bureau of Labor Statistics, the number of unemployed workers (including so-called "discouraged" and "underemployed" workers) in August 2007 was 16.4 million, while the number of job vacancies was 4.1 million. No amount of investment in human capital is going to change the fact that there simply aren't enough jobs to go around.

Advocates of ELR also consistently reject the Keynesian rubric, with its focus on demand-management strategies—that is, policies aimed at increasing aggregate demand for the output of the economy. This approach has been pursued either directly, through government spending on goods and services (including transfer payments to households), or indirectly, largely through policies intended to increase private investment. Such an approach exacerbates inequality by biasing policy in favor of the already well-to-do, through tax cuts and investment credits to wealthy individuals and powerful corporations. These policies also tend to privilege the more highly skilled and better-paid workers found in the industries that generally benefit from the government's largesse (often arms manufacturers and other military-related companies). For example, much of the increase in government spending during the Cold War era went into the high-tech, capital-intensive, and oligopolized sectors of the economy. Capital-intensive industries require relatively small amounts of labor, and, thus, produce little employment growth per dollar of government expenditure. Under this policy approach, the most that lower-paid or unemployed workers could hope for would be to snatch a few crumbs from the great corporate feast as the economy expanded over time.

In contrast to both the human-capital and demand-management approaches, ELR provides a means for rapidly achieving zero involuntary unemployment. By definition, anyone who is unemployed and chooses not to accept the ELR offer would be considered voluntarily unemployed. Many individuals with sufficient savings and decent job prospects may forgo the opportunity to participate in the ELR program, but ELR always provides them with a backup option.

In addition to the immediate effects of ELR on employment, the program acts as an "automatic stabilizer" in the face of cyclical fluctuations in the private sector of the economy. During a recession, the number of participants in the program can be expected to grow as people are laid off and/or find it increasingly difficult to find private-sector employment. The opposite happens during the recovery phase of the business cycle, as people find it easier to find private-sector employment at wages above the ELR minimum. As a result, ELR advocates argue, the existence of such a program would dampen fluctuations in private-sector activity by setting a floor to the decline in incomes and employment.

A final and less discussed benefit of the program is its socializing effect. The example of Argentina is instructive in this respect. The nature of employment in the *Jefes* program, oriented as it was toward community rather than market imperatives, created a sense of public involvement and responsibility. Participants reported increases in morale and often continued to work beyond the four hours a day for which they were getting paid; they appreciated the cooperative nature of most of the enterprises and their focus on meeting essential community needs as opposed to quarterly profit targets. By expanding the public sphere, the *Jefes* program created a spirit of democratic participation in the affairs of the community, unmediated by the impersonal relations of market exchange. These are the kinds of experiences that are essential if capitalist societies are to move beyond the tyranny of the market and toward more cooperative and democratic forms of social organization.

Some economists and advocates have pressed for a similar proposal, the *basic income guarantee* (BIG). Instead of guaranteeing jobs, under this proposal the government would guarantee a minimum income to everyone by simply giving cash assistance to anyone earning below that level, in an amount equal to the gap between his or her actual income and the established basic income. (Hence this proposal is sometimes referred to as a "negative income tax.") BIG is an important idea deserving wider discussion than it has so far received. But ELR advocates have a number of concerns. One is that a BIG program is inherently inflationary: by providing income without putting people to work, it creates an additional claim on output without directly increasing the production of that output. Another is that BIG programs are less politically palatable—and hence less sustainable—than ELR schemes, which benefit society at large through the provision of public works and other social goods, and which avoid the stigma attached to "welfare" programs. Finally, a job offers social and psychological benefits that an income payment alone does not: maintaining and enhancing work skills, keeping in contact with others, and having the satisfaction of contributing to society. When, for instance, participants in Argentina's *Jefes* program were offered an income in place of a job, most refused; they preferred to work. Consequently, ELR programs meet the same objectives as basic income guarantee schemes and more, without the negative side effects of inflation and stigmatization. Nonetheless, a BIG program may be appropriate for those who should not be expected to work.

Learning from the Past

The idea that the government in a capitalist economy should provide jobs for the unemployed is not new. In the United States, the various New Deal agencies created during the Great Depression of the 1930s offer a well-known example. Organizations such as the Works Progress Administration and the Civilian Conservation Corps were designed to deal with the massive unemployment of that period. Unemployment peaked at almost 25% of the civilian labor force in 1933 and averaged over 17% for the entire decade. These programs were woefully inadequate, largely due to their limited scale. It ultimately took the massive increases in government expenditure precipitated by the Second World War to pull the U.S. economy out of depression.

The onset of the postwar "Golden Age" and the dominance of Keynesian economics sounded the death knell of direct job creation as a solution to unemployment. The interwar public employment strategy was replaced with a "demand-management" strategy—essentially a sort of trickle-down economics in which various tax incentives and government expenditure programs, mainly military spending, were used to stimulate private investment. Policymakers believed that this would spur economic growth. The twin problems of poverty and unemployment would then be eliminated since, according to President Kennedy's famous aphorism, "a rising tide lifts all boats."

In the mid-1960s, the civil rights movement revived the idea of direct job creation as a solution to the problems of poverty and unemployment. Although the Kennedy and Johnson administrations had declared a so-called War on Poverty, the movement's call for direct job creation fell on deaf ears as the Johnson administration, at the behest of its Council of Economic Advisers, pursued a more conservative approach based on the standard combination of supply-side incentives to increase private investment and assorted strategies to "improve" workers' "human capital" so as to make them more attractive to private employers.

The rise to dominance of neoliberalism since the mid-1970s has resulted in a full-scale retreat from even the mildly social democratic policies of the early postwar period. While a commitment to full employment remains official U.S. policy, the concerns of central bankers and financial capitalists now rule the roost in government circles. This translates into a single-minded obsession with fighting inflation at the expense of all other economic and social objectives. Not only is fighting inflation seemingly the only concern of economic policy, it is seen to be in direct conflict with the goal of full employment (witness the widespread acceptance among economists and policymakers of the NAIRU, or "non-accelerating inflation rate of unemployment" theory, which posits that the economy has a set-point for unemployment, well above zero, below which rapidly rising inflation must occur). Whenever falling unemployment leads to concerns about "excessive" wage growth, central banks are expected to raise interest rates in an attempt to force slack on the economy and thereby decrease inflationary pressures. The resulting unemployment acts as a kind of discipline, tempering the demands of working-class people for higher wages or better working conditions in favor of the interests of large commercial and financial institutions. The postwar commitment to full employment has finally been sacrificed on the altar of price stability.

ELR and Capitalism

As demonstrated by the history of public employment programs in the United States and the example of Argentina, direct job-creation programs do not happen absent significant political pressure from below. This is the case whether or not those calling for change explicitly demand an ELR program. Given the hegemonic position of neoliberal ideology, there are many powerful forces today that would be hostile to the idea of governments directly creating jobs for the unemployed. These forces represent a critical barrier to the implementation of an ELR program. In fact, these forces represent a critical barrier to virtually any project for greater social and economic justice. The purpose of initiating a wider discussion of ELR proposals is to build them into more comprehensive programs for social and economic justice. As is always the case, this requires the building of mass-based social movements advocating for these and other progressive policies.

A significant objection to the ELR proposal remains: it's capitalism, stupid. If you don't like unemployment, poverty, and inequality—not to mention war, environmental destruction, and alienating and exploitative work—then you don't like capitalism, and you should seek alternatives instead of reformist employment policies. ELR advocates would not disagree. In the face of the overlapping and myriad problems afflicting a capitalist economy, the achievements of even a full-scale ELR program would be limited. The political difficulties involved in establishing an ELR program in the first place, in the face of opposition from powerful elements of society, would be immense. And certainly, the many experiments in non-capitalist forms of economic and social organization currently being carried out, for example, in the factories of Argentina and elsewhere, should be championed. But it is fair to ask: shouldn't we also champion living wage laws, a stronger social safety net for those who cannot or should not be expected to work, and universal health care—as well as an end to imperialist wars of aggression, environmentally unsustainable practices, and the degradation of work? In sum, shouldn't we seek to alleviate all of the symptoms of capitalism, even as we work toward a better economic system?

Sources: Joseph Halevi, "The Argentine Crisis," *Monthly Review*, April 2002; Pavlina Tcherneva, "Macroeconomic Stabilization Policy in Argentina: A Case Study of the 2002 Currency Collapse and Crisis Resolution through Job Creation," Bard College Working Paper, 2007; L. Randall Wray, *Understanding Modern Money: The Key to Full Employment and Price Stability*, Edward Elgar, 1998; Congressional Research Service, "The Cost of Iraq, Afghanistan and Other Global War on Terror Operations Since 9/11," www.fas.org/sgp/crs/natsec/RL33110.pdf, update 7/07; National Jobs for All Coalition, "September 2007 Unemployment Data," www.njfac.org/jobnews.html; Nancy Rose, "Historicizing Government Work Programs: A Spectrum from Workfare to Fair Work," Center for Full Employment and Price Stability, Seminar Paper No. 2, March 2000; Judith Russell, *Economics, Bureaucracy and Race: How Keynesians Misguided the War on Poverty*, Columbia Univ. Press, 2004; Fadhel Kaboub, "Employment Guarantee Programs: A Survey of Theories and Policy Experiences," Levy Econ. Inst., Working Paper No. 498, May 2007.

Article 4.2

RESPONDING TO REVISIONISM
Fiscal stimulus and recovery during the Great Depression

BY GERALD FRIEDMAN
May/June 2009

"THERE IS NO DISAGREEMENT THAT WE NEED ACTION BY OUR GOVERNMENT,
A RECOVERY PLAN THAT WILL HELP TO JUMPSTART THE ECONOMY."

—PRESIDENT-ELECT BARACK OBAMA, JANUARY 9, 2009

With all due respect, Mr. President, that is not true.

Notwithstanding reports that all economists are now Keynesians and that we all support a big increase in the burden of government, we the undersigned do not believe that more government spending is a way to improve economic performance. More government spending by Hoover and Roosevelt did not pull the United States economy out of the Great Depression in the 1930s. More government spending did not solve Japan's "lost decade" in the 1990s. As such, it is a triumph of hope over experience to believe that more government spending will help the U.S. today. To improve the economy, policymakers should focus on reforms that remove impediments to work, saving, investment and production. Lower tax rates and a reduction in the burden of government are the best ways of using fiscal policy to boost growth.
—Full-page Cato Institution ad in the *New York Times* and other major newspapers, signed by 200 economists, late January 2009.

In the 1930s, the Great Depression discredited laissez-faire capitalism, and President Franklin Roosevelt's New Deal showed the world how an active government could restore economic vitality and improve life. Since then, the claim that the New Deal failed to end the Great Depression of the 1930s has become central to conservative attacks on government fiscal policy. "More government spending by Hoover and Roosevelt," the Cato Institute claims in a recent advertisement, "did not pull the United States economy out of the Great Depression in the 1930s."

Such claims have some superficial credibility; official statistics, not including workers on federal emergency employment, report an unemployment rate of over 9% at the end of Roosevelt's first term, and over 12% in 1938. Indeed, economic historians have long recognized that New Deal fiscal policy did not end the Great Depression; E. Cary Brown concluded in 1956, for example, that fiscal policy "seems to have been an unsuccessful recovery device in the 'thirties." But he adds that this was "not because it did not work but because it was not tried." Christina D. Romer, now head of the President's Council of Economic Advisers, reached similar conclusions, also finding that fiscal policy was applied too timidly to end the Depression.

It is a nice piece of rhetoric for the Cato Institute and other conservatives to equate FDR with the failed policies of Herbert Hoover. Yes, FDR was not fiscally aggressive enough, but Hoover did not try to stimulate the economy with government spending at all. Instead, he greeted the onset of the Great Depression by trimming government spending to maintain budget balance. He ran surpluses during the early Depression years, 1929–30, only reversing course in 1932 when plunging revenues, which fell to half the 1930 level, forced a significant deficit. On the spending side, federal consumption and investment remained stuck at 1.8% of Gross Domestic Product (GDP) throughout the Hoover years.

Thus Cato is right: Hoover's policy of budget balance and spending restraint did not stem economic collapse. Instead, under Hoover, investment fell by 81%, consumption by 18%, and the GDP by over 25%. Unemployment rose from 2.9% of the civilian labor force to 23% and 8 million jobs disappeared. By the end of his term, collapse had spread to the banking system. The economy spiraled down when banks, fearing insolvency due to mortgages and loans unlikely to be repaid in a collapsing economy, further cut back on their lending. Depositors lined up to withdraw their money, driving the banks another step towards insolvency, and dragging the economy down further.

Arriving in office in March 1933, Roosevelt intervened aggressively in financial markets, averting further panic by closing all banks for a week. Eventually, only the stronger banks were allowed to reopen, and they were backed with a new federal system of depositor insurance to prevent further bank panics. Roosevelt pressed the Federal Reserve to inaugurate a policy of monetary ease. He also significantly increased government spending, running deficits that averaged 4.8% of GDP throughout his first term. Unlike Hoover's inadvertent 1932 deficit, Roosevelt's New Deal deficits reflected significantly increased spending even with rising revenues. During FDR's first term, real federal spending was over twice the Hoover level.

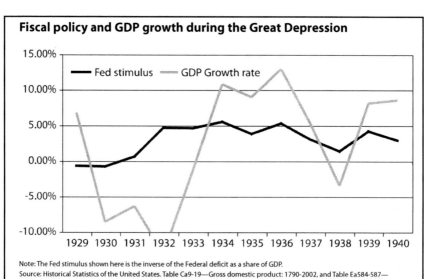

Fiscal policy and GDP growth during the Great Depression

Note: The Fed stimulus shown here is the inverse of the Federal deficit as a share of GDP.
Source: Historical Statistics of the United States. Table Ca9-19—Gross domestic product: 1790-2002, and Table Ea584-587—Federal government finances—revenue, expenditure, and debt: 1789-1939.

Critics who charge that Roosevelt's fiscal policy failed to cure the Depression ignore the very rapid economic recovery that came with the New Deal. Stimulated by his aggressive fiscal policy, the economy boomed during Roosevelt's first term at rates about double the size of the federal deficit. GDP growth averaged over 10% a year from 1934 to 1936, and the economy grew from 62% of its trend level in 1933 to 76% in 1936. By 1937, FDR's stimulus policies had lowered unemployment to 9%, less than half the rate when he assumed office.

While the New Deal did not end the Depression, had FDR remained on course through his second term, the Depression may have ended by 1940. But instead of continuing aggressive fiscal policy, FDR reversed course in 1937, dramatically reducing the federal deficit after 1936. This plunged the economy back into a severe depression. Unemployment shot up three points to 12% in 1938. Roosevelt quickly reversed course with enough deficit spending from 1939 to 1941 to revive the economy after the 1938 dip. But it was the massive Keynesian stimulus of WWII, with deficits as high as 27% of GDP in 1943, that finally ended the Great Depression.

Even this casual examination of the 1930s discredits conservative claims about the New Deal. But there are positive lessons here as well. Far from contradicting Keynesian expectations, the New Deal shows the power of fiscal policy, both to promote recovery (1933–37 and 1939–45) and to exacerbate depression (1929–30 and 1938). The New Deal could have done better with a larger deficit. Nonetheless, when combined with reform of the financial sector and the banks, the New Deal produced four years of rapid growth that by 1937 had more than halved the unemployment rate.

Cato is right that there are lessons for the Obama administration in the New Deal experience. But the lessons are the opposite of those they would preach. First, we will need a very large stimulus, probably significantly larger than the deficit of 6–8% of GDP planned for now. Between a sharp drop in consumption with falling housing and stock market prices, falling exports, and declining investment due to the financial crisis, we may have a decline in aggregate demand of as much 20% of GDP. This would suggest the need for a deficit of between 10% and 14% of GDP, significantly more than is currently planned by the administration.

Lesson two: facing a serious economic downturn, don't declare victory prematurely. An economic collapse builds a great deal of depressing inertia that may require a long period of sustained stimulus to overcome. By prematurely moving towards budget balance in 1937–38, the Roosevelt administration prolonged the Great Depression by several years. We may hope that the Obama administration will be in a position to make that mistake in 2010 or 2011; and let us hope that they learn from the past.

Sources: E. Cary Brown, "Fiscal Policy in the 'Thirties: A Reappraisal," *The American Economic Review* 46:5 (Dec. 1956), 857–79; John K. Galbraith, *The Great Crash of 1929* (New York, Harpers, 1955); Charles Kindleberger, *The World in Depression* (Berkeley, University of California Press, 1986); Christina D. Romer, "What Ended the Great Depression?" *The Journal of Economic History* 52:4 (Dec 1993), 757–84; Herbert Stein, *The Fiscal Revolution in America* (Chicago, University of Chicago Press, 1969); Peter Temin and Barrie Wigmore, "The End of One Big Deflation," *Explorations in Economic History* 27 (Oct. 1990), 483-502; Peter Temin, *Did Monetary Forces Cause the Great Depression?* (New York, Norton, 1976); Peter Temin, *Lessons from the Great Depression* (Cambridge, MIT Press, 1989).

Article 4.3

HOW I LEARNED TO STOP WORRYING AND LOVE THE DEFICIT

BY JOHN MILLER
November/December 2009

> THE PELOSI-OBAMA DEFICITS
> [C]urrent U.S. fiscal policy is "borrow and spend" on a hyperlink. The ...
> deficit for 2009 will be "only" $1.58 trillion ... . But the Obama fiscal plan
> envisions $9 trillion in new borrowing over the next decade.
>
> We've never fretted over budget deficits, at least if they finance tax
> cuts to promote growth or spending to win a war. But these deficit esti-
> mates are driven entirely by more domestic spending and already assume
> huge new tax increases.
>
> [T]he White House still hasn't ruled out another fiscal stimulus. ...
> Obamanomics has turned into an unprecedented experiment in runaway
> government with no plan to pay for it, save, perhaps, for a big future toll
> on the middle class such as a value-added tax.
> —from an op-ed in the *Wall Street Journal*, 9/26/09

You would have thought the federal budget deficit had morphed into Dr.
Strangelove's doomsday machine from the howling that followed the publica-
tion of the Congressional Budget Office (CBO) projections in August. The *Wall
Street Journal* editors were happy to join in despite assuring readers that they are
not deficit-phobic.

But the truth is, government spending and the budget deficit it engendered
are what stood between us and an economic doomsday that would have rivaled
the Great Depression of the 1930s. In that context, the Obama budget deficits are
neither all that big nor all that bad, although they sure could have been better had
the spending priorities been more progressive. And even larger deficits could have
done—and still could do—more to alleviate the economic suffering that continues
unabated even as the economy begins to stabilize.

How Big Is It?

Even after correcting for inflation, $1.58 trillion is a record federal budget deficit.
But this eye-popping number needs to be seen in context.

A trillion and a half dollar deficit will equal 11.2% of Gross Domestic Product
(GDP) for 2009, according to CBO estimates. That too is a record for "peacetime"
deficits. The Reagan deficits in their worst year reached 6% of GDP. During World
War II, however, military spending pushed the federal deficit to qualitatively different levels, reaching 31.3% of GDP and never dropping below 14.5% during the war
years 1942 to 1945.

Whatever its size, before pinning the 2009 deficit on runaway government spending, it's important to assess how much the collapsing economy contributed to the deficit. Big government bashers like the *Journal* editors would have you believe that the entire budget deficit was brought on by reckless government spending.

That is hardly the case. The collapsing economy added more to the deficit from 2007 to 2009 than any other factor. As economic activity dried up, personal and corporate income tax revenues plummeted: this year government revenues will drop to 14.9% of GDP, their lowest level since 1950. Plus, the crashing economy automatically pushed government spending on unemployment insurance and food stamps up, further widening the deficit. Even the financial-sector bailout and the Obama stimulus package taken together did less to swell the deficit than the economic collapse did.

To control for the effect of the business cycle on the budget deficit, economists look at the so-called standardized, or cyclically adjusted, deficit—the deficit that would occur if the economy was always operating at the peak of the business cycle, in other words, at its "potential GDP." Standardized deficit figures indicate that the 2009 budget is highly stimulative but hardly disproportionate to the economic emergency it confronted. In 2009 the cyclically adjusted deficit will reach 8.6% of potential GDP, and then shrink to 3.4% by 2011, according to CBO estimates. The previous high was 4.7% in 1986 (with data back to 1962), in the midst of the "borrow and squander" Reagan years when the only emergencies facing the nation were the desire of the rich for a tax cut and the drive to expand cold-war military spending. Under George W. Bush, tax cutter to the rich *extraordinaire*, the cyclically adjusted deficit reached 3.1% in 2004, the near equal of the projected 2011 figure.

The CBO projected deficits will add $9 trillion in the next decade to the national debt, the cumulative amount of money the government will have borrowed to finance its annual deficits.

That is another frightening number, but it too needs to be seen in context. For instance, publicly held federal-government debt will reach 67.8% of GDP in 2019, according to CBO projections. That number would be the largest ratio of debt to national output since 1952, but still not in the same ballpark as the 120% figure at the end of World War II.

But absent the stimulus, the federal government would face yet larger deficits as the economy and federal tax revenues fell further. And unlike World War II spending that sparked a 20-year economic boom, a do-nothing strategy would be followed by a depression that would impose far greater costs than escalating government debt.

Domestic Spending Gone Wild?

The *Journal*'s editors are correct that it is not the size of the deficit that is worrisome, but its content—the spending and taxing policies that brought it about. But on that count they really should not be complaining, because it was the tax cuts and military spending they favor that played a decisive role in pushing the federal budget out of the black and into the red.

When the Bush administration took office in 2001, the CBO projected the federal government would run a budget *surplus* of $710 billion in FY 2009. The CBO now projects a $1.6 trillion budget deficit. The Economic Policy Institute found that the bad economy (slow growth and then the crisis) and Bush administration tax and spending policies (from the 2001 and 2003 tax cuts, to spending on Afghanistan and Iraq, to Medicare prescription drug coverage) each caused about 42% of that $2.3 trillion budget swing. Following by quite a distance were the Obama stimulus package and the TARP bailout, accounting for 7.6% and 7.7% of the budget swing respectively. Supplemental defense allocations for the Iraq and Afghanistan wars accounted for more of the increase in the deficit (9.3%) than either program.

Nor do the CBO numbers justify the editors' claim that we are about to enter a period of runaway government and deficits "driven entirely by more domestic spending." Discretionary domestic spending (federal government spending on education, housing, infrastructure, and the like) will average 3.7% of GDP over the 2010 to 2019 period—no higher than in 2008, the last year of the Bush administration. Mandatory domestic spending (including Social Security, Medicare, Medicaid, and unemployment insurance) will average 12.8% of GDP over the next ten years, 1.6 percentage points more than in 2008. Even that jump in what is, after all, already-obligated spending will account for just two-fifths of the federal deficits that the CBO projects for the next ten years. That is hardly domestic spending gone wild.

The True Test

Obama administration policies might not have been the chief cause of the 2009 deficit or the $2.3 trillion budget swing from black to red ink over this decade, nor will they commission runaway domestic spending as the editors allege.

But that alone does not make the president's policies successful. The true test of any deficit spending policy is whether it makes people better off. The policies endorsed by the editors have failed that test miserably. Worse yet, they saddled us with large deficits that now block the very spending proposals that might pass that test. Whether it is spending for universal health care, green technology, infrastructure repair, or school renovations—or help for those who have lost their homes—the new refrain is that spending must not add one dime to "the deficit."

A second dose of deficit-financed stimulus spending, a notion the editors dismiss out of hand, would create jobs desperately needed as even official unemployment rates are likely remain at double-digit levels through much of 2010.

In a very real way, our jobs and our prospects for living in a fair society depend upon learning to stop worrying and love the deficit.

Sources: The Pelosi-Obama Deficits," *Wall Street Journal*, Sept. 26, 2009; "The Budget and Economic Outlook: An Update," Congressional Budget Office, August 2009; "Measuring the Effects of the Business Cycle on the Federal Budget: An Update," Congressional Budget Office, September 1, 2009; John Irons, Kathryn Edwards, and Anna Turner, "The 2009 Budget Deficit: How did we get here?" Economic Policy Institute, August 20, 2009.

Article 4.4

MYTHS OF THE DEFICIT

BY MARTY WOLFSON

May/June 2010

Nearly 15 million people are officially counted as unemployed in the United States, and more than 6 million of these have been unemployed for more than 26 weeks. Another 11 million are the "hidden" unemployed: jobless workers who have given up looking for work and part-time workers who want full-time jobs. Unemployment has especially affected minority communities; the official black teenage unemployment rate, for example, stands at 42%.

The *moral* case for urgently addressing the unemployment issue is clear. The costs of unemployment, especially prolonged unemployment, are devastating. Self-worth is questioned, homes are lost, families stressed, communities disrupted. Across the land, the number one issue is jobs, jobs, jobs.

The *economic* case for how to address the jobs issue is also clear. As Keynes argued during the Great Depression, federal government spending can directly create jobs. And the $787 billion stimulus package approved by Congress in February 2009 did help pull the economy back from disaster, when it was shedding 20,000 jobs *a day* in late 2008 and early 2009.

But we still have a long way to go. To get back just to where we were when the recession began in December 2007, the economy would need to create 11.1 million jobs: 8.4 million to replace the jobs lost and 2.7 million to absorb new workers who have entered the labor market since then.

Despite a pickup of economic activity recently, long-term projections are that the unemployment rate will fall only gradually over the next several years. The Congressional Budget Office forecast for the unemployment rate for 2012 is a stubbornly high 8%. So why are we not moving more aggressively to reduce unemployment?

The *ideological* opposition to government spending remains a major obstacle. There are those who see an increase in the role of government as something to be avoided at all costs—even if the cost is the jobs of the unemployed.

Even among those who are not subject to such ideological blinders, there is still a *political* argument that resonates strongly. The argument is that government spending to create jobs will create large budget deficits, which will have terrible consequences for the American people. Politicians, pundits, and other commentators—in a frenzied drumbeat of speeches, op-eds, and articles—have asserted that the most urgent priority *now* is to reduce the budget deficit.

It is important to note that this argument is focused on current policy, not just the long-term budgetary situation. There is room for debate about long-term budget deficits, but these are affected more by the explosive growth of health-care costs than by government discretionary spending to create jobs.

Why, then, are people taken in by an argument that says it is more important to reduce the budget deficit now than for the government to spend money to create jobs? Two myths constantly repeated in the public debate have contributed to this situation:

1) Families can't spend more than they have; neither should the government.

It seems to be common sense that a family can't spend more than it has. But of course that is exactly what the family does when it takes out a car loan or a student loan, or does any other kind of borrowing. The government, just like families, should be able to borrow. The real issue is whether or not the debt is affordable. For families, and for the government, that depends on the size of the debt relative to the income available to service the debt; it also depends on the nature of the borrowing.

For the federal government, the relevant debt-income measure is the ratio of outstanding debt of the federal government to gross domestic product. (*Outstanding debt* is the total amount owed at a particular time, roughly the result of debt accumulated over time by annual budget deficits; GDP, the value of goods and services produced, is equal to total income.) In 2009, this ratio was 53%. Although higher than the recent low point of 33% at the end of the 1990s expansion, the ratio in 2009 was still far lower than the record peak of 109% in 1946—after which the U.S. economy in the post-World War II period experienced the strongest economic growth in its history.

The U.S. ratio of 53% actually compares favorably to those of other advanced industrial countries. For example, IMF data indicate the following debt-to-GDP ratios for 2009: France (67%), Germany (70%), Japan (105%), and Italy (113%).

The nature of the borrowing also affects affordability. If a family runs up credit-card debt to finance a lavish lifestyle, after the fancy dinners are eaten the family still needs to figure out how to pay its debt. But if a family member borrows to buy a car to get to work, presumably the job will help provide the income to service the debt.

Likewise for the federal government: If the government borrows to finance tax cuts for the rich, and the rich use their tax cuts to purchase imported luxury goods, then the government still needs to figure out how to pay its debt. On the other hand, if the government borrows to put people to work creating long-term investments that increase the productivity of the U.S. economy, like infrastructure and education, then it is in a much better situation. The income generated by the more productive economy, as well as by the newly employed workers, can help to provide the tax revenue to service the debt.

So it is a myth to say that families can't spend more than they have. They can, and so can the government. And both are justified in borrowing if the size of the debt is manageable and if so doing helps to provide the income necessary to service the debt.

2) Large budget deficits create a burden for our grandchildren.

This is the issue that probably resonates most forcefully with public opinion. If we in the current generation run up a big debt, it may be left to our grandchildren to repay. The only difficulty with this reasoning is that the grandchildren who may be asked to repay the debt are paying it to other grandchildren. When the government incurs a debt, it issues a bond, an obligation to repay the debt to the holder of the bond. If the holders of the bond are U.S. residents, then paying off the debt means paying money to U.S. residents. In other words, debt that is an obligation of future

U.S. taxpayers is also a source of income to the U.S. holders of that debt. Thus there is not a generational burden that we today are imposing on "our grandchildren" as a collective entity.

Of course, the obvious exception to this reasoning is the debt held by non-U.S. residents. In that case, it is indeed true that future generations of Americans will need to pay interest to foreign holders of U.S. debt. But the basic reason for this situation is the trade deficit, not the budget deficit. When we pay more for imports than we receive from exports, and when U.S. multinational companies ship production abroad to take advantage of low-cost labor, foreigners are provided with dollars that they can use to invest in U.S. assets. And the real burden that this causes is the same whether foreigners invest in U.S. government debt or whether they invest in U.S. companies, real estate, the U.S. stock market, etc.

Borrowing by the federal government can in some situations create a real burden, but it has less to do with generational transfers and more to do with distributional issues and the nature of economic growth (discussed above). If the grandchildren who are taxed in the future to pay off government debt are poorer than the grandchildren who are paid, the distribution of income becomes more unequal.

Also, cutting taxes for the rich and spending money on wars in Iraq and Afghanistan do not lead to the kind of productive economic growth that generates strong tax revenue. So financing these by debt *does* create a real distributional burden: The rich and military contractors benefit, but the losers are those who might be taxed, or those whose government programs might be squeezed out of the budget, because of the need to pay interest on the debt.

Borrowing money to put people back to work does make sense. It helps people most in need, the unemployed. It provides them with income that they can use to pay taxes and to buy goods and services that create more jobs, more income, and more tax revenue. Indeed, our inability thus far to seriously tackle the unemployment problem is what has worsened the budget problem, as tax receipts have fallen and spending for unemployment benefits and food stamps have risen. An analysis by the Economic Policy Institute reveals that the largest source of the 2009 budget deficit (42%) was actually the recession itself.

We *will* leave a burden for our grandchildren if we don't address the urgent problem of unemployment, if we let parents and grandparents suffer the indignities and financial hardships of lost jobs. We *will* leave a burden for our grandchildren if we don't rebuild our aging infrastructure, break our reliance on fossil fuels, and provide all our children with an excellent education. It makes perfect sense to borrow money now to address these problems, and we shouldn't let myths about budget deficits get in the way of meeting these real needs.

Sources: Congressional Budget Office, "The Budget and Economic Outlook: Fiscal Years 2010 to 2020," January 2010; John Irons, Kathryn Edwards, and Anna Turner, "The 2009 Budget Deficit: How Did We Get Here?" Economic Policy Institute, August 20, 2009; Dean Baker, "The Budget Deficit Scare Story and the Great Recession," Center for Economic and Policy Research, February 2010; Office of Management and Budget, "The President's Budget For Fiscal Year 2011, Historical Tables: Table 7.1, Federal Debt at the End of Year: 1940-2015," February 2010.

Article 4.5

WHY ARE THINGS GETTING WORSE AND WORSE?

BY ARTHUR MacEWAN
March/April 2009

> Dear Dr. Dollar:
> *I learned in my economics classes that in a market economy, problems tend to be self-correcting: when a recession starts, demand weakens; then prices drop, people and firms start to buy more and the economy picks up again. So why don't we see this kind of self-correction now? Why does it seem as if things are getting worse and worse?* —Corina Chio, Los Angeles, Calif.

Life, it turns out, is more complicated than the way it is presented in many economics classes. "More complicated" means different.

One of the key differences between reality and the standard fare of some economics classes is that the standard fare does not take sufficient account of the time lapses between one event and another. These time lapses don't simply mean that adjustments take longer; they mean that the nature of those adjustments can be very different from what one learns in class.

When demand weakens, prices do tend to drop, but they don't drop immediately. So, for example, when demand weakens and people buy fewer cars, candy, cardigans, and computers, the prices of these goods don't fall right away. But, facing the fall-off in purchases, the firms that make these products cut back on production and lay off workers. So demand falls further because the unemployed have less money to buy all these products. In this situation, things can get worse and worse instead of being turned around by the falling prices. Which way things go is not automatic, but depends on the seriousness of the initial fall-off in demand and the speed with which that fall-off occurs.

A further problem with the simplistic analysis presented in some classes is that people's buying decisions are based on expectations about the future as well as on current prices. If auto dealers try to get me to buy a new car by lowering the price, I am not likely to respond positively if I think I may well lose my job soon and be unable to make the monthly payments. And if my main use for a car is to get to and from work, my expectation of lack of work will make me even less likely to buy a new car regardless of the price.

Firms behave similarly. Why should a firm hire more labor or invest in new plants and equipment if the firm expects that people will be cutting back on demand for the firm's products? Even if interest rates and the prices of labor and raw materials are all falling, firms are unlikely to expand operations if they do not think the demand will be there. Indeed, it is precisely the falling prices that signal to firms that a recession is developing—which means that demand will not be there.

Worse: as prices fall, both consumers and firms are likely to delay purchases, expecting that things will be even cheaper if they wait. But by waiting (i.e., by not spending) they create even more downward pressure. So falling prices (deflation) can make things worse, not better.

And even worse still: because consumers and firms act quite rationally in this manner—cutting back expenditures because they expect things to get worse—things do get worse! When each firm and consumer acts rationally in response to negative expectations, as a group they tend to insure that those negative expectations will become reality. Individual rationality and social rationality come in conflict with one another. This phenomenon is often referred to as "the paradox of thrift." People respond to the situation by being thrifty, doing what is good for them individually. But the outcome for society as a whole is bad. Under these circumstances, there is a need for collective action—that is, government action.

This collective action—this government action—will be most effective when it takes the form of deficit spending. And this is exactly what is meant when people talk about a "stimulus package." By engaging in deficit spending the government is increasing demand more by its spending than it is reducing demand through taxes. The difference is made up by borrowing, and the "stimulus" is greatest when the borrowed money would not have been spent—and it would not have been spent precisely because the private firms and individuals who have the money (the money the government is borrowing) also have poor expectations about the future.

Not every economic downturn gets worse and worse. There can be a process of self-correction. But when a serious downturn develops—as is the case right now—self-correction is not going to solve our problems. The collective action that we can take through government is essential to avoid economic disaster.

Article 4.6

STATE BUDGET BLUES
Looking for funds in all the wrong places.

BY MARIANNE HILL
November/December 2009

California's fiscal woes may have grabbed the national headlines, but states across the nation are slashing budgets to close gaps that are averaging a jaw-dropping 24% this year. Even before the economy nose-dived in late 2008, the Government Accountability Office (GAO) was warning states to expect growing revenue shortfalls over the coming decade. The recession and the staggering increase in the federal debt have worsened the GAO's predictions.

The GAO now estimates that, if programs are maintained at current levels, state and local revenues will fall short by an average of 7.6% annually over the coming decade.

To close the yawning gaps in their budgets, states are currently relying on stimulus funds and budget cuts. But fewer federal funds will be there to help as the country begins to pay down the huge national debt. Experts anticipate that federal dollars going to state programs will be scaled back, with funding levels increasing only in targeted areas such as health care and energy. So shortfalls in state budgets will continue for years to come unless states either enact more cuts or update their antiquated tax systems.

In fact, it is past time to overhaul current tax systems. Neither the federal government nor state and local governments are adequately capturing revenue from the high-income, high-growth segments of the economy. At the same time, lower- and middle-income families are unfairly burdened.

Trends in expenditures account for part of the problem. State and local spending on health care for Medicaid, employees, and retirees is projected to significantly outpace revenues. Federal grants-in-aid, which finance about 20% of state and local budget outlays, are dominated by grants to Medicaid. Half of federal grants-in-aid go to Medicaid and this proportion has been increasing with rising enrollment and the growing cost of health care. By 2012, 60% of grants-in-aid will be going to Medicaid, leaving fewer federal dollars for other programs.

Health care reform that succeeds in reducing the cost of medical services while expanding coverage could improve the states' budgetary outlook, but the outlook for revenue collections would remain problematic. The major factor is the erosion of state tax bases, particularly of the sales tax, which accounts for about a third of state and local revenues.

The fiscal crisis in the states will have a long-term impact on our quality of life since state and local governments, with federal assistance, provide most of the public services we receive. They employ almost seven times as many people as does the federal government, and state and local expenditures on public services are greater than federal expenditures, if Medicare and military spending are excluded.

The growing demands on the states are not taken into account by the GAO study, by the way, which only considers the cost of maintaining current service levels. The future scenario for state budgets, then, is likely to be more dire than the GAO predicts. Even with health care reform and improvements in revenue collection and program efficiency, the states will need new revenue sources, better aligned with their income bases, to carry out their vital role in the economy.

Traditionally, states have turned to the sales tax when seeking additional funds. The sales tax is the largest single revenue source for state and local budgets, accounting for a third of tax receipts. Statewide sales tax rates range from a low of 0% in the five states with no general sales tax to 7.25% in California. Recent expansions of the sales tax include the increased taxation of services and of Internet sales.

This reliance on the sales tax is increasingly a liability, however, since the most rapidly expanding industries are in services that are often not subject to the sales tax, such as health care, education. and financial services (credit cards, loans, etc.). A few states are now taxing gross receipts of all businesses to capture service industries, but economists are generally appalled: firms with high input costs but low profit margins can be crippled by a tax on receipts rather than on income net of costs.

Personal and corporate incomes, other potential revenue sources, offer an expanding tax base, but increases in exemptions and deductions have cut into taxable income. (Personal income taxes accounted for about 24% of state and local tax receipts, corporate income taxes 5%, and property taxes 30%, in 2007.)

How states raise needed revenues can be as critical as how they are spent. Equity—basing taxes on the ability to pay—is a prime concern: equity aids both revenue collections and the economic well-being of families. It is especially urgent given recent income trends.

Since the 1980s, progress in raising living standards has been hindered both in the states and nationally by rising income inequality. Output per employee more than doubled in the United States from 1960 to 2005, but earnings did not. In fact, real hourly earnings in 2005 were lower than in 1967, after adjusting for inflation.

The picture is very different for those at the top of the corporate ladder. The typical S&P 500 CEO had an income about 42 times as high as that of the average worker in 1980, but now this CEO gets 344 times as much, according to the Institute for Policy Studies. The top 5% of families currently have incomes about 20 times as high as the bottom 20% at present, up from 11 times as high in 1979.

These figures help to explain why the poverty rate in 1988, 1998, and 2008 remained stubbornly at 13%, despite rising average incomes.

Taxes can increase inequality. Sales taxes, for example, absorb a greater percentage of the income of low-income families than of high-income families, and so increase inequality. Figures on federal corporate taxation are especially disturbing for this reason: 30% of U.S. corporations with gross receipts of $50 million or more paid no taxes over the 1998-2005 period, according to the GAO. If smaller corporations are included as well, 65% paid no U.S. corporate income tax.

Corporations also avoid state taxes. The Multistate Tax Commission found that large, multi-state corporations avoided about $7 billion in state corporate taxes, due to such tactics as shifting their reported profits from high-tax states to low-tax states.

To combat such problems, 20-plus states have banded together and use combined reporting. This requires a multi-state corporation to add together the profits of all its subsidiaries, regardless of their location, into one report. The report provides each state with information needed to levy the appropriate tax, based on individual state tax provisions.

Combined reporting also makes it more difficult for companies to avoid reporting income altogether: one study of 252 large corporations found that in 2003 those companies on average failed to include two-thirds of their actual U.S. pretax profits on their state tax returns. The study found, for example, that Wal-Mart reported $77 billion in pretax profits to its shareholders but paid state income taxes on about half that sum.

The National Association of State Budget Officers suggests another reform: monitoring tax breaks offered to corporations. It notes that some states impose a surcharge on tax breaks offered under business incentive programs if the return to the state from these tax breaks is not as great as expected.

Other reforms could improve the states' revenue outlook. Currently, the personal income tax rate paid by those in the top bracket ranges from Vermont's 9.5% to zero: there are nine states with no personal income tax. An increase in the number of brackets and in rates could boost revenues, while increasing basic exemptions at the same time would protect middle-income families. The tax break on capital gains should be examined.

There are nontraditional means of raising funds as well. For example, penalties and fines for fraud and violations of labor and environmental regulations can be imposed or increased. A carbon emissions tax could be a major revenue source.

Stable, equitable revenue sources are found when taxes are levied in line with the distribution of income and wealth in a state. Taxes like the sales tax that push low-income families further into poverty don't make sense when alternative revenue sources are available that are both more lucrative and more equitable. It is time to look to these sources to close shortfalls in state and local budgets.

Sources: Center for Budget and Policy Priorities; Citizens for Tax Justice; Economic Policy Institute, Institute on Taxation and Economic Policy, *State of Working America 2007*; *Economic Report of the President 2008*; Federation of Tax Administrators; GAO documents GAO-09-210T, GAO-08-957 and GAO-07-1080SP.

Article 4.7

WE NEED A (GREEN) JOBS PROGRAM

Clean-energy investment would promote job growth for a wide swath of the U.S. workforce.

BY JEANNETTE WICKS-LIM
September/October 2010

Fourteen months of an unemployment rate at or near 10% clearly calls for the federal government to take a lead role in job creation. The White House should push its clean-energy agenda as a jobs program but steer clear of all the hype about "green-collar" jobs. Green-collar jobs are widely perceived as job opportunities accessible only to an elite segment of the U.S. workforce—those with advanced degrees, such as environmental engineers, lab technicians, and research scientists. Such jobs are inaccessible to the 52% of unemployed workers with no college experience. The truth is, however, that clean-energy investments could serve as a powerful engine for job growth for a wide swath of the U.S. workforce.

My colleagues at the Political Economy Research Institute and I examined a clean-energy program that includes making buildings more energy efficient, expanding and improving mass transit, updating the national electric grid, and developing each of three types of renewable energy sources: wind, solar, and biomass fuels. Here's what we found.

First, clean-energy activities produce more jobs, dollar for dollar, than fossil fuel-related activities. This is because clean-energy activities tend to be more labor intensive (i.e., more investment dollars go to hiring workers than buying machines), have a higher domestic content (i.e., more dollars are spent on goods and services produced within the United States) and have lower average wages than fossil fuel-related activities. The figures in the table below show how a $1 million investment in clean-energy activities would create more than three times the number of jobs that would be created by investing the same amount in fossil fuels.

Second, many clean energy sector jobs would be accessible to workers with no college experience. The table also shows how the jobs created by a $1 million investment in clean energy would be spread across three levels of education: high school degree or less, some college, and B.A. or more. Nearly half of the clean energy jobs would be held by workers with a high school degree or less. These include jobs for construction laborers, carpenters, and bus drivers. Fewer than one-quarter of clean-energy jobs would require a B.A. or more. The figures for the fossil fuels sector (second column) show that they are more heavily weighted toward jobs requiring college degrees.

Does this mean green investments will just create lots of low-paying jobs? No. The figures in the table below show that investing $1 million in green activities rather than fossil fuel-related activities would generate many more jobs for workers at *all three levels* of formal education credentials. Compared to the fossil fuels sector, the clean energy sector would produce nearly four times the number of jobs that require a high school degree or less, three times the number of jobs that require some college experience, and 2.5 times the number of jobs that require a B.A. or more. Green investments would produce more jobs at all education and wage levels, even while generating proportionately *more* jobs that are accessible to workers with a high school degree or less.

Workers are right to worry about whether these high school degree jobs would offer family-supporting wages. Construction laborers, for example, average at $29,000 annually—awfully close to the $22,000 official poverty line. In addition, women and workers of color have historically faced discrimination in the construction industry, which would be the source of a lot of the lower-credentialed jobs in the clean energy sector. Workers will need to do some serious organizing to put in place labor protections such as living-wage laws, strong collective bargaining rights, and affirmative action policies to insure that these jobs pay decent wages and are equally accessible to all qualified workers.

Sources: Robert Pollin, Jeannette Wicks-Lim, and Heidi Garrett-Peltier, *Green Prosperity: How Clean-Energy Policies Can Fight Poverty and Raise Living Standards in the United States*, Political Economy Research Institute, 2009, www.peri.umass.edu/green_prosperity.

Article 4.8

IS MILITARY KEYNESIANISM THE SOLUTION?

Why war is not a sustainable strategy for economic recovery.

BY HEIDI GARRETT-PELTIER

March/April 2010

The United States is currently preparing to send 30,000 additional troops to Afghanistan by summer 2010. Military contractors, deeply integrated into the U.S. economy, will continue to prosper and profit from increased military spending resulting from this surge of troops. At a time when unemployment in the domestic economy remains near 10%, it may seem convenient to fall back on the principle of military Keynesianism: War is good for the economy.

John Maynard Keynes, the British economist whose work has once again become popular in the wake of this most recent economic crisis, advocated increased government spending to lift an economy out of recession or depression. When consumers and businesses slow their spending, the government can step in to increase demand for goods and services so that businesses can continue to produce and people can remain employed. This fiscal stimulus could take the form of infrastructure projects, healthcare, education, or other productive endeavors. By this logic, military spending can lift an economy out of recession by creating demand for goods and services provided by military contractors, such as the production of tanks and ammunition or the provision of security services. Advocates of this strategy point not only to the widespread employment created by military spending, but also claim that military spending creates well-paying, stable jobs.

It is true that military spending creates jobs throughout the economy, and that many of those jobs are well-paying. But at a time when our jobless rate is high, infrastructure is crumbling, and global climate change is becoming an increasingly urgent matter, we must ask whether military spending is truly a solution to our economic woes or whether we might be able to create more jobs in productive areas that also help us meet longer-term goals.

In a recent paper that I co-authored with Robert Pollin, we show that dollar per dollar, more jobs are created through spending on clean energy, health care, and education than on the military. Further, we show that more middle-income and well-paying jobs are created in all of these areas. For each $1 billion of spending, over 17,000 jobs would be created in clean energy, close to 20,000 in health care, and over 29,000 in education. That same $1 billion would create only 11,600 jobs as a result of military spending. If we look at well-paying jobs, those that pay over $64,000 per year, these alternative domestic spending areas also outperform military spending. The same $1 billion would create 1,500 well-paying jobs in clean energy and just over 1,000 in the military—clean energy creates 50% *more* good jobs than military spending. Education, which is labor-intensive and creates many well-paying jobs per dollar of expenditure, creates close to 2,500 jobs paying over $64,000—that's 2.5 times as many as the military.

According to the National Priorities Project, military spending on the Iraq and Afghanistan wars has reached approximately $1 trillion since 2001, not including the cost of the surge of 30,000 troops. In fiscal year 2009, federal government outlays on the military were 17% of all outlays. Meanwhile, energy, resource conservation, and the environment accounted for only 1% of federal outlays, while education, training, and social services made up only 2%. Military spending is therefore *eight to seventeen times* as high as federal education- and energy-related spending.

The Obama administration is facing increased pressure to reduce the size of the fiscal deficit and the national debt, both of which have grown partly as a result of military spending. At the same time, there is an urgent need to put people back to work and to move the country toward a low-carbon future. While military Keynesianism offers one strategy for recovering from the recession, it is by no means the most effective, even putting aside the other reasons for objecting to a war economy. By reducing military spending, we can channel some of those savings to clean energy, healthcare, education, and other matters of national and global importance.

Sources: "The U.S. Employment Effects of Military and Domestic Spending Priorities: An Updated Analysis", by Robert Pollin and Heidi Garrett-Peltier, available at www.peri.umass.edu; National Priorities Project, www.nationalpriorities.org.

Article 4.9

THE TAX-CUT CON

BY PAUL KRUGMAN
September 2003

Bruce Tinsley's comic strip, "Mallard Fillmore," is, he says, "for the average person out there: the forgotten American taxpayer who's sick of the liberal media." In June 2003, that forgotten taxpayer made an appearance in the strip, attacking his TV set with a baseball bat and yelling: "I can't afford to send my kids to college, or even take 'em out of their substandard public school, because the federal, state and local governments take more than 50% of my income in taxes. And then the guy on the news asks with a straight face whether or not we can 'afford' tax cuts."

Nobody likes paying taxes, and no doubt some Americans are as angry about their taxes as Tinsley's imaginary character. But most Americans also care a lot about the things taxes pay for.

All politicians say they're for public education; almost all of them also say they support a strong national defense, maintaining Social Security and, if anything, expanding the coverage of Medicare. When the "guy on the news" asks whether we can afford a tax cut, he's asking whether, after yet another tax cut goes through, there will be enough money to pay for those things. And the answer is no.

But it's very difficult to get that answer across in modern American politics, which has been dominated for 25 years by a crusade against taxes.

I don't use the word "crusade" lightly. The advocates of tax cuts are relentless, even fanatical. An indication of the movement's fervor—and of its political power—came during the Iraq war. War is expensive and is almost always accompanied by tax increases. But not in 2003. "Nothing is more important in the face of a war," declared Tom DeLay, the House majority leader, "than cutting taxes." And sure enough, taxes were cut, not just in a time of war but also in the face of record budget deficits.

A result of the tax-cut crusade is that there is now a fundamental mismatch between the benefits Americans expect to receive from the government and the revenues government collects. This mismatch is already having profound effects at the state and local levels: teachers and policemen are being laid off and children are being denied health insurance. The federal government can mask its problems for a while by running huge budget deficits, but it, too, will eventually have to decide whether to cut services or raise taxes. And we are not talking about minor policy adjustments. If taxes stay as low as they are now, government as we know it cannot be maintained. In particular, Social Security will have to become far less generous; Medicare will no longer be able to guarantee comprehensive medical care to older Americans; Medicaid will no longer provide basic medical care to the poor.

How did we reach this point? What are the origins of the antitax crusade? And where is it taking us?

Supply-Siders, Starve-the-Beasters, and Lucky Duckies

It is often hard to pin down what antitax crusaders are trying to achieve. The reason is not, or not only, that they are disingenuous about their motives—though as we will see, disingenuity has become a hallmark of the movement in recent years. Rather, the fuzziness comes from the fact that today's antitax movement moves back and forth between two doctrines. Both doctrines favor the same thing: big tax cuts for people with high incomes. But they favor it for different reasons.

One of those doctrines has become famous under the name "supply-side economics." It's the view that the government can cut taxes without severe cuts in public spending. The other doctrine is often referred to as "starving the beast," a phrase coined by David Stockman, Ronald Reagan's budget director. It's the view that taxes should be cut precisely in order to force severe cuts in public spending. Supply-side economics is the friendly, attractive face of the tax-cut movement. But starve-the-beast is where the power lies.

The starting point of supply-side economics is an assertion that no economist would dispute: taxes reduce the incentive to work, save and invest. A businessman who knows that 70 cents of every extra dollar he makes will go to the IRS is less willing to make the effort to earn that extra dollar than if he knows that the IRS will take only 35 cents. So reducing tax rates will, other things being the same, spur the economy.

This much isn't controversial. But the government must pay its bills. So the standard view of economists is that if you want to reduce the burden of taxes, you must explain what government programs you want to cut as part of the deal. There's no free lunch.

What the supply-siders argued, however, was that there was a free lunch. Cutting marginal rates, they insisted, would lead to such a large increase in gross domestic product that it wouldn't be necessary to come up with offsetting spending cuts. What supply-side economists say, in other words, is, "Don't worry, be happy and cut taxes." And when they say cut taxes, they mean taxes on the affluent: reducing the top marginal rate means that the biggest tax cuts go to people in the highest tax brackets.

The other camp in the tax-cut crusade actually welcomes the revenue losses from tax cuts. Its most visible spokesman today is Grover Norquist, president of Americans for Tax Reform, who once told National Public Radio: "I don't want to abolish government. I simply want to reduce it to the size where I can drag it into the bathroom and drown it in the bathtub." And the way to get it down to that size is to starve it of revenue. "The goal is reducing the size and scope of government by draining its lifeblood," Norquist told *U.S. News & World Report*.

What does "reducing the size and scope of government" mean? Tax-cut proponents are usually vague about the details. But the Heritage Foundation, ideological headquarters for the movement, has made it pretty clear. Edwin Feulner, the foundation's president, uses "New Deal" and "Great Society" as terms of abuse, implying that he and his organization want to do away with the institutions Franklin Roosevelt and Lyndon Johnson created. That means Social Security, Medicare, Medicaid—most of what gives citizens of the United States a safety net against economic misfortune.

The starve-the-beast doctrine is now firmly within the conservative mainstream. George W. Bush himself seemed to endorse the doctrine as the budget surplus evaporated: in August 2001 he called the disappearing surplus "incredibly positive news" because it would put Congress in a "fiscal straitjacket."

Like supply-siders, starve-the-beasters favor tax cuts mainly for people with high incomes. That is partly because, like supply-siders, they emphasize the incentive effects of cutting the top marginal rate; they just don't believe that those incentive effects are big enough that tax cuts pay for themselves. But they have another reason for cutting taxes mainly on the rich, which has become known as the "lucky ducky" argument.

Here's how the argument runs: to starve the beast, you must not only deny funds to the government; you must make voters hate the government. There's a danger that working-class families might see government as their friend: because their incomes are low, they don't pay much in taxes, while they benefit from public spending. So in starving the beast, you must take care not to cut taxes on these "lucky duckies." (Yes, that's what the *Wall Street Journal* called them in a famous editorial.) In fact, if possible, you must raise taxes on working-class Americans in order, as the *Journal* said, to get their "blood boiling with tax rage."

So the tax-cut crusade has two faces. Smiling supply-siders say that tax cuts are all gain, no pain; scowling starve-the-beasters believe that inflicting pain is not just necessary but also desirable. Is the alliance between these two groups a marriage of convenience? Not exactly. It would be more accurate to say that the starve-the-beasters hired the supply-siders—indeed, created them—because they found their naive optimism useful.

A look at who the supply-siders are and how they came to prominence tells the story. The supply-side movement likes to present itself as a school of economic thought like Keynesianism or monetarism—that is, as a set of scholarly ideas that made their way, as such ideas do, into political discussion. But the reality is quite different. Supply-side economics was a political doctrine from Day 1; it emerged in the pages of political magazines, not professional economics journals.

That is not to deny that many professional economists favor tax cuts. But they almost always turn out to be starve-the-beasters, not supply-siders. And they often secretly—or sometimes not so secretly—hold supply-siders in contempt. N. Gregory Mankiw, now chairman of George W. Bush's Council of Economic Advisers, is definitely a friend to tax cuts; but in the first edition of his economic-principles textbook, he described Ronald Reagan's supply-side advisers as "charlatans and cranks."

It is not that the professionals refuse to consider supply-side ideas; rather, they have looked at them and found them wanting. A conspicuous example came earlier this year when the Congressional Budget Office tried to evaluate the growth effects of the Bush administration's proposed tax cuts. The new CBO head, Douglas Holtz-Eakin, is a conservative economist who was handpicked for his job by the administration. But his conclusion was that unless the revenue losses from the proposed tax cuts were offset by spending cuts, the resulting deficits would be a drag on growth, quite likely to outweigh any supply-side effects.

But if the professionals regard the supply-siders with disdain, who employs these people? The answer is that since the 1970s almost all of the prominent supply-siders have been aides to conservative politicians, writers at conservative publications like *National Review,* fellows at conservative policy centers like Heritage or economists at private companies with strong Republican connections. Loosely speaking, that is, supply-siders work for the vast right-wing conspiracy. What gives supply-side economics influence is its connection with a powerful network of institutions that want to shrink the government and see tax cuts as a way to achieve that goal.

Supply-side economics is a feel-good cover story for a political movement with a much harder-nosed agenda.

A Planned Crisis

Right now, much of the public discussion of the Bush tax cuts focuses on their short-run impact. Critics say that the 2.7 million jobs lost since March 2001 prove that the administration's policies have failed, while the administration says that things would have been even worse without the tax cuts and that a solid recovery is just around the corner.

But this is the wrong debate. Even in the short run, the right question to ask isn't whether the tax cuts were better than nothing; they probably were. The right question is whether some other economic-stimulus plan could have achieved better results at a lower budget cost. And it is hard to deny that, on a jobs-per-dollar basis, the Bush tax cuts have been extremely ineffective. According to the Congressional Budget Office, half of this year's $400 billion budget deficit is due to Bush tax cuts. Now $200 billion is a lot of money; it is equivalent to the salaries of four million average workers. Even the administration doesn't claim its policies have created four million jobs. Surely some other policy—aid to state and local governments, tax breaks for the poor and middle class rather than the rich, maybe even WPA-style public works—would have been more successful at getting the country back to work.

Meanwhile, the tax cuts are designed to remain in place even after the economy has recovered. Where will they leave us?

Here's the basic fact: partly, though not entirely, as a result of the tax cuts of the last three years, the government of the United States faces a fundamental fiscal shortfall. That is, the revenue it collects falls well short of the sums it needs to pay for existing programs. Even the U.S. government must, eventually, pay its bills, so something will have to give.

The numbers tell the tale. This year and next, the federal government will run budget deficits of more than $400 billion. Deficits may fall a bit, at least as a share of gross domestic product, when the economy recovers. But the relief will be modest and temporary. As Peter Fisher, undersecretary of the treasury for domestic finance, puts it, the federal government is "a gigantic insurance company with a sideline business in defense and homeland security." And about a decade from now, this insurance company's policyholders will begin making a lot of claims. As the baby boomers retire, spending on Social Security benefits and Medicare will steadily rise, as will spending on Medicaid (because of rising medical costs). Eventually, unless there are sharp cuts in benefits, these three programs alone will consume a larger share of GDP than the federal government currently collects in taxes.

Alan Auerbach, William Gale, and Peter Orszag, fiscal experts at the Brookings Institution, have estimated the size of the "fiscal gap"—the increase in revenues or reduction in spending that would be needed to make the nation's finances sustainable in the long run. If you define the long run as 75 years, this gap turns out to be 4.5% of GDP. Or to put it another way, the gap is equal to 30% of what the federal government spends on all domestic programs. Of that gap, about 60% is the result of the Bush tax cuts. We would have faced a serious fiscal problem even if those tax cuts had never happened. But we face a much nastier problem now that they are in place.

And more broadly, the tax-cut crusade will make it very hard for any future politicians to raise taxes.

So how will this gap be closed? The crucial point is that it cannot be closed without either fundamentally redefining the role of government or sharply raising taxes.

Politicians will, of course, promise to eliminate wasteful spending. But take out Social Security, Medicare, defense, Medicaid, government pensions, homeland security, interest on the public debt, and veterans' benefits—none of them what people who complain about waste usually have in mind—and you are left with spending equal to about 3% of gross domestic product. And most of that goes for courts, highways, education, and other useful things. Any savings from elimination of waste and fraud will amount to little more than a rounding-off error.

So let's put a few things back on the table. Let's assume that interest on the public debt will be paid, that spending on defense and homeland security will not be compromised, and that the regular operations of government will continue to be financed. What we are left with, then, are the New Deal and Great Society programs: Social Security, Medicare, Medicaid and unemployment insurance. And to close the fiscal gap, spending on these programs would have to be cut by around 40%.

It's impossible to know how such spending cuts might unfold, but cuts of that magnitude would require drastic changes in the system. It goes almost without saying that the age at which Americans become eligible for retirement benefits would rise, that Social Security payments would fall sharply compared with average incomes, that Medicare patients would be forced to pay much more of their expenses out of pocket—or do without. And that would be only a start.

All this sounds politically impossible. In fact, politicians of both parties have been scrambling to expand, not reduce, Medicare benefits by adding prescription drug coverage. It's hard to imagine a situation under which the entitlement programs would be rolled back sufficiently to close the fiscal gap.

Yet closing the fiscal gap by raising taxes would mean rolling back all of the Bush tax cuts, and then some. And that also sounds politically impossible.

For the time being, there is a third alternative: borrow the difference between what we insist on spending and what we're willing to collect in taxes. That works as long as lenders believe that someday, somehow, we're going to get our fiscal act together. But this can't go on indefinitely.

Eventually—I think within a decade, though not everyone agrees—the bond market will tell us that we have to make a choice.

In short, everything is going according to plan.

For the looming fiscal crisis doesn't represent a defeat for the leaders of the tax-cut crusade or a miscalculation on their part. Some supporters of President Bush may have really believed that his tax cuts were consistent with his promises to protect Social Security and expand Medicare; some people may still believe that the wondrous supply-side effects of tax cuts will make the budget deficit disappear. But for starve-the-beast tax-cutters, the coming crunch is exactly what they had in mind.

What Kind of Country?

The astonishing political success of the antitax crusade has, more or less deliberately, set the United States up for a fiscal crisis. How we respond to that crisis will determine what kind of country we become.

If Grover Norquist is right—and he has been right about a lot—the coming crisis will allow conservatives to move the nation a long way back toward the kind of limited government we had before Franklin Roosevelt. Lack of revenue, he says, will make it possible for conservative politicians—in the name of fiscal necessity—to dismantle immensely popular government programs that would otherwise have been untouchable.

In Norquist's vision, America a couple of decades from now will be a place in which elderly people make up a disproportionate share of the poor, as they did before Social Security. It will also be a country in which even middle-class elderly Americans are, in many cases, unable to afford expensive medical procedures or prescription drugs and in which poor Americans generally go without even basic health care. And it may well be a place in which only those who can afford expensive private schools can give their children a decent education.

But that's a choice, not a necessity. The tax-cut crusade has created a situation in which something must give. But what gives—whether we decide that the New Deal and the Great Society must go or that taxes aren't such a bad thing after all—is up to us. The American people must decide what kind of a country we want to be.

Excerpted from the *New York Times Magazine*, September 14, 2003.

Article 4.10

THAT HURT! LET'S DO IT AGAIN.

BY JOHN MILLER
November/December 2010

> It's official: The Great Recession ended 15 months ago, in June 2009. ... [T]he downturn that began in December 2007 lasted 18 months ... only two months longer than the 16-month downturns of 1973-75 and 1981-82 ... .
>
> What is different about this period is the relative weakness of the economic recovery. ... [I]n 1983 the recovery surpassed its previous peak in gross domestic product very rapidly from the recession's trough. ...
>
> This time, even after a year of recovery through June 2010, real GDP remained 1.3% below its previous peak ...
>
> Consider this contrast: In 1983, the Reagan cuts in marginal tax rates were finally kicking in, regulatory burdens were falling across the economy, and the Federal Reserve was cutting interest rates. In 2010, taxes are heading up, new regulations are piling up thanks to ObamaCare, et al., and the Fed can't keep interest rates near-zero forever. We think these different policy circumstances are very much related to the different pace of the two recoveries.
>
> —*Wall Street Journal* editorial, 9/22/10

"**S**lump Over, Pain Persists" read the *Wall Street Journal* headline the day after the announcement in September that the Great Recession had ended back in June 2009.

The editors' reaction? Let's have more tax cuts and deregulation, the very policies that brought on the recession. Their reason? Because the first year of recovery from the 1981-82 recession, following the Reagan tax cuts, was far more robust than the Obama recovery has been so far.

But before you get nostalgic about the Reagan recovery, read the fine print.

To begin with, while the 1981-82 downturn was lengthy and severe, it was no Great Recession. No financial collapse, as even the editors allow, is one profound difference. Others include less drop-off in output, fewer jobs lost, and less long-term unemployment.

Climbing out of a smaller hole than the one left by the Great Recession, the Reagan recovery did manage to post economic growth rates that just matched those of the typical recovery since World War II, something the Obama recovery has not done. But how much of that growth can rightly be attributed to tax cuts?

The answer is, not much. Enacted in 1981, the Reagan tax cuts slashed corporate and individual income tax rates, with the biggest cut in the top rate. "Reaganomics" claimed that drastic tax cuts would restore prosperity by encouraging work, savings, and investment.

But when mainstream economists, such as Barry Bosworth and Gary Burtless of the Brookings Institution, looked closely, they found that something quite different had happened. After the 1981 tax cuts, savings rates actually plummeted. There was no boom in investment, since the tax cuts created large deficits that drove up interest rates, in turn discouraging investment. Men did work somewhat more and married women in particular worked longer hours, yet most saw no increase in their earnings.

What Reagan's tax cuts and other economic policies did do was to usher in an era of rising inequality. During the 1982-89 expansion, the share of total income gains that went to the richest one percent of households exceeded the share going to the bottom 90% for the first time since the 1920s.

The editors do not cite the next round of pro-rich tax cuts, passed in 2001 and 2003 during the Bush administration. That's probably because they were nearly devoid of expansionary powers. From 2001 to 2007, the U.S. economy grew more slowly and created fewer jobs than during any expansion since World War II. This was also the only expansion in 60 years that failed to lift real median household income.

If those dismal results are not enough to convince you that more tax cuts are the wrong medicine, consider this. Today, tax rates for the rich—the top income tax bracket, estate taxes, and dividend and capital gains taxes—are lower than they were *after* the Reagan tax cuts, and would remain so even if the Bush tax cuts for families with incomes over $250,000 were allowed to expire. So much for the economic-growth magic of low tax rates.

It is not taxes or overregulation but poor sales that are the largest single problem facing small businesses, according to the National Federation of Independent Business. But boosting sales remains no mean feat. With persistent high unemployment, wages virtually frozen, and foreclosures continuing unabated, there is no reason to expect consumer spending to rescue the U.S. economy.

Additional government stimulus spending would help, but more than that needs to be done: the deregulatory, inequality-inducing policies initiated during the Reagan recovery need to be undone. And what better place to start than with eliminating the Bush tax cuts for the rich.

Sources: Barry Bosworth and Gary Burtless, "The Effect of Tax Reform on Labor Supply, Investment, and Savings," *Journal of Economic Perspectives*, Winter 1992; Avi Feller and Chad Stone, "Top 1 Percent of Americans Reaped Two-Thirds of Income Gains in the Last Expansion," Center on Budget and Policy Priorities, Sept. 9, 2009; NFIB Small Business Economic Trends, Sept. 2010.

Article 4.11

SAND IN THE WHEELS, NOT IN THE FACE

Why a transaction tax is a really good *idea.*

BY JOHN MILLER
March/April 2010

WHY TAXING STOCK TRADES IS A REALLY BAD IDEA

[S]urely it is "socially useful" to let free people transact freely, without regulators and legislators micromanaging them. … It's Economics 101 that the free actions of market participants cause supply and demand to reach equilibrium. And isn't that what investors—indeed even speculators—do? Can they do it as well when facing the dead-weight costs of a transaction tax?

If not, then trading volume in our stock markets will fall. Beyond the tax, everyone— investors and speculator, great and small—who buys or sells stocks will pay more to transact in markets that are less liquid. In such a world, markets would necessarily be more risky, and the cost of capital for business would necessarily rise. The consequence of that is that innovation, growth, and jobs would necessarily fall. That would be the full and true cost of the trading tax.

—Donald L. Luskin and Chris Hynes, "Why Taxing Stock Trades Is a Really Bad Idea," *Wall Street Journal*, January 5, 2010

"**S**ome financial activities which proliferated over the last 10 years were socially useless," Britain's Finance Service Authority Chairman Adiar Turner told a black-tie gathering of financial executives in London in September 2009. That is why he had proposed a transaction tax for the United Kingdom and why British Prime Minister Gordon Brown would propose an international transaction tax at the November G-20 summit.

The gathered bankers "saw red," as one report described their reaction. Investment bankers Donald L. Luskin and Chris Hynes are still irate.

In some ways their reaction is surprising. A financial transaction tax is nothing other than a sales tax on trading stocks and other securities. Transaction taxes are already in place in about 30 countries, and a transaction tax applied to the sale of stock in the United States from 1914 to 1964.

In addition, the transaction tax rates on a single trade are typically quite low. For instance, the "Let Wall Street Pay for the Restoration of Main Street Act of 2009," proposed by U.S. Representative Peter DeFazio (D-Ore.), would assess a one quarter of one percent (.25%) tax on the value of stock transactions, and two one hundredths of one percent (.02%) tax on the sale on a variety of derivative assets—including credit default swaps, which played such a large role in the mortgage crisis. To target speculators, the bill exempts retirement accounts, mutual funds, education and health savings accounts, and the first $100,000 of transactions annually.

In other ways, Luskin's and Hynes's reaction is not surprising at all. At its heart, a transaction tax is a radical measure. Its premise is that faster-acting financial markets driven by speculation don't bring relief to the economy—instead, they loot the economy. Its purpose, as Nobel Prize-winning economist James Tobin put it when he proposed his original transaction tax on international money markets during the 1970s, is to "throw sand in the wheels" of our financial markets.

Also, while its tax rate is low, the burden of a transaction tax adds up as securities are repeatedly traded, as is the practice on Wall Street today. For instance, even after accounting for its exemptions and allowing for a sizable decline in trading, the DeFazio bill would still raise $63.5 billion annually, according to the estimates of Dean Baker, co-director of the Center for Economic Policy Research.

Luskin and Hynes have two main objections to the transaction tax. The first is that a transaction tax would affect every single person who owns and invests in stocks, not just speculators. Customers would not have to pay a tax to buy or sell mutual funds, but, as Luskin and Hynes emphasize, the mutual funds themselves would have to pay a tax every time they trade stocks. So everyone holding mutual funds would still end up paying the tax.

What Luskin and Hynes don't say is this: Mutual funds that actively trade stocks would pay three times the transaction taxes of an average fund, as the Investment Company Institute, the fund industry trade group, reports. And stock index funds, which hold a sample of all stocks but seldom trade them, are taxed the least. Those funds have historically outperformed other mutual funds. So a transaction tax would work to push mutual fund customers to invest their savings more wisely, providing some with higher rates of return with a transaction tax than their previous funds provided without it. And that would mean fewer broker fees and lower profits for the fund industry.

But what really sticks in Luskin's and Hynes's craw is the assertion that financial trading is not socially useful. That claim flies in face of the long-held contention, buttressed by much of finance theory, that the equilibrium outcomes of financial markets are efficient. And if financial markets are efficient, there is no need for a tax that will reduce trading.

But much of what Luskin and Hynes have to say is not right. First, as anyone who *paid attention* in Economics 101 would know, reaching an equilibrium is not in and of itself desirable. To endorse the outcomes of today's speculative financial markets as desirable because they reach an equilibrium is the equivalent of describing a gambler in a poker game raking in a big pot as desirable because it clears the table. And the gamblers in our financial markets did rake in some awfully big pots betting that subprime borrowers would default on their loans. The last few years show us just how undesirable that equilibrium turned out to be.

Second, speculation dwarfs financing investment in U.S. stock markets. During the 1970s, for every dollar of new investment in plants and equipment, $1.30 in stocks were traded on the U.S. exchanges, reports Robert Pollin, co-director of the Political Economy Research Institute. But from 1998 to 2007, $27 in stocks were traded on the U.S. exchanges for every dollar of corporate investment in plant equipment. Such a rapid stock turnover has diverted the attention of managers of enterprises from long-term planning. Whatever damage that churning caused on Main Street, it paid off handsomely on Wall Street. From 1973 to 2007, the size of the financial (and insurance) sector relative to the economy doubled, financial sector profits went from one-quarter to two-fifths of domestic profits, and compensation in the finance industry went from just about average to 180% of the private industry average.

By counteracting these trends, a transactions tax can actually enhance, not diminish, the efficiency of financial markets. If it forces the financial sector to fulfill its function of transferring savings to investment with less short-term churning, then the tax will have freed up resources for more productive uses.

A transaction tax would surely be a step in the right direction toward reducing the bloat of the finance industry, righting the balance of speculation over enterprise, and restoring the focus on long-term planning and job-creation in the economy.

None of that will happen unless every last grain of the decades' worth of sand the bullies on Wall Street have kicked in our faces gets thrown into the wheels of finance. That is a tall order. But as DeFazio's and Turner's example shows, some of today's policymakers are up to the task.

Sources: "The Benefits of a Financial Transaction Tax," by Dean Baker, Center For Economic and Policy Research, December 2008; ""Public Investment, Industrial Policy, and U.S. Economic Renewal," by Robert Pollin and Dean Baker, Political Economy Research Institute, December 2009; "Turner Plan on 'Socially Useless' Trades Make Bankers See Red," by Caroline Binham, Bloomberg.com; "Taxing Wall Street Today Wins Support for Keynes Idea (Update 1)," by Yaiman Onaran, Bloomberg.com; "The Potential Revenue from Financial Transactions Taxes, by Dean Baker, Robert Pollin, Travis McArthur, and Matt Sherman, Political Economy Research Institute, Working paper no. 212, December 2009; "Why Taxing Stock Trades Is a Really Bad Idea," by Donald L. Luskin and Chris Hynes, *Wall Street Journal*, January 5, 2010; "Lawmakers Weigh A Wall Street Tax," by John McKinnon, *Wall Street Journal*, December 19, 2009; Tobin Tax, freerisk. org/wiki/index.php/Tobin_tax; text of HR 4191—"Let Wall Street Pay for the Restoration of Main Street Act of 2009," www.govtrack.us.

Article 4.12

SOCIAL SECURITY ISN'T BROKEN
So why the rush to "fix" it?

BY DOUG ORR
November/December 2004

Federal Reserve Chairman Alan Greenspan told Congress earlier this year [2004] that everyone knows there's a Social Security crisis. That's like saying "everyone knows the earth is flat."

Starting with a faulty premise guarantees reaching the wrong conclusion. The truth is there is no Social Security crisis, but there is a potential crisis in retirement income security and there may be a crisis in the future in U.S. financial markets. It's this latter crisis that Greenspan actually is worried about.

Social Security is the most successful insurance program ever created. It insures millions of workers against what economists call "longevity risk," the possibility they will live "too long" and not be able to work long enough, or save enough, to provide their own income. Today, about 10% of those over age 65 live in poverty. Without Social Security, that rate would be almost 50%.

Social Security was originally designed to supplement, and was structured to resemble, private-sector pensions. In the 1930s, all private pensions were defined-benefit plans. The retirement benefit was based on a worker's former wage and years of service. In most plans, after 35 years of service the monthly benefit, received for life, would be at least half of the income received in the final working year.

Congress expected that private-sector pensions eventually would cover most workers. But pension coverage peaked at 40% in the 1960s. Since then, corporations have systematically dismantled pension systems. Today, only 16% of private-sector workers are covered by defined-benefit pensions. Rather than supplementing private pensions, Social Security has become the primary source of retirement income for almost two-thirds of retirees. Thus, Congress was forced to raise benefit levels in 1972.

What has happened to private-sector defined benefit pensions? They've been replaced with defined-contribution (DC) savings plans such as 401(k)s and 403(b)s. These plans provide some retirement income but offer no real protection from longevity risk. Once a retiree depletes the amount saved in the plan, their retirement income is gone.

In a generous DC plan, a firm might match the worker's contribution up to 3% of his or her pay. With total contributions of 6%, average wage growth of 2% a year, and an average return on the investment portfolio of 5%, after 35 years of work, a retiree would exhaust the plan's savings in just 8.5 years even if her annual spending is only half of her final salary. If she restricts spending to just one-third of the final salary, the savings can stretch to 14 years.

At age 65, life expectancy for women today is about 20 years, and for men about 15 years, so DC savings plans will not protect the elderly from longevity risk. The conversion of defined-benefit pensions to defined-contribution plans is the source of the real potential crisis in retirement income. Yet Greenspan did not mention this in his testimony to Congress.

No Crisis

Opponents of Social Security have hated it since its creation in 1935. The first prediction of a Social Security crisis was published in 1936! The Heritage Foundation and Cato Institute are home to many of the program's opponents today, and they fixate on the concept of a "demographic imperative." In 1960, the United States had 5.1 workers per retiree, in 1998 we had 3.4, and by 2030 we will have only 2.1. Opponents claim that with these demographic changes, revenues will eventually be insufficient to pay Social Security retirement benefits.

The logic is appealingly simple, but wrong for two reasons. First, this "old-age dependency" ratio in itself is irrelevant. No amount of financial manipulation can change this fact: all current consumption must come from current physical output. The consumption of all dependents (non-workers) must come from the output produced by current workers. It's the overall dependency ratio—the number of workers relative to all non-workers, including the aged, the young, the disabled, and those choosing not to work—that determines whether society can "afford" the baby boomers' retirement years. In the 1960s we had only 0.62 workers for each dependent, and we were building new schools and the interstate highway system and getting ready to put a man on the moon. No one bemoaned a demographic crisis or looked for ways to cut the resources allocated to children; in fact, the living standards of most families rose rapidly. In 2030, we will have 0.98 workers per dependent. We'll have more workers per dependent in the future than we did in the past. While it is true a larger share of total output will be allocated to the aged, just as a larger share was allocated to children in the 1960s, society will easily produce adequate output to support all workers and dependents, and at a higher standard of living.

Second, the "demographic imperative" ignores productivity growth. Average worker productivity has grown by about 2% per year, adjusted for inflation, for the past half-century. That means real output per worker doubles every 36 years. This productivity growth is projected to continue, so by 2040, each worker will produce twice as much as today. Suppose each of three workers today produces $1,000 per week and one retiree is allocated $500 (half of his final salary)—then each worker gets $833. In 2040, two such workers will produce $2,000 per week each (after adjusting for inflation). If each retiree gets $1,000, each worker still gets $1,500. The incomes of both workers and retirees go up. Thus, paying for the baby boomers' retirement need not decrease their children's standard of living. A larger share of output going to retirees does not imply that the standard of living of those still working will be lower. Those still working will have a slightly smaller share of a much larger pie.

So why the talk of a Social Security crisis? Social Security always has been a pay-as-you-go system. Current benefits are paid out of current tax revenues. But in the 1980s, a commission headed by Greenspan recommended raising payroll taxes to expand the trust fund in order to supplement tax revenues when the baby boom generation retires. Congress responded in 1984 by raising payroll taxes significantly. As a result, the Social Security trust fund, which holds government bonds as assets, has grown every year since. As the baby boom moves into retirement, these assets will be sold to help pay their retirement benefits.

Each year, Social Security's trustees must make projections of the system's status for the next 75 years. In 1996, they projected the trust fund balance would go to zero in 2030. In 2000, they projected a zero balance in 2036 and today they project a zero balance in 2042. The projection keeps changing because the trustees continue to make unrealistic assumptions about future economic conditions. The current projections are based on the assumption that annual GDP growth will average 1.8% for the next 75 years. In no 20-year period, even including the Great Depression, has the U.S. economy grown that slowly. Each year the economy grows faster than 1.8%, the zero balance date moves further into the future. But the trustees continue to suggest that if we return to something like the Great Depression, the trust fund will go to zero.

Opponents of Social Security claim the system will then be "bankrupt." Bankruptcy implies ceasing to exist. But if the trust fund goes to zero, Social Security will not shut down and stop paying benefits. It will simply revert to the pure pay-as-you-go system that it was before 1984 and continue to pay current benefits using current tax revenues. Even if the trustees' worst-case assumptions come true, the payroll tax paid by workers would need to increase by only about two percentage points, and only in 2042, not today.

If the economy grows at 2.4%—which is still slower than the stagnant growth of the 1980s—the trust fund never goes to zero. The increase in real output and real incomes will generate sufficient revenues to pay promised benefits. By 2042, we will need to lower payroll taxes or raise benefits to reduce the surplus.

The claim that benefits of future retirees must be reduced in order to not reduce the standard of living of future workers is simply wrong. It is being used to drive a wedge between generations and panic younger workers into supporting Bush's plan to destroy Social Security. Under the most likely version of his privatization proposal, according to Bush's own Social Security Commission, the guaranteed benefits from Social Security of a 20-year-old worker joining the labor force today would be reduced by 46%. That Commission also admitted that private accounts are unlikely to make up for this drop in benefits. An estimate made by the Goldman Sachs brokerage firm suggests that even with private accounts, retirement income of younger workers would be reduced by 42% compared to what they would receive if nothing is done to change the Social Security system. Private accounts are a losing proposition for younger workers.

The Real Fear: An Oversupply of Bonds

So why did Greenspan claim cutting benefits would become necessary? To understand the answer, we need to take a side trip to look at how bonds and the financial markets affect each other. It turns out that rising interest rates reduce the selling price of existing financial assets, and falling asset prices push up interest rates (see box "How Does the Bond Market Work?").

For example, in the 1980s, President Reagan cut taxes and created the largest government deficits in history up to that point. This meant the federal government had to sell lots of bonds to finance the soaring government debt; to attract enough buyers, the Treasury had to offer very high interest rates. During the 1980s, real interest rates (rates adjusted for inflation) were almost four times higher than the historic average. High interest rates slow economic growth by making it more expensive for consumers to buy homes or for businesses to invest in new infrastructure. The GDP growth rate in the 1980s was the slowest in U.S. history apart from the Great Depression.

But high interest rates also depress financial asset prices. A five percentage point rise in interest rates reduces the selling price of a bond (loan) that matures in 10 years by 50%. It was the impact of the record-high interest rates of the 1980s on the value of the loan portfolios of the savings and loan industry that caused the S&L crisis and the industry's collapse.

Greenspan is worried because he sees history repeating itself in the form of President Bush's tax cuts. In his testimony, Greenspan expressed concern over a potentially large rise in interest rates. This is his way of warning about an excess supply of bonds. Starting in 2020, Social Security will have to sell about $150 billion (in 2002 dollars) in trust fund bonds each year for 22 years. At the same time, private-sector pension funds will be selling $100 billion per year of financial assets to make their pension payments. State and local governments will be selling $75 billion per year to cover their former employees' pension expenses, and holdings in private mutual funds will fall by about $50 billion per year as individual retirees cash in their

HOW DOES THE BOND MARKET WORK?

A bond is nothing more than an IOU. A company or government borrows money and promises to pay a certain amount of interest annually until it repays the loan. When you buy a newly issued bond, you are making a loan. The amount of the loan is the "face value" of the bond. The initial interest rate at which the bond is issued, the "face rate," multiplied by this face value determines the amount of interest paid each period. Until the debt is paid back, events in the financial markets affect the bond's value.

If market interest rates fall, prices of existing bonds rise. Why? Suppose you buy a bond with a face value of $100 that pays 10%. You then collect $10 per year. If the current interest rate falls to 5%, newly issued bonds will pay that new rate. Since your bond pays 10%, people would rather buy that one than one paying 5%. They are willing to pay more than the face value to get it, so the price will be bid up until interest rates equalize. The price at which you could sell your bond will rise to $200, since $10 is 5% of $200.

But changes in bond prices also affect interest rates. If more people are selling bonds than buying them, an excess supply exists, and prices will fall. If you need to sell your bond to get money to pay your rent, you might have to lower the price of the bond you hold to $50. Because the bond still pays $10 per year to the owner, the new owner gets a 20% return on the $50 purchase. Anyone trying to issue new bonds will have to match that return, so the new market interest rate becomes 20%.

401(k) assets. Private firms will still need to issue about $100 billion of new bonds a year to finance business expansion. Combined, these asset sales could total $475 billion per year.

This level of bond sales is more than double the record that was set in the 1980s following the Reagan tax cuts. But back then, the newly issued bonds were being purchased by "institutional investors" such as private-sector pension funds and insurance companies. After 2020, these groups will be net sellers of bonds. The financial markets will strain to absorb this level of asset sales. It's unlikely they will be able to also absorb the extra $400 billion per year of bond sales needed to cover the deficit spending that will occur if the new Bush tax cuts are made permanent. This oversupply of bonds will drive down the value of all financial assets.

In a 1994 paper, Sylvester Schieber, a current advisor to President Bush on pension and Social Security reform, predicted this potential drop in asset prices. After 2020, the value of assets held in 401(k) plans, already inadequate, will be reduced even more. More importantly, at least to Greenspan, the prices of assets held by corporations to fund their defined benefit pension promises will fall. Thus, pension payments will need to come out of current revenues, reducing corporate profits and, in turn, driving down stock prices.

It's this potential collapse in the prices of financial assets that worries Greenspan most. In order to reduce the run-up of long-term interest rates, some asset sales must be eliminated. Greenspan said, "You don't have the resources to do it all." But rather than rescinding Bush's tax cuts, Greenspan favors reducing bond sales by the Social Security trust fund. Doing that requires a reduction in benefits and raising payroll taxes even more.

Framing a question incorrectly makes it impossible to find a solution. The problem is not with Social Security, but rather with blind reliance on financial markets to solve all economic problems. If the financial markets are likely to fail us, what is the solution? The solution is simple once the question is framed correctly: where will the real output that baby boomers are going to consume in retirement come from?

The federal budget surplus President Bush inherited came entirely from Social Security surpluses resulting from the 1984 payroll tax increase. Bush gave away revenues meant to provide for workers' retirement as tax cuts for the wealthiest 10% of the population.

We should rescind Bush's tax cuts and use the Social Security surpluses to really prepare for the baby boom retirement. Public investment or targeted tax breaks could be used to encourage the building of the hospitals, nursing homes, and hospices that aging baby boomers will need. Such investment in public and private infrastructure would also stimulate the real economy and increase GDP growth. Surpluses could be used to fund the training of doctors, nurses and others to staff these facilities, and of other high skilled workers more generally. The higher wages of skilled labor will help generate the payroll tax revenues needed to fund future benefits. If baby boomers help to fund this infrastructure expansion through their payroll taxes while they are still working, less output will need to be allocated when they retire. These expenditures will increase the productivity of the real economy, which will help keep the financial sector solvent to provide for retirees.

Destroying Social Security in order to "save" it is not a solution.

Sources: Dean Baker and Mark Weisbrot, *Social Security: The Phony Crises*, University of Chicago Press, 1999; William Wolman and Anne Colamosca, *The Great 401(k) Hoax*, Perseus Publishing, 2002; Sylvester J. Schieber and John B. Shoven, "The Consequences of Population Aging on Private Pension Fund Saving and Asset Markets," National Bureau of Economic Research, Working Paper No. 4665, 1994.

Chapter 5

MONETARY POLICY AND FINANCIAL MARKETS

INTRODUCTION

Ben Bernanke replaced Alan Greenspan as the man behind the curtain of the Federal Reserve Board just in time to oversee the worst financial crisis since the Great Depression.

Bernanke needed all the wizard-like powers the business press sometimes attributed to Greenspan, given it was his job to pull the economy's fat out of the fire. And those powers were in awfully short supply when Greenspan himself confessed before Congress in October 2008 that the financial crisis had left him "in a state of shocked disbelief" and that he had "made a mistake in presuming that banks … were capable of protecting their own shareholders."

Bernanke did avert a complete economic meltdown. Limited steps have been undertaken to resolve the nearly intractable mortgage debt crisis and to put in place the measures that might prevent another financial crisis, both of which receive plenty of attention in this chapter, Still working people have fared no better under Bernanke than they did under maestro Greenspan. Even before the financial crisis, Greenspan worried that, under his tenure, inequality had worsened to levels that threatened our democratic institutions, and that the unprecedented level of U.S. reliance on foreign borrowing had become unsustainable. Bernanke has acknowledged the seriousness of both problems as well, but seems just as incapable as his predecessor of remedying them.

But why should it matter who chairs the Federal Reserve Board? The Fed is charged with using monetary policy to keep inflation in check and provide liquidity to keep the economy going (or bolster a flagging economy). The Fed is supposed to use its three tools—the reserve requirement, the discount and federal funds rates, and open market operations—to manipulate banking activity, control the money supply, and direct the economy to everyone's benefit.

It all sounds value-free. But what the Fed really does is serve those who hold financial assets. And that is just what's wrong with Fed monetary policy. When it comes to making monetary policy, the Fed puts the interests of bondholders first, well before those of job seekers and workers. Investors look to the Fed to protect the value of their stocks and bonds by keeping inflation low—and if that means keeping a cap on employment growth, so be it.

That is why monetary policy is not just a matter for financial market junkies, but for anyone concerned with the social policies it holds hostage. As Doug Orr and Ellen Frank argue in this chapter, "Whenever any policy is proposed, be it in health care, housing, or transportation, the first question politicians ask is, 'What will the bond market think about it?'" The authors go on to show just how monetary policy under Greenspan has worked against most of us and even helped push the economy into a slowdown in 2000 (Article 5.2).

Other articles in this chapter look closely at diverse aspects of Fed policy-making. Doug Orr explains in everyday language what money is and how the Fed attempts to control the money supply (Article 5.1). Arthur MacEwan compares monetary and fiscal policy, highlighting the greater powers of fiscal policy to counteract recessions (Article 5.3). The explosion in the excess reserves held by U.S. banks, as economist Gerald Friedman shows, confirms that the Fed can do little to get the economy going using conventional monetary policy if banks won't make loans (Article 5.4). The Fed's recent decision to purchase long-term bonds, instead of its usual practice of buying and selling short-term bonds, is economist Alejandro Reuss's focus in Article 5.5. He argues that the continued reluctance of banks to lend and the skittishness of investors will stand in the way of the Fed's newest attempt to boost investment by lowering long-term interest rates.

The next few articles tally up the damage inflicted by the financial crisis. Arthur MacEwan explicates the role that a giant pool of money (actually, financial assets) played in the home mortgage crisis (Article 5.6). Marty Wolfson gives a down-to-earth description of the financial instruments and deregulatory measures at the heart of the crisis. He calls for a regulatory structure that puts limits on financial risk and manipulation (Article 5.7). Mary Bottari, director of the Real Economy Project, gives readers a visual sense of the how the money spent to bail out Wall Street exceeds the total of government spending on the wars in Iraq and Afghanistan, the 2010 health care reform law, the 2009 economic stimulus package, and the savings-and-loan bailout three decades earlier (Article 5.8).

Deregulation, the financial crisis, the bailout of major banks, and finally the Dodd-Frank Act of 2010 have transformed the banking and financial industries. Economist Rob Larson begins our coverage with a careful analysis of how deregulation permitted banks to become too big to fail. He traces the changes wrought by interstate banking, economies of scale in the banking industry, and expansion of commercial banks into insurance and investment banking. Larson reports that the financial crisis and the bailout led only to further concentration in the banking industry (Article 5.9). Economist and one-time bank regulator William K. Black tells the story of how the banking crisis was driven by an "epidemic of lending fraud," primarily mortgage lenders, and how regulators blinded by near theological faith in the self-regulating powers of markets failed to check it. Black concludes that none of the reforms to date have corrected the incentive structure that has produced intensifying and recurrent financial crises (Article 5.10). Banks are back: Short-term stability has returned, profits are soaring, and bonuses are as plump as ever. But, as Larson reports in a second article, banks are still stuck with a backlog of bad loans that threatens their long-term viability. And with loan volume still depressed, banks continue to rely on profits from market bubbles and on their considerable political power to hold off the hell they will have to pay for their slumping core business (Article 5.11).

Two other economists, Fred Moseley and Robert Pollin, close the chapter with proposals for what to do about the home mortgage crisis, the banking industry, and the Fed. Moseley analyzes the bailout of the public mortgage lending agencies, Fannie Mae and Freddie Mac. He makes the case for a reinvented public home mortgage agency whose sole purpose would be to provide affordable housing (Article 5.12). Pollin makes the case for transforming the Fed into a democratically controlled investment bank that serves the interests of all of us (Article 5.13).

Discussion Questions

1. (Article 5.1) What are the mechanisms the Fed uses to "control" the creation of money by the banking system. Why, according to Orr, is the Fed's control over the creation of money "limited"?

2. (Article 5.2) According to Orr and Frank, monetary policy serves the interests of bondholders at the expense of people seeking work and of everyone who benefits from social spending. What evidence do they provide to demonstrate this? Do you find it convincing?

3. (Article 5.3) What advantage is there in using monetary policy to slow down the economy? Why might fiscal policy be a more effective tool for lifting the economy out of a recession?

4. (Article 5.4) Why does Friedman, like others before him, liken monetary policy to "pushing on a string"? What evidence does Friedman offer to show that this analogy is an apt description of monetary policy today?

5. (Article 5.5) What is the goal of the Fed's decision to purchase long-term bonds. What obstacles will the Fed have to overcome if this new policy initiative is to be successful?

6. (Article 5.6) Who filled "the giant pool money" that flowed into the United States; how did it affect the U.S. economy?

7. (Article 5.7) So what exactly is a derivative and what role did derivatives play in the financial crisis?

8. (Article 5.8) Why would government spending for the 2009 economic stimulus law receive far more scrutiny from Congress than government spending on the Wall Street bailout, which was four times the spending on the stimulus package?

9. (Article 5.9) Describe the changes in bank regulation and the economic forces that contributed to creating banks that were "too big to fail"?

10. (Article 5.10) What are the fraudulent activities that Black says are at the heart of the financial crisis? And why did financial regulators do so little to put a stop to those activities?

11. (Article 5.11) According to Larson, why are banks still in trouble despite soaring profits and fat executive bonuses?

12. (Article 5.12) Who is to blame for the financial troubles of Fannie Mae and Freddie Mac? How should Fannie and Freddie be reformed? Should the provision of affordable housing be their sole focus?

13. (Article 5.13) What are the chief elements of Pollin's proposal to transform the Fed? How would the Fed's focus and decision-making change? Do you think Pollin's proposal would be effective?

Article 5.1

WHAT IS MONEY?

BY DOUG ORR
November/December 1993; revised October 2010

We all use money every day. Yet many people do not know what money actually is. There are many myths about money, including the idea that the government "prints" all of it and that it has some intrinsic value. But actually, money is less a matter of value, and more a matter of faith.

Money is sometimes called the universal commodity, because it can be traded for all other commodities. But for this to happen, everyone in society must believe that money will be accepted. If people stop believing that it will be accepted, the existing money ceases to be money. Recently in Poland, people stopped accepting the zloty, and used vodka as money instead.

In addition to facilitating exchanges, money allows us to "store" value from one point in time to another. If you sell your car today for $4,000, you probably won't buy that amount of other products today. Rather, you store the value as money, probably in a bank, until you want to use it.

The "things" that get used as money have changed over time, and "modern" people often chuckle when they hear about some of them. The Romans used salt (from which we get the word "salary"), South Sea Islanders used shark's teeth, and several societies actually used cows. The "Three Wise Men" brought gold, frankincense and myrrh, each of which was money in different regions at the time.

If money does not exist, or is in short supply, it will be created. In POW camps, where guards specifically outlaw its existence, prisoners use cigarettes instead. In the American colonies, the British attempted to limit the supply of British pounds, because they knew that by limiting the supply of money, they could hamper the development of independent markets in the colonies. Today, the United States uses a similar policy, through the International Monetary Fund, in dealing with Latin America.

To overcome this problem, the colonists began to use tobacco leaves as money. This helped the colonies to develop, but it also allowed the holders of large plots of land to grow their own money! When the colonies gained independence, the new government decreed gold to be money, rather than tobacco, much to the dismay of Southern plantation owners. Now, rather than growing money, farmers had to find or buy it.

To aid the use of gold as money, banks would test its purity, put it in storage, and give the depositor paper certificates of ownership. These certificates, "paper money," could then be used in place of the gold itself. Since any bank could store gold and issue certificates, by the beginning of the Civil War, over 7,000 different types of "paper money" were in circulation in the United States, none of it printed by the government.

While paper money is easier to use than gold, it is still risky to carry around large amounts of cash. It is safer to store the paper in a bank and simply sign over its ownership to make a purchase. We sign over the ownership of our money by writing a check. Checking account money became popular when, in an unsuccessful attempt to control the amount of money created by banks, the government outlawed the printing of paper money by private banks in 1864.

How Banks Create Money

Banks are central to understanding money, because in addition to storing it, they help to create it. Bankers realize that not everyone will withdraw their money at the same time, so they loan out much of the money that has been deposited. It is from the interest on these loans that banks get their profits, and through these loans the banking system creates new money.

If you deposit $100 cash in your checking account at Chase Manhattan Bank, you still have $100 in money to use, because checks are also accepted as money. Chase must set aside some of this cash as "reserves," in case you or other depositors decide to withdraw money as cash. Current regulations issued by the Federal Reserve Bank (the Fed) require banks to set aside an average of three cents out of each dollar. So Chase can make a loan of $97, based on your deposit. Chase does not make loans by handing out cash but instead by putting $97 in the checking account of the person, say Emily, taking out the loan. So from your initial deposit of $100 in cash, the economy now has $197 in checking account money.

The borrower, Emily, pays $97 for some product or service by check, and the seller, say Ace Computers, deposits the money in its checking account. The total amount of checking account money is still $197, but its location and ownership have changed. If Ace Computer's account is at Citibank, $97 in cash is transferred from Chase to Citibank. This leaves just $3 in cash reserves at Chase to cover your original deposit. However, Citibank now has $97 in "new" cash on hand, so it sets aside three cents on the dollar ($2.91) and loans out the rest, $94.09, as new checking account money. Through this process, every dollar of "reserves" yields many dollars in total money.

If you think this is just a shell game and there is only $100 in "real" money, you still don't understand money. Anything that is accepted as payment for a transaction is "real" money. Cash is no more real than checking account money. In fact, most car rental companies will not accept cash as payment for a car, so for them, cash is not money!

As of June 2010, there was $883 billion of U.S. currency, i.e. "paper money," in existence. However, somewhere between 50% to 70% of it is held outside the United States by foreign banks and individuals. U.S. $100 bills are the preferred currency of choice used to facilitate illegal international transactions, such as the drug trade. The vast majority of all money actually in use in the United States is not cash, but rather checking account money. This type of money, $1,590 billion, was created by private banks, and was not "printed" by anyone. In fact, this money exists only as electronic "bits" in banks' computers. (The less "modern" South Sea Islanders could have quite a chuckle about that!)

The amount of money that banks can create is limited by the total amount of reserves, and by the fraction of each deposit that must be held as reserves. Prior to

1914, bankers themselves decided what fraction of deposits to hold as reserves. Since then, this fraction has been set by the main banking regulator, the Fed.

Until 1934, gold was held as reserves, but the supply of gold was unstable, growing rapidly during the California and Alaska "gold rushes," and very slowly at other times. As a result, at times more money was created than the economy needed, and at other times not enough money could be created. Starting in 1934, the U.S. government decided that gold would no longer be used as reserves. Cash, now printed by the Fed, could no longer be redeemed for gold, and cash itself became the reserve asset.

Banks, fearing robberies, do not hold all of their cash reserves in their own vaults. Rather, they store it in an account at a regional Fed bank. These accounts count as reserves. What banks do hold in their vaults is their other assets, such as Treasury bonds and corporate bonds.

The Fed and Bank Reserves

The only role of the government in creating money is indirectly through the Fed, which is controlled by neither the Congress nor the executive branch. If the Fed wants to expand the money supply, it must increase bank reserves. To do this, the Fed buys Treasury bonds from a bank, and pays with a check drawn on the Fed itself. By depositing the check in its reserve account at the Fed, the bank now has more reserves, so the bank can now make more loans and create new checking account money.

By controlling the amount of reserves, the Fed attempts to control the size of the money supply. But as recent history has shown, this control is limited. During the late 1970s, the Fed tried to limit the amount of money banks could create by reducing reserves, but banks simply created new forms of money, just like the POW camp prisoners and colonial farmers. In 1979, there was only one form of checking account money. Today, there are many, with odd names such as NOWs, ATSs, repos, and money market deposit accounts. If there is a profit to be made creating money, banks will find a way.

In 2010, we have the opposite problem. The Fed is trying to expand the money supply, but banks are refusing to create new money. In good times, banks hold as few reserves as possible, so they can profit from making loans. In times of crisis, banks fear that we will lose faith in the commercial banking system and all try to take out our "money" as cash. Since there is far more electronic money than cash, this is impossible. But if the bank cannot give us our money in the form we want it, the bank fails and ceases to exist. Since the start of 2007, over 300 banks, with assets totally more than $637 billion, have failed.

Since all banks fear they will be next, they want as many reserves as possible. Excess reserves are any reserves above those required by the Fed. During the 1990s, these averaged about $1 billion for the entire banking system. During the crisis of 2001, they spiked to the then unheard of level of $19 billion. As of June 2010, excess reserves in the banking system were $1,035 billion! This is the classic case of trying to push on a string. The Fed can create reserves, but only banks can create money and they are not yet willing to make any new loans.

These amorphous forms of money function only because we believe they will function, which is why the continued stability of the banking system is so critical. While it is true that the bailout of the banking system was not handled very well, and that many people who created the crisis are still profiting from it, the bailout was a necessary evil. In a modern market economy, banks create the money, and no market economy can function without its money. Money only exists if we believe in it, so we have to maintain the faith. To maintain the faith we need more democratic control over money creation, which can only come if regulation of the financial system is greatly expanded.

Sources: Money supply: Federal Reserve Board, www.federalreserve.gov/releases/h6/current/; excess reserves: St. Louis Federal Reserve Bank, research.stlouisfed.org/fred2/series/EXCRESNS; bank failures: Federal Deposit Insurance Corporation (FDIC), www.fdic.gov/bank/individual/failed/banklist.html.

Article 5.2

FOCUS ON THE FED
The "Bond Market" versus the Rest of Us

BY DOUG ORR AND ELLEN FRANK
October 1999; revised October 2010

Why should anyone involved in environmental issues, education reform efforts, efforts to house the homeless, or anyone else, care about monetary policy? After all, it only affects the financial markets, right? Wrong. Monetary policy is holding all other social policy hostage, and is part of the cause of the rapid increase in income inequality in the United States. Whenever any policy change is proposed, be it in health care, housing or transportation, the first question politicians ask is, "What will the 'bond market' think about this?"

"The bond market" is a euphemism for the financial sector of the U.S. economy and the Federal Reserve Bank (known as "the Fed"), which regulates that sector. The Fed is the central bank of the United States. It controls monetary policy, and uses its power to help the banking industry and the holders of financial assets, while thwarting government attempts to deal with pressing social problems.

Since 1979, the Fed has had an unprecedented degree of independence from government control. This independence has put it in a position to veto any progressive fiscal policy that the Congress might propose. To understand how this situation developed, we must understand the function of banks, the structure of the Fed, and the role of monetary policy.

Banks and Instability

Government regulates the banking industry because private sector, profit-driven banking is inherently unstable. Banks do more than just store money—they help create it. If you deposit a dollar in the bank, you still have that dollar. Commercial banks will set aside three cents as "reserves" to "cover" your deposit, and the remaining 97 cents is loaned out to someone else who now has "new money." By making loans, banks create new money and generate profit. The drive to maximize profits often leads banks to become overextended—making too many loans and holding too few reserves. This drive for profits can undermine a bank's stability.

If depositors think the bank is holding too few reserves, or is making overly speculative loans, they might try to withdraw their money as cash. Large numbers of depositors withdrawing cash from a bank at the same time is called a "run on the bank." Since banks only hold 3% of their deposit liabilities as cash, even a moderate-sized "run" would be enough to drain the bank of its cash reserves. If a bank has no reserves, it is insolvent and is forced to close. At that point, all remaining deposits in the bank cease to exist, and depositors lose their money.

The failure of a bank affects more than just that bank's depositors. One bank's excesses tend to shake people's faith in other banks. If the run spreads, "bank panics" can occur. During the 1800s, such panics erupted every five to ten years, bankrupting between 10% and 25% of the banks in the United States and creating a major recession each time.

The Creation of the Fed

The panic of 1907 bankrupted some of the largest banks and led to demands by the public for bank reforms that would stabilize the system. Reform proposals ranged from doing almost nothing to nationalizing the entire banking industry. As a compromise, the Federal Reserve was created in 1913. The U.S. government saw the Fed as a way for bankers to regulate themselves, and structured the Federal Reserve System so that it could be responsive to its main constituents: banks and other financial-sector businesses that are now called, euphemistically, "the bond market." While ideally it should serve the interests of the general public when it conducts monetary policy, in reality the Fed balances two, conflicting goals: maintaining the stability of "the bond market" and maximizing financial-sector profits. Over time, Congress and the president have varied the degree of independence that they have given to the Fed to choose between these goals.

Initially, the Fed enjoyed a high degree of independence. During the 1920s, the Fed allowed member banks to engage in highly speculative activities, including using depositors' money to play the stock market. While many banks were very profitable, speculative excesses caused almost 20% of the banks in existence in 1920 to fail during the following decade. With the onset of the Great Depression, between 1929 and 1933, more than 9,000 banks, 38% of the total, failed. Since the Fed had not achieved its first goal, in 1935 Congress responded with laws that put many new regulations on banks, and reduced the Fed's independence.

Fed Independence Lost

Under the new regulations, "investment banks" were not allowed to take deposits, but were allowed to play the markets, while "commercial banks" were restricted to taking deposits and making commercial loans. Deposits were now insured by the FDIC. Thus, the only opportunity for making a profit was to maintain a "spread" between the interest rate paid on deposits and that charged on loans. Loans are made for relatively long terms, and deposits are not. If the short-term interest rate on deposits varies widely, the spread will grow and shrink, which makes bank profits unstable. In order to stabilize bank profits, during the 30 years after 1935, the Treasury mandated that the Fed keep the short-term rate approximately constant.

Under this arrangement, Congress indirectly controlled monetary policy. If Congress wanted to stimulate the economy it could increase government spending or cut taxes. Both led to an increase in spending and an increase in the demand for money. To keep interest rates, which are the price of money, from rising, the Fed had to increase the supply of money. Thus, the Fed "accommodated" fiscal policy decisions made by Congress and the president.

During most of this period, growth was moderate and prices were stable. The Fed went along because this arrangement did not threaten bank profits. Starting in the mid-1960s, however, stimulative fiscal policy started to push up the inflation rate, which did threaten bank profits. A confrontation over Fed independence ensued and grew in intensity throughout the 1970s.

Inflation's Impact

Contrary to the view commonly propagated by the media, inflation does not affect everyone equally. In fact, there are very clear winners and losers. Inflation is an increase in the average level of prices, but some prices rise faster than average and some rise slower. If the price of the thing you are selling is rising faster than average, you win. Otherwise, you lose. Inflation redistributes income, but in an arbitrary manner. This uncertainty makes inflation unpopular, even to the winners. However, one industry always loses from unexpected inflation, and that industry is finance.

Banks make loans today that will be repaid, with interest, in the future. If inflation reduces the value of those future payments, the banks' profits will be reduced. So bankers are interested in the "real interest rate," that is, the actual ("nominal") interest rate on the loan minus the rate of inflation. If the interest rate on commercial bank loans is 7% and the rate of inflation is 3%, the real rate of interest is 4%. In the early postwar period, real interest rates were relatively stable at about 2%.

From 1965 on, unexpected increases in inflation reduced the real interest rate. This cheap credit was a boon to home buyers, farmers, and manufacturers, but it greatly reduced bank profits. Banks wanted inflation cut. The Keynesian view of monetary policy offered a simple but unpopular solution: raise interest rates enough to cause a recession. High unemployment and falling incomes would take the steam out of inflation.

But, putting people out of work to help bankers would be a hard sell. The Fed needed a different story to justify shifting its policy from stabilizing interest rates to fighting inflation. That story was "monetarism," a theory that claims that changes in the money supply affect prices, but nothing else in the economy.

The Monetarist Experiment

On October 6, 1979, Fed Chair Paul Volcker, using monetarist theory as a justification, announced that the Fed would no longer try to keep interest rates at targeted levels. He argued that Fed policy should concentrate on controlling inflation, and to do so he would now focus on limiting the money supply growth rate. Since neither Congress nor the president attempted to overrule Volcker, this change ushered in an era of unprecedented independence for Fed monetary policy.

During the next three years, the Fed reduced the rate of growth in the money supply, but this experiment did not yield the results predicted by the monetarists. Instead of a swift reduction in the rate of inflation, the most immediate outcome was a rapid rise in the real interest rate and the start of the worst recession since the Great Depression.

As the Keynesian view predicted, the recession occurred because high interest rates slowed economic growth and increased unemployment. In 1979, the unemployment rate was 5.8%. By 1982 it had reached 10.7%, the first double-digit rate since the Depression. With fewer people working and buying products, the inflation rate, which had been 8.7% in 1979, finally started to slow in 1981 and was approaching 4% by the end of 1982. The Fed's tight money policies kept nominal interest rates from falling as fast as inflation. This raised real interest rates on commercial loans from 0.5% in 1979 to 10% in 1982.

The Fed's fight against inflation had a severe impact on the entire economy. All businesses, especially farming and manufacturing, run on credit. The rise in interest rates, combined with lower prices, squeezed the profits of farmers and manufacturers.

Both of these industries rely heavily on exports, and so were also hurt by the negative effect of high interest rates on the competitiveness of U.S. exports. Real interest rates in the United States were the highest in the world, thereby attracting financial investment from abroad. In order for foreigners to buy financial assets in the United States, they first had to buy dollars. This demand for dollars drove up their value in international markets. While a "strong" dollar means imports are relatively cheap, it also means that U.S. exports are expensive. Foreign countries could not afford to buy our "costly" agricultural and manufactured exports. As a result, during this period, bankruptcy rates in these two industries were massive, higher than during the 1930s.

Despite its high cost to the rest of the economy, the monetarist experiment did not benefit many banks. Initially, the high real interest rates appeared to help bank profits. Regulations capped the interest rates banks could pay on deposits, but rates charged on loans were not regulated. This increased the profit on loans. Many investors, however, started moving their deposits to less regulated financial intermediaries, such as mutual funds and new forms of "shadow banks", that could pay higher rates on deposits. In addition, the recession forced many borrowers to declare bankruptcy and default on their loans. Both of these factors pushed banks toward insolvency.

Reversing Course

It was bank losses, not the pain in the rest of the economy, that led Volcker to announce in September 1982 that he was abandoning monetarism. His new policy aimed to provide enough reserves to keep most banks solvent and to allow a *slow* recovery from the recession. Unemployment remained high for the next five years, so inflation continued to slow. Real interest rates stayed near 8% through 1986, so interest-sensitive industries such as farming and manufacturing did not take part in the recovery.

Volcker made his allegiance to the banking industry very clear during a meeting, in February 1985, with a delegation of state legislators, laborers, and farmers who were demanding easier money and lower interest rates. He told them, "Look, your constituents are unhappy, mine aren't."

Yet by 1985, the crisis in the savings and loan industry was spreading into commercial banking. To provide cash ("liquidity") to the banks, Volcker allowed the money supply to grow by 12% during 1985 and by 17% in 1986. Monetarists raised the specter of a return to double-digit inflation. Instead, the rate of inflation continued to slow, demonstrating that a simple link between the money supply and inflation hypothesized by monetarist theory does not exist.

The Veto

Despite the failure and subsequent abandonment of monetarist policies, the Fed still uses monetarist *theory* to justify its continued focus on "fighting inflation." The myth that monetary policy only affects inflation provides a convenient "cover" that allows the Fed to serve its narrow constituency: "the bond market." From the end of World War II to 1979, real interest rates averaged 2.1%. Since 1980, they have averaged 5.7%. Real interest rates remain high because "the bond market" worries about any possible increase in future inflation, but high rates continue to hollow out the manufacturing sector.

Fighting inflation benefits the bond market. However, despite the near-depression that monetarism caused in the 1980s and the extremely slow rate of economic growth that has occurred since, the Fed continues to claim that fighting inflation serves the interests of the entire country. The public's widespread belief in this myth denies progressives in Congress the support they need to force the Fed back into accommodating fiscal policy. It also provides support for those in Congress that want to block any expansion of social programs.

If Congress decides to spend more for environmental clean-up, housing the homeless, or education, "the bond market" will raise the specter of renewed inflation. The Fed will then raise interest rates, as it did in June 1999, as a "preemptive strike" to prevent inflation, and sent the economy into a recession. The increase in interest rates slowed the economy, increased unemployment, reduced government revenues, and returned the federal budget to a deficit. Since Congress knows it will be incorrectly blamed for this outcome, Congress won't pass any legislation "the bond market" doesn't like. This is how the bond market holds Congress hostage. As long as Congress and the president allow the Fed to follow an inflation-fighting policy, the Fed can maintain a veto threat over the elected government.

In the most recent recession (and anemic recovery), the Fed has not vetoed Obama's fiscal policy stimulus because Fed Chairman Ben Bernanke realizes that the second premise of monetarist theory, that the Fed can always increase the money supply, is also wrong. The Fed has pumped more than $1 trillion in reserves into the banking system, and almost all of them sit as excess reserves. This is a classic example of what Keynes called a "liquidity trap." In this case, monetary policy is powerless to stimulate the economy. Only fiscal policy can bring us out of the "Great Recession." Unfortunately, the veto power of the Fed has been replaced by the veto power of the Republican "Party of No," which has filibustered every attempt to revive the economy. Apparently, making Obama look ineffective is more important to them than the well-being of the American people.

The Fed has also played a large role in the rapid increase in income and wealth inequality that started in the 1980s and has accelerated ever since. The two decades following World War II are often called the "golden age" of the U.S. economy. On average, Gross Domestic Product (GDP) grew 4.3% each year, and unemployment averaged 4.6%. Average real wages, that is, wages adjusted for inflation, grew at an annual rate of 2.1%, rising from $10.86 an hour in 1950 to $18.21 in 1973 (both measured in 2005 dollars). This period saw the creation of a true middle class in the United States.

In the three decades since 1980, GDP growth has averaged 2.7% each year, unemployment has averaged 6.2% (2.3% and 6.7% if we exclude the higher-growth Clinton years). Average real wages *declined* every year from 1980 to 1996. In fact, the real median wage in 2009 was $16.40 an hour, exactly the same as in 1966. If wages had continued to grow at 2.1%, the average wage today would be $38.50. Without the slow-growth policies of the Fed and the anti-labor policies that started under Reagan, the average income of the majority of the people in the United States would be more than twice as large. Instead, we've seen a hollowing out of the middle class, and a rapid transfer of wealth and income to those already wealthy.

Where Do Interest Payments Go?

By focusing on inflation rather than interest rates, the media deflect attention from a critical social issue—how high interest rates transfer income from the indebted middle class to the very rich. If ownership of financial assets was evenly distributed among households, the growth in interest income would not be of much importance. But ownership of financial assets is heavily concentrated. As of 2007, the top 5% of households, those with incomes more than $183,000, controlled 60.5% of all wealth in the U.S. The top 10% controlled 71.6%. Yet these numbers understate the concentration of financial wealth. Almost 80% of families in the United States have almost no assets, outside of the equity in their homes and vehicles. Despite the media hype about the "democratization" of the stock market, between 1989 and 1995 the concentration of stock ownership increased. Detailed studies of wealth data collected by the Fed report that in 2007 the wealthiest 5% of households owned 93.6% of all directly owned bonds and 82.4% of all directly owned stocks. The top 10% if households owned 98.4% of all bonds and 90.4% of all stocks.

The "poorest" nine-tenths of the U.S. population—that is, most of us—have virtually no financial assets. Such families gain little from rising interest rates. But the higher mortgage, credit card, and auto payments that result take a real toll on living standards. Each uptick in the real interest rate entails a transfer of income from the lowest 90% of the population to the highest 10%. And most of that income goes to the very, very wealthy who are yet another part of "the bond market" served by the Fed.

Economist James Galbraith has called today's high interest rates a form of taxation without representation. The term is apt. Tax increases are passed by Congress, which has at least some public oversight. Interest rate hikes are decided by the Fed, an institution over which the president, Congress and the public have virtually no control.

Like taxes, rising interest rates are a drain on the resources and income of the vast majority of U.S. households. But unlike tax revenues, which can be used to provide education, environmental clean-up, homeless shelters, roads, airports, and other infrastructure, interest payments flow into the pockets of the very rich, who become ever so much richer.

Resources: Arthur B. Kennickell, "Ponds and Streams: Wealth and Income in the U.S,, 1989 to 2007," Federal Reserve Working Paper 2009-13 (Jan. 2009); Lawrence Mishel, Jared Bernstein, and Heidi Shierholz, The State of Working America 2008/2009.

Article 5.3

HOW DO FISCAL AND MONETARY POLICY COMPARE?

BY ARTHUR MacEWAN
July/August 1997

The Federal Reserve influences the economy through monetary policy—the actions the Fed takes to affect the cost and availability of credit. For example, in March of this year, the Fed, led by its chairman Alan Greenspan, decided that it was time to slow economic growth. So it induced banks and other lenders to raise their interest rates. Higher interest rates mean fewer businesses and individuals will take out loans and spend the borrowed money. Lower spending means slower economic growth.

The federal government can also influence economic growth and the demand for goods and services through fiscal policy—the way it taxes and spends. If the government wants to slow down the economy, for example, it can raise taxes and reduce its own spending. Less money ends up in people's hands if the government hires fewer construction workers to build roads, or if it cuts back on education programs.

One problem with fiscal policy is that changing the budget takes time—except for programs whose spending levels change automatically when the economy does, like unemployment compensation. To slow down the economy, Congress has to pass new laws raising taxes—certainly a "no no" these days—or cutting spending. Then the President has to accept Congress's new law, which might require negotiations, or more legislative action. All this is to say that the political process involves considerable delays and might result in no action at all.

Monetary policy is different because the Fed does not have to bother with this messy political process that we call democracy. It is "independent" since its members, appointed by the President, serve long terms. They decide whether to ease or tighten the availability of credit, without any role for Congress or the President. To be sure, the "independence" of the Fed is not enshrined in the Constitution. Yet for Congress and the President to pass new laws which directed or restricted the Fed's action would be a serious disruption of well-established policy.

The law governing the Fed says that it should pursue both stable prices (low inflation) and full employment. In fact, the Fed focuses almost exclusively on the goal of stable prices. If unemployment has to rise to meet this goal, well, too bad. It is easy to see why the Fed does its work best when it doesn't have to worry about getting democratic approval.

Fiscal policy is somewhat more constrained by democratic processes than is monetary policy. For example, conservative attacks on Medicare and Social Security have not gotten very far because these programs are very popular.

But the recent mania to balance the budget makes it difficult to use fiscal policy to stimulate economic expansion by increasing spending. This may present some serious problems during economic downturns. The monetary policy of the Fed, it turns out, is not nearly so effective in stimulating economic expansion during a recession as it is in slowing growth during relatively good times. In a recession, the Fed can induce commercial banks to lower their interest rates. But if the recession leads investors to worry that demand for products and services will fall, the lower interest rates might not reignite economic growth. What's the point, for example, in building a new office building when it doesn't look like it will be possible to rent out the space in existing buildings for quite a while?

In a recession, then, trying to use monetary policy to get the economy going can be like pushing on a string. It simply won't do any good. Fiscal policy, however, might directly create demand, present businesses with the reality of a new expansion, and generate a new period of investment and growth.

Article 5.4

PUSHING ON STRINGS

The explosion of U.S. banks' excess reserves since last fall illustrates the dramatic failure of monetary policy.

BY GERALD FRIEDMAN
May/June 2009

Monetary policy is not working. Since the economic crisis began in July 2007, the Federal Reserve has dramatically cut interest rates and pumped out over a trillion dollars, increasing the money supply by over 15% in less than two years. These vast sums have failed to revive the economy because the banks have been hoarding liquidity rather than lending.

The Federal Reserve requires that banks hold money on reserve to back up deposits and other bank liabilities. In the past, beyond these required reserves, banks would hold very small amounts of excess reserves, holdings that they minimized because reserves earn very little or no interest. Between the 1950s and September 2008, U.S. banks held over $5 billion in total excess reserves only once, after the September 11 attacks. This changed with the collapse of Lehman Brothers. Beginning with less than $2 billion in August 2008, excess reserves soared to $60 billion in September and then to $559 billion in November before peaking at $798 billion in January 2009. (They have since dropped to $644 billion in the last accounting month.)

This explosion of excess reserves represents a signal change in bank policy that threatens the effectiveness of monetary policy in the current economic crisis. Aware of their own financial vulnerability, even insolvency, frightened bank managers

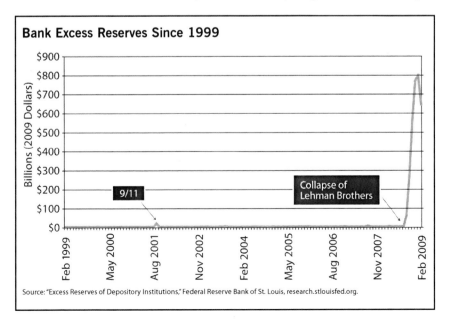

Bank Excess Reserves Since 1999

Source: "Excess Reserves of Depository Institutions," Federal Reserve Bank of St. Louis, research.stlouisfed.org.

responded to the collapse of major investment houses like Lehman Brothers by grab-bing and hoarding all the cash that they could get. At the same time, a general loss of confidence and spreading economic collapse persuaded banks that there are few to whom they could lend with confidence that the loans would be repaid. Clearly, our banks have decided that they need, or at least want, the money more than consum-ers and productive businesses do.

Banks could have been investing this money by lending to businesses need-ing liquidity to buy material inputs or pay workers. Had they done so, monetar-ist economists would be shouting from the rooftops, or at least in the university halls, about how monetary policy prevented another Great Depression. Instead, even the *Wall Street Journal* is proclaiming that "We're All Keynesians Again" because monetary policy has failed. Monetary authorities, the *Journal* ex-plains, can create money but they cannot force banks to lend or to invest it in productive activities. The Federal Reserve confronts a reality shown in the graph above: it can't "push on a string," as Fed Chair Marriner Eccles famously put it in testimony before Congress in 1935, in the depths of the Great Depression.

If the banks won't lend, then we need more than monetary policy to get out of the current crisis. No bailout, no TARP program, can revive the economy if banks hoard all the cash they receive. The Obama stimulus was an appropriate response to the failure of string-pushing. But much more government stimulus will be needed to solve a crisis this large, and we will need programs to move liquidity from bank vaults to businesses and consumers. It may be time to stop waiting on the banks, and to start telling them what to do with our money.

Article 5.5

WHY IS THE GOVERNMENT BUYING LONG-TERM BONDS?

BY ALEJANDRO REUSS

January 2011

I *heard that the government is now buying long-term bonds. What's that all about?*
Basically, the government is purchasing long-term bonds in order to push down long-term interest rates. (While the Federal Reserve is buying both government and private bonds, here we will focus just on purchases of government bonds.) The reduction in long-term interest rates, in turn, is meant to stimulate investment and other forms of spending.

Wait a minute. Don't banks decide what interest rates to charge—like on business loans, home mortgages, car loans, or whatever? How would the government force banks to charge the interest rates that the government wants? And what does buying bonds have to do with it anyway?
Those are all good questions. Let's start with how the government influences interest rates.

When we hear about government policies designed to change the money supply or influence interest rates (monetary policy), we are talking about the role of the Federal Reserve (or "the Fed"). This is the central monetary-policy making authority for the United States.

The main way that the Fed influences interest rates is by buying and selling government bonds. It decides whether to increase or decrease interest rates depending on whether it aims to pump up or rein in overall demand for goods and services. When Fed policymakers decide that they want to raise interest rates, the Fed sells government bonds. This sale reduces the price of bonds and raises the interest rate on these bonds. (We can also think of this as the Fed reducing the money supply. This makes money less plentiful and drives up the price of borrowing.) When Fed policymakers decide they want to lower interest rates, the Fed buys government bonds. This purchase increases the price of bonds and lowers the interest rate on these bonds. (We can think of this as the Fed increasing the money supply, which makes money more plentiful and drives down the price of borrowing.)

Usually, the Fed buys and sells short-term government bonds in order to change a very short-term interest rate called the "federal funds rate." Now, the Fed is buying and selling longer-term government bonds, with the aim of influencing longer-term rates.

When the Fed buys government bonds, does that just mean paper is shuffling back and forth between one part of the government and another?
No, the Fed buys bonds previously sold by the U.S. Treasury to "members of the public" (to some extent to individuals, but mostly to financial firms, in the United States and abroad) and to the central banks of other countries.

When the government needs to borrow, the U.S. Treasury sells bonds. (A bond is basically an IOU, the government's promise to pay the owner of the bond a certain amount of money at a specific date in the future. In the meantime, the government can spend the money it received in exchange for the bond.) At any time, there are lots and lots (and lots) of bonds owned by people or institutions who have either bought them directly from the Treasury, or bought them from someone else in the "bond market." Bonds may change hands lots of times after their initial sale by the Treasury. When the Fed wants to lower interest rates, it buys some of these bonds from their owners.

You said that when the bond price goes up the interest rate goes down, and vice versa. Why do the bond price and the interest rate move in opposite directions?
That's a good question. Suppose that you can buy a bond today for $100 and it promises you $110 in a year. The interest rate is the difference between what you will get and what you paid ($110 - $100 = $10), divided by the purchase price ($100). That comes to 10%. Suppose the purchase price for that bond increases to $105, but it still promises $110 in a year. Now the difference between what you get and what you paid is only $5. Divide that by the purchase price ($105), and you get an interest rate of less than 5%. So when the bond price goes up, the interest rate goes down. (It works just the same in the opposite direction.)

More demand for bonds (including demand from the Fed) means a higher bond price, and that pushes down interest rates. So when the Fed wants to push interest rates down, it buys bonds.

OK, so the Fed can push down the interest rate on government bonds, but how does that push down interest rates that banks charge and consumers or businesses pay?
Imagine a bank deciding to whom to lend. The bank can lend to the government (by buying government bonds), or it can lend to private businesses, to individuals, and so on. If the risk of lending to one borrower is the same as the risk of lending to another, the bank will make whichever loan fetches the higher interest rate.

The U.S. government is a very safe borrower, so much so that government bonds are considered "risk free." Let's set risk aside for now, and assume that there are other borrowers that are just as safe as the U.S. government. Suppose that the interest rates on government bonds and these very safe borrowers' bonds are both equal to, say, 2%. So the bank can buy either bond for $100 today and be promised $102 in a year.

Suppose the Fed starts buying government bonds, and that makes the bond price go up to almost $101 (pushing the interest rate on government bonds down to 1%). Let's think about what the bank will do now. Suppose that it had just paid $100 for a government bond that promises $102 in a year. The bank can hold onto that bond and still get $102 in a year. But it can also sell the bond for $101 and buy a private company's bond for $100. The private company's bond still promises $102 in a year, but the bank, having sold a government bond for $101 and bought a private bond for $100, also gets to pocket the difference of $1. If the bank were to sell 100 government bonds, it could buy 100 private-company bonds, plus use the extra $100 it pocketed to buy one extra bond. A bank that wants to make as much profit as possible, then, will sell the government bonds it holds and buy private-company bonds.

If banks start buying private-company bonds (with the money they made by selling government bonds), then the price of private-company bonds will go up and the interest rate on those bonds will go down. In other words, private companies will now be able to borrow at a lower interest rate than before.

So how low will interest rates for private companies go?

If the risk on private-company bonds were the same as on government bonds, as we assumed in our example, then the process would continue as long as the interest rate on the private bonds remained higher than that on the government bonds. The two would eventually end up equal.

In reality, however, the risk on a loan to a private company (even the most rock-solid) is greater than the risk on a loan to the U.S. government. When lending to a private company or individual (or, for that matter, to state or local governments, or national governments deemed less credit-worthy than the U.S. government), lenders insist on a higher interest rate to compensate them for the greater perceived risk. The difference in interest rate between a risky loan (like a business loan, home mortgage, car loan, etc.) and a "risk-free" loan (as to the U.S. government) is called the "risk premium."

If the risk premiums between different loans (to different borrowers) do not change, then lowering the interest-rate on a risk-free loan will lower the interest-rate on risky loans by the same amount. You can think of different interest rates, associated with different levels of risk, as being "stacked" on top of each other. The idea behind Fed policy is that, by lowering the interest rate on the bottom of the "stack," the interest rates above it will also come down. In real life, the "spreads" between interest rates may increase, especially during a crisis, when investors are desperately looking for safe places to park their money. So the interest rates on top of the stack may not come down as much as the interest rate on the bottom.

Why does the Fed want to bring down interest rates now?

The idea is that lower interest rates encourage people and companies to spend, adding to demand for goods and services and stimulating production and employment.

Economists especially emphasize the relationship between interest rates and investment spending. In this context, "investment" means the purchase of highly durable goods, like machinery, new factories and office buildings, and new houses (not purchases of stock or other "paper" assets). When companies make investment decisions, they decide whether the cost of buying new factories or new machines is justified by the expected profits from the sale of goods (made with those factories or machines). The idea behind government policies to lower interest rates is that some projects that would not have been profitable for a company at a higher interest rate would be profitable at a lower interest rate. So, if the government can bring down interest rates, companies will undertake some projects that they would not have otherwise, increasing production and employment.

Hasn't the government been bringing down interest rates for a couple of years now? Why keep on doing the same thing if it's not working?

Yes, the Fed has brought interest rates down in response to the current economic crisis. As mentioned earlier, during a recession the Fed usually buys short-term government bonds, which has the effect of driving down short-term interest rates. The Fed usually targets a certain level of the "federal funds rate," the interest rate that banks charge each other on very short-term (overnight) loans. The federal funds rate has basically been 0% for a couple of years now.

There are a couple of problems with this policy:

First, the interest rates that the Fed directly targets are not directly relevant to the decisions made by businesses and households. Neither businesses nor families can typically borrow at the same rates that banks can. Moreover, long-term interest rates are usually more important to businesses and individuals than very-short-term rates. When businesses buy factories or expensive machinery, or people buy cars or houses, they usually take out loans for five, ten, twenty, or thirty years (certainly not overnight).

Second, once the government has pushed the federal funds rate to 0%, it cannot go any lower. If that's not enough to stimulate substantial new spending and pull the economy out of a recession, there's nothing more that the government can do using "conventional" monetary policy (that is, a policy that focuses on short-term rates).

This is why the Fed is now turning toward policies aimed at bringing down longer-term interest rates.

If the Fed keeps this up, isn't it going to cause runaway inflation?

The U.S. economy is currently operating far below capacity. There are about 15 million unemployed workers, plus millions more who are working part-time but want full-time jobs. This is not at all like a situation where the economy is already operating close to full capacity. Under conditions of full employment, additional demand cannot result in more goods being produced. Instead, prices are bid up, causing inflation. When there is lots of excess capacity, however, more demand can result in increased production of goods and services. Even though demand has increased, so has supply, so prices need not increase (at least not very much).

Even if the inflation rate were to increase a bit, that would not be such a bad thing.

First, the current inflation rate is very low. The risk right now is deflation, a decrease in the general price level. If people expect prices tomorrow to be lower than prices today, they tend to put off purchases. For this reason, deflation would exacerbate the depressed demand that is causing high unemployment. In addition, deflation means that people's money incomes decline. (People's incomes are largely based on prices of one kind or another, so as prices fall across the board, so do people's incomes in dollar terms.) Their debts, however, stay the same. So deflation would make real debt burdens larger.

Low-income people tend to be net debtors (to owe more than they are owed) and high-income people tend to be net creditors (to owe less than they are owed). Therefore, deflation has the effect of redistributing income from low-income people to high-income people. People with low incomes also tend to spend all or almost all of their incomes, while people with high incomes tend to save more of their incomes. If income is redistributed from people who would spend it to people who would save more of it, overall spending will decrease. So deflation, by redistributing income from debtors to creditors, would likely reduce overall spending.

Second, just as deflation would depress spending now, modest positive inflation would encourage spending now. If people expect that prices tomorrow will be higher than prices today, they will tend to spend now, rather than put off purchases. Given widespread fears of unemployment and reluctance to spend, this effect will not, by itself, pull the economy back to full employment, but it would probably boost spending somewhat. A bit of inflation would also reduce real debt burdens.

I've also heard that the policy will weaken the dollar. Is that true?

This policy is, indeed, likely to "weaken" the dollar. This means that the same number of dollars would buy fewer units of another currency, like the euro (€).

A weaker dollar means that goods produced in other countries will become more expensive in terms of dollars. Suppose you want to buy a t-shirt that sells for 10€. If you can get 10€ for $10, then the t-shirt costs you $10. If the dollar weakens against the euro, and now you can only get 10€ for $11, the same 10€ T-shirt now costs you $11. This effect would cause domestic prices to increase as well, since domestic producers would face less international competition. While this contributes to inflation, remember that a bit of inflation would not be all bad, for the reasons described above.

A weaker dollar also has the effect of making goods produced in the United States cheaper to people in other countries. If someone in Europe can get $10 for 10€, then they can buy a $10 t-shirt for 10€. Suppose the dollar weakens against the euro, and now they can get $10 for 9€. This means that the European buyer can get the same $10 t-shirt for 9€. This increases demand for U.S. exports—and that extra export demand, just like extra domestic demand, tends to increase U.S. output and employment.

A weaker dollar, by making U.S. exports cheaper for buyers in other countries and those other countries' exports more expensive in the United States, could mean less demand for goods produced in other countries (and therefore reduce output and employment in those countries). Remember that the policy is also intended to boost overall U.S. demand for goods, which would tend to increase U.S. demand for imports. It's not clear whether the exchange-rate effect or the demand effect would be larger, so we can't say for sure that the policy would reduce demand for goods produced in other countries. Nonetheless, the governments of Germany and China have criticized the Fed's plan, evidently fearing the effects on their trade balances, and on employment in exporting industries.

U.S. politicians and the mainstream media often talk about boosting the U.S. trade balance (reducing the trade deficit, or bringing about a trade surplus) as if it were obviously a good thing. One's conclusion about whether it would be good or bad, however, depends on whether one thinks that increased employment in the United States—even at the expense of employment in other countries (even much lower-income countries)—is a good thing or not.

OK, is this new strategy likely to work?

There are major problems.

First, it's not clear how effective the policy will be at lowering long-term interest rates. The Fed has increased the money supply dramatically over the last few years. Banks have sold bonds to the Fed and received cash in return. The Fed's idea was that the banks would try to loan out as much of that money as possible, lowering the interest rates they charged in order to find new borrowers. In fact, however, banks have held onto much of that money in the form of "excess reserves" (over and above the amount they are required to hold by law). Uncertain about the value of assets they held (especially those related to home mortgages), banks held on to reserves as a hedge against the risk of insolvency. It's possible that the new infusion of money into the banking system will, likewise, remain in banks' coffers.

Second, it's not clear that lower interest rates (even long-term rates) would have much of an effect on investment demand. Remember, investment means purchases of highly durable goods, like machinery, new buildings (including new housing), and so on. Right now, businesses still have negative expectations of future sales, and so are not trying to increase output very quickly. Moreover, they have vast amounts of excess capacity—meaning shuttered buildings, unused machinery, and so on. Under such conditions, lower interest rates are not very likely to entice businesses to run out and buy new plant and equipment. New construction of residential housing is even less unlikely to resume soon, given the excessive construction during the housing boom and looming foreclosures, which will dump enormous numbers of existing houses on the market.

If this won't work, is there anything that might?

One possible answer is another round of fiscal stimulus. In contrast to the policies discussed above, which involve changes in the money supply and interest rates and are therefore termed "monetary" policies, "fiscal" policies involve changes in government expenditures and taxes. A fiscal stimulus involves increased government expenditures or decreased taxes, with the idea of boosting demand, and therefore output and employment.

It's not that the first fiscal stimulus "didn't work," and that the government should try the same thing while expecting a different result. The first stimulus was way too small—as serious economists pointed out at the time. It did not create nearly enough demand (through increases in spending and reduction in taxes) to counteract the collapse in private consumption and investment, as well as the decline in state-level spending.

Some fiscal policies that make sense now include: 1) Increases in unemployment insurance payments (making payments more generous and extending their duration). Unemployment insurance both provides some relief to the unemployed and helps boost demand, since unemployed people are likely to spend all or nearly all of their benefits. 2) Federal government grants to prevent state budget cuts. Budget cuts at the state level are not only eliminating essential services, but also reducing demand, both directly and indirectly (by putting people out of work, which causes them to cut back their spending as well). 3) Additional government spending on real goods and services. Some obvious possibilities would be infrastructure investments, like renovations of school buildings, public housing, and so on. Investments in alternative energy (such as windmills or solar energy) and new transportation systems (like high-speed rail) could not only boost demand now but also plant seeds for new "green" technologies and industries. 4) Direct government hiring, like under the Works Progress Administration (WPA) and other "alphabet soup" programs during the Great Depression.

None of these things is theoretically very complicated. If they seem unlikely now, which they are, the reasons lie in the distribution of political power, rather than any inherent mystery about our predicament or what can be done about it.

Article 5.6

THE GIANT POOL OF MONEY

BY ARTHUR MacEWAN
September/October 2009

> Dear Dr. Dollar:
>
> *On May 9, the public radio program* This American Life *broadcast an explanation of the housing crisis with the title: "The Giant Pool of Money." With too much money looking for investment opportunities, lots of bad investments were made—including the bad loans to home buyers. But where did this "giant pool of money" come from? Was this really a source of the home mortgage crisis?*
> —Gail Radford, Buffalo, N.Y.

The show was both entertaining and interesting. A good show, but maybe a bit more explanation will be useful.

There was indeed a "giant pool of money" that was an important part of the story of the home mortgage crisis—well, not "money" as we usually think of it, but financial assets, which I'll get to in a moment. And that pool of money is an important link in the larger economic crisis story.

The giant pool of money was the build-up of financial assets—U.S. Treasury bonds, for example, and other assets that pay a fixed income. According to the program, the amount of these assets had grown from roughly $36 trillion in 2000 to $70 trillion in 2008. That's $70 *trillion*, with a T, which is a lot of money, roughly the same as total world output in 2008.

These financial assets built up for a number of reasons. One was the doubling of oil prices (after adjusting for inflation) between 2000 and 2007, largely due to the U.S. invasion of Iraq. This put a lot of money in the hands of governments in oil-producing countries and private individuals connected to the oil industry.

A second factor was the large build up of reserves (i.e., the excess of receipts from exports over payments for imports) by several low-income countries, most notably China. One reason some countries operated in this manner was simply to keep the cost of their currency low in terms of U.S. dollars, thus maintaining demand for their exports. (Using their own currencies to buy dollars, they were increasing both the supply of their currencies and the demand for dollars; this pushed the price of their currencies down and of dollars up.) But another reason was to protect themselves from the sort of problems they had faced in the early 1980s, when world recession cut their export earnings and left them unable to meet their import costs and pay their debts—thus the debt crisis of that era.

This build-up of dollar reserves by governments (actually, central banks) of other countries was also a result of the budgetary deficits of the Bush administration. Spending more than it was taking in as taxes (after the big tax cuts for the wealthy and with the heavy war spending), the Bush administration needed to borrow. Foreign governments, by buying the U.S. securities, were providing the loans.

Still a third factor explaining the giant pool of financial assets was the high level of inequality within the United States and elsewhere in the global economy. Since 1993, half of all income gains in the United States have gone to the highest-income 1% of households. While the very rich spend a good share of their money on mansions, fancy cars, and other luxuries, there was plenty more money for them to put into investments—the stock market but also fixed-income securities (i.e., bonds).

So there is the giant pool of money or, again, of financial assets.

The financial assets became a problem for two connected reasons. First, in the recovery following the 2001 recession, economic growth was very slow; there were thus very limited real investment opportunities. Between 2001 and 2007, private fixed investment (adjusted for inflation) grew by only 11%, whereas in the same number of years following the recession of the early 1990s, investment grew by 59%.

Second, in an effort to stimulate more growth, the Federal Reserve kept interest rates very low. But the low interest rates meant low returns on financial assets—U.S. government bonds in particular, but financial assets in general. So the holders of financial assets went searching for new investment opportunities, which, as the radio program explained, meant pushing money into high-risk mortgages. The rest, as they say, is history.

So the giant pool of money was the link that tied high inequality, the war, and rising financial imbalances in the world economy (caused in large part by the U.S. government's budgetary policies) to the housing crisis and thus to the more general financial crisis.

Article 5.7

DERIVATIVES AND DEREGULATION

BY MARTY WOLFSON

November/December 2008

It has become commonplace to describe the current financial crisis as the most serious since the Great Depression. Although we have more tools now to avoid a depression, the current crisis presents in some ways more significant challenges than did the banking crises of the 1930s.

And it's not over.

The form of the current crisis is similar to others we have seen in the past: a speculative increase in asset prices, overly optimistic expectations, and an expansion of debt sustainable only if the speculative bubble continues. Then the bubble pops, debt can't be repaid, and losses mount at financial institutions. The risk of bank failures rises and lenders get scared. They panic, refuse to lend to anyone that seems at all risky, and seek safety in cash or super-safe assets.

In the early 1930s, there was no federal deposit insurance and little federal government intervention. Depositor runs took down the banking system.

In more recent crises, though, the Federal Reserve successfully developed and used its powers as a lender of last resort. Deposit insurance helped to reassure small depositors and, if needed, the Federal Deposit Insurance Corporation stepped in and bailed out threatened banks. It could guarantee all liabilities of a failing bank and arrange mergers with healthier banks. These tools generally worked to reduce panicked reactions and prevent the freezing up of credit.

But this time, after the collapse of the speculative bubble in housing prices, the course of events has been different. The Federal Reserve was forced to expand the concept of a lender of last resort in unprecedented ways. It has lent to investment banks and insurance companies, not just regulated depository institutions. It has taken all kinds of assets as collateral for its loans, not just the high-grade securities it traditionally accepted. It has even lent to nonfinancial corporations (by buying their commercial paper).

What is surprising is that these dramatic actions and expensive bailouts of financial institutions, such as American International Group (AIG) and even Fannie Mae and Freddie Mac, were insufficient to reassure lenders about the ability of financial institutions to honor their repayment commitments. Treasury Secretary Paulson's plan to use $700 billion to buy "toxic assets" from financial institutions, signed into law by President Bush on October 3rd, failed to stop what had become by then a generalized panic and freeze-up of credit. It took a coordinated global initiative to inject capital directly into financial institutions, plus a federal guarantee on bank debt and unlimited FDIC insurance on non-interest-bearing (mostly business) accounts at banks, announced on October 12th, to begin to have an effect on unfreezing credit markets.

The "TED spread," a widely watched measure of credit risk that had spiked sharply during the panic, began to reverse its path following the October 12 announcement. The TED spread measures the difference between an interest rate that banks charge when lending to each other (the London Interbank Offered Rate, or LIBOR) and the interest rate on U.S. Treasury bills. Because the Treasury is assumed to be "risk-free," the difference between it and LIBOR measures the perceived relative risk of lending to banks.

Why has this panic been so much more difficult to control? The answer has to do with the widespread use of complicated and opaque securities, known as derivatives, in a deregulated, interconnected, and global financial system.

A derivative is a financial contract that derives its value from something else, such as an asset or an index. At the root of the current crisis are derivatives known as mortgage-backed securities (MBSs). MBSs are claims to payments from an underlying pool of mortgages. The ability of MBS issuers to repay their debt, and thus the value of the MBS, is derived from the ability of homeowners to meet their mortgage payments.

In the process leading up to the crisis, a mortgage broker typically extended a mortgage to a borrower, and then turned to a commercial bank to fund the loan. The bank might sell the loan to Fannie Mae, which would pool a group of mortgages together and sell the resulting MBS to an investment bank like Lehman Brothers. Lehman, in turn, repackaged the MBS in various ways, and issued even more complicated derivatives called collateralized debt obligations (CDOs). Buyers of the CDOs might be other banks, hedge funds, or other lenders.

At the base of this complicated pyramid of derivatives might be a subprime borrower whose lender did not explain an adjustable-rate loan, or another borrower whose ability to meet mortgage payments depended on a continued escalation of home prices. As subprime borrowers' rates reset, and especially as housing price speculation collapsed, the whole house of cards came crashing down.

Why were mortgage loans made that could not be repaid? And why did supposedly sophisticated investors buy MBSs and CDOs based on these loans? First of all, the mortgage brokers and commercial banks that made and funded these loans quickly sold them off and no longer had any responsibility for them. Second, rating agencies like Moody's and Standard & Poor's gave these derivatives stellar AAA ratings, signifying a credit risk of almost zero. Recent Congressional hearings have highlighted the conflict of interest that these rating agencies had: they were being paid by the issuers of the derivatives they were rating. Third, financial institutions up and down the line were making money and nobody was limiting what they could do. In the deregulated financial environment, federal regulators stood aside as housing speculation spun out of control and did little to regulate, or even document, the growth of complicated derivatives.

Finally, financial institutions' concerns about the creditworthiness of the derivatives they held were eased because they thought they could protect themselves against possible loss. For example, by using another type of derivative known as a credit default swap, holders of MBSs and CDOs could make periodic premium payments to another financial institution, like American International Group (AIG), to insure themselves against default by the issuers of the MBSs and CDOs. (This insurance contract was technically classified as a derivative rather than insurance in order to escape regulation.) However, if an insurer like AIG is unable to honor all its insurance contracts, then the protection against loss is illusory.

The total value of all the securities insured by credit default swaps at the end of 2007 was estimated by the Bank of International Settlements to be $58 trillion, and by the International Swaps and Derivatives Association to be $62 trillion. (The estimates could vary by as much as $4 trillion because unregulated credit default swaps do not have to be officially reported to regulatory agencies. Moreover, even greater ambiguity surrounds these contracts because insurers can transfer their liability to other parties, and the insured party may be unaware of the creditworthiness or even the identity of the new insurer.)

Surprisingly, though, the value of the actual securities that form the basis of these credit default swaps was only about $6 trillion. How could $6 trillion worth of assets be insured at ten times that amount? The discrepancy is due to the fact that it is possible to speculate on the likelihood of default of a security without actually owning the security: all the speculator has to do is enter into a credit default swap contract with an insurer. The total volume of "insured securities" can thus escalate dramatically.

Because derivatives are so complex, because so much speculation and debt are involved, and because it is so hard to know how much is at risk (and exactly who is at risk), regulators are unsure of the implications of the failure of a particular financial institution. That is why they have been so fearful of the consequences of letting a troubled institution fail.

The exception that did indeed prove the rule was Lehman Brothers. The Federal Reserve and Treasury did not bail it out, and its failure led to an intensification of the problems in credit markets. A money market fund, the Reserve Primary Fund, announced that it would only pay 97 cents on the dollar to its investors, because its investments in Lehman Brothers could not be redeemed. The Treasury moved quickly to announce that it would insure money market funds, in order to prevent a run on the funds. However, the Lehman failure raised further concerns that lenders had about the derivatives portfolios of other banks, and about the possibility that the banks would not have enough capital to cover potential losses.

Secretary Paulson's initial plan to buy "toxic" assets (including MBSs and CDOs) from financial institutions was designed to address these concerns about bank capital. However, his plan was probably also negatively affected by uncertainty. Because these "toxic" assets are complex and nobody wants to buy them, there is no market for them and their value is uncertain. And because the Paulson plan's unstated objective was to boost bank capital by overpaying for these assets, the difficulties in pricing the assets raised the prospects of long delays and questions about whether the plan to increase bank capital would be successful. Lenders continued to hold back. They may also have hesitated because of concern about a political backlash against a taxpayer subsidy for the very banks that many people blamed for the crisis.

By injecting capital directly into the banks, the global initiative announced on October 12th raised the prospect of returns on the capital investment for taxpayers. It also avoided the uncertainties of buying individual assets and helped to reduce the panic.

But the crisis isn't over. Reducing the panic is only the first step. There is now likely to be a longer-term credit crunch that will continue to threaten the broader economy. Banks and other lenders will be wary for quite some time. Losses on mortgage-related assets will continue as years of housing speculation—financed with heaps of borrowed money—continues to unwind. Bank lending will lag as banks rebuild their capital and overcome their pessimistic expectations.

It will be up to the federal government to pick up the slack that the banks will leave. We will need programs to enable people to stay in their homes and stabilize their communities. We will need to create jobs by investing in infrastructure, renewable energy, and education. We will need a "trickle-up" approach that puts people first and raises living standards and opportunities.

At the same time, we need a regulatory structure for the financial system that puts limits on risk and manipulation. It is clear that deregulation, and the entire neoliberal model that has dominated economic policy for the past 30 years, has run aground. It has sown the seeds of financial crisis, and this crisis has led us to the edge of an abyss. Only by dramatically reorienting our economic and financial structure can we avoid the abyss and create the kind of society that meets our needs. The nature of that new structure should be the subject of intensive democratic discussion and debate in the days to come.

Article 5.8

OF BUBBLES AND BAILOUTS

New Wall Street bailout accounting puts the numbers in perspective.

BY MARY BOTTARI
July/August 2010

The collapse of the U.S. housing bubble led directly to the largest industry bailout in U.S. history. While it will be many years yet before we can put a hard number to the amount of taxpayer dollars actually lost in the bailout, the Center for Media and Democracy (CMD) has developed an assessment of the dollars disbursed in the bailout that graphically illustrates the extraordinary lengths to which the federal government has gone to bail out the financial sector. This original Wall Street bailout accounting includes all the major bailout programs of the U.S. Treasury Department, the Federal Reserve, and other government agencies including the FDIC and the Federal Housing Authority. The tally is updated monthly and does not include stimulus funds, unemployment insurance payments, student loans, the auto-industry bailout, or other initiatives to create jobs or support ordinary people, as other bailout tallies do. CMD's total for taxpayer dollars that have gone out the door to date: $4.7 trillion, with $2 trillion still outstanding as of June 2010. The chart below puts this extraordinary expenditure of $4.7 trillion into perspective.

This assessment of dollars disbursed demonstrates that the hotly contested $700 billion Troubled Asset Relief Program (aka "TARP") was only a small portion of the funds that the U.S. government rapidly deployed to aid the financial sector. Without Congressional discussion or debate, the Fed has provided the bulk of the money in the form of loans and purchases of toxic assets and other securities that may—or

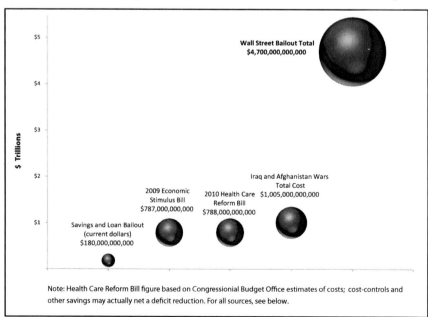

Note: Health Care Reform Bill figure based on Congressional Budget Office estimates of costs; cost-controls and other savings may actually net a deficit reduction. For all sources, see below.

may not—be sellable, amounting to 80% of the $4.7 trillion. And contrary to popular belief, the bailout continues unabated as the Fed pumps money into Fannie Mae and Freddie Mac, amounting to a $1.6 trillion "stealth" bailout. The full accounting for the various Fed programs is still murky, as the Fed has fought court battle after court battle to prevent the release of information regarding certain programs. Hopefully the unprecedented Federal Reserve audit provided for in the 2010 financial-reform package will finally shed light on these "Secrets of the Temple."

Sources: S&L bailout: "Financial Audit: Resolution Trust Corporation's 1995 and 1994 Financial Statements" (adjusted here to 2010 dollars), gao.gov; *Economic Stimulus Bill:* Track the Money, recovery.gov; *Health Care Reform:* Congressional Budget Office, Final Reconciliation, www.cbo. gov; *Wars:* National Priorities Project, nationalpriorities.org; *Wall Street bailout:* Total Wall Street Bailout Cost Table, sourcewatch.org.

Article 5.9

NOT TOO BIG ENOUGH
Where the big banks come from.

BY ROB LARSON
July/August 2010

The government bailout of America's biggest banks set off a tornado of public anger and confusion. When the House of Representatives initially rejected the bailout bill, the *Wall Street Journal* attributed it to "populist fury," and since then the public has remained stubbornly resentful over the bailout of those banks considered "too big to fail." Now, the heads of economic policy are trying to gracefully distance themselves from bailouts, claiming that future large-scale bank failures will be avoided by stronger regulation and higher insurance premiums.

Dealing with the collapse of these "systemically important banks" is a difficult policy issue, but the less-discussed issue is how the banking industry came to this point. If the collapse of just one of our $100 billion megabanks, Lehman Brothers, was enough to touch off an intense contraction in the supply of essential credit, we must know how some banks became "too big to fail" in the first place. The answer lies in certain incentives for bank growth, which after the loosening of crucial industry regulations drove the enormous waves of bank mergers in the last thirty years.

Geographical Growth

Prior to the 1980s, American commercial banking was a small-scale affair. State-chartered banks were prohibited by state laws from running branches outside their home state, or sometimes even outside their home county. Nationally chartered banks were likewise limited, and federal law allowed interstate acquisitions only if a state legislature specifically decided to permit out-of-state banks to purchase local branches. No states allowed such acquisition until 1975, when Maine and other states began passing legislation allowing at least some interstate banking. The trend was capped in 1994 by the Riegle-Neal Act, which removed the remaining restrictions on interstate branching and allowed direct cross-state banking mergers.

This geographic deregulation allowed commercial banks to make extensive acquisitions, in state and out. When Wells Fargo acquired another large California bank, Crocker National, in 1986 it was the largest bank merger in U.S. history. Since "the regulatory light was green," a single banking company could now operate across the uniquely large U.S. market, opening up enormous new opportunities for economies of scale in the banking industry.

Economies of scale are savings that companies enjoy when they grow larger and produce more output. The situation is similar to a cook preparing a batch of cookies for a Christmas party, and then preparing a batch for New Year's while all the ingredients and materials are already out. Producing more output (cookies) in one afternoon is more efficient than taking everything out again later to make the New Year's batch separately. In enterprise, this corresponds to spreading the large costs of startup investment over more and more output, and is often thought of as lower per-unit costs as the level of production increases. In other words, there's less effort per cookie if you make them all at once. Economies of scale, when present in an industry, create a strong incentive for firms to grow larger, since profitability will improve. But they also give larger, established firms a valuable cost advantage over new competitors, which can put the brakes on competition.

Once unleashed by the policy changes, these economies of scale played a major role in the industry's seemingly endless merger activity. "In order to compete, you need scale," said a VP for Chemical Bank when buying a smaller bank in 1994. Of course, in 1996 Chemical would itself merge with Chase Manhattan Bank.

Economies of Scale in Banking and Finance

Economies of scale are savings that companies benefit from as they grow larger and produce more output. While common in many industries, in banking and finance, these economies drove bank growth after industry deregulation in the 1980s and 90s. Some of the major scale economies in banking are:

- **Spreading investment over more output.** With the growth in importance of large-scale computing power and sophisticated systems management, the costs of setting up a modern banking system are very large. However, as a firm grows it can "spread out" the cost of that initial investment over more product, so that its cost per unit decreases as more output is produced.

- **Consolidation of functions.** The modern workforce is no stranger to the mass firings of "redundant" staff after mergers and acquisitions. If one firm's payroll staff and computer systems can handle twice the employees with little additional expense, an acquired bank may see its payroll department harvest pink slips while the firm's profitability improves. When Citicorp merged with the insurance giant Travelers Group in 1998, the resulting corporation laid off over 10,000 workers—representing 6% of the combined company's total workforce and over $500 million in reduced costs for Citigroup. This practice can be especially lucrative in a country like the United States, with a fairly unregulated labor market where firms are quite free to fire. Despite the economic peril inflicted on workers and their families, this consolidation is key to increasing company efficiency post-merger. Beyond back-office functions, core profit operations may also benefit from consolidation. When Bank of America combined its managed mutual funds into a single fund, it experienced lower total costs, thanks to trimming overhead from audit and prospectus mailing expenses. Consolidating office departments in this fashion can yield savings of 40% of the cost base of the acquired bank.

- **Funding mix.** The "funding mix" used by banks refers to where banks get the capital they then package into loans. Smaller institutions, having only limited deposits from savers, must "purchase funds" by borrowing from other institutions. This increases the funding cost of loans for banks, but larger banks will naturally have access to larger pools of deposits from which to arrange loans. This funding cost advantage for larger banks relative to smaller ones represents another economy of scale.

- **Advertising.** The nature of advertising requires a certain scale of operation to be viable. Advertising can reach large numbers of potential customers, but if a firm is small or local, many of those customers will be too far afield to act on the marketing. Large firm size, and especially geographic reach, can make the returns on ad time worth the investment.

Spreading big investment costs over more output is the main source of generic economies of scale, and in banking, the large initial investments are in sophisticated computer systems. The cost of investing in new computer hardware and systems development is now recognized as a major investment obstacle for new banks, although once installed by banks large enough to afford them, they are highly profitable. The *Financial Times* describes how "the development of bulk computer processing and of electronic data transmission…has allowed banks to move their back office operations away from individual branches to large remote centers. This had helped to bring real economies of scale to banking, an industry which traditionally has seen diseconomies set in at a very modest scale."

Economies of scale are common in manufacturing, and in the wake of deregulation the banking industry was also able to exploit a number of them. Besides spreading out the cost of computer systems, economies of scale may be present in office consolidation, in the funding mix used by banks, and in advertising. (See box.)

Industry-to-Industry Growth

BusinessWeek's analysis is that the banking industry "has produced large competitors that can take advantage of economies of scale…as regulatory barriers to interstate banking fell," although not until the banks could "digest their purchases." The 1990s saw hundreds of bank purchases annually and hundreds of billions in acquired assets.

But an additional major turn for the industry came with the Gramm-Leach-Bliley Act of 1999 (GLB), which further loosened restrictions on bank growth, this time not geographically but industry-to-industry. After earlier moves in this direction by the Federal Reserve, GLB allowed for the free combination of commercial banking, insurance, and the riskier field of investment banking. These had been separated by law for decades, on the grounds that the availability of commercial credit was too important to the overall economy to be tied to the volatile world of investment banking.

GLB allowed firms to grow further, through banks merging with insurers or investment banks. The world of commercial credit was widened, and financial mergers this time exploited economies of scope—where production of multiple products jointly is cheaper than producing them individually. As commercial banks, investment banks, and insurers have expanded into each others' fields in the wake of GLB, their different lines of business can benefit from single expenses—for example, banks perform research on loan recipients that can also be used to underwrite bond issues. Scope economies such as these allow the larger banks to both run a greater profit on a per-service basis and attract more business. Thanks to the convenience of "one stop shopping," Citigroup now does more business with big corporations, like IT giant Unisys, than its component firms did pre-merger.

Exploiting economies of scope to diversify product lines in this fashion can also help a firm by reducing its dependence on any one line of business. Bank of America weathered the stock market downturn of 2001 in part because its corporate debt underwriting business was booming. Smaller, more specialized banks can become "one-trick ponies" as the *Wall Street Journal* put it—outdone by larger competitors with low-cost diversification thanks to scope economies.

These economies of scope are parallel to the scale economies, since both required deregulatory policy changes to be unleashed. Traditionally, banking wasn't seen as an industry with the strong economies of scale seen in, say, manufacturing. But the deregulation and computerization of the industry have allowed these firms to realize returns to greater scale and wider scope, and this has been a main driver of the endless acquisitions in the industry in recent decades.

Market Power

The enormous proportions that the banking institutions have taken on following deregulation have meant serious consequences for market performance. A number of banks have reached sufficient size to exercise market power—the ability of firms to influence prices and to engage in anticompetitive behavior. The market power of our enormous banks allows them to take positions as price leaders in local markets, where large firms use their dominance to elevate prices (i.e., increase fees and rates on loans, and decrease interest rates on deposits). Large firms can do this because smaller firms may perceive that lowering their prices to take market share could be met by very drastic reductions in prices from the larger firm in retaliation. Large firms, having deeper pockets, may be able to withstand longer periods of operating at a loss than the smaller firms.

Small banks are likely to perceive that the colossal size and resources of the megabanks make them unprofitable to cross—better to follow along and charge roughly what the dominant, price-leading firm does. Empirical research by Federal Reserve Board senior economist Steven Pilloff supported this analysis, finding that the arrival of very large banks in local markets tended to increase bank profitability for reasons of price leadership, due to the larger banks' economies of scale and scope, financial muscle, and diversification.

Examples of the use of banking industry market power are easy to find. Several bills now circulating in Congress deal with the fees retail businesses pay to the banks and the credit card companies. When consumers make purchases with their Visas or MasterCards, an average of two cents of each dollar goes not to the retailer but to the credit card companies that run the payment network and the banks that supply the credit. These "interchange fees" bring in over $35 billion in profit in the United States alone, and they reflect the strong market power of the banks and credit card companies over the various big and small retailers. The 2% charge comes to about $31,000 for a typical convenience store, just below the average per-store yearly profit of $36,000, and this has driven a coalition of retailers to press for congressional action.

Visa has about 50% of the credit card market (including debit cards), and MasterCard has 25%, which grants them profound market power and strong bargaining positions. Federal Reserve Bank of Kansas City economists found the United States "maintains the highest interchange fees in the world, yet its costs should be among the lowest, given economies of scale and declining cost trends." The *Wall Street Journal*'s description was that "these fees…have also been paradoxically tending upward in recent years when the industry's costs due to technology and economies of scale have been falling." Of course, there's only a paradox if market power is omitted from the picture. The dominant size and scale economies of the banks and the credit card oligopoly allow for high prices to be sustained—bank muscle in action against a less powerful sector of the economy. The political action favored by the retailers includes proposals for committees to enact price ceilings or (interestingly) collective bargaining by the retailers. As is often the case, the political process is the reflection of the different levels and positions of power of various corporate institutions, and the maneuvering of their organizations.

Market power brings with it a number of other advantages. A powerful company is likely to have a widespread presence, make frequent use of advertising, and be able to raise its profile by contributing to community organizations like sports leagues. This allows the larger banks to benefit from stronger brand identity—their scale and resources make customers more likely to trust their services. This grants a further advantage in the form of customer tolerance of higher prices due to brand loyalty.

Political Clout

Crucially, large firms with market power are free to participate meaningfully in politics—using their deep pockets to invest in electoral campaigns and congressional lobbying. The financial sector is among the highest-contributing industries in the United States, with total 2008 campaign contributions approaching half a billion dollars, according to the Center For Public Integrity. So it's unsurprising that they receive so many favors from the government, since they fund the careers of the decision-making government personnel. This underlying reality is why influential Senator Dick Durbin said of Congress, "The banks own the place."

Finally, banks may grow so large by exploiting scale economies and market power that they become "systemically important" to the nation's financial system. In other words, the scale and interconnectedness of the largest banks is considered to have reached a point where an abrupt failure of one or more of them may have "systemic" effects—meaning the broader economic system will be seriously impaired. These "too big to fail" banks are the ones that were bailed out by act of Congress in the fall 2008. Once a firm becomes so enormous that the government must prevent its collapse for the good of the economy, it has the ultimate advantage of being free to take far greater risks. Riskier investments come with higher returns and profits, but the greater risk of collapse that accompanies them will be less intimidating to huge banks that have an implied government insurance policy.

Some analysts have expressed doubt that such firms truly are too large to let fail, and that the banks have pulled a fast one. It might be pointed out in this connection that in the past the banks themselves have put their money where their mouths are—they have paid out of pocket to rescue financial institutions they saw as too large and connected to fail. An especially impressive episode took place in 1998, when several of Wall Street's biggest banks and financiers agreed to billions in emergency loans to rescue Long Term Capital Management. LTCM was a high-profile hedge fund that borrowed enormous sums of capital to make billion-dollar gambles on financial markets.

America's biggest banks aren't in the habit of forking over $3.5 billion of good earnings, but they had loaned heavily to LTCM and feared losing their money if the fund went under. The Federal Reserve brought the bankers together, and in the end, they paid up to bail out their colleagues, and the *Wall Street Journal* reported that it was the Fed's "clout, together with the self-interest of several big firms that already had lent billions of dollars to Long-Term Capital, that helped fashion the rescue." Interestingly, the banks insisted on real equity in the firm they were pulling out of the fire, and they gained a 90% stake in the hedge fund. Comparing this to the less-valuable "preferred stock" the government settled for in its 2008 bailout package of the large banks is instructive. The banks also got a share of control in the firm they rescued, again in stark contrast to the public bailout of some of the same banks.

Even Bigger?

In fact, the financial crisis and bailout led only to further concentration of the industry. The crisis gave stronger firms an opportunity to pick up sicker ones in another "wave of consolidation," as *BusinessWeek* put it. And a large part of the government intervention itself involved arranging hasty purchases of failing giants by other giants, orchestrated by the Federal Reserve. For example, the Fed helped organize the purchase of Bear Stearns by Chase in March 2008 and the purchase of Wachovia by Wells Fargo in December 2008. Even the bailout's "capital infusions" were used for further mergers and acquisitions by several recipients. The Treasury Department was "using the bailout bill to turn the banking system into the oligopoly of giant national institutions," as the *New York Times* reported.

The monumental growth of the largest banks owes a lot to the industry's economies of scale and scope, once regulations were relaxed so firms could exploit them. While certainly not unique to finance, these dynamics have brought the banks to such enormous size that their bad bets can put the entire economy in peril. Banking therefore offers an especially powerful case for the importance of these economies and the role of market power, since it's left the megabanks holding all the cards.

In fact, many arguments between defenders of the market economy and its critics center on the issue of competition vs. power—market boosters reliably insist that markets mean efficient competition, where giants have no inherent advantage over small, scrappy firms. However, the record in banking clearly shows that banks have enjoyed a variety of real benefits from growth. The existence of companies of great size and power is a quite natural development in many industries, due to the appeal of returns to scale and power. This is why firms end up with enough power to influence government policy, or such absurd size that they can blackmail us for life support.

And leave us crying all the way to the bank.

Sources: Judith Samuelson and Lynn Stout, "Are Executives Paid Too Much?" *Wall Street Journal*, February 26, 2009; Tom Braithwaite, "Geithner Presses Congress for Action on Reform," *Financial Times*, September 23, 2009; Phillip Zweig, "Intrastate Mergers Between Banking Giants Might Not Be Out of the Question Anymore," *Wall Street Journal*, March 25, 1986; Bruce Knecht, "Chemical Banking plans acquisition of Margaretten," *Wall Street Journal*, May 13, 1994;

Eric Weiner, "Banks Will Post Good Quarterly Results," *Wall Street Journal*, January 10, 1997; Gabriella Stern, "Four Big Regionals To Consolidate Bank Operations," *Wall Street Journal*, July 22, 1992; "Pressure for change grows," *Financial Times*, September 27, 1996; Tracy Corrigan and John Authers, "Citigroup To Take $900 Million Charge: Cost-cutting Program to Result in Loss of 10,400 Jobs," *Financial Times*, December 16, 1998; Eleanor Laise, "Mutual-Fund Mergers Jump Sharply," *Wall Street Journal*, March 9, 2006; Steven Pilloff, "Banking, commerce and competition under the Gramm-Leach-Bliley Act," *The Antitrust Bulletin*, Spring 2002; David Humphrey, "Why Do Estimates of Bank Scale Economies Differ?" *Economic Review* of Federal Reserve Bank of Richmond, September/October 1990, note four; Michael Mandel and Rich Miller, "Productivity: The Real Story," *BusinessWeek*, November 5, 2001; John Yang, "Fed Votes to Give 7 Bank Holding Firms Additional Power in Securities Sector," *Wall Street Journal*, July 16, 1987; "Banking Behemoths—What Happens Next: Many Companies Like to Shop Around For Their Providers of Financial Services," *Wall Street Journal*, September 14, 2000; Carrick Mollenkamp and Paul Beckett, "Diverse Business Portfolios Boost Banks' Bottom Lines," *Wall Street Journal*, July 17, 2001; *Journal of Financial Services Research*, "Does the Presence of Big Banks Influence Competition in Local Markets?" May 1999; "Credit-Card Wars," *Wall Street Journal*, March 29, 2008; *Economic Review* of the Federal Reserve Bank of Kansas City, "Interchange Fees in Credit and Debit Card Markets: What Role for Public Authorities," January-March 2006; "Credit Where It's Due," *Wall Street Journal*, January 12, 2006; Keith Bradsher, "In One Pocket, Out the Other," *New York Times*, November 25, 2009; Center For Public Integrity, Finance/Insurance/Real Estate: Long-Term Contribution Trends, opensecrests.org; Dean Baker, "Banks own the U.S. government," *Guardian*, June 30, 2009; Anita Raghavan and Mitchell Pacelle, "To the Rescue? A Hedge Fun Falters, So the Fed Persuades Big Banks to Ante Up," *Wall Street Journal*, September 24, 1998; Theo Francis, "Will Bank Rescues Mean Fewer Banks?" *BusinessWeek*, November 25, 2008; Joe Nocera, "So When Will Banks Give Loans?" *New York Times*, October 25, 2008.

Article 5.10

STILL BANKING ON FRAUD
Reforms fail to address the "control fraud" that caused the financial crisis.

BY WILLIAM K. BLACK
Janurary/February 2011

A truly amazing thing has happened in banking. After the worst financial crisis in 75 years sparked the "Great Recession," we have

- Failed to identify the real causes of the crisis
- Failed to fix the defects that caused the crisis
- Failed to hold the CEOs, professionals, and anti-regulators who caused the crisis accountable—even when they committed fraud
- Bailed out the largest and worst financial firms with massive public funds
- Covered up banking losses and failures—impairing any economic recovery
- Degraded our integrity and made the banking system even more encouraging of fraud
- Refused to follow policies that have proved extremely successful in past crises
- Made the systemically dangerous megabanks even more dangerous
- Made our financial system even more parasitic, harming the real economy

And pronounced this travesty a brilliant success.

The Bush and Obama administrations have made an already critically flawed financial system even worse. The result is that the banking industry's future is bad for banking, terrible for the real economy, horrific for the public—and wonderful for the top executives at the largest banks. This is significantly insane, especially given that over the past 30 years, the savings-and-loan fiasco and other crises provided ample opportunity to learn about those flaws. It appears that we will need to suffer another depression before we are willing to put aside the crippling dogmas that have so degraded the financial system, the real economy, democracy, and the ethical standards of private and public elites.

The Economics Blindfold

Why did most of the experts neither foresee nor understand the forces in the U.S. banking industry that caused this meltdown? The short answer is: their dogmatic belief in neoclassical economic theory that is impervious to the facts, or what I like to call "theoclassical" economics.

Theoclassical economics is premised on the asserted effectiveness of private market discipline. This (oxymoronic) discipline is the basis for the "efficient markets" and "efficient contracts" hypotheses that are the pillars of faith supporting modern finance theory and much of neoclassical microeconomics. Collectively, these hypotheses lead to absolute faith that markets exclude fraud. "A rule against fraud is not an essential or even necessarily an important ingredient of securities markets," wrote eminent corporate law scholars Frank Easterbrook and Daniel Fischel in their 1991 *The Economic Structure of Corporate Law*, in a typical statement of that faith.

How are markets supposed to exclude fraud? Easterbrook and Fischel offer two reasons. The first, a circular argument, lies in theoclassical economists' core belief that markets are by nature efficient. Markets that allow frauds cannot be efficient. Therefore, markets must exclude fraud.

The other argument rests on "signaling" theory. The logical premise is that honest firms have a financial incentive to signal to investors and creditors that they are honest. The false premise is that honest firms have the *unique* ability to signal that they are honest. Easterbrook and Fischel claim that there are three signals of honesty that only honest firms can transmit: hiring a top-tier audit firm, having the CEO own substantial stock in the firm, and operating with extreme leverage, i.e., a high ratio of debt to capital.

The reality, which Fischel knew before he co-authored the treatise, was that firms engaging in so-called control fraud can mimic each of these signals. Control fraud occurs when the executives at a seemingly legitimate firm use their control to loot the firm and its shareholders and creditors. In banking, accounting is the weapon of choice for looting. Accounting control frauds have shown the consistent ability to get "clean" accounting opinions from top tier audit firms; their CEOs use their stock ownership to loot the firm; and they love to borrow extensively, as that allows them to loot the firm's creditors.

In fact, the claim that markets inherently exclude fraud runs contrary to all of our experience with securities markets. The role of epidemics of accounting control frauds in driving recent financial crises is well documented. The national commission that investigated the causes of the savings-and-loan debacle found that at the "typical large failure," "fraud was invariably present." Similarly, the Enron and WorldCom scandals were shown to be accounting control frauds.

Theoclassical economists, however, refused to acknowledge these frauds because recognizing the existence of control fraud would challenge the assumptions underlying their faith-based economic theories. This economic dogma was so dominant that it drove regulatory policy in the United States, Europe, and Japan during the last three decades. Regulations ignored control fraud and assumed that paper profits produced by fraud were real. The result, from the mid-1990s on, was regulatory complacency endorsed by economists who actually praised the worst of the emerging control frauds because of their high reported profits.

So it is no surprise that the recent U.S. banking crisis was driven by an epidemic of lending fraud, primarily mortgage lenders making millions of "liar's loans" annually. According to Credit Suisse, for instance, 49% of all mortgage originations in 2006 were stated-income loans, meaning loans based on applicants' self-reported incomes with no verification. MARI, the Mortgage Bankers Association experts on fraud, warned in 2006 that these loans caused endemic fraud:

Stated income and reduced documentation loans ... are open invitations to fraudsters. It appears that many members of the industry have little historical appreciation for the havoc created by low-doc/no-doc products that were the rage in the early 1990s. Those loans produced hundreds of millions of dollars in losses for their users.

One of MARI's customers recently reviewed a sample of 100 stated income loans upon which they had IRS Forms 4506. When the stated incomes were compared to the IRS figures, the resulting differences were dramatic. Ninety percent of the stated incomes were exaggerated by 5% or more. More disturbingly, almost 60% of the stated amounts were exaggerated by more than 50%. These results suggest that the stated income loan deserves the nickname used by many in the industry, the "liar's loan."

Why would scores of lenders specialize in making liar's loans after being warned by their own experts and even by the FBI that such loans led to endemic fraud? (Not that they needed any warnings. Bankers have known for centuries that underwriting is essential to survival in mortgage lending. Even the label "liar's loan," widely used in the industry, shows that bankers knew such loans were commonly fraudulent.) How could these fraudulent loans be sold to purportedly the most sophisticated underwriters in the history of the world at grossly inflated values blessed by the world's top audit firms? How could hundreds of thousands of fraudulent loans be pooled into securities, the now-infamous collateralized debt obligations (CDOs), and receive "AAA" ratings from the top rating agencies? How could markets that are supposed to exclude all fraud instead accommodate millions of fraudulent loans that hyper-inflated the largest financial bubble in history and triggered the Great Recession?

The answer is the financial system is riddled with incentives so perverse that it is criminogenic—it creates fraud epidemics instead of preventing fraud. When compensation levels for banking executives and professionals are very large and based substantially on reported short-term income, financial firms become superb vehicles for control fraud. Add in deregulation and desupervision, and the result is an environment ripe for a fraud epidemic.

Accounting is the weapon of choice for financial sector control frauds. The recipe for a lender to maximize (fictional) reported accounting income has four ingredients:

- Extremely rapid growth
- Lending regardless of borrower creditworthiness, at premium yields
- Extreme leverage
- Minimal loss reserves

The first two ingredients are related. A U.S. housing lender operates in a mature, reasonably competitive industry. A mortgage lender cannot grow extremely rapidly by making high-quality mortgages. If it tried to do so, it would have to cut its yield substantially in order to gain market share. Its competitors would respond by cutting their yields and the result would be modest growth and a serious loss of yield, reducing reported profits. Any lender, however, can guarantee extremely rapid growth and charge borrowers a premium yield simply by making loans to borrowers who most likely cannot repay them. Worse, hundreds of lenders can follow this same recipe because there are tens of millions of potential homebuyers in the United States who would not be able to repay their loans. Indeed, when hundreds of firms follow the same recipe, they hyper-inflate the resultant financial bubble, which in turn allows borrowers to refinance their loans and thereby delay their defaults for years.

Economists George Akerlof and Paul Romer explained in 1993 that accounting fraud is a "sure thing" and explained why it caused bubbles to hyper-inflate, then burst. Note that the same recipe that produces record *fictional* income in the short-term eventually produces catastrophic *real* losses. The lender will fail (unless it is bailed out or able to sell to the "greater fool"), but with their compensation largely based on reported income, the senior officers can walk away wealthy. This paradox—the CEO prospers by causing the firm's collapse—explains Akerlof and Romer's title, *Looting: The Economic Underworld of Bankruptcy for Profit.*

Senior executives can also use their ability to hire, promote, compensate, and fire to suborn employees, officers, and outside professionals. As Franklin Raines, chairman and CEO of Fannie Mae, explained to *BusinessWeek* in 2003:

Investment banking is a business that's so denominated in dollars that the temptations are great, so you have to have very strong rules. My experience is where there is a one-to-one relation between if I do X, money will hit my pocket, you tend to see people doing X a lot. You've got to be very careful about that. Don't just say: "If you hit this revenue number, your bonus is going to be this." It sets up an incentive that's overwhelming. You wave enough money in front of people, and good people will do bad things.

Raines knew what he was talking about: he installed a compensation system at Fannie Mae that produced precisely these perverse incentives among his staff and made him wealthy by taking actions that harmed Fannie Mae.

In an earlier work, Akerlof had explained how firms that gained a competitive advantage through fraud could cause a "Gresham's" dynamic in which bad ethics drove good ethics from the marketplace. The national commission that investigated the savings and loan debacle documented this criminogenic dynamic: "[A]busive operators of S&L[s] sought out compliant and cooperative accountants. The result was a sort of "Gresham's Law" in which the bad professionals forced out the good." The same dynamic was documented by N.Y. Attorney General Andrew Cuomo's 2007 investigation of appraisal fraud, which found that Washington Mutual blacklisted appraisers who refused to inflate appraisals. An honest secured lender would never inflate, or permit the inflation of, appraisals.

Failure to Respond

The U.S. government's response to the meltdown has been not merely inadequate, but actually perverse. The Bush and Obama administrations' banking regulators have left frauds in charge of failed banks and covered up the banks' losses, allowed the behemoths of the industry to become even larger and more dangerous, and passed a "reform" law that fails to mandate the most critical reforms.

In March 2009, Congress, with the explicit encouragement of Federal Reserve Board Chairman Bernanke and the implicit acceptance of the Obama administration, successfully extorted the Financial Accounting Standards Board on behalf of the banking industry to force it to change the banking rules so that banks did not have to recognize losses on their bad assets until they sold them. Normal accounting rules sensibly require banks to recognize losses on bad loans when the problems with the loans are not "temporary." The losses at issue in the recent crisis were caused by system-wide fraud and the collapse of the largest financial bubble in world history. They were not temporary—moreover, they were (and are) massive. If banks had recognized these losses as they were required to do under pre-existing accounting rules, many of them would have had to report that they were unprofitable, badly undercapitalized, or even insolvent.

Gimmicking the accounting rules so bankers could lie about their asset values has caused the usual severe problems. First, it allows CEOs to pretend that unprofitable banks are profitable and so continue to pay themselves massive bonuses. This is not only unfair; it contributes to a broadly criminogenic environment. Second, it leads banks to hold onto bad home loans and other assets at grossly inflated prices, preventing markets from clearing and prolonging the recession. This is the Japanese scenario that led to the country's "lost decade" (now extended). Third, it makes it harder for regulators to supervise vigorously, should they try to do so, because many regulatory powers are triggered only when losses occur with the resulting failure to meet capital requirements. Indeed, the assault on honest accounting was launched with the express purpose of evading the Prompt Corrective Action law, passed in 1991 on the basis of bitter experience: when savings-and-loan CEOs who had looted "their" institutions were allowed to remain in control of them by using fraudulent accounting, the losses and the fallout of the S&L crisis kept growing. Fourth, it embraces dishonesty as an official policy. Indeed, it implies that the solution to the accounting fraud that massively inflated asset valuations is to change the accounting rules to encourage the massive inflation of those same asset values. Effective regulation is impossible without regulatory integrity; lying about asset values destroys integrity.

Even in the case of the roughly 20 massive U.S. financial institutions considered "too big to fail," the public policy response has been perverse. The terminology itself demonstrates how economists err in their analysis—and how much they identify with the CEOs who helped cause the Great Recession. They refer to the largest banks as "systemically important institutions," as if these banks deserved gold stars. By the prevailing logic, however, the massive banks are the opposite: ticking time bombs that can take down the global financial system if they fail. So "systemically dangerous institutions," or SDIs, would be more apt.

It should be a top public policy priority to end the ability of any single bank to pose a global systemic risk. That means that the SDIs should be forbidden to grow, required to shrink over a five-year period to a size at which they no longer pose a systemic risk, and intensively supervised until they shrink to that size. These reforms are vital for all banks but particularly urgent for the SDIs, with their potential to cause massive damage.

Instead, the opposite has been done. Both administrations have responded to the financial crisis by allowing (indeed, encouraging) SDIs, even insolvent ones, to acquire other failed financial firms and become even larger and more systemically dangerous to the global economy. The SDIs' already perverse incentives were made worse by giving them a bailout plus the accounting cover-up of their losses on terms that made the U.S. Treasury and the Federal Reserve the "fools" in the market.

With small- and medium-size banks likely to continue to fail in high numbers due to residential and commercial real estate losses, the financial crisis has increased the long-term trend toward extreme concentration in the financial industry. The SDIs will pursue diverse business strategies. Some will continue their current strategy of borrowing short-term at extremely low interest rates and reinvesting the proceeds primarily in government bonds. They will earn material, not exceptional, profits but will do little to help the real economy recover. Others will invest in whatever asset category offers the best (often fictional) accounting income. They will drive the next U.S.-based crisis.

What about the long-awaited bank reform law, which Congress finally delivered in July 2010 in the form of the Dodd-Frank Act? The law does not address the fundamental factors that have caused recurrent, intensifying financial crises: fraud, accounting, executive and professional compensation, and regulatory failure. The law does create a regulatory council that is supposed to identify systemic risks. The council, however, will be dominated by economists of the same theoclassical stripe who not only failed to identify the systemic risks that produced the recent financial crises, but actually praised the criminogenic incentives that caused those crises.

The chief international reform, the Basel III accord, shares the fundamental deficiency of the Dodd-Frank Act. Dominated as they were by theoclassical economists, the Basel negotiations not surprisingly produced an agreement that ignores the underlying causes of the crisis. Instead, it focuses on one symptom of the crisis—extreme leverage, the third ingredient of the recipe for optimizing accounting control fraud. The remedy was to restore capital requirements to roughly the levels required under Basel I (Basel II eviscerated European banks' capital requirements). Fortunately, the United States did not fully implement the Basel II capital reserve reductions, which means that the leverage of non-fraudulent U.S. banks has been significantly lower than their European counterparts. However, capital requirements only have meaning under honest accounting. Once one takes into account the fictional "capital" produced by fraudulent lending— along with the revised accounting rules that are helping banks hide their losses—the irrelevance of the proposed Basel III capital requirements becomes clear. (For more on the Dodd-Frank Act as well as Basel III, see "Underwater" in this volume.)

If the Dodd-Frank Act of 2010 and the Basel III proposals are the limits of our response to the crisis, then the most probable outcome in the near- and medium-term is the Japanese scenario—a weak, delayed, and transitory recovery followed by periodic recessions. Banks will remain weak and a poor provider of capital for economic expansion.

With private market "discipline" having become criminogenic, the only hope for preventing the current crisis was vigorous regulation and supervision. Effective supervision *is* possible. For instance, in 1990-91, savings-and-loan regulators used their hard-won understanding of accounting control fraud to stop a developing pattern of fraud in California involving S&Ls making stated-income loans. Unfor-tunately, at the federal level the dogmatic belief that markets automatically prevent fraud led to complacency and the appointment of anti-regulators chosen for their willingness to praise and serve their banking "customers." (The "reinventing government" initiative championed by former Vice President

Al Gore and by George W. Bush when he was Texas' governor indeed instructed banking regulators to refer to bankers as their "customers.") President Obama has generally left in office, reappointed, or promoted the heads (or their "acting" successors) of the Office of the Comptroller of the Currency, the Office of Thrift Supervision, the Federal Reserve, the Federal Reserve Bank of New York, and the Federal Housing Finance Agency. Several of these leaders did not simply fail as federal regulators; they actually made things worse by aggressively preempting state regulatory efforts against fraudulent and predatory mortgage lenders.

None of the reforms to date addresses the fundamental criminogenic incentive structures that have produced recurrent, intensifying financial crises. True, liar's loans have been largely eliminated, and in 2008 the Federal Reserve finally used its regulatory authority under the Home Ownership and Equity Protection Act of 1994 to regulate mortgage bankers (after most of the worst ones had failed), but none of this came soon enough to contain the current crisis and none of it will prevent the next one. The accounting control frauds merely need to switch to a different asset category for a time.

Sources: George A. Akerlof, 1970, "The Market for 'Lemons': Quality Uncertainty and the Market Mechanism," *Quarterly Journal of Economics* 84(3):488–500; George A. Akerlof and Paul G. Romer, 1993, "Looting: The Economic Underworld of Bankruptcy for Profit," in W. Brainard and G. Perry, eds., *Brookings Papers on Economic Activity* 2:1-73; William K. Black, 2003, "Reexamining the Law-and-Economics Theory of Corporate Governance," *Challenge* 46(2):22-40; William K. Black, 2005, *The Best Way to Rob a Bank Is to Own One: How Corporate Executives and Politicians Looted the S&L Industry,* Austin: University of Texas Press; Frank Easterbrook and Daniel Fischel, 1991, *The Economic Structure of Corporate Law,* Cambridge, Mass.: Harvard University Press; National Commission on Financial Institution Reform, Recovery and Enforcement (NCFIRRE), 1993, *Origins and Causes of the S&L Debacle: A Blueprint for Reform.* Washington, D.C.: Government Printing Office.

Article 5.11

UNDERWATER

Profits and pay are sky-high, even as bad loans are sinking the megabanks.

BY ROB LARSON
January/February 2011

Since the catastrophic bank collapses of 2008 and the government rescue of the finance industry, Wall Street has staged a dramatic comeback. Since the bailout, profits are up, capital reserves are up, stock prices are up, government direct aid has been paid back, and executive compensation is exploding. But a closer look shows bank stability is just skin-deep, and dense accounting rules hide a powder keg of bad debt and mounting funding issues. While the recent paper-thin reregulation of finance was a major political victory, the banks' core business is headed downhill and even worse trouble seems to lie ahead.

All of the big four U.S. megabanks—Bank of America, Citigroup, Chase, and Wells Fargo—reported either decreases or very modest increases in their massive profitability during 2010. But this surprisingly weak performance would have been even more disappointing without a pair of accounting maneuvers. One was a bookkeeping measure allowing banks to book projected profit from buying back their debt when their bonds become cheaper. But the banks rarely buy back their debt, so this is essentially a paper gain. The other penstroke that boosted profit was consumption of money set aside to protect against losses on loans—as banks have grown more outwardly confident about the economic recovery, they have lowered their stated expectations of bad loans and designated some of their capital cushions as profit.

But these shallow techniques for elevating profit weren't enough to compensate for the decline in banks' core business—interest income, the money collected from loans minus that paid out to depositors. That income has consistently dropped this year, mainly due to falling loan volume. Banks are making fewer loans to consumers and businesses, citing a "lack of demand," which obscures the quite favorable credit rating now required to get a loan. The lower supply of qualified applicants as job losses persist, combined with locking out applicants with spottier credit history and a general consumer preference to reduce total debt, have all caused bank loan books to continue to shrink in the feeble recovery.

The market has not rewarded the banks for the elaborate camouflage of this core weakness, and their stock prices have lately sagged as a result. But executive compensation is another story, and traders' pay is also rebounding into the $200,000to-$500,000 range, while tens of millions of Americans struggle to keep food on the table. Meanwhile Obama's much-hailed "pay czar" in charge of monitoring finance executive compensation, Kenneth Feinberg, has reported that within three months of receiving their bailouts, the megabanks had paid out $1.6 billion in bonuses—up to a quarter of their TARP rescue totals. However, the "czar" has no formal power to rescind exorbitant pay now that the majors have repaid their government capital infusions, and compensation will now be monitored by a rather unintimidating consortium of regulators. With the CEOs of the banking majors making about a million a year each in straight salary, no upward limit is in sight for financier compensation. But the banking institutions themselves may have some bumpy days ahead.

Extend and Pretend and Descend

While the banking majors were relieved of much of their bad home mortgage-based investments by government purchases in the course of the financial crisis and aftermath, large loans related to commercial real estate remained on their books. Many of these loans were to growing businesses and overoptimistic developers, and have frequently failed to perform, as the recession has rendered projects unprofitable, reducing borrowers' ability to repay.

But the loans are often for sobering amounts, upwards of tens of millions of dollars, and rather than foreclose on such large credit lines, banks large and small are engaging in what has come to be called "extend and pretend." The practice involves not taking legal measures on underperforming commercial real-estate loans, but rather "restructuring" loans with new, more favorable terms for the borrowers, like below-market interest rates or extended timelines for repayment. The goal of the practice is to prevent foreclosure on large loans, with the hope that extending maturities will give borrowers enough time to recover their business and repay.

ONE HAND REGULATES THE OTHER

July's Wall Street Reform and Consumer Protection Act was expected to be a return to at least moderate finance regulation, even if a far cry from the more sweeping controls of the 1930s. But the slap-on-the-wrist nature of the bill became clear when stock prices of the megabanks rose 3% on its passage. The bill delegates dozens of important decisions, from what constitutes a systemically important bank to credit ratings disclosure, to the regulatory agencies themselves. Crucially, bank regulators are expecting what the press calls a "lobbying blitz," as former employees of the regulators are bankrolled by Wall Street to lobby for industry discretion and relaxed standards on every rule. Highlights include:

- While now stuck with limits on overdraft fees and the "interchange fees" charged to merchants for debit card processing, banks are phasing out free checking accounts and elevating fees elsewhere, since they have the market power to do so. Many depositors are unable to afford checking account fees, of course, but the New York Times expects the banks to "jettison unprofitable customers."

- The Volcker Rule would limit banks' "proprietary trading," investments made with a bank's own money rather than clients' funds. The practice was damaging during the financial crisis, but banks have already found a work-around for the new rule. Banks are moving star proprietary traders to client desks, where they will primarily conduct derivatives trade for clients, but will also be able to engage in the barred practice on the side, further blurring the client/proprietary distinction.

- Derivatives will now be listed on established indexes and will require collateral as a cushion against losses, having previously been traded ad-hoc by individual banks. This removes significant risk from the banks themselves, reducing them to competing on

There are several problems with this practice. First, it conceals the real condition of the commercial real-estate market. Second, the restructured loans are usually still foreclosed upon in the end—in the first quarter of fiscal year 2010, 44% of restructured loans were still a month or more delinquent, a fact related to the startling two-thirds of commercial real-estate loans maturing by 2014 that are underwater—meaning that the property is worth less than the bank loan itself. Finally, the bad loans take up space on bank balance sheets that could go to real lending. This suggests that the banks' current predicament may lead to a miniature version of 1990s Japan, where refusal to accept real-estate loan losses led to a decade of slow growth, in part due to banks' inability to make fresh loans when demand recovered.

However, the "extend and pretend" policy presents one major benefit to the big banks: restructuring these loans allows banks to count them as "performing" rather than delinquent or worse, which means banks may reduce their capital reserves against losses. This enables banks to claim their capital cushions as profit; banks remain in denial about their bad loans, and this itself allows the recent profit increases. And when banks are one day obliged to confront these serious losses, they may find they no longer have the capital cushion to absorb the damage.

This ominous hidden liability is on top of the better-publicized problem of banks' under-performing residential mortgage holdings. The mortgage delinquency rate is now hovering around 10% nationwide, and including those behind on pay-

---

service rather than generating large securitization fees. Importantly, businesses that use derivatives for legitimate purposes, such as farmers buying futures contracts to secure favorable grain prices, are exempted from the bill's indexing and collateralizing requirements.

- The bill includes a resolution authority that gives regulators a procedure to "unwind" a bank—overseeing its bankruptcy in an orderly fashion and at its creditors' expense. Additionally, the Kanjorski amendment to the bill gives regulators the authority to break up any financial institution considered to be a systemic threat to the financial system. But it seems unlikely that regulators, typically close to the firms they regulate, would let a titan go down regardless of their resolution authority.

- The new Consumer Financial Protection Bureau requires more information transparency from banks in their communications with customers. However, despite apocalyptic predictions from bank spokespeople, it is notable that banks with under $10 billion in assets are exempt from its rules. This excludes the small and medium-sized lenders that make up 98% of U.S. banks, but does include the large proportion of the industry run by the majors.

Sources: Congressional Oversight Panel, *Small Banks In the Capital Purchase Program*, July 14, 2010; Eric Dash and Nelson Schwartz, "Banks Seek to Keep Profits as New Oversight Rules Loom," *New York Times*, July 15, 2010; Aaron Lucchetti and Jenny Strasburg, "What's a 'Prop' Trader Now?—Banks Move Those Who Wager With Firms' Money to Client-Focused Jobs," *Wall Street Journal*, July 6, 2010; Randall Smith and Aaron Luchetti, "The Financial-Regulation Overhaul," *Wall Street Journal*, June 26, 2010; Damian Paletta, "Late Change Sparks Outcry Over Finance-Overhaul Bill," *Wall Street Journal*, July 2, 2010; Michael Phillips, "Finance Overhaul Casts Long Shadow on the Plains," *Wall Street Journal*, July 14, 2010; "Killing Them Softly," *The Economist*, August 26, 2010; "Not All On the Same Page," *The Economist*, July 1, 2010; Eric Lichtblau, "Ex-Regulators Get Set to Lobby on New Financial Rules," *New York Times*, July 27, 2010.

ments and those on the verge of eviction, fully one U.S. mortgage in seven is in some kind of trouble. Importantly, the bad mortgage debt on banks' books has ceased to be a primarily "subprime" phenomenon of low-income loan recipients; over a third of new foreclosures early this year were prime fixed-rate loans, as the layoff-intensive recovery pulls the rug out from under mortgage recipients.

Notably, the home mortgages still held by the banks are listed on bank balance sheets at inflated values since they are for homes bought at the housing bubble peak, and government has not forced the banks to account them at any reasonable value. And beside this additional hidden weakness and the space taken up on bank balance sheets by this bad mortgage debt, the banking majors are vulnerable to moves by insurers and other investors to force the banks to repurchase securitized home loans sold to them at wildly inflated prices. So far, losses on affected and expected repurchases have cost the biggest four U.S. banks nearly $10 billion, with further losses anticipated.

Meanwhile, the banks have allowed extremely few mortgage borrowers to modify their mortgages or reduce their principal—the National Bureau of Economic Research has found that just 8% of delinquent borrowers received any modification, while a pitiful 3% have received reductions in their total owed principal. However, about half of all seriously delinquent borrowers have had foreclosure proceedings brought by their bank. Of course, banks ultimately benefit more from a renegotiated loan that is paid off than from a foreclosure, but the long timeline required in the foreclosure process allows the banks to once again push back acknowledgement of the loss.

The banks' rush to foreclose is reflected in the recent suspension of the practice by several megabanks, after discovery that foreclosure standards were not being followed, with single employees overseeing upwards of 400 foreclosures daily, far more than can be properly reviewed according to legal standards. The investigation by state attorneys general adds to the legal swamp that may slow down the flood of foreclosures, but also testifies to the large banks' preference for foreclosure over loan modification.

Lending On Borrowed Time

Banks face other market difficulties in the near future. One involves the increased reliance of the large banks on short-term borrowing to fund their loan portfolios. While banks have issued bonds to raise loan capital for years, in recent years they have grown increasingly dependent on short-term borrowing—the average maturity of recent bank bond issues is under five years, the shortest in decades. This is in fact why the seizing up of the credit markets in 2008 was such a big deal—banks were in immediate trouble if they couldn't borrow. Of course, the government bailout included guarantees for short-term bonds, leading the banks to become even more reliant upon them.

This means banks must "turn over" their debt more frequently—they must issue fresh bonds to raise capital to pay off the maturing older bonds—and U.S. banks must refinance over a trillion dollars through 2012. The problem is that the banks will be competing with huge bond rollovers from state and federal government, which are heavily indebted because of upper-class tax cuts, as well as expensive wars and recent rounds of stimulus at the federal level. Even the powerful megabanks may struggle in this environment—as the *New York Times* puts it, "The cost of borrowing is likely to rise faster than banks can pass it on to customers." The total demand for institutional credit may significantly spike in coming years, meaning perhaps higher interest rates as states and finance houses compete for the bond market's favor, or a further decline in lending by banks due to prohibitive funding costs.

Meanwhile, smaller banks have experienced a different post-crisis environment. Despite some TARP bailout crumbs, they have gone under in record numbers—140 failed in 2009, with 2010 on track for a yet larger figure. Most of these smaller fry succumb to losses or suffocate under bad loans following the real-estate bubble of the last decade. This sector of the industry is ironically on track to cause more taxpayer losses from non-repayment of bailout funds than the majors, which have attracted the most scorn for taking TARP funds.

BASEL FAULTY

The Basel III bank guidelines are meant to be the G-20's coordinated global response to the crisis of 2008, establishing consistent rules limiting banking risk. But like the American bill, the lightweight standards were greeted by stock jumps for the bank majors, since the process was heavily influenced by massive financial industry lobbying and other, nationalist factors.

Perhaps most notably, the biggest banks' minimum leverage ratio—how much hard capital banks must hold to cushion against sudden losses—has been set at a modest 7% of assets. However, banks need not meet this requirement until 2019, with only a 2.5% requirement by 2015. Further, the Basel Committee has caved to industry demands to count assets like deferred-tax funds, mortgage-service rights, and investments in other firms as capital. These are now allowed to make up 15% of a bank's capital cushion, despite being illiquid and thus not very helpful in a crisis. Notably, some U.S. megabanks had reserve levels close to these on the eve of the finance crisis, and of course found them to be insufficient.

A related issue is how much long-term funding (vs. short-term bonds) the banks issue, making them less-vulnerable to sudden credit-market lockups as in 2008. The committee failed to reach agreement on this issue, and the rule has been postponed until 2015, along with many others, including "calibration," the specific required reserve level banks must maintain based on their importance to the overall finance system.

One obstacle to progress is the distinctly nationalist approach taken by the regulators, who aim to minimize the weight of regulations that will affect the banks based in their home countries. The United States has pushed aggressively for broader definitions of capital, since U.S. banks still hold large volumes of mortgage-securitization rights. Germany wants "flexible" enforcement of the reserve requirements for its undercapitalized banks; France wants allowances for its banks to continue to own insurers, and so on. The result is banking regulators fighting tooth and nail against regulating their own banks.

In this way, the standards meant to prevent banks from reverting to their old systemically risky ways have been heavily diluted, diminishing Basel to a fig leaf. As the *Wall Street Journal* accurately predicted, "significant moves by the Basel Committee to back away from its initial proposals...[are] likely to provoke criticism that regulators are caving to industry pressure and missing a chance to impose restraints that could reduce the risk of future costly crises."

Sources: Damian Paletta and David Enrich, "Banks Gain in Rules Debate," *Wall Street Journal*, July 15, 2010; Damian Paletta and David Enrich, "Risks Rulebooks Is Nearly Done—Key Aspects of Banks' New Restraints Are Agreed Upon," *Wall Street Journal*, July 27, 2010; Damien Paletta, "Banks Get New Restraints," *Wall Street Journal*, September 13, 2010.

Compounding these stabilized but still shaky banking positions, the industry is now subject to a significantly reshaped regulatory environment. In addition to the major finance reform bill enacted in July, banks face new international capital standards in the Basel Rules and new regulatory scope for the Federal Reserve as well. But all these reforms have been limited by massive lobbying spending by Wall Street, coming to over $700 million in the last 18 months alone, as estimated by the Center For Responsive Politics. (See sidebars.)

A crucial part of the picture is the uncertainty caused by the notorious secrecy of the financial world. Large parts of the modern finance system do not accept deposits as commercial banks do, and therefore face far less regulation, allowing them to disclose much less information about their investments and leverage. Additionally, even the commercial banks are not obliged to report changes to the terms of their commercial real-estate holdings, obscuring the full extent of "extend-and-pretend" practices. And the Federal Reserve, for its part, has fought to preserve its own institutional secrecy. The Wall Street reform bill does include provisions for limited audits of the Fed's open-market operations and discount window, the basic monetary policy tools used to manipulate interest rates and to modulate economic activity. But this casts little light on the Fed's expansive holdings in mortgage securities and other paper bought from the banks in the course of the 2008-9 bailout. From the banks to the regulators, secrecy—and thus uncertainty—colors the picture.

In the end, moderately higher capital requirements and the public listing and indexing of derivatives may take the financial system back to short-term stability, but banks remain stuck with significant bad loans limiting core interest income, and continue to rely on market bubbles and on their outsized political power. They also face a difficult short-term bond market in the near future in addition to some higher regulatory costs, and crucially, their core business is further limited by weak credit demand in the low-expectations recovery. Unsurprisingly, compensation has rocketed back into seven figures in spite of these circumstances.

So while ordinary Americans limp along in a jobless recovery, the banks have their execs instead of Hell to pay.

Sources: Eric Dash, "JPMorgan Chase Profit Rises as Loans Provisions Fall," *New York Times*, October 13, 2010; Eric Dash, "Citigroup Reports $2.2 Billion Profit in Third Quarter," *New York Times*, October 18, 2010; Bradley Keoun, "Bank Profits Are Worse Than They Look," *Bloomberg Businessweek*, July 22, 2010; Matthias Rieker and Marshall Eckblad, "Banks Generate Profits, but Struggle to Lend," *Wall Street Journal*, July 22, 2010; Eric Dash, "Federal Report Faults Banks on Huge Bonuses," *New York Times*, July 22, 2010; "Bankers' Pay," *New York Times*, July 27, 2010; Carrick Mollenkamp and Lingling Wei, "To Fix Sour Property Deals, Lenders 'Extend and Pretend,'" *Wall Street Journal*, July 7, 2010; David Streitfeld, "Mortage Data Leaves Bankers Uncertain of Trend," *New York Times*, May 19, 2010; Floyd Norris, "Banks Stuck With Bill for Bad Loans," *New York Times*, August 19, 2010; Manuel Adelino et al, "Why Don't Lenders Renegotiate More Home Mortgages? Redefaults, Self-Curse and Securitization," NBER, July 2009; Jack Ewing, "Crisis Awaits World's Banks as Trillions Come Due," *New York Times*, July 11, 2010; AP, FDIC Closes 6

Banks, Including 3 in Florida," *New York Times*, July 16, 2010; Randall Smith and Robin Sidel, "Banks Keep Failing, No End in Sight," *Wall Street Journal*, September 27, 2010; Binyamin Appelbaum, "Mortgage Securities It Holds Pose Sticky Problem for Fed," *New York Times*, July 22, 2010; Peter Goodman, "Policy Options Dwindle as Economic Fears Grow," *New York Times*, August 28, 2010; Center For Responsive Politics, Lobbying Spending Database, FIRE 2010, opensecrets.org.

Article 5.12

THE BAILOUT OF FANNIE MAE AND FREDDIE MAC

BY FRED MOSELEY

September/October 2008

On Sunday, September 7 [2008], Treasury Secretary Henry Paulson announced that the U.S. government was taking control of Fannie Mae and Freddie Mac, the two giant home mortgage companies, which together either own or guarantee almost half of the mortgages in the United States. This takeover stands in striking contrast to the generally laissez-faire philosophy of the U.S. government, especially the Republican Party. Why did Paulson take this highly unusual action? And what will be the future of Fannie and Freddie? To delve into these questions is to underscore the critical fault line between private profits and public aims—in this case, the aim of making homeownership affordable—a fault line that ran right through the hybrid structure of Fannie and Freddie.

A Brief History

Fannie Mae (short for the Federal National Mortgage Association) was created as an agency of the federal government in 1938 in an attempt to provide additional funds to the home mortgage market and to help the housing industry recover from the Great Depression. Fannie Mae purchased approved mortgages from commercial banks, which could then use the funds to originate additional mortgages. It continued to fulfill this function on a modest scale in the early postwar years.

Fannie Mae was privatized in 1968, in part to help reduce the budget deficit caused by the Vietnam War (a short-sighted goal, if ever there was one). In 1970, Freddie Mac (Federal Home Loan Mortgage Corporation) was created as a private company in order to provide competition for Fannie Mae. Chartered by the federal government, both are (or were, until the takeover) so-called government-sponsored enterprises: private enterprises whose main goal is to maximize profit for the shareholders who own them, but also quasi-public enterprises with a mandated goal of increasing the availability of affordable mortgages to families in the United States. In the end, this dual mandate proved to be untenable.

In order to obtain funds to purchase mortgages, Fannie and Freddie sell short-term bonds. In other words, their business plan involves borrowing short-term and lending long-term, because interest rates are higher on long-term loans than on short-term loans. However, such "speculative finance" is risky because it depends on the willingness of short-term creditors to continue to loan to Fannie and Freddie by rolling over or refinancing their short-term loans. If creditors were to lose confidence in Fannie and Freddie and refuse to do so, then they would be in danger of bankruptcy. This is what almost happened in the recent crisis.

Beginning in the 1970s, Fannie and Freddie began to develop and sell "mortgage-backed securities"—hundreds of mortgages bundled together and sold to investors as a security, similar to a bond. They also guaranteed these securities (so that if a mortgage defaulted, they would repurchase it from the investors) and made money by charging a fee for this guarantee (like an insurance premium). The major financial innovation enabled the two companies to buy more mortgages from commercial banks, thereby increasing the supply of credit in the home mortgage market, which in turn was supposed to push mortgage interest rates lower, making houses more affordable. These early mortgage-backed securities consisted entirely of "prime" mortgages—that is, loans at favorable interest rates, typically made to creditworthy borrowers with full documentation and a substantial down payment.

The securities that Fannie and Freddie sold were widely perceived by investors to carry an implicit government guarantee: if Fannie or Freddie were ever in danger of bankruptcy, then the federal government would pay off their debts (even though this government guarantee was explicitly denied in legislation and in the loan agreements themselves). This perceived guarantee enabled Fannie and Freddie to borrow money at lower interest rates because loans to them were viewed as less risky.

In the 1980s, Wall Street investment banks also began to package and sell mortgage-backed securities. In the 1990s and 2000s, these "private label" mortgage-backed securities expanded rapidly in volume and also in reach, coming to include "subprime" mortgages—loans at higher interest rates with less favorable terms, geared toward less credit-worthy borrowers and typically requiring little or no documentation and little or no down payment.

The subprime innovation was entirely the work of the investment banks; as of 2000, Fannie and Freddie owned or guaranteed almost no subprime mortgages. This innovation greatly increased the supply of credit for home mortgages and led to the extraordinary housing boom of the last decade, and also eventually to the crisis. As a result of these changes, the share of mortgage-backed securities sold by Fannie and Freddie fell to around 40% by 2005.

In the recent housing boom, the companies—especially Freddie—began to take greater risks. While continuing to bundle prime mortgages into securities and sell them to investors, Fannie and Freddie began to buy mortgage-backed securities issued by investment banks, including some based on subprime and Alt-A (between prime and subprime) mortgages. Why did they begin buying as well as selling mortgage-backed securities? Buying these private-label securities gave Fannie and Freddie a way to get in on the subprime action—while still avoiding direct purchases of subprime mortgages from the banks and mortgage companies that originated them. It was a way both to increase their profits at the behest of their shareholders, and, in response to pressure from the government, to make more mortgages available to low- and middle-income families. Of course, it also opened them up to the risks of the subprime arena. Moreover, the prime mortgages they continued to buy and guarantee were increasingly at inflated, bubble prices, making them vulnerable to the eventual bust and the decline of housing prices.

Anatomy of a Crisis

When the subprime crisis began in the summer of 2007, Fannie and Freddie at first appeared to be relatively unaffected, and were even counted on to increase their purchases of mortgages in order to support the mortgage market and help overcome the crisis. Congress facilitated this by relaxing some of its regulations on the two com-panies: the maximum value of mortgages that they could purchase was increased substantially; their reserve capital requirements, already much lower than for com-mercial banks, were reduced further; and restrictions on their growth were lifted. As a result of these changes and the drying up of private label mortgage-backed securi-ties, the share of all mortgage-backed securities sold by Fannie and Freddie doubled to approximately 80%. Without Fannie and Freddie, the mortgage and housing cri-ses of the last year would have been much worse.

As the overall crisis unfolded, however, the financial situation of Fannie and Freddie deteriorated. Delinquency and foreclosure rates for the mortgages they own or guarantee, while lower than for the industry as a whole, increased rapidly and beyond expectations. The two companies together reported losses of $14 billion in the last year. Their actual losses have been much worse. As of mid-2008, the two had lost about $45 billion due to the decline in the value of their mortgage-backed securities, mostly those backed by subprime and Alt-A mortgages. But by labeling that decline "temporary," they could leave the losses off their balance sheets. If these losses were counted, as they should be, then Freddie's capital would be completely wiped out (a value of -$5.6 billion), and Fannie's would be reduced to a razor-thin margin of $12.2 billion (less than 2% of its assets), likely becoming negative in the coming quarters. In addition, both Fannie and Freddie count as assets "tax deferred losses" that can be used in future years to offset tax bills—if they make a profit. Without this dubious (but legal) accounting trick, the net assets of both Fannie and Freddie would be below zero, -$20 billion and -$32 billion respectively.

The financial crisis of Fannie and Freddie worsened in early July. The price of their stock, which had already fallen by more than half since last summer, declined another 50% in a few weeks, for a total decline of over 80%. Fear spread that Fannie and Freddie's creditors would refuse to roll over their short-term loans to the two. If that were to happen, then the U.S. home mortgage market and the housing construc-tion industry probably would have collapsed completely, and the U.S. economy would have fallen into an even deeper recession. Furthermore, approximately 20% of the mortgage-backed securities and debt of Fannie and Freddie are owned by foreign in-vestors. Mainly these are foreign governments, most significantly China. If these for-eign investors became unwilling to continue to lend Fannie and Freddie money, this would have precipitated a steep fall in the value of the dollar which, on top of recent significant declines, would have dealt another blow to the U.S. economy. Clearly, the potential crisis here was serious enough to spur government action.

In late July, Congress passed a law authorizing the Treasury to provide unlimited amounts of money to Fannie and Freddie, either by buying new issues of stock or by making loans, and also to take over the companies in a conservator arrangement if necessary.

Government Takeover

Through August [2008] the financial condition of Fannie and Freddie continued to deteriorate (especially Freddie), and confidence in their ability to survive waned. Foreign investors in particular reduced their purchases of the companies' debt, and mortgage rates increased. The Treasury concluded that it had to implement a takeover in order to reassure creditors and restore stability to the home mortgage market.

The Treasury plan has three main components:

• It commits up to $200 billion over the next 15 months for purchases of preferred shares of Fannie and Freddie as necessary to keep the companies solvent;

• It establishes a special lending facility that will provide emergency loans in case of a liquidity crisis;

• It commits to purchase unspecified amounts of Fannie and Freddie's mortgage-backed securities "as deemed appropriate."

The day after Paulson's announcement, William Poole, ex-president of the Federal Reserve Bank of St. Louis, estimated that the total cost to taxpayers would be in the neighborhood of $300 billion.

The top managers and the boards of directors of both companies will be dismissed and replaced by new, government-appointed managers. Other than that, the Treasury hopes that day-to-day operations at Fannie and Freddie will be "business as usual." They will continue to borrow money from creditors, now reassured by the government's intervention and more willing to lend to them, and they will continue to purchase and guarantee prime mortgages. In fact, Treasury Department plans call for the volume of mortgages purchased by the two companies to increase over the next year in order to push the supply of mortgage loans up and mortgage interest rates down.

The Treasury plan is a complete bailout of the creditors of Fannie and Freddie, who will be repaid in full, with taxpayer money if necessary. In contrast, owners of Fannie or Freddie stock will lose to some degree: dividends will be suspended for the foreseeable future, and their stock is now worth very little. But their stock was not expropriated. Nor was it wiped out entirely; it could regain value in the future as the home mortgage market recovers. Without the intervention, both companies would have gone bankrupt and the stockowners would have lost everything. So the intervention does represent at least a modest bailout for shareholders.

The most controversial issue in the months ahead will be the future of Fannie and Freddie. Should they become public enterprises permanently? Should they be re-privatized? Should they be sold off in pieces and cease to exist? Secretary Paulson made it clear that the government's current conservatorship is a holding action, and that decisions about the companies' ultimate status will only be made once the next administration and the next Congress are in office. Paulson said that Fannie and Freddie's current structure is unworkable because of its dual and conflicting goals of making housing affordable and maximizing profit—a radical statement, if you think about it! And he suggested that the two should either be fully public enterprises, or else they should be fully private enterprises without any government backing.

In the upcoming debate, the left should advocate forcefully for a public home mortgage agency, one whose sole purpose is to provide affordable housing without the conflicting purpose of maximizing profit. This would stabilize the home mortgage market and help it avoid the boom/bust cycle of private mortgage markets that has brought on the current crisis.

More fundamentally, because decent affordable housing is a basic economic right, providing credit for home purchases should be a function of the government rather than of private businesses whose primary goal is maximum profit. The provision of credit for housing should not be an arena where enormous profits are made, as has been the case in recent years. Without these huge profits, mortgages would be cheaper and houses more affordable. Plus, the kinds of fraudulent lending practices that played a significant role in the recent housing boom would be minimized.

With the presidential election just weeks away, the crisis of Fannie, Freddie, and the whole home lending market is poised to become a major campaign issue. McCain has said that he wants Fannie and Freddie to "go away"—i.e., to be broken up and disappear, leaving the mortgage market entirely to private enterprises. Obama has emphasized the conflict between the public aim of making housing widely affordable and the private aim of making a profit, but so far he has not come down on one side or the other. Now he will have to decide. I hope that he will be a strong advocate of a public home mortgage agency, and I think this would help him to get elected.

Article 5.13

TRANSFORMING THE FED

BY ROBERT POLLIN
November 1992

The U.S. financial system faces deep structural problems. Households, businesses, and the federal government are burdened by excessive debts. The economy favors short-term speculation over long-term investment. An unrepresentative and unresponsive elite has extensive control over the financial system. Moreover, the federal government is incapable of reversing these patterns through its existing tools, including fiscal, monetary, and financial regulatory policies.

I propose a dramatically different approach: transforming the Federal Reserve System (the "Fed") into a public investment bank. Such a bank would have substantial power to channel credit in ways that counter financial instability and support productive investment by private businesses. The Fed would use its powers to influence how and for what purposes banks, insurance companies, brokers, and other lenders loan money.

The U.S. government has used credit allocation policies, such as low-cost loans, loan guarantees, and home mortgage interest deductions, extensively and with success. Its primary accomplishment has been to create a home mortgage market that, for much of the period since World War II, provided non-wealthy households with unprecedented access to home ownership.

I propose increasing democratic control over the Federal Reserve's activities by decentralizing power to the 12 district Fed banks and instituting popular election of their boards of directors. This would create a mechanism for extending democracy throughout the financial system.

My proposal also offers a vehicle for progressives to address two separate but equally serious questions facing the U.S. economy:

- how to convert our industrial base out of military production and toward the development and adoption of environmentally benign production techniques; and
- how to increase opportunities for high wage, high productivity jobs in the United States. The U.S. needs such jobs to counteract the squeeze on wages from increasingly globalized labor and financial markets.

Transforming the Federal Reserve system into a public investment bank will help define an economic path toward democratic socialism in the United States.

My proposal has several strengths as a transitional program. It offers a mechanism for establishing democratic control over finance and investment—the area where capital's near-dictatorial power is most decisive. The program will also work within the United States' existing legal and institutional framework. We could implement parts of it immediately using existing federal agencies and with minimal demands on the federal budget.

At the same time, if an ascendant progressive movement put most of the program in place, this would represent a dramatic step toward creating a new economic system. Such a system would still give space to market interactions and the pursuit of greed, but would nevertheless strongly promote general well-being over business profits.

How the Fed Fails

At present the Federal Reserve focuses its efforts on managing short-term fluctuations of the economy, primarily by influencing interest rates. When it reduces rates, it seeks to increase borrowing and spending, and thereby stimulate economic growth and job opportunities. When the Fed perceives that wages and prices are rising too fast (a view not necessarily shared by working people), it tries to slow down borrowing and spending by raising interest rates.

This approach has clearly failed to address the structural problems plaguing the financial system. The Fed did nothing, for example, to prevent the collapse of the savings and loan industry. It stood by while highly speculative mergers, buyouts, and takeovers overwhelmed financial markets in the 1980s. It has failed to address the unprecedented levels of indebtedness and credit defaults of private corporations and households.

New Roles for the Fed

Under my proposal, the Federal Reserve would shift its focus from the short to the long term. It would provide more and cheaper credit to banks and other financiers who loan money to create productive assets and infrastructure—which promote high wage, high productivity jobs. The Fed would make credit more expensive for lenders that finance speculative activities such as the mergers, buyouts, and takeovers that dominated the 1980s.

The Fed would also give favorable credit terms to banks that finance decent affordable housing rather than luxury housing and speculative office buildings. It would make low-cost credit available for environmental research and development so the economy can begin the overdue transition to environmentally benign production. Cuts in military spending have idled many workers and productive resources, both of which could be put to work in such transformed industries.

Finally, the Fed would give preferential treatment to loans that finance investment in the United States rather than in foreign countries. This would help counter the trend of U.S. corporations to abandon the domestic economy in search of lower wages and taxes.

The first step in developing the Fed's new role would be for the public to determine which sectors of the economy should get preferential access to credit. One example, suggested above, is industrial conversion from military production to investment in renewable energy and conservation.

Once the public establishes its investment goals, the Fed will have to develop new policy tools and use its existing tools in new ways to accomplish them. I propose that a transformed Federal Reserve use two major methods:

- set variable cash ("asset reserve") requirements for all lenders, based on the social value of the activities the lenders are financing; and

- increase discretionary lending activity by the 12 district Federal Reserve banks.

Varying Banks' Cash Requirements

The Fed currently requires that banks and other financial institutions keep a certain amount of their assets available in cash reserves. Banks, for example, must carry three cents in cash for every dollar they hold in checking accounts. A bank cannot make interest-bearing loans on such "reserves." I propose that the Fed make this percent significantly lower for loans that finance preferred activities than for less desirable investment areas. Let's say the public decides that banks should allocate 10% of all credit to research and development of new environmental technologies, such as non-polluting autos and organic farming. Then financial institutions that have made 10% of their loans in environmental technologies would not have to hold any cash reserves against these loans. But if a bank made no loans in the environmental area, then it would have to hold 10% of its total assets in reserve. The profit motive would force banks to support environmental technologies without any direct expenditure from the federal budget.

All profit-driven firms will naturally want to avoid this reserve requirement. The Fed must therefore apply it uniformly to all businesses that profit through accepting deposits and making loans. These include banks, savings and loans, insurance companies, and investment brokerage houses. If the rules applied only to banks, for example, then banks could circumvent the rules by redefining themselves as another type of lending institution.

Loans to Banks That Do the Right Thing

The Federal Reserve has the authority now to favor some banks over others by making loans to them when they are short on cash. For the most part, however, the Fed has chosen not to exercise such discretionary power. Instead it aids all banks equally, through a complex mechanism known as open market operations, which increases total cash reserves in the banking system. The Fed could increase its discretionary lending to favored banks by changing its operating procedures without the federal government creating any new laws or institutions. Such discretionary lending would have several benefits.

First, to a much greater extent than at present, financial institutions would obtain reserves when they are lending for specific purposes. If a bank's priorities should move away from the established social priorities, the Fed could then either refuse to make more cash available to it, or charge a penalty interest rate, thereby discouraging the bank from making additional loans. The Fed, for example, could impose such obstacles on lenders that are financing mergers, takeovers, and buyouts.

In addition, the Fed could use this procedure to more effectively monitor and regulate financial institutions. Banks, in applying for loans, would have to submit to the Fed's scrutiny on a regular basis. The Fed could more closely link its regulation to banks' choices of which investments to finance.

Implementing this procedure will also increase the authority of the 12 district banks within the Federal Reserve system, since these banks approve the Fed's loans. Each district bank will have more authority to set lending rates and monitor bank compliance with regulations.

The district banks could then more effectively enforce measures such as the Community Reinvestment Act, which currently mandates that banks lend in their home communities. Banks that are committed to their communities and regions, such as the South Shore Bank in Chicago, could gain substantial support under this proposed procedure.

Other Credit Allocation Tools

The Fed can use other tools to shift credit to preferred industries, such as loan guarantees, interest rate subsidies, and government loans. In the past the U.S. government has used these techniques with substantial success. They now primarily support credit for housing, agriculture, and education. Indeed, as of 1991, these programs subsidized roughly one-third of all loans in the United States.

Jesse Jackson's 1988 Presidential platform suggested an innovative way of extending such policies. He proposed that public pension funds channel a portion of their money into a loan guarantee program, with the funds used to finance investments in low cost housing, education, and infrastructure.

There are disadvantages, however, to the government using loan guarantee programs and similar approaches rather than the Fed's employing asset reserve requirements and discretionary lending. Most important is that the former are more expensive and more difficult to administer. Both loan guarantees and direct government loans require the government to pay off the loans when borrowers default. Direct loans also mean substantial administrative costs. Interest subsidies on loans are direct costs to government even when the loans are paid back.

In contrast, with variable asset reserve requirements and discretionary lending policies, the Fed lowers the cost of favored activities, and raises the cost of unfavored ones, without imposing any burden on the government's budget.

Increasing Public Control

The Federal Reserve acts in relative isolation from the political process at present. The U.S. president appoints seven members of the Fed's Board of Governors for 14 year terms, and they are almost always closely tied to banking and big business. The boards of directors of the 12 district banks appoint their presidents, and these boards are also composed of influential bankers and business people within each of the districts.

The changes I propose will mean a major increase in the central bank's role as an economic planning agency for the nation. Unless we dramatically improve democratic control by the public over the Fed, voters will correctly interpret such efforts as an illegitimate grasp for more power by business interests.

Democratization should proceed through redistributing power downward to the 12 district banks. When the Federal Reserve System was formed in 1913, the principle behind creating district banks along with the headquarters in Washington was to disperse the central bank's authority. This remains a valuable idea, but the U.S. government has never seriously attempted it. Right now the district banks are highly undemocratic and have virtually no power.

One way to increase the district banks' power is to create additional seats for them on the Open Market Committee, which influences short-term interest rates by expanding or contracting the money supply.

A second method is to shift authority from the Washington headquarters to the districts. The Board of Governors would then be responsible for setting general guidelines, while the district banks would implement discretionary lending and enforcement of laws such as the Community Reinvestment Act.

The most direct way of democratizing the district banks would be to choose their boards in regular elections along with other local, regional, and state-wide officials. The boards would then choose the top levels of the banks' professional staffs and oversee the banks' activities.

Historical Precedents

Since World War II other capitalist countries have extensively employed the types of credit allocation policies proposed here. Japan, France, and South Korea are the outstanding success stories, though since the early 1980s globalization and deregulation of financial markets have weakened each of their credit policies. When operating at full strength, the Japanese and South Korean programs primarily supported large-scale export industries, such as steel, automobiles, and consumer electronics. France targeted its policies more broadly to coordinate Marshall Plan aid for the development of modern industrial corporations.

We can learn useful lessons from these experiences, not least that credit allocation policies do work when they are implemented well. But substantial differences exist between experiences elsewhere and the need for a public investment bank in the United States.

In these countries a range of other institutions besides the central bank were involved in credit allocation policies. These included their treasury departments and explicit planning agencies, such as the powerful Ministry of International Trade and Industry (MITI) in Japan. In contrast, I propose to centralize the planning effort at the Federal Reserve.

We could create a new planning institution to complement the work of the central bank. But transforming the existing central banking system rather than creating a new institution minimizes both start-up problems and the growth of bureaucracies.

A second and more fundamental difference between my proposal and the experiences in Japan, France, and South Korea is that their public investment institutions were accountable only to a business-oriented elite. This essentially dictatorial approach is antithetical to the goal of increasing democratic control of the financial system.

The challenge, then, is for the United States to implement effective credit allocation policies while broadening, not narrowing, democracy. Our success ultimately will depend on a vigorous political movement that can fuse two equally urgent, but potentially conflicting goals: economic democracy, and equitable and sustainable growth. If we can meet this challenge, it will represent a historic victory toward the construction of a democratic socialist future.

Resources: Robert Pollin, "Transforming the Federal Reserve into a Public Investment Bank: Why it is Necessary; How it Should Be Done," in G. Epstein, G. Dymski and R. Pollin, eds., *Transforming the U.S. Financial System,* M.E. Sharpe, 1993.

Chapter 6

UNEMPLOYMENT AND INFLATION

INTRODUCTION

In June of 2009, with the economy still in the throes of its worst crisis since the Great Depression, supply-side economist Arthur Laffer warned of the threat of inflation. In an op-ed piece in the *Wall Street Journal* Laffer wrote that "we can expect rapidly rising prices over the next four or five years." He argued that the Fed's unprecedented expansion of the money supply during the crisis has the potential to unleash an inflation spiral more virulent than that of the 1970s.

There might be something to Laffer's concerns about price stability over the longer term. But why voice those concerns just three days after the economy had registered its highest unemployment rate in 26 years? Do conservative economists think it is more important to address a threat of inflation that will not manifest itself for another year or more than to deal with record-setting unemployment today?

The short answer is yes. This is hardly a surprise when considering that investors and stockholders feel precisely the same way because rising prices eat into their real rate of return or profits, after accounting for inflation.

Why is that? The explanation comes down to the trade-off between inflation and unemployment. Standard macroeconomics textbooks depict that trade-off as a "Phillips curve" in which rising employment pushes up prices.

Why does this textbook trade-off affect the returns of stockholders and other investors? The answer, as economist Robert Pollin points out, is "all about class conflict." Wall Street investors, out to protect the value of their assets and their investment profits, are hyper-concerned with price stability, and this pits them against workers on Main Street, who care about employment and wage growth. Higher unemployment rates and fewer jobs eat away at the bargaining power of workers, keeping wage growth and inflation in check and corporate profit margins wide.

Pollin captures that dynamic in Article 6.1, "The 'Natural Rate' of Unemployment." As he sees it, the unemployment rate consistent with price stability—the so-called "natural rate"—declined dramatically in the 1990s because workers' economic power eroded during the decade. Economist Chris Tilly attributes the long-term decline in pay, benefits, and working conditions for U.S. workers to slower economic growth; the business offensive against workers' protections, such as unions and the minimum wage; and businesses pushing more risks onto workers in the form of temporary work, mass layoffs, and reduced benefits (Article 6.2). U.S. labor markets have also been haunted by offshore outsourcing, which began with manufacturing jobs and has now spread to back office work and a wide swath of service-sector jobs. Economist John Miller notes that the alarming estimates of the scope of offshore outsourcing have given even some inveterate free-traders second thoughts (Article 6.3).

Economists Miller and Jeannette Wicks-Lim take on the claim that the persistently elevated unemployment rates in the U.S. economy are due to a skills deficit among those looking for work. They examine closely the data on job openings, hires, and unemployment and find that there are plenty of experienced workers still looking for work even in the industries doing most of the hiring. For them, a jobs deficit, not a skills deficit, is the cause of today's unemployment problems (Article 6.4). Next, economist Sylvia Allegretto and labor analyst Steven Pitts document how black workers fared in the Great Recession and the current jobless economic recovery. During the downturn black unemployment rates increased faster than white unemployment rates, despite starting from a higher level. And after white unemployment rates eventually stopped rising and began to come down, black unemployment rates continued to rise (Article 6.5).

What can be done to raise wages and get workers a better deal? Wicks-Lim's answer is to reverse the decline in workers' political muscle and bargaining power. She argues that pushing U.S. workers' unionization rate back up is a key strategy for creating jobs with decent compensation in the coming decade (Article 6.6).

Economist Ramaa Vasudevan takes a careful look at the macroeconomic relationship between inflation and unemployment and how that trade-off changed during the stagflation of the 1970s and the productivity boom of the 1990s. Like Pollin, she attributes the combination of sustained low inflation and low unemployment during the 1990s to the relatively weak bargaining position of workers (Article 6.7).

Research analyst Ben Collins closes out the chapter by looking at the forces driving the rise of food prices across the globe. Food and other commodities have become a hot new target for investment as housing and stocks turn sour. The financialization of food, just another in a long list of ills visited upon the global economy by unregulated financial markets, has not only contributed to economic instability but is also changing how people around the world eat and who doesn't eat at all (Article 6.8).

Discussion Questions

1. (Article 6.1) What is the concept of the non-accelerating inflation rate of unemployment (the NAIRU, or "natural rate of unemployment")? Is there a natural rate? What is it?

2. (Article 6.1) Given the class conflict inherent in the trade-off between inflation and unemployment, what policies might lead to improved standards of living for workers in today's economy?

3. (Article 6.2) In Tilly's view, What forces have led to a "raw deal" for workers in the long run?

4. (Article 6.2) How have the "paradox of corporate thrift," the "neoliberal paradox," and the "Arkansas paradox" complicated the task of winning a fair deal for workers?

5. (Article 6.3) Just how big a problem is offshore outsourcing? For whom?

6. (Article 6.3) What policies would best address the negative impacts of offshore outsourcing?

7. (Article 6.4) What data do those who argue that today's high unemployment rates can be attributed to a mismatch between job openings and workers' skills use to make their case? How do Miller and Wicks-Lim respond to their arguments?

8. (Article 6.5) How did the pattern of white unemployment and black unemployment differ in the jobless recovery from the 2001 recession? Have the same differences held during the jobless recovery from the Great Recession?

9. (Articles 6.6, 6.7) How might strengthening unions raise wages and help to create decent jobs?

10. (Article 6.7) What are the costs of higher inflation and who bears those costs? According to Vasudevan's evidence, what is the relationship between inflation and growth?

11. (Article 6.1, 6.7) What forces led to sustained low inflation and low unemployment during the 1990s? How are those conditions changing today?

12. (Article 6.8) What forces have transformed food commodities into a hot speculative investment? What steps, if any, do you think governments should take to regulate speculation in food commodities and its dangerous consequences for the world's food supply?

Article 6.1

THE "NATURAL RATE" OF UNEMPLOYMENT
It's all about class conflict.

BY ROBERT POLLIN
September/October 1998

In 1997, the official U.S. unemployment rate fell to a 27-year low of 4.9%. Most orthodox economists had long predicted that a rate this low would lead to uncontrollable inflation. So they argued that maintaining a higher unemployment rate—perhaps as high as 6%—was crucial for keeping the economy stable. But there is a hitch: last year the inflation rate was 2.3%, the lowest figure in a decade and the second lowest in 32 years. What then are we to make of these economists' theories, much less their policy proposals?

Nobel prize-winning economist Milton Friedman gets credit for originating the argument that low rates of unemployment would lead to accelerating inflation. His 1968 theory of the so-called "natural rate of unemployment" was subsequently developed by many mainstream economists under the term "Non-Accelerating Inflation Rate of Unemployment," or NAIRU, a remarkably clumsy term for expressing the simple concept of a threshold unemployment rate below which inflation begins to rise.

According to both Friedman and expositors of NAIRU, inflation should accelerate at low rates of unemployment because low unemployment gives workers excessive bargaining power. This allows the workers to demand higher wages. Capitalists then try to pass along these increased wage costs by raising prices on the products they sell. An inflationary spiral thus ensues as long as unemployment remains below its "natural rate."

Based on this theory, Friedman and others have long argued that governments should never actively intervene in the economy to promote full employment or better jobs for workers, since it will be a futile exercise, whose end result will only be higher inflation and no improvement in job opportunities. Over the past generation, this conclusion has had far-reaching influence throughout the world. In the United States and Western Europe, it has provided a stamp of scientific respectability to a whole range of policies through which governments abandoned even modest commitments to full employment and workers' rights.

This emerged most sharply through the Reaganite and Thatcherite programs in the United States and United Kingdom in the 1980s. But even into the 1990s, as the Democrats took power in the United States, the Labour Party won office in Britain, and Social Democrats won elections throughout Europe, governments remained committed to stringent fiscal and monetary policies, whose primary goal is to prevent inflation. In Western Europe this produced an average unemployment rate of over 10% from 1990-97. In the United States, unemployment rates have fallen sharply in the 1990s, but as an alternative symptom of stringent fiscal and monetary policies, real wages for U.S. workers also declined dramatically over the past generation. As of 1997, the average real wage for nonsupervisory workers in the United States was 14% below its peak in 1973, even though average worker productivity rose between 1973 and 1997 by 34%.

Why have governments in the United States and Europe remained committed to the idea of fiscal and monetary stringency, if the natural rate theory on which such policies are based is so obviously flawed? The explanation is that the natural rate theory is really not just about predicting a precise unemployment rate figure below which inflation must inexorably accelerate, even though many mainstream economists have presented the natural rate theory in this way. At a deeper level, the natural rate theory is bound up with the inherent conflicts between workers and capitalists over jobs, wages, and working conditions. As such, the natural rate theory actually contains a legitimate foundation in truth amid a welter of sloppy and even silly predictions.

The "Natural Rate" Theory Is about Class Conflict

In his 1967 American Economic Association presidential address in which he introduced the natural rate theory, Milton Friedman made clear that there was really nothing "natural" about the theory. Friedman rather emphasized that: "by using the term 'natural' rate of unemployment, I do not mean to suggest that it is immutable and unchangeable. On the contrary, many of the market characteristics that determine its level are man-made and policy-made. In the United States, for example, legal minimum wage rates ... and the strength of labor unions all make the natural rate of unemployment higher than it would otherwise be."

In other words, according to Friedman, what he terms the "natural rate" is really a social phenomenon measuring the class strength of working people, as indicated by their ability to organize effective unions and establish a livable minimum wage.

Friedman's perspective is supported in a widely-read 1997 paper by Robert Gordon of Northwestern University on what he terms the "time-varying NAIRU." What makes the NAIRU vary over time? Gordon explains that, since the early 1960s, "The two especially large changes in the NAIRU... are the increase between the early and late 1960s and the decrease in the 1990s. The late 1960s were a time of labor militancy, relatively strong unions, a relatively high minimum wage and a marked increase in labor's share in national income. The 1990s have been a time of labor peace, relatively weak unions, a relatively low minimum wage and a slight decline in labor's income share."

In short, class conflict is the spectre haunting the analysis of the natural rate and NAIRU: this is the consistent message stretching from Milton Friedman in the 1960s to Robert Gordon in the 1990s.

Stated in this way, the "Natural Rate" idea does, ironically, bear a close family resemblance to the ideas of two of the greatest economic thinkers of the left, Karl Marx and Michal Kalecki, on a parallel concept—the so-called "Reserve Army of Unemployed." In his justly famous Chapter 25 of Volume I of *Capital*, "The General Law of Capitalist Accumulation," Marx argued forcefully that unemployment serves an important function in capitalist economies. That is, when a capitalist economy is growing rapidly enough so that the reserve army of unemployed is depleted, workers will then utilize their increased bargaining power to raise wages. Profits are correspondingly squeezed as workers get a larger share of the country's total income. As a result, capitalists anticipate further declines in profitability and they therefore reduce their investment spending. This then leads to a fall in job creation, higher unemployment, and a replenishment of the reserve army. In other words, the reserve army of the unemployed is the instrument capitalists use to prevent significant wage increases and thereby maintain profitability.

Kalecki, a Polish economist of the Great Depression era, makes parallel though distinct arguments in his also justly famous essay, "The Political Aspects of Full Employment." Kalecki wrote in 1943, shortly after the 1930s Depression had ended and governments had begun planning a postwar world in which they would deploy aggressive policies to avoid another calamity of mass unemployment. Kalecki held, contrary to Marx, that full employment can be beneficial to the profitability of businesses. True, capitalists may get a smaller share of the total economic pie as workers gain bargaining power to win higher wages. But capitalists can still benefit because the size of the pie is growing far more rapidly, since more goods and services can be produced when everyone is working, as opposed to some significant share of workers being left idle.

But capitalists still won't support full employment, in Kalecki's view, because it will threaten their control over the workplace, the pace and direction of economic activity, and even political institutions. Kalecki thus concluded that full employment could be sustainable under capitalism, but only if these challenges to capitalists' social and political power could be contained. This is why he held that fascist social and political institutions, such as those that existed in Nazi Germany when he was writing, could well provide one "solution" to capitalism's unemployment problem, precisely because they were so brutal. Workers would have jobs, but they would never be permitted to exercise the political and economic power that would otherwise accrue to them in a full-employment economy.

Broadly speaking, Marx and Kalecki do then share a common conclusion with natural rate proponents, in that they would all agree that positive unemployment rates are the outgrowth of class conflict over the distribution of income and political power. Of course, Friedman and other mainstream economists reach this conclusion via analytic and political perspectives that are diametrically opposite to those of Marx and Kalecki. To put it in a nutshell, in the Friedmanite view mass unemployment results when workers demand more than they deserve, while for Marx and Kalecki, capitalists use the weapon of unemployment to prevent workers from getting their just due.

From Natural Rate to Egalitarian Policy

Once the analysis of unemployment in capitalist economies is properly understood within the framework of class conflict, several important issues in our contemporary economic situation become much more clear. Let me raise just a few:

1. Mainstream economists have long studied how workers' wage demands cause inflation as unemployment falls. However, such wage demands never directly cause in-

flation, since inflation refers to a general rise in prices of goods and services sold in the market, not a rise in wages. Workers, by definition, do not have the power to raise prices. Capitalists raise prices on the products they sell. At low unemployment, inflation occurs when capitalists respond to workers' increasingly successful wage demands by raising prices so that they can maintain profitability. If workers were simply to receive a higher share of national income, then lower unemployment and higher wages need not cause inflation at all.

2. There is little mystery as to why, at present, the so-called "time-varying" NAIRU has diminished to a near vanishing point, with unemployment at a 25-year low while inflation remains dormant. The main explanation is the one stated by Robert Gordon—that workers' economic power has been eroding dramatically through the 1990s. Workers have been almost completely unable to win wage increases over the course of the economic expansion that by now is seven years old.

3. This experience over the past seven years, with unemployment falling but workers showing almost no income gains, demonstrates dramatically the crucial point that full employment can never stand alone as an adequate measure of workers' well-being. This was conveyed vividly to me when I was working in Bolivia in 1990 as part of an economic advising team led by Keith Griffin of the University of California-Riverside. Professor Griffin asked me to examine employment policies.

I began by paying a visit to the economists at the Ministry of Planning. When I requested that we discuss the country's employment problems, they explained, to my surprise, that the country *had no employment problems*. When I suggested we consider the situation of the people begging, shining shoes, or hawking batteries and Chiclets in the street just below the window where we stood, their response was that these people *were* employed. And of course they were, in that they were actively trying to scratch out a living. It was clear that I had to specify the problem at hand far more precisely. Similarly, in the United States today, we have to be much more specific as to what workers should be getting in a fair economy: jobs, of course, but also living wages, benefits, reasonable job security, and a healthy work environment.

4. In our current low-unemployment economy, should workers, at long last, succeed in winning higher wages and better benefits, some inflationary pressures are likely to emerge. But if inflation does not accelerate after wage increases are won, this would mean that businesses are not able to pass along their higher wage costs to their customers. Profits would therefore be squeezed. In any case, in response to *either* inflationary pressures or a squeeze in profitability, we should expect that many, if not most, segments of the business community will welcome a Federal Reserve policy that would slow the economy and raise the unemployment rate.

Does this mean that, as long as we live in a capitalist society, the control by capitalists over the reserve army of labor must remain the dominant force establishing the limits of workers' strivings for jobs, security, and living wages? The challenge for the progressive movement in the United States today is to think through a set of policy ideas through which full employment at living wages can be achieved and sustained.

Especially given the dismal trajectory of real wage decline over the past generation, workers should of course continue to push for wage increases. But it will also be crucial to advance these demands within a broader framework of proposals. One important component of a broader package would be policies through which labor and capital bargain openly over growth of wages and profits after full employment is achieved. Without such an open bargaining environment, workers, with reason, will push for higher wages once full employment is achieved, but capitalists will then respond by either raising prices or favoring high unemployment. Such open bargaining policies were conducted with considerable success in Sweden and other Nordic countries from the 1950s to the 1980s, and as a result, wages there continued to rise at full employment, while both accelerating inflation and a return to high unemployment were prevented.

Such policies obviously represent a form of class compromise. This is intrinsically neither good nor bad. The question is the terms under which the compromise is achieved. Wages have fallen dramatically over the past generation, so workers deserve substantial raises as a matter of simple fairness. But workers should also be willing to link their wage increases to improvements in productivity growth, i.e., the rate at which workers produce new goods and services. After all, if the average wage had just risen at exactly the rate of productivity growth since 1973 and not a penny more, the average hourly wage today for nonsupervisory workers would be $19.07 rather than $12.24.

But linking wages to improvements in productivity then also raises the question of who controls the decisions that determine the rate of productivity growth. In fact, substantial productivity gains are attainable through operating a less hierarchical workplace and building strong democratic unions through which workers can defend their rights on the job. Less hierarchy and increased workplace democracy creates higher morale on the job, which in turn increases workers' effort and opportunities to be inventive, while decreasing turnover and absenteeism. The late David Gordon of the New School for Social Research was among the leading analysts demonstrating how economies could operate more productively through greater workplace democracy.

But improvements in productivity also result from both the public and private sector investing in new and better machines that workers put to use every day, with the additional benefit that it means more jobs for people who produce those machines. A pro-worker economic policy will therefore also have to be concerned with increasing investments to improve the stock of machines that workers have at their disposal on the job.

In proposing such a policy approach, have I forgotten the lesson that Marx and Kalecki taught us, that unemployment serves a purpose in capitalism? Given that this lesson has become part of the standard mode of thinking among mainstream economists ranging from Milton Friedman to Robert Gordon, I would hope that I haven't let it slip from view. My point nevertheless is that through changing power relationships at the workplace and the decision-making process through which investment decisions get made, labor and the left can then also achieve a more egalitarian economy, one in which capitalists' power to brandish the weapon of unemployment is greatly circumscribed. If the labor movement and the left neglect issues of control over investment and the workplace, we will continue to live amid a Bolivian solution to the unemployment problem, where full employment is the by-product of workers' vulnerability, not their strength.

Sources: A longer version of this article appears as "The 'Reserve Army of Labor' and the 'Natural Rate of Unemployment': Can Marx, Kalecki, Friedman, and Wall Street All Be Wrong?," *Review of Radical Political Economics*, Fall 1998. Both articles derive from a paper originally presented as the David Gordon Memorial Lecture at the 1997 Summer Conference of the Union for Radical Political Economics. See also Robert Pollin and Stephanie Luce, *The Living Wage: Building a Fair Economy*, 1998; David Gordon, *Fat and Mean*, 1997; David Gordon, "Generating Affluence: Productivity Gains Require Worker Support," *Real World Macro*, 15th ed., 1998.

Article 6.2

RAW DEAL FOR WORKERS

BY CHRIS TILLY
July/August 2003

F ew people have seen the inside of a "secondary meat processor"—a factory where large cuts of beef are turned into hamburger patties, roast beef, and other beef products. The workers who process beef do not have it easy. Many stand for long hours on wet floors. They are in constant contact with raw meat. In a typical plant the temperature ranges from 50° down to 3°F. Some workers rake 30-pound beef slabs from a huge bin onto a scale. Others heave giant roasts from one transmission belt to another. The work is repetitive and boring, but at the same time requires extreme attention to detail because of the potential for injury as well as food safety regulations. At one typical plant, entry-level pay is $7.75 an hour, or $16,000 a year—a poverty-level wage. There is no question that meat processors are getting a raw deal.

But the raw deal for workers is not limited to those workers who deal with raw meat. Pay, opportunities, and job quality have gotten worse for most workers in the United States over the past 30 years, across most sectors of the economy.

Obviously, the 2001 recession and the current jobless recovery have meant two-plus years of severe job shortages. But the deterioration of U.S. labor market conditions is a longer-term phenomenon. The spread of second-class jobs in the past three decades relates to fundamental changes in the economy and society, including sluggish productivity growth and employer assaults on workers' rights and protections.

The strongest evidence for the raw deal comes from looking at how workers were doing at the peak of the 1990s boom, three years ago. It was the longest boom in recorded U.S. history (lasting from March 1991 to March 2001). The expansion drove unemployment down to its lowest level in 30 years and spurred talk about a "new economy" that would turn productivity growth into endless prosperity. It should have been the best of times. But as a glance at the numbers reveals, it was not the best of times for working people.

Why the Raw Deal?

Why are workers getting such a raw deal? First, the economic pie is growing more slowly. Productivity growth during the "new economy" 1990s was only two-thirds as fast as in the "old economy" 1960s. That reflects the fact that companies have not invested as much in upgrading their equipment and training their workers as they once did—although the numbers are up compared to the 1980s, when productivity growth was even slower.

Why are these investments down? Businesses make an investment when they expect a payoff. But total global demand for goods and services grew only about half as fast in the 1980s and 1990s as it did in the 1960s and 1970s, and the increasing globalization of trade and investment meant that businesses were much more likely to face new competitors.

Second, over the last 20 years, businesses have aggressively attacked the protections that workers had built up for themselves. They have busted and blocked unions, shredded the unspoken agreements that governed many non-union workplaces, and lobbied to weaken pro-worker legislation. One consequence of these efforts: private sector workers are now less than one-third as likely to belong to a union now as they were in the mid-1950s. The minimum wage is only worth about two-thirds as much as it was at its high point in the late 1960s (after taking inflation into account). Because the low-wage workforce includes disproportionate numbers of women and people of color, the minimum wage and unions particularly benefit these groups.

Republican presidents have joined in the attacks on these protections. Every Republican administration since Ronald Reagan has doggedly opposed minimum wage increases. When Reagan fired striking air traffic controllers in 1981, he set a precedent for the permanent replacement of strikers. George W. Bush out-did Reagan in 2002 when he demanded that the Department of Homeland Security not have civil service protections and announced plans to privatize half of the federal workforce. Republicans in the White House have also stacked the National Labor Relations Board (NLRB), other federal agencies, and the courts with anti-labor appointees. As a result, these agencies offer at best weak enforcement of labor protections. To provide two recent examples: the NLRB recently ruled that unions have no right to hand out leaflets in company parking lots, and the Supreme Court ruled in 2002 that if a company terminates an undocumented worker, it need not pay the worker his or her back pay. Further, under-funding of the Occupational Safety and Health Administration (OSHA) has reduced inspections in hazardous workplaces—like meat processors. Self-styled New Democrats have backed many of these changes in the name of aiding business.

Of course, at the same time as corporations have attacked rank-and-file workers' protections, they have increased the rewards to top executives and stockholders. CEO pay kept growing through 2001, even while profits and stock values declined.

The third reason for the raw deal is that businesses have pushed more and more risk onto workers. The most extreme example of this is the growth of temporary work, which has expanded more than twenty-fold since the late 1960s. (Temporary work has been shrinking for the last two years—which of course is exactly the point: you hire temporary workers so you can dump them when the economy goes south.) But beyond the temps themselves, the frequency of mass layoffs highlights the fact that really, almost all jobs are temporary today.

Benefits are another area where workers bear more and more risk. Twenty-five years ago, most workers with pensions had "defined benefit" plans which specified the amount they would be paid upon retirement. Today, fewer than half of all workers are covered by any retirement plan, and fewer than one in five has a defined-benefit pension plan. Businesses prefer to offer defined-contribution plans like 401(k)s which require employee contributions and tie retirement income to market returns. In the last two years, we saw the results for those who had invested their 401(k) savings in Wall Street. Similarly, employers who offer health insurance have made workers take on more and more of the cost of health benefits—with the result that a growing number of workers decide they can't afford their health plan and go without coverage.

Because They Can

Why are businesses attacking worker protections and demanding that workers bear more risk? The first answer that many people give is "globalization"—and the increased competition that comes with it. Globalization has certainly had an important impact, but it does not offer an adequate explanation for business's newly combative stance. After all, it is the National Restaurant Association—representing an industry that experiences absolutely no global competition—that has fought hardest to keep the minimum wage low. To a large extent, businesses have gone on the offensive not because they *must*, but because they *can*.

Of course, businesses have always had the ability to lobby against the minimum wage, to cut health benefits, and to run anti-union campaigns. What has changed is the social acceptability of such actions. Princeton economist Paul Krugman recently argued that this is what accounts for the stratospheric rise of CEO pay: businesses have torn up the old social contract that placed important restraints on corporate self-seeking. Once a few large companies did this, the pressure mounted for other companies to go along or else face a competitive disadvantage, both in the stock market and in the market for goods and services. And as the social contract got rewritten, the government stopped enforcing the old rules. Cases in point are recent changes by the Supreme Court, the NLRB, and OSHA, mentioned earlier.

What can be done about this raw deal? It's tempting to think about the Arnold Schwarzenegger solution. In the 1986 movie *Raw Deal* ("They gave him a raw deal. *Nobody* gives him a raw deal."), Schwarzenegger used fists, guns, and explosives to wipe out the Chicago mob. But leveling the playing field for workers is no Hollywood action film. Complicating the task of winning a fairer share are three paradoxes.

Three Paradoxes

The first is the *paradox of corporate thrift*. Again, businesses are spending less on investments in equipment and training, and are also doing their best to keep wages and benefits low, all because the demand for the goods and services they sell is not growing very fast. For any business individually, this kind of thrift makes sense. But the paradox is that for businesses taken as a whole, it's counterproductive. Because if businesses are keeping down their own spending, and giving workers as little as possible, the overall result is to keep down the demand for goods and services. It's a vicious circle.

Handing another million dollars to a CEO is not a good way to stimulate the economy. True, some CEOs, like Tyco's Dennis Kozlowski, found creative ways to spend the money—on art, furniture, boats, and travel. But in general, rich people save most of their income. If you took a million dollars of executive pay and divided it among 1,000 poor families, you would get a lot more economic impact.

The second paradox is what University of Massachusetts economist James Crotty calls the *neoliberal paradox*. With slow global growth and increased global competition, it's become harder for most businesses to keep profits up. But at the same time, changes in the stock market mean that investors now demand consistently high profits. The growth of large institutional investors and the invention of the hostile takeover have made it possible for investors to threaten companies with takeover or destruction unless they generate high returns. Crotty points out that profit for nonfinancial corporations actually peaked in 1997. But corporations knew what would happen if they told their shareholders this bad news. In this context, the pressures for accounting games and even fraud became irresistible.

These first two paradoxes point out that the economy is far too important to let businesses run it. But when we think about how to take more control away from businesses, we run into the third paradox, the *Arkansas Traveler paradox*, named for an old song in which a traveler comes upon a man whose roof is leaking in a rainstorm. When the traveler asks him why he doesn't fix the roof, he says, "I can't fix it when it's raining." Asked why he doesn't then repair the roof when it's sunny, he replies, "When it's sunny, there's no need to fix it."

Similarly, when the economy is booming, workers have more economic leverage. Businesses run up against labor shortages, so they're more willing to make concessions to in order to ensure they can get the workers they need. It's a good time to organize a union, push for a higher minimum wage, or demand that employers provide a training program. Governments have the money to enforce regulations or to help pay for training.

But when the economy is booming, many workers don't see as much need to band together to defend their interests. Why form a union or lobby for a higher minimum wage when you can hop to a better paying job? Why push for a training program when even unskilled workers are getting jobs? The 1990s may not have amounted to a workers' paradise, but employment rates and wages were relatively edenic compared to the two decades that came before.

On the other hand, when the economy crashes, all of a sudden even the corporate media and mainstream politicians begin to focus on all the ways that business falls short. But when businesses are struggling for survival, they will fight desperately against any attempt to give workers a bigger share. The large numbers of unemployed job seekers put a damper on any attempts to organize unions or boost minimum wages. Governments face budget shortfalls, so they are not inclined to take on new activities.

The only way out of this box is not economic, but political. We have to build a movement that sees beyond the current situation in any given year. In the boom years, we have to remember all the problems of a business-dominated economy and use our economic leverage to strengthen institutions and business practices that help workers. In the bust years, like now, we have to keep in mind that economic resources will soon enough be growing again, and put in place rules that will more equitably distribute and effectively use them. We know what rules make a difference: the most important are strong wage floors and collective bargaining protections. By making businesses work under a better set of rules, we can actually help grow those resources by steering the economy out of the paradox of thrift and the neoliberal paradox.

If the problem is a raw deal, the solution is a new New Deal. The New Deal of the 1930s and 1940s saved U.S. capitalism from itself. It looks like we're going to have to do it again.

Article 6.3

OUTSIZED OFFSHORE OUTSOURCING

The scope of offshore outsourcing gives some economists and the business press the heebie-jeebies.

BY JOHN MILLER
September/October 2007

At a press conference introducing the 2004 *Economic Report of the President*, N. Gregory Mankiw, then head of President Bush's Council of Economic Advisors, assured the press that "Outsourcing is probably a plus for the economy in the long run [and] just a new way of doing international trade."

Mankiw's comments were nothing other than mainstream economics, as even Democratic Party-linked economists confirmed. For instance Janet Yellen, President Clinton's chief economist, told the *Wall Street Journal*, "In the long run, outsourcing is another form of trade that benefits the U.S. economy by giving us cheaper ways to do things." Nonetheless, Mankiw's assurances were met with derision from those uninitiated in the economics profession's free-market ideology. Sen. John Edwards (D-N.C.) asked, "What planet do they live on?" Even Republican House Speaker Dennis Hastert (Ill.) said that Mankiw's theory "fails a basic test of real economics."

Mankiw now jokes that "if the American Economic Association were to give an award for the Most Politically Inept Paraphrasing of Adam Smith, I would be a leading candidate." But he quickly adds, "the recent furor about outsourcing, and my injudiciously worded comments about the benefits of international trade, should not eclipse the basic lessons that economists have understood for more than two centuries."

In fact Adam Smith never said any such thing about international trade. In response to the way Mankiw and other economists distort Smith's writings, economist Michael Meeropol took a close look at what Smith actually said; he found that Smith used his invisible hand argument to favor domestic investment over far-flung, hard-to-supervise foreign investments. Here are Smith's words in his 1776 masterpiece, *The Wealth of Nations*:

> By preferring the support of domestic to that of foreign industry, he [the investor] intends only his own security; and by directing that industry in such a manner as its produce may be of the greatest value, he intends only his own gain, and he is in this, as in many other cases, led by an invisible hand to promote an end, which was no part of his intention.

Outsized offshore outsourcing, the shipping of jobs overseas to take advantage of low wages, has forced some mainstream economists and some elements of the business press to have second thoughts about "free trade." Many are convinced that the painful transition costs that hit before outsourcing produces any ultimate benefits may be the biggest political issue in economics for a generation. And some recognize, as Smith did, that there is no guarantee unfettered international trade will leave the participants better off even in the long run.

Keynes's Revenge

Writing during the Great Depression of the 1930s, John Maynard Keynes, the pre-eminent economist of the twentieth century, prescribed government spending as a means of compensating for the instability of private investment. The notion of a mixed private/government economy, Keynes's prosthesis for the invisible hand of the market, guided U.S. economic policy from the 1940s through the 1970s.

It is only fitting that Paul Samuelson, the first Nobel Laureate in economics, and whose textbook introduced U.S. readers to Keynes, would be among the first mainstream economist to question whether unfettered international trade, in the context of massive outsourcing, would necessarily leave a developed economy such as that of the United States better off—even in the long run. In an influential 2004 article, Samuelson characterized the common economics wisdom about outsourcing and international trade this way:

> Yes, good jobs may be lost here in the short run. But …the gains of the winners from free trade, properly measured, work out to exceed the losses of the losers. … Never forget to tally the real gains of consumers alongside admitted possible losses of some producers. … The gains of the American winners are big enough to more than compensate the losers.

Samuelson took on this view, arguing that this common wisdom is "dead wrong about [the] *necessary* surplus of winning over losing" [emphasis in the original]. In a rather technical paper, he demonstrated that free trade globalization can sometimes give rise to a situation in which "a productivity gain in one country can benefit that country alone, while permanently hurting the other country by reducing the gains from trade that are possible between the two countries."

OFFSHORED? OUTSOURCED? CONFUSED?

The terms "offshoring" and "outsourcing" are often used interchangeably, but they refer to distinct processes:

Outsourcing – When a company hires another company to carry out a business function that it no longer wants to carry on in-house. The company that is hired may be in the same city or across the globe; it may be a historically independent firm or a spinoff of the first company created specifically to outsource a particular function.

Offshoring or *Offshore Outsourcing* – When a company shifts a portion of its business operation abroad. An offshore operation may be carried out by the same company or, more typically, outsourced to a different one.

Many in the economics profession do admit that it is hard to gauge whether intensified offshoring of U.S. jobs in the context of free-trade globalization will give more in winnings to the winners than it takes in losses from the losers. "Nobody has a clue about what the numbers are," as Robert C. Feenstra, a prominent trade economist, told *BusinessWeek* at the time.

The empirical issues that will determine whether offshore outsourcing ultimately delivers, on balance, more benefits than costs, and to whom those benefits and costs will accrue, are myriad. First, how wide a swath of white-collar workers will see their wages reduced by competition from the cheap, highly skilled workers who are now becoming available around the world? Second, by how much will their wages drop? Third, will the U.S. workers thrown into the global labor pool end up losing more in lower wages than they gain in lower consumer prices? In that case, the benefits of increased trade would go overwhelmingly to employers. But even employers might lose out depending on the answer to a fourth question: Will cheap labor from abroad allow foreign employers to out-compete U.S. employers, driving down the prices of their products and lowering U.S. export earnings? In that case, not only workers, but the corporations that employ them as well, could end up worse off.

Bigger Than A Box

Another mainstream Keynesian economist, Alan Blinder, former Clinton economic advisor and vice-chair of the Federal Reserve Board, doubts that outsourcing will be "immiserating" in the long run and still calls himself "a free-trader down to his toes." But Blinder is convinced that the transition costs will be large, lengthy, and painful before the United States experiences a net gain from outsourcing. Here is why.

First, rapid improvements in information and communications technology have rendered obsolete the traditional notion that manufactured goods, which can generally be boxed and shipped, are tradable, while services, which cannot be boxed, are not. And the workers who perform the services that computers and satellites have now rendered tradable will increasingly be found offshore, especially when they are skilled and will work for lower wages.

Second, another 1.5 billion or so workers—many in China, India, and the former Soviet bloc—are now part of the world economy. While most are low-skilled workers, some are not; and as Blinder says, a small percentage of 1.5 billion is nonetheless "a lot of willing and able people available to do the jobs that technology will move offshore." And as China and India educate more workers, offshoring of high-skill work will accelerate.

ATTRIBUTES OF JOBS OUTSOURCED

- No Face-to-Face Customer Servicing Requirement
- High Information Content
- Work Process is Telecommutable and Internet Enabled
- High Wage Differential with Similar Occupation in Destination Country
- Low Setup Barriers
- Low Social Networking Requirement

Third, the transition will be particularly painful in the United States because the U.S. unemployment insurance program is stingy, at least by first-world standards, and because U.S. workers who lose their jobs often lose their health insurance and pension rights as well.

How large will the transition cost be? "Thirty million to 40 million U.S. jobs are potentially offshorable," according to Blinder's latest estimates. "These include scientists, mathematicians and editors on the high end and telephone operators, clerks and typists on the low end."

Blinder arrived at these figures by creating an index that identifies how easy or hard it will be for a job to be physically or electronically "offshored." He then used the index to assess the Bureau of Labor Statistics' 817 U.S. occupational categories. Not surprisingly, Blinder classifies almost all of the 14.3 million U.S. manufacturing jobs as offshorable. But he also classifies more than twice that many U.S. service sector jobs as offshorable, including most computer industry jobs as well as many others, for instance, the 12,470 U.S. economists and the 23,790 U.S. multimedia artists and animators. In total, Blinder's analysis suggests that 22% to 29% of the jobs held by U.S. workers in 2004 will be potentially offshorable within a decade or two, with nearly 8.2 million jobs in 59 occupations "highly offshorable." Table 2 (next page) provides a list of the broad occupational categories with 300,000 or more workers that Blinder considers potentially offshorable.

Mankiw dismissed Blinder's estimates of the number of jobs at risk to offshoring as "out of the mainstream." Indeed, Blinder's estimates are considerably larger than earlier ones. But these earlier studies either aim to measure the number of U.S. jobs that will be outsourced (as opposed to the number at risk of being outsourced), look at a shorter period of time, or have shortcomings that suggest they underestimate the number of U.S. jobs threatened by outsourcing. (See "Studying the Studies," p. 228.)

Global Arbitrage

Low wages are the reason U.S. corporations outsource labor. Table 1 shows just how large the international wage differentials were for computer programmers in 2002.

TABLE 1: AVERAGE SALARIES OF PROGRAMMERS

Country	Salary Range
Poland and Hungary	$4,800 to $8,000
India	$5,880 to $11,000
Philippines	$6,564
Malaysia	$7,200
Russian Federation	$5,000 to $7,500
China	$8,952
Canada	$28,174
Ireland	$23,000 to $34,000
Israel	$15,000 to $38,000
USA	$60,000 to $80,000

Source: *CIO* magazine, November 2002, from Merrill Lynch *Smart Access Survey*.

TABLE 2: MAJOR OCCUPATIONS RANKED BY OFFSHORABILITY

Occupation	Category	Index Number	Number of Workers
Computer programmers	I	100	389,090
Telemarketers	I	95	400,860
Computer systems analysts	I	93	492,120
Billing and posting clerks and machine operators	I	90	513,020
Bookkeeping, accounting, and auditing clerks	I	84	1,815,340
Computer support specialists	I and II	92/68	499,860
Computer software engineers: Applications	II	74	455,980
Computer software engineers: Systems software	II	74	320,720
Accountants	II	72	591,311
Welders, cutters, solderers, and brazers	II	70	358,050
Helpers—production workers	II	70	528,610
First-line supervisors/managers of production and operating workers	II	68	679,930
Packaging and filling machine operators and tenders	II	68	396,270
Team assemblers	II	65	1,242,370
Bill and account collectors	II	65	431,280
Machinists	II	61	368,380
Inspectors, testers, sorters, samplers, and weighers	II	60	506,160
General and operations managers	III	55	1,663,810
Stock clerks and order fillers	III	34	1,625,430
Shipping, receiving, and traffic clerks	III	29	759,910
Sales managers	III	26	317,970
Business operations specialists, all other	IV	25	916,290

Source: Alan Blinder, "How Many U.S. Jobs Might Be Offshorable?" *CEPS Working Paper* #142, March 2007, figures from Bureau of Labor Statistics and author's judgments.

Programmers in the United States make wages nearly *ten times* those of their counterparts in India and the Philippines, for example.

Today, more and more white-collar workers in the United States are finding themselves in direct competition with the low-cost, well-trained, highly educated workers in Bangalore, Shanghai, and Eastern and Central Europe. These workers often use the same capital and technology and are no less productive than the U.S. workers they replace. They just get paid less.

This global labor arbitrage, as Morgan Stanley's chief economist Stephen Roach calls it, has narrowed international wage disparities in manufacturing, and now in services too, by unrelentingly pushing U.S. wages down toward international norms. ("Arbitrage" refers to transactions that yield a profit by taking advantage of a price differential for the same asset in different locations. Here, of course, the "asset" is wage labor of a certain skill level.) A sign of that pressure: about 70% of laid-off workers in the United States earn less three years later than they did at the time of

---

STUDYING THE STUDIES

When economist Alan Blinder raised alarm bells in 2006 about the potentially large-scale offshoring of U.S. jobs, his results were inevitably compared to earlier research on offshore outsourcing. Three studies have been especially influential. The 2002 study (revised in 2004) by Forrester Research, a private, for-profit market research firm, which estimated that 3.3 million U.S. service sector jobs would move offshore by 2015, caused perhaps the biggest media stir. It was picked up by *BusinessWeek* and the *Wall Street Journal*, and hyped by Lou Dobbs, the CNN business-news anchor and outspoken critic of offshoring.

Forrester researcher John McCarthy developed his estimate by poring over newspaper clippings and Labor Department statistics on 505 white-collar occupations and then making an educated guess about how many jobs would be shipped offshore by 2015.

The Forrester study projects actual offshoring, not the number of jobs at risk of offshoring, so its estimate is rightfully lower than Blinder's. But the ample possibilities for technological change between now and 2015 convince Blinder that the Forrester estimate is nonetheless too low.

A 2003 study by University of California economists Ashok Bardhan and Cynthia Kroll estimated that about 11% of all U.S. jobs in 2001 were vulnerable to offshoring. Bradhan and Kroll applied the "outsourceability attributes" listed in "Attributes of Jobs Outsourced" to occupations where at least some outsourcing either has already taken place or is being planned.

Blinder considers the Bardhan and Kroll estimate for 2001 to be comparable to his estimate that 20% to 30% of the employed labor force will be at risk of offshore outsourcing within the next ten to twenty years, especially considering that Bardhan and Kroll do not allow for outsourcing to spread beyond the occupations it is currently affecting. This is like "looking only slightly beyond the currently-visible tip of the iceberg," according to Blinder.

The McKinsey Global Institute (MGI), a research group known for its unabashedly favorable view of globalization, has done its best to put a positive spin on offshore outsourcing. Its 2003 study, which relied on the Forrester offshoring estimates, concluded

the layoff; on average, those reemployed earn 10% less than they did before.

And it's not only laid-off workers who are hurt. A study conducted by Harvard labor economists Lawrence F. Katz, Richard B. Freeman, and George J. Borjas finds that every other worker with skills similar to those who were displaced also loses out. Every 1% drop in employment due to imports or factories gone abroad shaves 0.5% off the wages of the remaining workers in that occupation, they conclude.

Global labor arbitrage also goes a long way toward explaining the poor quality and low pay of the jobs the U.S. economy has created this decade, according to Roach. By dampening wage increases for an ever wider swath of the U.S. workforce, he argues, outsourcing has helped to drive a wedge between productivity gains and wage gains and to widen inequality in the United States. In the first four years of this decade, nonfarm productivity in the United States has recorded a cumulative increase of 13.3%—more than double the 5.9% rise in real compensation per hour over the same period. ("Compensation" includes wages, which have been stagnant

---

that offshoring is already benefiting the U.S. economy. For instance, MGI calculates that for every dollar spent on a business process outsourced to India, the U.S. economy gains at least $1.12. The largest chunk—58 cents—goes back to the original employer in the form of cost savings, almost exclusively in the form of lower wages. In addition, 30% of Indian offshoring is actually performed by U.S. companies, so the wage savings translate into higher earnings for those companies. The study also argues that offshore outsourcing frees up U.S. workers to do other tasks.

A second MGI study, in 2005, surveyed dozens of companies in eight sectors, from pharmaceutical companies to insurers. The study predicted that multinational companies in the entire developed world will have located only 4.1 million service jobs in low-wage countries by 2008—a figure equal to only 1% of the total number of service jobs in developed countries.

But the MGI outsourcing studies have serious limitations. For instance, Blinder points out that MGI's analysis looks at a very short time frame, and that the potential for outsourcing in English-speaking countries such as the United States is higher than elsewhere, a fact lost in the MGI studies' global averages.

In their 2005 book *Outsourcing America*, published by the American Management Association, public policy professors Ron Hira and Anil Hira argue that MGI's 2003 report "should be viewed as a self-interested lobbying document that presents an unrealistically optimistic estimate of the impact of offshore outsourcing." For instance, most of the data for the report came from case studies conducted by MGI that are unavailable to the public and unsupported by any model. Moreover, the MGI analysis assumes that the U.S. economy will follow its long-term trend and create 3.5 million jobs a year, enough to quickly reemploy U.S. workers displaced by offshoring. But current U.S. job creation falls far short of that trend. A recent White House fact sheet brags that the U.S. economy has created 8.3 million jobs since August 2003. Still, that is less than 2.1 million jobs a year, and only 1.8 million jobs over the last 12 months.

MGI's Farrell is right about one thing. "If the economy were stronger," she says, "there wouldn't be such a negative feeling" about work getting offshored. But merely assuming high job growth doesn't make it so.

for the average worker, plus employer spending on fringe benefits such as health insurance, which has risen even as, in many instances, the actual benefits have been cut back.) Roach reports that the disconnect between pay and productivity growth during the current economic expansion has been much greater in services than in manufacturing, as that sector weathers the powerful forces of global labor arbitrage for the first time.

Doubts in the Business Press?!

Even in the business press, doubts that offshore outsourcing willy-nilly leads to economic improvement have become more acute. Earlier this summer, a *BusinessWeek* cover story, "The Real Cost of Offshoring," reported that government statistics have underestimated the damage to the U.S. economy from offshore outsourcing. The problem is that since offshoring took off, *import* growth, adjusted for inflation, has been faster than the official numbers show. That means improvements in living standards, as well as corporate profits, depend more on cheap imports, and less on improving domestic productivity, than analysts thought.

Growing angst about outsourcing's costs has also prompted the business press to report favorably on remedies for the dislocation brought on by offshoring that deviate substantially from the non-interventionist, free-market playbook. Even the most unfazed pro-globalization types want to beef up trade adjustment assistance for displaced workers and strengthen the U.S. educational system. But both proposals are inadequate.

More education, the usual U.S. prescription for any economic problem, is off the mark here. Cheaper labor is available abroad up and down the job-skill ladder, so even the most rigorous education is no inoculation against the threat of offshore outsourcing. As Blinder emphasizes, it is the need for face-to-face contact that stops jobs from being shipped overseas, not the level of education necessary to perform them. Twenty years from now, home health aide positions will no doubt be plentiful in the United States; jobs for highly trained IT professionals may be scarce.

Trade adjustment assistance has until now been narrowly targeted at workers hurt by imports. Most new proposals would replace traditional trade adjustment assistance and unemployment insurance with a program for displaced workers that offers wage insurance to ease the pain of taking a lower-paying job and provides for portable health insurance and retraining. The pro-globalization research group McKinsey Global Institute (MGI), for example, claims that for as little as 4% to 5% of the amount they've saved in lower wages, companies could cover the wage losses of all laid-off workers once they are reemployed, paying them 70% of the wage differential between their old and new jobs (in addition to health care subsidies) for up to two years.

While MGI confidently concludes that this proposal will "go a long way toward relieving the current anxieties," other globalization advocates are not so sure. They recognize that economic anxiety is pervasive and that millions of white-collar workers now fear losing their jobs. Moreover, even if fears of actual job loss are overblown, wage insurance schemes do little to compensate for the downward pressure offshoring is putting on the wages of workers who have not been laid off.

Other mainstream economists and business writers go even further, calling for not only wage insurance but also taxes on the winners from globalization. And globalization has produced big winners: on Wall Street, in the corporate boardroom, and among those workers in high demand in the global economy.

Economist Matthew Slaughter, who recently left President Bush's Council of Economic Advisers, told the *Wall Street Journal*, "Expanding the political support for open borders [for trade] requres making a radical change in fiscal policy." He proposes eliminating the Social Security-Medicare payroll tax on the bottom half of workers—roughly, those earning less than $33,000 a year—and making up the lost revenue by raising the payroll tax on higher earners.

The goal of these economists is to thwart a crippling political backlash against trade. As they see it, "using the tax code to slice the apple more evenly is far more palatable than trying to hold back globalization with policies that risk shrinking the economic apple."

Some even call for extending global labor arbitrage to CEOs. In a June 2006 *New York Times* op-ed, equity analyst Lawrence Orlowski and New York University assistant research director Florian Lengyel argued that offshoring the jobs of U.S. chief executives would reduce costs and release value to shareholders by bringing the compensation of U.S. CEOs (on average 170 times greater than the compensation of average U.S. workers in 2004) in line with CEO compensation in Britain (22 times greater) and in Japan (11 times greater).

Yet others focus on the stunning lack of labor mobility that distinguishes the current era of globalization from earlier ones. Labor markets are becoming increasingly free and flexible under globalization, but labor enjoys no similar freedom of movement. In a completely free market, the foreign workers would come here to do the work that is currently being outsourced. Why aren't more of those workers coming to the United States? Traditional economists Gary Becker and Richard Posner argue the answer is clear: an excessively restrictive immigration policy.

Onshore and Offshore Solidarity

Offshoring is one of the last steps in capitalism's conversion of the "physician, the lawyer, the priest, the poet, the man of science, into its paid wage laborers," as Marx and Engels put it in the *Communist Manifesto* 160 years ago. It has already done much to increase economic insecurity in the workaday world and has become, Blinder suggests, the number one economic issue of our generation.

Offshoring has also underlined the interdependence of workers across the globe. To the extent that corporations now organize their business operations on a global scale, shifting work around the world in search of low wages, labor organizing must also be global in scope if it is to have any hope of building workers' negotiating strength.

Yet today's global labor arbitrage pits workers from different countries against each other as competitors, not allies. Writing about how to improve labor standards, economists Ajit Singh and Ann Zammit of the South Centre, an Indian non-governmental organization, ask the question, "On what could workers of the world unite" today? Their answer is that faster economic growth could indeed be a positive-sum game from which both the global North and the global South could gain. A pick-up in the long-term rate of growth of the world economy would generate higher employment, increasing wages and otherwise improving labor standards in both regions. It should also make offshoring less profitable and less painful.

The concerns of workers across the globe would also be served by curtailing the ability of multinational corporations to move their investment anywhere, which weakens the bargaining power of labor both in advanced countries and in the global South. Workers globally would also benefit if their own ability to move between countries was enhanced. The combination of a new set of rules to limit international capital movements and to expand labor mobility across borders, together with measures to ratchet up economic growth and thus increase worldwide demand for labor, would alter the current process of globalization and harness it to the needs of working people worldwide.

Sources: Alan S. Blinder, "Fear of Offshoring," CEPS Working Paper #119, Dec. 2005; Alan S. Blinder, "How Many U.S. Jobs Might Be Offshorable?" CEPS Working Paper #142, March 2007; N. Gregory Mankiw and P. Swagel, "The Politics and Economics of Offshore Outsourcing," Am. Enterprise Inst. Working Paper #122, 12/7/05; "Offshoring: Is It a Win-Win Game?" McKinsey Global Institute, August 2003; Diane Farrell et al., "The Emerging Global Labor Market, Part 1: The Demand for Talent in Services," McKinsey Global Institute, June 2005; Ashok Bardhan and Cynthia Kroll, "The New Wave of Outsourcing," Research Report #113, Fisher Center for Real Estate and Urban Economics, Univ. of Calif., Berkeley, Fall 2003; Paul A. Samuelson, "Where Ricardo and Mill Rebut and Confirm Arguments of Mainstream Economists Supporting Globalization," *J Econ Perspectives* 18:3, Summer 2004; Alan S. Blinder, "Free Trade's Great, but Offshoring Rattles Me," *Wash. Post,* 5/6/07; Michael Mandel, "The Real Cost of Offshoring," *BusinessWeek,* 6/18/07; Aaron Bernstein, "Shaking Up Trade Theory," *BusinessWeek,* 12/6/04; David Wessel, "The Case for Taxing Globalization's Big Winners," *WSJ,* 6/14/07; Bob Davis, "Some Democratic Economists Echo Mankiw on Outsourcing," *WSJ;* N. Gregory Mankiw, "Outsourcing Redux," gregmankiw. blogspot.com/2006/05/outsourcing-redux; David Wessel and Bob Davis, "Pain From Free Trade Spurs Second Thoughts," *WSJ,* 3/30/07; Ajit Singh and Ann Zammit, "On What Could Workers of the World Unite? Economic Growth and a New Global Economic Order," from *The Global Labour Standards Controversy: Critical Issues For Developing Countries,* South Centre, 2000; Michael Meeropol, "Distorting Adam Smith on Trade," *Challenge,* July/Aug 2004.

Article 6.4

UNEMPLOYMENT: A JOBS DEFICIT OR A SKILLS DEFICIT?

BY JOHN MILLER AND JEANNETTE WICKS-LIM

January/February 2011

Millions of Americans remain unemployed nearly a year and a half after the official end-date of the Great Recession, and the nation's official unemployment
rate continues at nearly 10%.

Why? We are being told that it is because—wait for it—workers are not qualified
for the jobs that employers are offering.

Yes, it's true. In the aftermath of the deepest downturn since the Great Depression, some pundits and policymakers—and economists—have begun to pin persistently high unemployment on workers' inadequate skills.

The problem, in this view, is a mismatch between job openings and the skills of
those looking for work. In economics jargon, this is termed a problem of "structural
unemployment," in contrast to the "cyclical unemployment" caused by a downturn
in the business cycle.

The skills-gap message is coming from many quarters. Policymaker-in-chief
Obama told Congress in February 2009: "Right now, three-quarters of the fastest-
growing occupations require more than a high school diploma. And yet, just over
half of our citizens have that level of education." His message: workers need to go
back to school if they want a place in tomorrow's job market.

The last Democrat in the White House has caught the bug too. Bill Clinton explained in a September 2010 interview, "The last unemployment report said that for
the first time in my lifetime, and I'm not young … we are coming out of a recession
but job openings are going up twice as fast as new hires. And yet we can all cite cases
that we know about where somebody opened a job and 400 people showed up. How
could this be? Because people don't have the job skills for the jobs that are open."

Economists and other "experts" are most likely the source of the skills-gap
story. Last August, for instance, Narayana Kocherlakota, president of the Federal
Reserve Bank of Minneapolis, wrote in a Fed newsletter: "How much of the current unemployment rate is really due to mismatch, as opposed to conditions that the
Fed can readily ameliorate? The answer seems to be a lot." Kocherlakota's point was
that the Fed's monetary policy tools may be able to spur economic growth, but that
won't help if workers have few or the wrong skills. "The Fed does not have a means
to transform construction workers into manufacturing workers," he explained.

The skills-mismatch explanation has a lot to recommend it if you're a federal or Fed
policymaker: it puts the blame for the economic suffering experienced by the 17% of the
U.S. workforce that is unemployed or underemployed on the workers themselves. Even
if the Fed or the government did its darndest to boost overall spending, unemployment
would be unlikely to subside unless workers upgraded their own skills.

The only problem is that this explanation is basically wrong. The weight of the
evidence shows that it is not a mismatch of skills but a lack of demand that lies at
the heart of today's severe unemployment problem.

High-Skill Jobs?

President Obama's claim that new jobs are requiring higher and higher skill levels would tend to support the skills-gap thesis. His interpretation of job-market trends, however, misses the mark. The figure that Obama cited comes from the U.S. Department of Labor's employment projections for 2006 to 2016. Specifically, the DOL reports that among the 30 fastest growing occupations, 22 of them (75%) will typically require more than a high school degree. These occupations include network systems and data communications analysts, computer software engineers, and financial advisors. What he fails to say, however, is that these 22 occupations are projected to represent less than 3% of all U.S. jobs.

What would seem more relevant to the 27 million unemployed and underemployed workers are the occupations with the *largest* growth. These are the occupations that will offer workers the greatest number of new job opportunities. Among the 30 occupations with the largest growth, 70%—21 out of 30—typically do not require more than a high school degree. To become fully qualified for these jobs, workers will only need on-the-job training. The DOL projects that one-quarter of all jobs in 2016 will be in these 21 occupations, which include retail salespeople, food-preparation and food-service workers, and personal and home care aides.

In fact, the DOL employment projections estimate that more than two-thirds (68%) of the jobs in 2016 will be accessible to workers with a high school degree or less. Couple this with the fact that today, nearly two-thirds (62%) of the adult labor force has at least some college experience, and an alleged skills gap fails to be convincing as a driving force behind persistent high unemployment.

LABOR MARKET MUSICAL CHAIRS

To understand the data discussed here, try picturing the U.S. labor market as a game of musical chairs, with a few twists. At any time, chairs (job openings) can be added to the circle and players can sit down (get hired). When the music stops at the end of the month, not all the chairs are filled. Still, many people—far more people than the number of empty chairs—are left standing.

Each month, the Bureau of Labor Statistics reports on what happened in that month's game of labor market musical chairs in its various measures of unemployment and in the Job Openings and Labor Turnover Survey (JOLTS). Here's how the BLS scorecard for labor market musical chairs works.

- **Job openings** is a snapshot of the number of jobs available on the last day of the month—the number of empty chairs when the music stops.

- **Hires** are all the new additions to payroll during the month—the number of people who found a chair to sit in while the music was playing. Because many chairs are added to the circle and filled within the same month, the number of hires over a month is typically greater than the number of openings available on the last day of that month.

- **Unemployed person**s are those who looked for a job that month but couldn't find one—the number of people who played the game but were left standing when the music stopped at the end of the month.

Low-Skill Workers?

If employers were having a hard time finding qualified workers to fill job openings, you'd think that any workers who are qualified would be snapped right up. But what the unemployment data show is that there remains a substantial backlog of experienced workers looking for jobs or for more hours in their existing part-time jobs in those major industries that have begun hiring—including education, healthcare, durable goods manufacturing, and mining.

Most telling are the *underemployed*—those with part-time jobs who want to work full-time. Today there are more underemployed workers in each of the major industries of the private economy than during the period from 2000 to 2007, as Arjun Jayadev and Mike Konczal document in a recent paper published by the Roosevelt Institute. Even in the major industries with the highest number of job openings—education and health services, professional and business services, transportation and utilities, leisure and hospitality, and manufacturing—underemployment in 2010 remains at levels twice as high or nearly twice as high as during the earlier period (measured as a percentage of employed workers).

Purveyors of the mismatch theory would have a hard time explaining how it is that underemployed workers who want full-time work do not possess the skills to do the jobs full time that they are already doing, say, 20 hours a week.

More broadly, workers with a diverse set of skills—not just construction workers—lost jobs during the Great Recession. Workers in manufacturing, professional and business services, leisure and hospitality, transportation and utilities, and a host of other industries were turned out of their jobs. And many of these experienced workers are still looking for work. In each of the 16 major industries of the economy unemployment rates in September 2010 were still far higher than they had been at the onset of the Great Recession in December 2007. In the industries with a large number of (cumulative) job openings during the recovery—education and health services, professional and business services, and manufacturing—experienced workers face unemployment rates twice what they were back in December 2007.

There are plenty of experienced workers still looking for work in the industries with job openings. To be faithful to the data, Kocherlakota and the other mismatch proponents would need to show that experienced workers no longer possess the skills to work in their industry, even though that industry employed them no more than three years ago. That seems implausible.

Statistical Errors

Still, the statistical oddity that Bill Clinton and many economists have pointed to does seem to complicate the picture. If the number of job openings is rising at a good clip yet the number of new hires is growing more slowly and the unemployment rate is stagnant, then maybe employers *are* having trouble finding qualified folks to hire.

Once you take a closer looks at the numbers, though, there is less here than meets the eye.

First, the *rate* at which job openings and new hires numbers change over time is not the right place to look. What we really need to know is how the number of unfilled job posts compares to the number of qualified workers employers hire over the same month. If employers in today's recovery are having a hard time finding workers, then the job openings left unfilled at the end of the month should be relatively high compared to the number of newly hired workers that month. In other words, if the number of positions left unfilled at the end of the month relative to the number of new hires rises *above* what we've seen during past recoveries, this would mean that employers are finding it harder to fill their positions with the right workers this time around.

But it turns out that the ratio of unfilled job openings to new hires is approximately the same during this recovery as in the recovery from the 2001 recession. In September 2010, fifteen months into the current economic recovery, the ratio of job posts left unoccupied at the end of the month to the number of monthly new hires stood at 69%—very close to its 67% level in February 2003, fifteen months into the last recovery. In other words, today's employers are filling their job openings with the same rate of success as yesterday's employers.

Comparisons that focus on the unemployment rate rather than on the number of new hires are even less meaningful. As hiring picks up at the beginning of an economic recovery, workers who had given up the job search start looking again. This brings them back into the official count of the unemployed, keeping the unemployment rate from dropping even as both job openings and new hires rise.

WHERE MISMATCHES MAY MATTER

The skills-mismatch theory does not go very far toward explaining stubbornly high U.S. unemployment. Still, there are unquestionably some unemployed and underemployed workers whose job prospects are limited by "structural" factors.

One kind of structural unemployment that does seem to fit the contours of the Great Recession to at least some degree is that caused by a mismatch of geography: the workers are in one part of the country while the jobs they could get are in another. The housing crisis surely has compromised the ability of unemployed workers to unload their single largest asset, a house, and move to another part of the country. Plus, job losses have been particularly heavy in regions where the housing crisis hit hardest.

But at the same time, lost jobs have been widespread across industries and there is little real evidence of geographic mismatch between job openings and unemployed workers. As labor economist Michael Reich reports, "economic decline and the growth of unemployment have been more widespread than ever before, making it unclear where the unemployed should migrate for greater job opportunities."

Even where there is a skills mismatch, that doesn't mean the government shouldn't get involved. On the contrary, government policies to boost economic demand can help significantly. When demand is high, labor markets become very tight and there are few available workers to hire. Workers previously viewed as "unemployable" get hired, get experience and on-the-job training, and see their overall career prospects brighten.

And, of course, government can fund expanded job-training programs. If the economy continues to slog along with low growth rates and persistent unemployment, the ranks of the long-term unemployed will rise. As they go longer and longer without work, their skills will atrophy or become obsolete and they will face a genuine skills-mismatch problem that will make job-training programs more and more necessary.

Not Enough Jobs

The reality of the situation—the widespread job losses and the long, fruitless job searches of experienced workers—make it clear that today's employment problem is a jobs deficit across the economy, not a skills deficit among those looking for work.

While it's true that any given month ends with some number of unfilled job openings, the total number of jobs added to the economy during this recovery has simply been inadequate to put the unemployed back to work. In fact, if every job that stood open at the end of September 2010 had been filled, 11.7 million officially unemployed workers would still have been jobless.

This recovery has seen far fewer job openings than even the so-called "jobless" re-covery following the 2001 recession. Economists Lawrence Mishel, Heidi Shierholz, and Kathryn Edwards of the Economic Policy Institute report that cumulative job open-ings during the first year of this recovery were roughly 25% lower than during the first year of the recovery following the 2001 recession—that's 10 million fewer jobs. Even in the industries generating the most job openings in the current recovery—education and health services, professional and business services, leisure and hospitality, and manufac-turing—the cumulative number of job openings has lagged well behind the figure for those industries during the first year of the recovery from the 2001 recession. (Only the mining and logging category, which accounted for just 0.5% of employment in 2007, has had more job openings during the first year of this recovery than during the first year of the 2001 recovery.)

Why has the pick-up in jobs following the Great Recession been worse than usual? The simple answer is that the recession was worse than usual. The sharp and extreme decline of output and employment in the Great Recession has severely dampened de-mand—that is, people have not had money to buy things. With the resulting lack of sales, businesses were not willing to either invest or hire; and this in turn has meant a continuing lack of demand.

If businesses have barely resumed hiring, it has not been for lack of profits. By the middle of 2010, corporate profits (adjusted for inflation) were about 60% above their low point at the end of 2008, well on their way back to the peak level of mid-2006. Also, in early 2010 non-financial firms were sitting on almost $2 trillion in cash. There was no lack of ability to invest and hire, but there was a lack of incentive to invest and hire, that is, a lack of an expectation that demand (sales) would rise. As is well known, small busi-nesses have generally accounted for a disproportionately large share of job growth. Yet, since the onset of the Great Recession, small business owners have consistently identified poor sales as their single most important problem—and thus, presumably, what has pre-vented them from expanding employment.

The Role of Demand

Regardless of the lack of evidence to support it, the skills-mismatch story has seeped into media coverage of the economy. Take, for example, National Public Radio's re-cent Morning Edition series titled "Skills gap: holding back the labor market." In one segment, reporter Wendy Kaufman presents anecdotes about employers turning down record numbers of applicants and leaving job openings unfilled. Economist Peter Capelli then comes on and remarks, "You know, a generation ago you'd never expect that somebody could come into a reasonably skilled, sophisticated position in your organization and immediately make a contribution. That's a brand new demand." Now, that comment does not point to today's workers possessing fewer skills or qualifications. Rather, it suggests that employers have raised the bar: they are pickier than in the past.

That makes sense. We've seen that employers are successfully filling positions at about the same rate as in the recent past. What's different this time around is that employers have had up to six unemployed workers competing for every job opening left vacant at the close of the month. This is by far the highest ratio on record with data back to 2000. During the 2001 recession, that ratio rose to just over two unemployed workers for each opening. (In the first years of the "jobless recovery" following the 2001 recession, the ratio continued to rise, but it remained below three to one.) Clearly, these numbers favor the alternative explanation. Unfortunately, Kaufman doesn't even consider it.

That's too bad. Recognizing that a lack of demand for goods and services is to blame for the severe crisis of unemployment puts the focus squarely back on the federal government and on the Fed, which could help to remedy the problem —*if* they had the political will to do so. Millions of unemployed workers, organized and armed with an accurate diagnosis of the problem, could create that political will— unless they are distracted by a wrong-headed diagnosis that tries to blame them for the problem.

Sources: Bureau of Labor Statistics Table A-14, Unemployed persons by industry and class of workers, not seasonally adjusted, historical data (bls.gov); Lawrence Mishel, Heidi Shierholz, and Kathryn Anne Edwards, "Reasons for Skepticism About Structural Unemployment," Economic Policy Institute, Briefing Paper #279, September 22, 2010 (epi.org); Arjun Jayadev and Mike Konczal, "The Stagnating Labor Market," The Roosevelt Institute, September 19, 2010 (rooseveltinstitute. org); Bureau of Labor Statistics, Job Openings and Labor Turnover (JOLTS) Highlights, September 2010 (bls.gov); Michael Reich, "High Unemployment after the Great Recession: Why? What Can We Do?," Policy Brief from the Center on Wage and Employment Dynamics, Institute for Research on Labor and Employment, University of California, Berkeley, June 2010 (irle.berkeley.edu/cwed); Narayana Kocherlakota, President Federal Reserve Bank of Minneapolis, "Inside the FOMC," Marquette, Michigan, August 17, 2010 (minneapolisfed.org); Lawrence Mishel and Katherine Anne Edwards, "Bill Clinton Gets It Wrong," Economic Policy Institute, Economic Snapshot, September 27, 2010 (epi.org); "Remarks of President Barack Obama—Address to Joint Session of Congress," February 24, 2009 (whitehouse.gov); "The Skills Gap: Holding Back the Labor Market," Morning Edition, National Public Radio, November 15, 2010 (npr.org).

Article 6.5

HOW BLACKS MIGHT FARE IN THE JOBLESS RECOVERY

BY SYLVIA ALLEGRETTO AND STEVEN PITTS

October 2010

There have been seemingly contradictory announcements recently concerning the economy. In September another 95,000 jobs were shed as the official unemployment rate remained at 9.6%. Unemployment has been at 9.5% or higher for well over a year now. About the same time this bad news about employment came out, it was announced that the recession, which began in December 2007, had actually ended in June of 2009—thus we are several months into the second year of recovery.

How could the recession be over, even amidst continued job losses and stubbornly high unemployment? And how might black workers, whose levels of unemployment have (as usual) been much higher than white workers' in this recession, fare in a "jobless recovery"?

The Dating of the Business Cycle

The task of officially declaring the start and end dates of recessions is performed by the Business Cycle Dating Committee of the National Bureau of Economic Research. The Committee is currently comprised of seven economists (an eighth is on leave) from prominent universities. The Committee examines the data trends of several economic indicators, including measures of:

- Overall output
- Overall national income
- Total employment
- Aggregate hours worked

The Committee did not say that the economy had returned to its pre-recession level of activity or that the economy was strong; it just stated that the decline in several economic measures that began in December 2007 had ended and any new decline in economic activity would represent a new recession. That the economy is not officially in recession does not mean that it doesn't feel as if it is for many workers and their families. There is often not a palpable difference between a recessionary economy and a weak recovery—this is especially true with what are called "jobless recoveries."

What Is Meant by a "Jobless Recovery"?

An economy officially in recovery that continues to shed jobs as if in recession, or experiences prolonged tepid job growth, is deemed a "jobless recovery." In a jobless recovery it takes an inordinate amount of time to recoup the jobs lost during the downturn. While the recession officially ended in June 2009, the employment picture remains quite dismal. At the lowest point for jobs, in December 2009, 8.4 million jobs were lost, which represented 6.1% of all jobs. To date job losses are still at 7.7 million, which represents 5.6% of all jobs. Since the onset of recovery, the monthly employment reports have been mixed, but the net employment level has fallen by an additional 439,000.

Figure 1 depicts the dynamics of recessionary job losses and jobless recoveries. Each line represents the trajectory of job growth from the onset of recession until jobs were finally recouped (when the line crosses the horizontal axis—which represents months since the onset of recession). The solid black line represents average job losses for recessions prior to 1990. (On average the pre-1990 recessions were about eleven months long and it took about 21 months to recoup pre-recessionary job level.)

Job losses due to the 1990 recession (the solid gray line) were just about 1.5%—quite shallow comparatively and the recession was officially just eight months long. But employment lingered at the trough for a long time and it took about 31 months to recoup those lost jobs. The downturn in 2001 (dotted black line) was also eight months long and about 2% of jobs were lost—again relatively mild—but it took 46 months to recoup those lost jobs.

It is clear from the figure that the recession that started in December 2007 (dotted gray line) led to a reduction in employment that far exceeded that of the previous recessions. This recession was 18 months long and ended in June 2009. Job losses were catastrophic. At its worst point jobs were down 8.4 million. Job growth turned positive in the spring of 2010—mostly due to the temporary hiring of Census workers. But shortly after Census workers were hired they were let go, and job growth once again turned negative. At this point it is clear that the labor market is in the realm of a jobless recovery—a prolonged period of negative or weak job growth. It will be a very long time before this economy recoups the enormous amount of jobs lost over this recession.

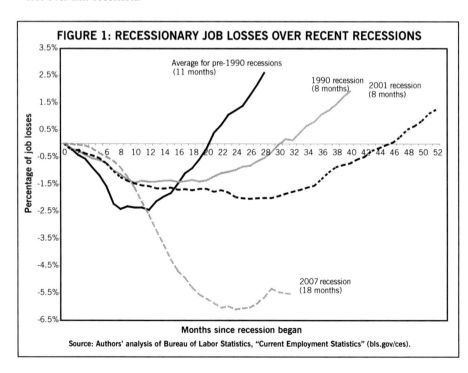

FIGURE 1: RECESSIONARY JOB LOSSES OVER RECENT RECESSIONS

Average for pre-1990 recessions (11 months)

1990 recession (8 months)

2001 recession (8 months)

2007 recession (18 months)

Percentage of job losses

Months since recession began

Source: Authors' analysis of Bureau of Labor Statistics, "Current Employment Statistics" (bls.gov/ces).

How Might Blacks Fare During a Jobless Recovery?

While it is difficult to predict exactly what might happen to black workers during this jobless recovery, it is instructive to examine what happened to black unemployment during the last jobless recovery, which followed the 2001 recession. Chart 2 provides key information.

The gray bars in the chart mark key dates of the last two recessions and recoveries. In examining the trend in black unemployment since the 2001 recession, there are six key dates:

- The beginning of the recession (March 2001)
- The official end of the recession (November 2001)
- When job creation turned positive (September 2003)
- When the employment levels returned to pre-recession level (January 2005)
- The beginning of recession (December 2007)
- The official end of the recession (June 2009)

As Figure 2 indicates, unemployment rates continued to rise after the official end of the recession in November 2001. Over the jobless recovery—from November 2001 to September 2003—unemployment increased from 9.8% to 11% for blacks and 4.9% to 5.4% for whites. Black unemployment rates did not begin to steadily fall until the total number of jobs had reached the pre-recession level (January 2005). The unemployment rates for whites started to fall just prior to September 2003—near the end of the jobless recovery.

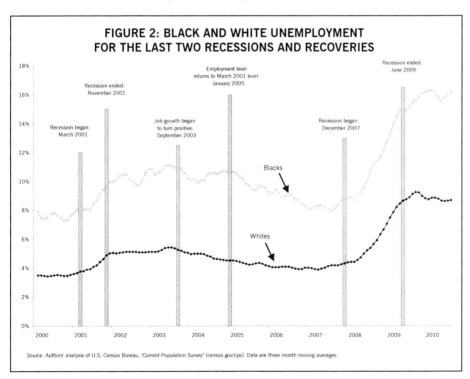

FIGURE 2: BLACK AND WHITE UNEMPLOYMENT FOR THE LAST TWO RECESSIONS AND RECOVERIES

Source: Authors' analysis of U.S. Census Bureau, "Current Population Survey" (census.gov/cps). Data are three month moving averages.

Starting with the onset of the 2007 recession, again the black unemployment rate increased at a faster rate than did that of whites. Since the onset of recovery—in June 2009—the unemployment rate of blacks has increased by 1.4 percentage points, from 14.8% to 16.2%. The rate for whites at the start of recovery was 8.7%, and after an initial increase it is back to that same rate today.

If the 2001 pattern holds, it may well be that the current black unemployment rates will not begin to significantly abate until the employment level returns to its pre-recessionary level of December 2007. This will almost certainly take several years as the shortfall in jobs is currently at 7.7 million. In order to return the national unemployment rate to its December 2007 rate, the economy would need to create 290,000 jobs per month for five years; so far this year job creation has averaged 68,000 per month, even as the last four months have averaged -98,000.

In other words, for many black workers and their families, the recovery will continue to feel like a deep recession for many years to come.

Resources: Bureau of Labor Statistics, "Current Employment Statistics" (bls.gov/ces); National Bureau of Economic Research, "The NBER's Business Cycle Dating Committee" (nber.org/cycles/recessions.html and nber.org/cycles/sept2010.html).

Article 6.6

CREATING DECENT JOBS: THE ROLE OF UNIONS

BY JEANNETTE WICKS-LIM
January/February 2010

The turmoil of the current recession is deflecting attention from a longer-term challenge facing the U.S. economy: how to create decent jobs. Even before the recession, nearly two-thirds of U.S. jobs failed the "decent job" test—they paid too little to cover a small family's basic needs. Between now and 2016, the strongest job growth will be largely in low-pay occupations, according to Department of Labor projections. So barring any structural changes, the U.S. economy will be no better at producing jobs that can support a worker and his or her family at a very basic living standard in 2016 than it was in 2006.

Collective bargaining through labor unions could brighten this forecast, raising the quality of future jobs even if the economy continues to produce the same types of jobs. Bringing the unionized share of the U.S. workforce back up to around its level in the 1970s—admittedly no easy task—would lift an estimated 2.5 million additional jobs over the decent-job threshold in 2016.

A reasonable definition of a decent job is one with the minimum pay and benefits necessary to provide a healthy and safe standard of living for a small family. This benchmark is substantially above the U.S. Census Bureau's official poverty threshold, widely viewed as far too low. Based on very basic family budgets the Economic Policy Institute has developed, a decent job has to pay at least $17 an hour with health and retirement benefits, or $22 an hour without.

A recent Labor Department report examines trends through 2006 to predict the jobs picture in 2016. Here are the ten occupations slated to add the most jobs: orderlies and nursing/home-health aides; registered nurses; retail salespersons; customer service representatives; food preparation and serving workers; general office clerks; personal/home-care aides; postsecondary teachers; janitors; and accounting clerks. In only two—RNs and postsecondary teachers—do the majority of existing jobs meet the decent job standard. The other eight fall short.

It's no surprise, then, that an analysis of the complete 2016 jobs projection shows little change in the overall proportion of decent jobs. By my estimates, in 2016 some 35.2% of all jobs will meet this standard, barely changed from the 2006 figure of 34.8%. These projections pre-date the current recession, and so reveal a long-term problem likely to persist well after the economy revives.

If we cannot count on a raft of novel, more lucrative occupations in the next several years, then expanding the number of decent jobs will require improving the compensation of jobs in existing occupations. Unions enable workers to do exactly that. Suppose union representation rose by a meaningful amount, say 10 percentage points to about 24%, by 2016. The proportion of decent jobs in 2016 would rise by an estimated 1.5 percentage points to 36.7%, representing an additional 2.5 million decent jobs. This is four times the projected increase if union representation levels remain the same.

But what about globalization? Forget about more decent jobs—how can U.S. workers stop decent jobs from disappearing in an increasingly integrated world economy with a large supply of labor that is cheaper than any in the United States, whether unionized or not?

One answer is to focus on jobs that are not off-shore-able and on sectors in which U.S.-based firms have a competitive edge. Clean energy initiatives fit the bill: they involve activities that can only be done locally such as retrofitting buildings, plus, renewable energy is an area where U.S.-based firms' technological edge counts.

This strategy has another potential benefit for workers: greater international solidarity. By reducing the pressure they face from the global "race to the bottom," robust clean-energy job growth would better position U.S. workers to focus on cross-border organizing that can raise the floor of the global labor market.

What would it take to bring an additional 10% of U.S. workers into unions? That is the subject of another article. But the fact that the Employee Free Choice Act, which would make it easier for workers to join unions, is under serious consideration in Congress gives reason for hope. Any policies that expand opportunities for workers to join unions would help ensure that employment growth in the coming years produces decent jobs.

Sources: *Creating Decent Jobs in the United States: The Role of Labor Unions and Collective Bargaining*, peri.umass.edu; Constance F. Citro and Robert T. Michael, eds., *Measuring Poverty: A New Approach*, National Academy Press, 1995; Arlene Dohm and Lyn Shniper, "Employment outlook 2006-2016: Occupational employment projections to 2016," *Monthly Labor Review*, Nov. 2007; David Howell, Dean Baker, Andrew Glyn, and John Schmitt, "Are Protective Labor Market Institutions at the Root of Unemployment? A Critical Review of the Evidence," *Capitalism and Society* 2(1), 2007; James Heckman, "Comments on 'Are Protective Labor Market Institutions at the Root of Unemployment? A Critical Review of the Evidence'," *Capitalism and Society* (2)1, 2007; James Lin and Jared Bernstein, What We Need To Get By, Economic Policy Institute, 2008.

Article 6.7

THE RELATIONSHIP OF UNEMPLOYMENT AND INFLATION

BY RAMAA VASUDEVAN

September/October 2006

Dear Dr. Dollar:

Back in first-year economics we learned that there is a tradeoff between un-employment and inflation, so you can't really have both low inflation and low unemployment at the same time. Do economists still consider that to be true?
—Edith Bross, Cambridge, Mass.

The trade-off between inflation and unemployment was first reported by A. W. Phillips in 1958—and so has been christened the Phillips curve. The simple intuition behind this trade-off is that as unemployment falls, workers are empowered to push for higher wages. Firms try to pass these higher wage costs on to consumers, resulting in higher prices and an inflationary buildup in the economy. The trade-off suggested by the Phillips curve implies that policymakers can target low inflation rates or low unemployment, but not both. During the 1960s, monetarists emphasized price stability (low inflation), while Keynesians more often emphasized job creation.

The experience of so-called stagflation in the 1970s, with simultaneously high rates of both inflation and unemployment, began to discredit the idea of a stable trade-off between the two. In place of the Phillips curve, many economists began to posit a "natural rate of unemployment." If unemployment were to fall below this "natural" rate, however slightly, inflation would begin to accelerate. Under the "natural rate of unemployment" theory (also called the Non-Accelerating Inflation Rate of Unemployment, or NAIRU), instead of choosing between higher unemployment and higher inflation, policymakers were told to focus on ensuring that the economy remained at its "natural" rate: the challenge was to accurately estimate its level and to steer the economy toward growth rates that maintain price stability, no matter what the corresponding level of unemployment.

The NAIRU has been extremely difficult to pin down in practice. Not only are estimates of it notoriously imprecise, the rate itself evidently changes over time. In the United States, estimates of the NAIRU rose from about 4.4% in the 1960s, to 6.2% in the 1970s, and further to 7.2% in the 1980s. This trend reversed itself in the 1990s, as officially reported unemployment fell. In the latter half of the 1990s, U.S. inflation remained nearly dormant at around 3%, while unemployment fell to around 4.6%. In the later Clinton years many economists warned that if unemployment was brought any lower, inflationary pressures might spin out of control. But growth in these years did not spill over into accelerating inflation. The United States, apparently, had achieved the Goldilocks state—everything just right!

What sustained this combination of low inflation and low unemployment? Explanations abound: a productivity boom, the high rates of incarceration of those who would otherwise fall within the ranks of the unemployed, the openness of the U.S. economy to world trade and competition, among others.

The full story, however, has to do with class conflict and the relatively weak position of workers in the 1990s. Both the breakdown of the Phillips curve in the 1970s and the recent "disappearance" of the natural rate of unemployment are in essence a reflection of institutional and political changes that affect the bargaining strength of working people—in other words, their ability to organize effective unions and establish a decent living wage.

Following the Reagan offensive against trade unions, workers' power fell dramatically. Consequently, unionization rates and the real value of the minimum wage each fell precipitously between the late 1970s and the 1990s. The period of stagflation, in contrast, had been one of labor militancy and rising wages. (Although "stagflation" has a negative ring, by many measures nonsupervisory workers—i.e., the vast majority of the U.S. labor force—fared better in the economy of the early- to mid-1970s than they do today, even after the long 1990s economic expansion.) Labor's weaker position in the 1990s meant that despite low unemployment, workers were not able to win higher wages that would have spurred inflation.

The long period of stable prices and low interest rates in the United States now seems to be coming to a close. The cost of the Iraq War and rising oil prices, among other factors, have fueled expectations of a resurgence of inflation. At the same time, the near jobless recovery from the last recession might suggest that the "natural rate" of unemployment is on the rise again—and that we are witnessing yet another twist in the strange history of the Phillips curve!

With inflation rising (albeit slowly, and still relatively mild at around 4.2%), some business sectors will no doubt begin clamoring for tighter monetary policies that sacrifice job-creation and wage growth by slowing the economy growth. But these fears of inflation are probably misplaced. A moderate rate of inflation is conducive to the growth of real investment, and in the context of a decades-long squeeze on workers' wage share, there is room to expand employment without setting off a wage-price spiral. What workers need is not greater fiscal and monetary austerity, but rather a revival of a Keynesian program of "employment targeting" that would sustain full employment and empower workers to push for higher wages. It's not likely, however, that the owners of capital and their political allies would sit idly by were such a program to be enacted.

Article 6.8

HOT COMMODITIES, STUFFED MARKETS, AND EMPTY BELLIES

What's behind higher food prices?

BY BEN COLLINS
July/August 2008

Since 2003, prices of basic agricultural commodities such as corn, wheat, soybeans, and rice have skyrocketed worldwide, threatening to further impoverish hundreds of millions of the world's poor.

Shifts in fundamental supply and demand factors for food grains have undoubtedly contributed to higher food prices. Prominent among these shifts are the increasing diversion of food crops for biofuel production in the United States and Europe; sustained drought and water scarcity in Australia's wheat-growing regions; flooding in the U.S. grain belt; rising prices for oil and fertilizer worldwide; and the adoption of European and American meat-rich diets by the growing middle classes throughout Asia.

On top of these recent developments, long-term threats to worldwide agricultural output have eroded the world food system's resilience in the face of changing supply and demand. Although decades in the making, a loss of agricultural capacity worldwide caused by soil depletion, climate change, water scarcity, and urbanization has begun to take its toll on food production. Moreover, half a century of import restrictions and cheap agricultural exports by wealthy countries has devastated domestic food production capacity in poorer countries, forcing many countries that were once self-sufficient to rely on imported food from the world market.

At the same time, however, the growing presence of buy-and-hold investors in commodity markets has prompted heated debate among commodity traders, economists, and politicians over other possible causes of higher commodity prices apart from supply and demand shifts.

Since 2001, the declining value of the U.S. dollar, low U.S. interest rates, weak stock market returns, and accelerating inflation have drawn investment dollars away from stocks and into non-traditional investments such as commodities. This flight to perceived safety in commodity markets turned into a stampede in 2007 and early 2008, as a credit-induced financial crisis in the United States compounded these existing stresses on global financial markets.

Rising commodity prices and financial speculation on food are not new phenomena. The 1970s saw a similar rise in commodity prices in the United States, and in the 1920s, U.S. investors formed commodity pools to bet on commodity price movements. But the quantity and liquidity of money flowing through today's global markets is unprecedented in history. The current commodities boom could be a sign of looming agricultural scarcity, or it may prove to be a short-lived speculative bubble that will deflate over the next few months or years. But regardless of where agricultural commodity prices are headed, the boom has already begun to transform how food is financed, grown, and sold, and may dramatically change how people around the world eat (or don't).

Commodity Investment Goes Retail

Commodity exchanges exist as a mechanism for the producers and consumers of grains, energy, and livestock to transfer risk to financial institutions and other traders. For example, wheat farmers might seek to reduce the risk of price fluctuations by selling a contract for the future delivery of their wheat crop on a commodity exchange. This futures contract will guarantee a price for the farmer selling the contract, enabling them to pay for their planting costs, and avoid the risk that the price of wheat may decrease between the date they sell the contract and the date they agree to deliver the wheat. Food giants such as Kraft and Nabisco, as well as smaller bakers and grain consumers, typically purchase commodity futures contracts to avoid the opposite risk—that the price of their raw materials may increase in the future. (Commodity markets also trade "spot" contracts, which entitle the purchaser to the immediate delivery of a commodity.)

Because producers and consumers seek to reduce risk, they function as so-called hedgers in commodity markets. In contrast, commercial trading firms and other speculators bet on the price of a commodity rising or falling, buying and selling futures contracts frequently in order to profit from short-term changes in their prices.

Since 2001, commodity funds have gained in popularity as a mechanism for institutions and individuals to profit from increases in commodity prices. These funds purchase commodity futures contracts in order to simulate ownership of a commodity. By periodically rolling over commodity futures contracts prior to their maturity date and reinvesting the proceeds in new contracts, the funds allow investors to gain investment returns equivalent to the change in price of a single commodity, or an "index" of several commodities (hence the name "index investor").

Investors in these commodity index funds include public pension funds, university endowments, and even individual investors, through mutual funds, for example. Although these investors are similar to traditional commodity speculators in that both seek to profit from changes in price, traditional speculators zero in on short-term price shifts, while index investors are almost exclusively long-term buyers betting on higher commodity prices in the future.

Some observers have argued that index investors themselves may have pushed already-high prices of commodities even higher. Hedge fund manager Michael Masters testified to the U.S. Senate that the total holdings of commodity index investors on regulated U.S. exchanges have increased from $13 billion in 2003 to nearly $260 billion as of March 2008. And as of April 2008, index investors owned approximately 35% of all corn futures contracts on regulated exchanges in the United States, 42% of all soybean contracts, and 64% of all wheat contracts, compared to minimal holdings in 2001. As Masters emphasized, these are immense commodity holdings. The wheat contracts, for example, are good for the delivery of 1.3 billion bushels of wheat, equivalent to twice the United States' annual wheat consumption.

Index fund managers have defended against charges that commodity index investment contributes to higher prices, arguing that because index funds never take delivery on their futures contracts, they simulate commodity price shifts for their investors without affecting the price of the underlying commodity. Some economists have also expressed skepticism that investment demand has driven commodity prices higher. Paul Krugman of Princeton University has noted that there is no evidence of "the usual telltale signs of a speculative price boom" such as physical hoarding of commodities. Furthermore, Krugman and others have pointed to non-exchange traded commodities such as iron ore that have also experienced rapid price increases during recent years, arguing that fundamental supply and demand factors, not investors, are to blame for higher commodity prices.

Other economists and commodity market observers have argued that despite price increases in non-exchange traded commodities, and an absence of physical hoarding, the recent flood of money into commodity markets has altered the balance between speculators and hedgers, leading to higher prices and greater price volatility. Mack Frankfurter, a commodities trading advisor at Cervino Capital Management, suggests that the influx of commodity index investors has transformed commodity futures from tools for risk management to long-term investments, "causing a self-perpetuating feedback loop of ever higher prices."

One reason the precise impact of index investors on commodity prices is difficult to determine is that the U.S. commodity trading regulator, the Commodity Futures Trading Commission (CFTC), does not collect data on so-called "over-the-counter" commodity trading—that is, trading on unregulated markets—even though the agency estimated that 85% of commodity index investment takes place on these markets. Because Masters's data on the holdings of commodity index investors only include the 15% of index investor contracts that are held on CFTC-regulated exchanges, total commodity index investor holdings may be much higher than his estimates.

In testimony that warned of the influence of these unregulated markets on commodity prices, Michael Greenberger, the former head of the CFTC's Division of Trading and Markets, estimated that if unregulated trading of energy and agricultural commodities were eliminated, the price of oil would drop by 25% to 50% "overnight." If Greenberger is correct, the effect on food commodity prices would likely be similar. However, index investment is just one of many avenues through which money can enter commodity markets, making it difficult to assess the impact of index investors without taking into account the recent deregulation of U.S. commodity markets that has facilitated the current boom in food and energy investments.

Commodity Trading Regulation, Enron-Style

Commodity index investment is deeply intertwined with the growth of unregulated commodity trading authorized by the Commodity Futures Modernization Act of 2000. Before 2000, U.S. commodity futures contracts were traded exclusively on regulated exchanges under the oversight of the CFTC. Traders were required to disclose their holdings of each commodity and adhere to strict position limits, which set a maximum number of futures contracts that an individual institution could hold. These regulations were intended to prevent market manipulation by traders who might otherwise attempt to build up concentrated holdings of futures contracts in order to manipulate the price of a commodity.

The 2000 law effectively deregulated commodity trading in the United States by exempting over-the-counter commodity trading outside of regulated exchanges from CFTC oversight. Soon after the bill was passed, several unregulated commodity exchanges opened for trading, allowing investors, hedge funds, and investment banks to trade commodities futures contracts without any position limits, disclosure requirements, or regulatory oversight. Since then, unregulated over-the-counter commodity trading has grown exponentially. The total value of all over-the-counter commodity contracts was estimated to be $9 trillion at the end of 2007, or nearly twice the value of the $4.78 trillion in commodity contracts traded on regulated U.S. exchanges.

Once these unregulated commodity markets were created, energy traders and hedge funds began to use them to place massive bets on commodity prices. Enron famously exploited deregulated electricity markets in 2001, when the firm managed to generate unheard-of profits by using its trading operations to effectively withhold electricity and charge extortionate rates from power grids in California and other western states.

Although Enron went bankrupt later that year, the hedge fund Amaranth later exploited unregulated natural gas markets prior to its 2006 collapse. The fund had been heavily invested in complicated bets on the price of natural gas, borrowing eight times its assets to trade natural gas futures, and lost $6.5 billion when natural gas prices moved in the wrong direction. One month prior to Amaranth's collapse, the New York Mercantile Exchange (NYMEX), which is regulated by the CFTC, asked Amaranth to reduce its huge natural gas position. Amaranth reduced its position at NYMEX's request, but purchased identical positions on the unregulated InterContinental Exchange, where its transactions were invisible to regulators until the fund finally collapsed.

Amaranth's implosion demonstrated the ineffectiveness of regulating some commodity exchanges but not others. Thanks to the Commodity Futures Modernization Act, traders could flout position limits and disclosure rules with impunity, simply by re-routing trades to unregulated exchanges. Although index investment in commodities does not typically involve white-knuckle, leveraged bets on a single commodity's short-term performance, index investment was made possible by the same deregulated environment exploited by Amaranth and Enron. Like Amaranth, commodity index investors commonly purchase futures contracts on unregulated markets when they exceed CFTC position limits on futures contracts for a particular commodity. And other financial actors such as investment banks, hedge funds, or even the sovereign wealth funds of other countries may also be heavily invested in these over-the-counter commodity contracts, but since this trading is unregulated and unreported, the holders of these $9 trillion worth of contracts remain anonymous.

This year, the CFTC has faced intense scrutiny from investors, politicians, farmers, and agricultural traders over the unprecedented volatility and price increases of several agricultural and energy commodities traded on U.S. exchanges. A lively CFTC roundtable on commodity markets in April appeared to confirm arguments made by Frankfurter, Greenberger, Masters, and other critics of commodity index investment. Representatives for farmers, grain elevator operators, and commercial bankers at the hearing repeatedly stressed that commodity markets were "broken," while the only pleas for calm came from CFTC economists and representatives for index investors and the financial industry. Unlike index investors, farmers have not benefited greatly from higher commodity prices, because extremely high levels of market volatility have made it difficult for some farmers to finance crop planting. National Farmers Union president Tom Buis sounded a particularly dire warning about the consequences of tight commodity supplies and burgeoning index investment demand: "We've got a train wreck coming in agriculture that's bigger than anything else we've seen."

Following these warnings from farmers and food producers about the presence of index investors in commodity markets, the CFTC's acting chair publicly acknowledged the ongoing debate over "whether the massive amount of money coming into the markets is overwhelming the system." Despite this admission, Greenberger, the former CFTC official, remains skeptical of the agency's capacity and willingness to regulate commodity markets effectively. He urged Congress and the Federal Trade Commission to circumvent the CFTC's authority and eliminate unregulated over-the-counter commodity trading. Recently, faced with strong criticism from Congress, the CFTC retreated further from its claim that commodity markets are functioning normally. A CFTC commissioner admitted: "We didn't have the data that we needed to make the statements that we made, and the data we did have didn't support our declarative statements. If we were so right, why the heck are we doing a study now?"

The Consequences of Financializing Food

Facing political pressure by constituents over high oil and food prices, several members of Congress have sponsored legislation that would bar index investors from commodity markets. One bill proposed by Sen. Joseph Lieberman (Ind-Conn.) would prohibit public and private pension funds with more than $500 million in assets from trading in commodity futures, and other bills would limit the maximum number of futures contracts an index investor could hold. These bills may stem the flood of money from index investors into commodities, but comprehensive reform is needed to reverse the Commodity Futures Modernization Act's authorization of over-the-counter commodity trading. Absent an outright repeal of this so-called "Enron loophole," energy and agricultural commodities will continue to be traded outside the reach of government regulation, making future Enron- and Amaranth-style market disruptions inevitable.

Ultimately, eliminating unregulated commodity trading cannot address the fundamental causes of higher agricultural prices. Even if speculative buying is curtailed, supply and demand factors such as falling crop yields, destructive trade policies, and the growing use of biofuels have likely brought the age of cheap food to an end. However, if the critics of commodity index investment are correct, then these investors have amplified recent food price shocks and are needlessly contributing to the impoverishment of the world's poorest citizens. Even though commodity market transparency and regulatory oversight will not solve the global food crisis, eliminating unregulated commodity trading can help resolve the debate over the effects of index investors on commodity prices and restore the accountability of commodity markets to the social interests they were originally established to serve.

Sources: Michael Masters, testimony before the Committee on Homeland Security and Government Affairs, United States Senate, May 20, 2008; Daniel P. Collins, "CFTC to up spec limits," *Futures,* May 1, 2005; Paul Krugman, "Fuels on the Hill," *New York Times,* June 27, 2008; Michael Frankfurter, *The Mysterious Case of the Commodity Conundrum, Securitization of Commodities, and Systemic Concerns,* Parts 1-3, www.marketoracle.co.uk; Michael Frankfurter and Davide Accomazzo, "Is Managed Futures an Asset Class? The Search for the Beta of Commodity Futures," December 31, 2007, *Graziadio Business Report*; "Regulator Admits to Futures Tracking Volatility," Associated Press, June 4, 2008; Commodity Futures Trading Commission, *CFTC Announces Agricultural Market Initiatives.* June 3, 2008; Michael Greenberger, testimony before the Committee on Commerce, Science, and Transportation, United States Senate, June 3, 2008; Sinclair Stewart and Paul Waldie. "Who is responsible for the global food crisis?" *Globe and Mail,* May 30, 2008; Commodity Futures Trading Commission, *Agricultural Markets Roundtable,* April 22, 2008; Ann Davis, "Commodities Regulator Under Fire—CFTC Scrutinized As Congress Looks Into Oil-Price Jump," *Wall Street Journal,* July 7, 2008; Ed Wallace, "ICE, ICE, Baby," *Houston Chronicle,* May 19, 2008; Laura Mandaro, "Lieberman plans would bar funds from commodities," *Marketwatch,* June 18, 2008; "Our Confusing Economy, Explained," *Fresh Air,* April 3, 2008, www.npr.org.

Chapter 7

PERSPECTIVES ON MACROECONOMIC POLICY

INTRODUCTION

A few years back, political economist Bob Sutcliffe developed a sure-fire economic indicator that he called the Marx/Keynes ratio—the ratio of references to Karl Marx to references to John Maynard Keynes in Paul Samuelson's *Economics*, the best-selling introductory economics textbook during the decades following World War II. In a recession or a period of sluggish economic growth, the Marx/Keynes ratio would climb, as social commentators and even economists fretted over the future of capitalism. In economic booms, however, Marx's predictions of the collapse of capitalism disappeared from the pages of Samuelson's textbook, while the paeans to Keynesian demand-management policies multiplied.

Today Sutcliffe's ratio wouldn't work very well. Marx has been pushed off the pages of most introductory macroeconomics textbooks altogether, and even Keynes has been given only a minor role. Mainstream textbooks now favor the "New Classical" economics, which depicts the private economy as inherently stable and self-regulating, and dismiss Keynesian demand-management policies as ineffectual or counterproductive. Our authors disagree. In this chapter, they reintroduce schools of thought that have been removed from economics textbooks in recent decades and critically assess New Classical economics. And they offer a critical assessment of the forces that brought on the economic crisis of 2008 and 2009 and what to do about it.

John Miller and Gina Neff start with a down-to-earth account of New Classical "rational expectations" models, in which markets clear instantaneously and bungling government bureaucrats can only make a mess of things. Drawing on the writings of Keynesian and New Keynesian economists, Miller and Neff argue that rational expectations models are contradicted by the historical record, which shows that bigger government has brought milder, not more severe, business cycle fluctuations (Article 7.1).

Robert Pollin (Article 7.2) attacks the underpinnings of the neoliberal policy prescription for the global economy. As he sees it, the unfettered globalization of free markets will be unable to resolve three basic problems: an ever-larger reserve army of the unemployed that reduces the bargaining power of workers in all countries (the Marx problem); the inherent instability and volatility of investment and financial markets (the Keynes problem); and the erosion of the protections of the welfare state (the Polanyi problem).

Alejandro Reuss takes a close look at what Keynes actually had to say about the efficacy of fiscal policy in his most famous book, *The General Theory of Employment, Interest and Money*. Keynes was a strong advocate of fiscal policy, especially government spending. Reuss explains how Keynes challenged the "Treasury view" that government spending could not get the economy going because it would "crowd out" private investment, the same argument today's conservatives have invoked against the Obama stimulus package (Article 7.3).

Reuss also contributes a primer on Marxist economics. Marx rejected the idea of a self-equilibrating economy, and argued that capitalism was inherently dynamic and unstable. Reuss describes some of Marx's key ideas, including the nature of capitalist exploitation, and what Marx saw as two ingredients of an eventual crisis of capitalism: overproduction and the falling rate of profit (Article 7.6).

Randy Albelda offers a feminist analysis of poverty and gender. Feminist economists have illuminated the ways in which having and caring for children alters the economic status of women—including those who are not mothers but are still relegated to poorly paid care-giving jobs. Feminist economists, argues Albelda, provide the best understanding of the obstacles low-income families face and the options that might improve their position in today's economy (Article 7.7).

The other two articles in the chapter examine the recent financial and economic crisis through the wider lens offered by a political-economy perspective. Arthur MacEwan identifies three root causes of the crisis—growing economic and social power in the hands of the wealthy, free-market ideology, and rising inequality. He argues that addressing these factors through expanded social programs, stronger unions, and market regulation are all crucial steps to making the economy more egalitarian, and will go a long way toward resolving capitalism's current problems (Article 7.4). Economist James Cypher argues that while Keynesian demand management put a floor under the Great Recession, more needs to be done to get the economy going again. Drawing on the work of Depression-era economist Irving Fisher, Cypher argues that millions of middle-class and poor families are caught in a debt trap that continues to hold down consumer spending, the key to a robust recovery (Article 7.5).

Discussion Questions

1. (Article 7.1) How do classical economists argue that macroeconomies are inherently stable, and that government intervention is ineffective or counterproductive? Are their arguments convincing?

2. (Article 7.1) Why are Keynesians convinced that markets don't clear instantaneously, and that government intervention can and must stabilize market economies? Evaluate the evidence for their position.

3. (Article 7.2) Summarize the Marx, Keynes, and Polanyi problems. Why does Pollin think that neoliberal globalization policies will be unable to resolve them?

4. (Article 7.3) Why did Keynes think that the dollar-for-dollar crowding-out argument (the "Treasury view") is mistaken? And how might Keynes respond to the arguments today's conservatives have leveled against the Obama stimulus package?

5. (Article 7.4) In MacEwan's analysis, how did inequality, power, and ideology lead to the recent economic crisis? In what ways would addressing these causes alleviate the crisis?

6. (Article 7.5) How does Cypher apply Fisher's debt-trap argument to today's economy? What does it suggest about the effectiveness of Keynesian stimulus policies and how the government could stimulate more rapid economic growth?

7. (Article 7.6) In Marxist theory, how is a dynamic capitalist economy felled by instability? What roles do a "falling rate of profit," a "reserve army of the unemployed," and "overproduction" play in Marx's theory of how capitalism will fall into crisis? Do you think today's macroeconomy displays any of those tendencies?

8. (Article 7.7) How does feminist economics' focus on gender challenge other theories of poverty? How are feminist theories of poverty different from Keynesian, Marxist, Institutionalist, and neoclassical analyses?

Article 7.1

THE REVENGE OF THE CLASSICS

BY JOHN MILLER AND GINA NEFF
May/June 1996, revised April 2002

Nineteen ninety-five was not a good year for the welfare state. A Gingrich-led Congress attempted to pull the plug on universal entitlements for the poor, from welfare to Medicaid. And the Royal Swedish Academy of Science awarded the Nobel Prize in economics to Robert Lucas, a 58-year-old University of Chicago economist, for his "insights into the difficulties of using economic policy to control the economy."

Using sophisticated mathematics and economic models, Lucas has persuaded much of the economics profession that the economic policies John Maynard Keynes developed to combat the Great Depression—the economic underpinnings of the welfare state and the mixed economy—are ineffective.

What would Lucas do instead? Forsake those policies, dismantle the welfare state, and embrace the market. That was a job that, back in the mid-1990s, Gingrich and his crowd seemed only too happy to take up. They were glad to join forces with a Federal Reserve Board (the "Fed") already under the influence of the conservative counterrevolution in macroeconomics, led initially by Milton Friedman, another University of Chicago monetary theorist, and then by Lucas.

The Fed has accepted the futility of using monetary policy to promote long-run employment, leaving inflation alone as the ultimate target of its policies. In addition, the Fed's practice of making early announcements of changes in monetary policy, which is probably a good thing, can be directly attributed to Lucas. He has argued that unannounced changes provoke instability in the private sector instead of muting it.

Lucas and his school of followers call themselves New Classical economists. Like the classical economists who predated Keynes, these modern conservatives believe the economy possesses powerful self-correcting forces that guarantee full employment. Their vision of a stable market economy rests on three building blocks: rational expectations, market clearing, and imperfect information.

Let's look first at rational expectations, a notion which does seem rational enough. After all, every one of our economic actions is directed toward the future. Using whatever economic information we can get our hands on about prices, growth, and other economic activity, we predict our economic future. And usually we are good at it. When fellow workers are getting laid off at the company we are employed in, for instance, chances are that buying an expensive house is not at the top of our to-do list.

When we do get things wrong, we reevaluate our predictions. And, says Lucas, we keep up this process of prediction and evaluation until there is no way to improve those predictions, ensuring that we won't consistently make the same forecasting mistakes. In that way we form what Lucas calls "rational expectations." As he sees it, people act much like experienced bettors at the track. They get good at picking horses, but are never able to pick the winning horse every time.

Lucas has made a career out of expressing these ideas in mathematical terms. He argues that predictions about the rates of interest, unemployment, and inflation shape how consumers, workers, and business people decide their economic future. From consumers buying a new home to workers looking for a new job to bosses hiring or laying off employees, rational expectations theory seeks to describe what motivates economic actors.

Adam Smith Returns

But Lucas does not stop there—with merely a theory of how people make economic decisions. New Classical economic theory also assumes that markets "clear" instantaneously. In the bat of an eye, prices adjust so that how much sellers bring to market just matches whatever buyers take away. For instance, in a labor market, wages (the price of labor) fall quickly enough to guarantee that every worker willing to work (or sell their labor) at the going wage finds a job with an employer (or buyer of labor). For New Classical economists that constitutes full employment. Only workers unwilling to work at the market clearing wage are out of a job. Those workers are voluntarily unemployed—they chose not to work and brought unemployment upon themselves.

The point here is simple: Market capitalism is stable. "Price flexibility" and "market clearing" guarantee a booming full-employment economy—one that does not need economic policymaking to stabilize it. In fact, in Lucas's framework, government attempts to fine tune the economy actually backfire.

Here's why. If people expect the government to change economic policy, they too change their economic actions. That is rational expectations at work. And when prices and wages adjust instantaneously as people scramble to match their economic actions to their new expectations, those adjustments nullify the government's actions.

For instance, suppose the Fed tries to reduce unemployment by increasing the money supply, in the hope of raising spending and putting people to work. Lucas's rational workers anticipate that more spending and hiring will bring not only higher wages but also instantaneously higher prices, leaving their purchasing power unchanged. In this world people are not forced to work to avoid starving, but rather choose to offer their services only when their inflation-adjusted wages are sufficiently high. So no rational worker is lured into the market. The Fed's actions fail to lower unemployment, and succeed only in driving up prices.

As far-fetched as this theory might seem, the stagflation (simultaneous stagnation and inflation) of the 1970s lent these ideas plausibility. New Classical economics gathered adherents as Keynesian policies seemed increasingly ineffectual.

In New Classical economics, meddlesome government is not only ineffective, it is the enemy. Why does Lucas's inherently stable capitalism suffer through the ups and downs of the business cycle? His answer: Washington types trying to fine tune the economy. This is where imperfect information, the third building block of Lucas' theory, enters the model. Even Lucas's rational actors in this market-clearing world possess only limited information and can be fooled by bungling bureaucrats and re-election minded politicians who launch surprise (unannounced) changes in government policy.

People know the economy around them—their own wages or profits, the prices of the products they sell and those that they buy—better than what is going on across the economy. So if the Federal Reserve, without announcing it, increases the money supply in order to beef up spending and lower unemployment, even people with rational expectations can be confounded. They see their prices or wages go up, but don't anticipate prices going up elsewhere in the economy.

And that causes a problem. Corporate managers, for instance, hike up production, thinking that a higher price must signal a soaring demand for their products. Output rises across the economy. But soon inventories pile up, because the price increases were due to general inflation rather than greater demand. Corporate managers realize that the higher production levels were unwarranted, and they order a cutback—below even the initial output. The economy contracts, causing a recession.

What can return stability to the economy? Forsaking government intervention into the economy. In Lucas's world, unannounced changes in government policy cause the ups and downs of the business cycle. And announced changes in government policies are fully anticipated and therefore ineffective. For Lucas, the only rational course of action is to turn our backs on active government attempts to soften the blows of the market economy.

Keynesian Critics

Not all economists are convinced by Lucas's arguments or support the draconian policy implications of New Classical economics. The proponents of Keynesian economic policy have been among the most vocal critics. While Keynesians may accept the idea of rationally formed expectations, they find the ideas of flexible prices and clearing markets preposterous. One Nobel laureate, James Tobin, called these ideas a "great myth"—powerful in its effect on how we see the economy, but nonetheless a myth.

Another Keynesian Nobel winner, Franco Modigliani, railed that it is as if "what happened in the United States in the 1930s was a severe attack of contagious laziness." For these dyed-in-the-wool Keynesians, the private economy will not necessarily be driven toward full employment even in the long run and Keynes's fundamental message still holds: "a modern monetized economy needs to be stabilized, can be stabilized, and should be stabilized" by government intervention.

More recently, "New Keynesian" economists have fashioned a different critique of New Classical economics. These modern Keynesians accept not only the idea that people form rational expectations about what will happen in the economy, but also the idea that in the long run the private economy tends toward full employment. Still, they argue that for good economic reasons, wages and prices are "sticky" and much slower to adjust than Lucas suggests. For instance, given the high cost of negotiating a wage settlement, most labor contracts are long term. In the United States, nearly 80% of union contracts are for three years and only about two-fifths of them contain cost-of-living adjustments. Corporations also often rely on long-term pricing agreements to afford them the price stability necessary to bid on contracts.

Thus, while the economy might eventually reach the full employment outcome Lucas' model predicts, the wait is likely to be intolerably long. What's needed is active government intervention designed for the workable policy time frame of three to five years, for as Keynes once wrote, "in the long run we are all dead."

More fundamentally, Lucas's way of thinking exaggerates the amount of power people really have over their economic lives. Economist E. Ray Canterbery writes mockingly that in the New Classical school, "The marginal blue collar worker on his way to the factory anticipates an increase in the money supply then fully anticipates the inflation within his monetarist model ... and a fall in the real interest rates and a fall in real wages. The worker does a U-turn, drives home, and voluntarily disemploys himself." In New Classical economics bosses raise their workers' wages when the economy is doing well rather than pocketing the extra profits. And workers have the power to choose whether or not to work, to ask for higher wages when they expect inflation to go up, or to move into a different industry when they fear the worst for their own job. This is indeed a great myth.

Perhaps the most mythical aspect of New Classical economics is its claim that capitalism is stable—that if only policy makers would cease their interventions, economic stability would be assured and full employment guaranteed. But the instability of capitalism has been with us since long before Keynesian economic policy, which after all was a response to the Great Depression of the 1930s.

And that instability will worsen if New Classical economics is able to undo what Keynesian policy makers have done to mitigate the instability of capitalism since World War II. Current economic anxiety will heighten as workers struggle with real-life adjustments like stagnant wages and rising layoffs. At the same time, Lucas and his New Classical followers will continue to construct mathematical paeans to the rationality of these adjustments and the inherent stability of capitalism, even if that stability is evident only in their seminar rooms and the the Royal Swedish Academy of Science.

Resources: Robert J. Gordon, *Macroeconomics*, 6th ed., 1994; Robert Lucas, *Studies in Business Cycle Theory*, 1989; N. Gregory Mankiw, "A Quick Refresher Course in Macroeconomics," *Journal of Economic Literature*, December 1990; James Tobin, *Asset Accumulation and Economic Activity*, 1980; *The End of Economic Man*, reviewed by E. Ray Canterbery in *Challenge*, Nov./Dec. 1995.

Article 7.2

WHAT'S WRONG WITH NEOLIBERALISM?
The Marx, Keynes, and Polanyi problems.

BY ROBERT POLLIN
May/June 2004

During the years of the Clinton administration, the term "Washington Consensus" began circulating to designate the common policy positions of the U.S. administration along with the International Monetary Fund (IMF) and World Bank. These positions, implemented in the United States and abroad, included free trade, a smaller government share of the economy, and the deregulation of financial markets. This policy approach has also become widely known as *neoliberalism*, a term which draws upon the classical meaning of the word *liberalism*.

Classical liberalism is the political philosophy that embraces the virtues of free-market capitalism and the corresponding minimal role for government interventions, especially as regards measures to promote economic equality within capitalist societies. Thus, a classical liberal would favor minimal levels of government spending and taxation, and minimal levels of government regulation over the economy, including financial and labor markets. According to the classical liberal view, businesses should be free to operate as they wish, and to succeed or fail as such in a competitive marketplace. Meanwhile, consumers rather than government should be responsible for deciding which businesses produce goods and services that are of sufficient quality as well as reasonably priced. Businesses that provide overexpensive or low-quality products will then be out-competed in the marketplace regardless of the regulatory standards established by governments. Similarly, if businesses offer workers a wage below what the worker is worth, then a competitor firm will offer this worker a higher wage. The firm unwilling to offer fair wages would not survive over time in the competitive marketplace.

This same reasoning also carries over to the international level. Classical liberals favor free trade between countries rather than countries operating with tariffs or other barriers to the free flow of goods and services between countries. They argue that restrictions on the free movement of products and money between countries only protects uncompetitive firms from market competition, and thus holds back the economic development of countries that choose to erect such barriers.

Neoliberalism and the Washington Consensus are contemporary variants of this longstanding political and economic philosophy. The major difference between classical liberalism as a philosophy and contemporary neoliberalism as a set of policy measures is with implementation. Washington Consensus policy makers are committed to free-market policies when they support the interests of big business, as, for example, with lowering regulations at the workplace. But these same policy makers become far less insistent on free-market principles when invoking such principles might damage big business interests. Federal Reserve and IMF interventions to bail out wealthy asset holders during the frequent global financial crises in the 1990s are obvious violations of free-market precepts.

Broadly speaking, the effects of neoliberalism in the less developed countries over the 1990s reflected the experience of the Clinton years in the United States. A high proportion of less developed countries were successful, just in the manner of the United States under Clinton, in reducing inflation and government budget deficits, and creating a more welcoming climate for foreign trade, multinational corporations, and financial market investors. At the same time, most of Latin America, Africa, and Asia—with China being the one major exception—experienced deepening problems of poverty and inequality in the 1990s, along with slower growth and frequent financial market crises, which in turn produced still more poverty and inequality.

If free-market capitalism is a powerful mechanism for creating wealth, why does a neoliberal policy approach, whether pursued by Clinton, Bush, or the IMF, produce severe difficulties in terms of inequality and financial instability, which in turn diminish the market mechanism's ability to even promote economic growth? It will be helpful to consider this in terms of three fundamental problems that result from a free-market system, which I term "the Marx Problem," "the Keynes problem," and "the Polanyi problem." Let us take these up in turn.

The Marx Problem

Does someone in your family have a job and, if so, how much does it pay? For the majority of the world's population, how one answers these two questions determines, more than anything else, what one's standard of living will be. But how is it decided whether a person has a job and what their pay will be? Getting down to the most immediate level of decision-making, this occurs through various types of bargaining in labor markets between workers and employers. Karl Marx argued that, in a free-market economy generally, workers have less power than employers in this bargaining process because workers cannot fall back on other means of staying alive if they fail to get hired into a job. Capitalists gain higher profits through having this relatively stronger bargaining position. But Marx also stressed that workers' bargaining power diminishes further when unemployment and underemployment are high, since that means that employed workers can be more readily replaced by what Marx called "the reserve army" of the unemployed outside the office, mine, or factory gates.

Neoliberalism has brought increasing integration of the world's labor markets through reducing barriers to international trade and investment by multinationals. For workers in high-wage countries such as the United States, this effectively means that the reserve army of workers willing to accept jobs at lower pay than U.S. workers expands to include workers in less developed countries. It isn't the case that businesses will always move to less developed countries or that domestically produced goods will necessarily be supplanted by imports from low-wage countries. The point is that U.S. workers face an increased *credible* threat that they can be supplanted. If everything else were to remain the same in the U.S. labor market, this would then mean that global integration would erode the bargaining power of U.S. workers and thus tend to bring lower wages.

But even if this is true for workers in the United States and other rich countries, shouldn't it also mean that workers in poor countries have greater job opportunities and better bargaining positions? In fact, there are areas where workers in poor countries are gaining enhanced job opportunities through international trade and multinational investments. But these gains are generally quite limited. This is because a long-term transition out of agriculture in poor countries continues to expand the reserve army of unemployed and underemployed workers in these countries as well. Moreover, when neoliberal governments in poor countries reduce their support for agriculture—through cuts in both tariffs on imported food products and subsidies for domestic farmers—this makes it more difficult for poor farmers to compete with multinational agribusiness firms. This is especially so when the rich countries maintain or increase their own agricultural supports, as has been done in the United States under Bush. In addition, much of the growth in the recently developed export-oriented manufacturing sectors of poor countries has failed to significantly increase jobs even in this sector. This is because the new export-oriented production sites frequently do not represent net additions to the country's total supply of manufacturing firms. They rather replace older firms that were focused on supplying goods to domestic markets. The net result is that the number of people looking for jobs in the developing countries grows faster than the employers seeking new workers. Here again, workers' bargaining power diminishes.

This does not mean that global integration of labor markets must necessarily bring weakened bargaining power and lower wages for workers. But it does mean that unless some non-market forces in the economy, such as government regulations or effective labor unions, are able to counteract these market processes, workers will indeed continue to experience weakened bargaining strength and eroding living standards.

The Keynes Problem

In a free-market economy, investment spending by businesses is the main driving force that produces economic growth, innovation, and jobs. But as John Maynard Keynes stressed, private investment decisions are also unavoidably risky ventures. Businesses have to put up money without knowing whether they will produce any profits in the future. As such, investment spending by business is likely to fluctuate far more than, say, decisions by households as to how much they will spend per week on groceries.

But investment fluctuations will also affect overall spending in the economy, including that of households. When investment spending declines, this means that businesses will hire fewer workers. Unemployment rises as a result, and this in turn will lead to cuts in household spending. Declines in business investment spending can therefore set off a vicious cycle: the investment decline leads to employment declines, then to cuts in household spending and corresponding increases in household financial problems, which then brings still more cuts in business investment and financial difficulties for the business sector. This is how capitalist economies produce mass unemployment, financial crises, and recessions.

Keynes also described a second major source of instability associated with private investment activity. Precisely because private investments are highly risky propositions, financial markets have evolved to make this risk more manageable for any given investor. Through financial markets, investors can sell off their investments if they need or want to, converting their office buildings, factories, and stock of machinery into cash much more readily than they could if they always had to find buyers on their own. But Keynes warned that when financial markets convert long-term assets into short-term commitments for investors, this also fosters a speculative mentality in the markets. What becomes central for investors is not whether a company's products will produce profits over a long term, but rather whether the short-term financial market investors *think* a company's fortunes will be strong enough in the present and immediate future to drive the stock price up. Or, to be more precise, what really matters for a speculative investor is not what they think about a given company's prospects per se, but rather what they think *other investors are thinking*, since that will be what determines where the stock price goes in the short term.

Because of this, the financial markets are highly susceptible to rumors, fads, and all sorts of deceptive accounting practices, since all of these can help drive the stock price up in the present, regardless of what they accomplish in the longer term. Thus, if U.S. stock traders are convinced that Alan Greenspan is a *maestro*, and if there is news that he is about to intervene with some kind of policy shift, then the rumor of Greenspan's policy shift can itself drive prices up, as the more nimble speculators try to keep one step ahead of the herd of Greenspan-philes.

Still, as with the Marx problem, it does not follow that the inherent instability of private investment and speculation in financial markets are uncontrollable, leading inevitably to persistent problems of mass unemployment and recession. But these social pathologies will become increasingly common through a neoliberal policy approach committed to minimizing government interventions to stabilize investment.

The Polanyi Problem

Karl Polanyi wrote his classic book *The Great Transformation* in the context of the 1930s depression, World War II, and the developing worldwide competition with Communist governments. He was also reflecting on the 1920s, dominated, as with our current epoch, by a free-market ethos. Polanyi wrote of the 1920s that "economic liberalism made a supreme bid to restore the self-regulation of the system by eliminating all interventionist policies which interfered with the freedom of markets."

Considering all of these experiences, Polanyi argued that for market economies to function with some modicum of fairness, they must be embedded in social norms and institutions that effectively promote broadly accepted notions of the common good. Otherwise, acquisitiveness and competition—the two driving forces of market economies—achieve overwhelming dominance as cultural forces, rendering life under capitalism a Hobbesian "war of all against all." This same idea is also central for Adam Smith. Smith showed how the invisible hand of self-interest and competition will yield higher levels of individual effort that increases the wealth of nations, but that it will also produce the corruption of our moral sentiments unless the market is itself governed at a fundamental level by norms of solidarity.

In the post-World War II period, various social democratic movements within the advanced capitalist economies adapted the Polanyi perspective. They argued in favor of government interventions to achieve three basic ends: stabilizing overall demand in the economy at a level that will provide for full employment; creating a financial market environment that is stable and conducive to the effective allocation of investment funds; and distributing equitably the rewards from high employment and a stable investment process. There were two basic means of achieving equitable distribution: relatively rapid wage growth, promoted by labor laws that were supportive of unions, minimum wage standards, and similar interventions in labor markets; and welfare state policies, including progressive taxation and redistributive programs such as Social Security. The political ascendancy of these ideas was the basis for a dramatic increase in the role of government in the post-World War II capitalist economies. As one indicator of this, total government expenditures in the United States rose from 8% of GDP in 1913, to 21% in 1950, then to 38% by 1992. The International Monetary Fund and World Bank were also formed in the mid-1940s to advance such policy ideas throughout the world—that is, to implement policies virtually the opposite of those they presently favor. John Maynard Keynes himself was a leading intellectual force contributing to the initial design of the International Monetary Fund and World Bank.

From Social Democracy to Neoliberalism

But the implementation of a social democratic capitalism, guided by a commitment to full employment and the welfare state, did also face serious and persistent difficulties, and we need to recognize them as part of a consideration of the Marx, Keynes, and Polanyi problems. In particular, many sectors of business opposed efforts to sustain full employment because, following the logic of the Marx problem, full employment provides greater bargaining power for workers in labor markets, even if it also increases the economy's total production of goods and services. Greater worker bargaining power can also create inflationary pressures because businesses will try to absorb their higher wage costs by raising prices. In addition, market-inhibiting financial regulations limit the capacity of financial market players to diversify their risk and speculate.

Corporations in the United States and Western Europe were experiencing some combination of these problems associated with social democratic capitalism. In particular, they were faced with rising labor costs associated with low unemployment rates, which then led to either inflation, when corporations had the ability to pass on their higher labor costs to consumers, or to a squeeze on profits, when competitive pressures prevented corporations from raising their prices in response to the rising labor costs. These pressures were compounded by the two oil price "shocks" initiated by the Oil Producing Exporting Countries (OPEC)—an initial fourfold increase in the world price of oil in 1973, then a second four-fold price spike in 1979.

These were the conditions that by the end of the 1970s led to the decline of social democratic approaches to policymaking and the ascendancy of neoliberalism. The two leading signposts of this historic transition were the election in 1979 of Margaret Thatcher as Prime Minister of the United Kingdom and in 1980 of Ronald Reagan as the President of the United States. Indeed, it was at this point that Mrs. Thatcher made her famous pronouncement that "there is no alternative" to neoliberalism.

This brings us to the contemporary era of smaller government, fiscal stringency and deregulation, i.e., to neoliberalism under Clinton, Bush, and throughout the less-developed world. The issue is not a simple juxtaposition between either regulating or deregulating markets. Rather it is that markets have become deregulated to support the interests of business and financial markets, even as these same groups still benefit greatly from many forms of government support, including investment subsidies, tax concessions, and rescue operations when financial crises get out of hand. At the same time, the deregulation of markets that favors business and finance is correspondingly the most powerful regulatory mechanism limiting the demands of workers, in that deregulation has been congruent with the worldwide expansion of the reserve army of labor and the declining capacity of national governments to implement full-employment and macroeconomic policies. In other words, deregulation has exacerbated both the Marx and Keynes problems.

Given the ways in which neoliberalism worsens the Marx, Keynes, and Polanyi problems, we should not be surprised by the wreckage that it has wrought since the late 1970s, when it became the ascendant policy model. Over the past generation, with neoliberals in the saddle almost everywhere in the world, the results have been straight-forward: worsening inequality and poverty, along with slower economic growth and far more unstable financial markets. While Margaret Thatcher famously declared that "there is no alternative" to neoliberalism, there are in fact alternatives. The experience over the past generation demonstrates how important it is to develop them in the most workable and coherent ways possible.

Article 7.3

FISCAL POLICY AND "CROWDING OUT"

BY ALEJANDRO REUSS
May/June 2009

In response to the deepest recession in the United States since the Great Depression, the Obama administration proposed a large fiscal "stimulus" plan. (Fiscal policies involve government spending and taxation. A fiscal stimulus involves increases in government spending or tax cuts, or both.) The current stimulus plan, after some compromises between the Obama administration and Republicans in Congress, included both substantial tax cuts and increases in government spending. Together, they would increase the federal government deficit by over $700 billion.

A fiscal stimulus is a standard "Keynesian" response to a recession. The logic behind these policies is that recessions can be caused by insufficient total demand for goods and services. If saving (a "leakage" from demand) exceeds investment (an "injection" of demand), there will not be enough demand to buy all the goods and services that the economy is capable of producing at the "full employment" level. Some goods will go unsold, and firms will reduce output. They will cut jobs, cancel supply orders, and even close production facilities. The economy will spiral into a recession.

In standard Keynesian models, either tax cuts or increased government spending can increase total demand, and therefore total output and employment. An initial increase in spending (by either the government or the recipients of the tax cuts) results in new income for other individuals, who then go on to spend part (not all) of this income, which results in new income for still other individuals, and so on. Ultimately, this series of additions to income results in a total increase in GDP greater than the original increase in government spending or reduction in taxes. The increase in real GDP divided by the initial spending increase is called the "multiplier." The standard Keynesian view implies a multiplier greater than one.

The Conservative Critique

Conservative economists, whose intellectual heritage includes decades-old attempts to refute Keynesian theory, disagree with this view. They argue that government spending cannot possibly increase overall economic activity, and that the stimulus plan is therefore doomed to fail. This position is sometimes known as the "Treasury view" (because it mirrors the arguments of the British Treasury Department during the Great Depression) or the theory of "crowding out." The new government spending, these economists argue, "has to come from somewhere," either from higher taxes or increased government borrowing. Either way, the increase in government spending will come at the expense of private spending.

If the spending is financed by tax increases, conservative economists argue, this will reduce individuals' after-tax incomes and therefore reduce their spending. If it is financed through borrowing, the increased government demand for loans will drive up interest rates, and this will "crowd out" private investment. (Some private investment projects that would have been profitable at lower interest rates would not be profitable at the higher rates, and therefore would not be undertaken.) Extreme versions of this theory, known as "dollar-for-dollar" crowding out, argue that the decrease in private investment will exactly offset the increase in government spending, and there will be no change in the overall output of goods and services.

Government intervention is not only incapable of pulling the economy out of a recession, conservative economists argue, it is also unnecessary. If there is more saving than investment, the quantity of funds people are willing to loan out will exceed the quantity that people are willing to borrow at the current interest rate. The surplus of loanable funds will drive down the interest rate. People will save less (since the reward to saving is lower) and borrow more and invest more (since the cost of borrowing is lower), until the injection of investment and the leakage of saving are equal. In short, if insufficient demand ever caused a recession, the economy would quickly pull itself back to full employment without any need for government intervention.

Keynes' Rejoinder

Keynes agreed with the idea that saving equals investment. In his view, however, this is true not only when the economy is producing at its full-employment capacity, but also when it is producing at far less than its capacity. Keynes argued that the "classical" economists (as he called the conservative orthodoxy of his time) had an incorrect view of the relationship between interest rates and savings, and that this was at the heart of their errors about the possibility of prolonged recessions.

The classicals believed that as interest rates increased, savings would increase, and that as interest rates declined, savings would decline. Keynes agreed that this was true at "a given income," but that a change in the interest rate would also affect the amount investment and therefore the level of income. A higher interest rate, he argued, was associated with lower investment, lower incomes, and therefore lower saving; a lower interest rate, with higher investment, higher incomes, and therefore higher saving. (As people's incomes increase, they spend more *and* save more; as their incomes decline, they spend less *and* save less.) In Keynes' view, saving will equal investment whether investment and saving are both high (at or near the full employment level of output) or if investment and saving are both low (in a low-output, high-unemployment economy). In the latter case, Keynes believed, there was no guarantee that the economy would pull itself back to full employment.

Keynes was also well aware, long before his critics, that government borrowing could crowd out some private investment. In *The General Theory* itself, he noted that the effects of the government directly increasing employment on public works may include "increasing the rate of interest and so retarding investment in other directions." This does not imply, however, dollar-for-dollar crowding out. Keynes still believed, and the empirical evidence confirms, that under depression conditions an increase in government spending can result in an increase in total output larger than the initial spending increase (a multiplier greater than one).

Of Spending and Multipliers

In a recent article in the *Wall Street Journal*, conservative economist Robert Barro declares, as a "plausible starting point," that the multiplier actually equals zero. That's what the dollar-for-dollar crowding-out theory means—an increase in government spending will be matched by equal decreases in private spending, and so will have zero effect on real GDP. When it comes to estimating the multiplier, based on historical data from 1943-1944, however, Barro finds that it is not zero, but 0.8.

First, contrary to Barro's intent, this is actually a disproof of dollar-for-dollar crowding out. It means that increased government spending brought about increased real GDP, though not by as much as the spending increase. It increased the production of public-sector goods by (much) more than it reduced the production of private-sector goods. Unless one views private-sector goods as intrinsically more valuable than public-sector goods, this is not an argument against government spending.

Second, Barro chose to base his study on two years at the height of the U.S. mobilization for World War II. When the economy is at or near full employment, the multiplier is bound to be small. If all resources are already being used, the only way to produce more of some kinds of goods (say, tanks and war planes) is to produce less of some others (say, civilian cars). Keynesian economists certainly understand this. Their point, however, is that government spending creates a large multiplier effect when the economy is languishing in a recession, not when it is already at full employment.

Economist Mark Zandi of Moody's Economy.com reports much higher multipliers for government spending. Zandi estimates multipliers between 1.3 and 1.6 for federal aid to states and for government infrastructure expenditures. The multipliers are even larger for government transfers (such as food stamps or unemployment compensation) to the hardest-hit, who are likely to spend all or almost all of their increase in income. Zandi estimates these multipliers at between 1.6 and 1.8. Tax cuts for high income individuals and corporations, who are less likely to spend their additional disposable income, have the lowest multipliers—between 0.3 and 0.4.

Why the General Theory?

The conservative case against standard Keynesian fiscal stimulus policy rests on the assumption that all of the economy's resources are already being used to the fullest. Keynes titled his most important work *The General Theory* because he thought that the orthodox economics of his time confined itself to this special case, the case of an economy at full employment. He did not believe that this was generally the case in capitalist economies, and he sought to develop a theory that explained this.

The argument conservatives make against government spending—"it has to come from somewhere"—is actually no less true for private investment. If dollar-for-dollar crowding out were true, therefore, it would be just as impossible for private investment to pull the economy out of a recession. This, of course, would be nonsense unless the economy was already at full employment (and an increase in one kind of production would have to come at the expense of some other kind of production).

If the economy were already operating at full capacity—imagine a situation in which all workers are employed, factories are humming with activity 24/7, and no unused resources would be available to expand production if demand increased—the argument that increased government spending could not increase overall economic output might be plausible. But that is manifestly not the current economic situation.

Real GDP declined at an annual rate of 6.3% in the fourth quarter of 2008. The official unemployment rate surged to 8.5%, the highest rate in 30 years, in March 2009. Over 15% of workers are unemployed, have given up looking for work, or can only find part-time work. Employment is plummeting by more than half a million workers each month. A theory that assumes the economy is already at full employment can neither help us understand how we got into this hole—or how we can get out.

Sources: John Maynard Keynes, *The General Theory of Employment, Interest, and Money*, 1964; Associated Press, "Obama: Stimulus lets Americans claim destiny," February 17, 2009; Paul Krugman, "A Dark Age of macroeconomics (wonkish)," January 27, 2009; J. Bradford DeLong, "More 'Treasury View' Blogging," February 5,2009; J. Bradford DeLong, "The Modern Revival of the 'Treasury View,'" January 18, 2009; Robert J. Barro,"Government Spending is No Free Lunch," *Wall Street Journal*, January 22, 2009; Paul Krugman, "War and non-remembrance," January 22, 2009; Paul Krugman, "Spending in wartime," January 23, 2009; Mark Zandi, "The Economic Impact of a $750 Billion Fiscal Stimulus Package," Moody'sEconomy.com, March 26, 2009; Bureau of Labor Statistics, Alternative measures of labor underutilization; Bureau of Labor Statistics Payroll Employment.

Article 7.4

INEQUALITY, POWER, AND IDEOLOGY
Getting it right about the causes of the current economic crisis.

BY ARTHUR MacEWAN
March/April 2009

I t is hard to solve a problem without an understanding of what caused it. For example, in medicine, until we gained an understanding of the way bacteria and viruses cause various infectious diseases, it was virtually impossible to develop effective cures. Of course, dealing with many diseases is complicated by the fact that germs, genes, diet, and the environment establish a nexus of causes.

The same is true in economics. Without an understanding of the causes of the current crisis, we are unlikely to develop a solution; certainly we are not going to get a solution that has a lasting impact. And determining the causes is complicated because several intertwined factors have been involved.

The current economic crisis was brought about by a nexus of factors that involved: a growing concentration of political and social power in the hands of the wealthy; the ascendance of a perverse leave-it-to-the-market ideology which was an instrument of that power; and rising income inequality, which both resulted from and enhanced that power. These various factors formed a vicious circle, reinforcing one another and together shaping the economic conditions that led us to the present situation. Several other factors were also involved—the growing role of credit, the puffing up of the housing bubble, and the increasing deregulation of financial markets have been very important. However, these are best understood as transmitters of our economic problems, arising from the nexus that formed the vicious circle.

What does this tell us about a solution? Economic stimulus, repair of the housing market, and new regulation are all well and good, but they do not deal with the underlying causes of the crisis. Instead, progressive groups need to work to shift each of the factors I have noted—power, ideology, and income distribution—in the other direction. In doing so, we can create a *virtuous* circle, with each change reinforcing the other changes. If successful, we not only establish a more stable economy, but we lay the foundation for a more democratic, equitable, and sustainable economic order.

A crisis by its very nature creates opportunities for change. One good place to begin change and intervene in this "circle"—and transform it from vicious to virtuous—is through pushing for the expansion and reform of social programs, programs that directly serve social needs of the great majority of the population (for example: single-payer health care, education programs, and environmental protection and repair). By establishing changes in social programs, we will have impacts on income distribution and ideology, and, perhaps most important, we set in motion *a power shift* that improves our position for preserving the changes. While I emphasize social programs as a means to initiate social and economic change, there are other ways to intervene in the circle. Efforts to re-strengthen unions would be especially important; and there are other options as well.

Causes of the Crisis: A Long Time Coming

Sometime around the early 1970s, there were some dramatic changes in the U.S. economy. The twenty-five years following World War II had been an era of relatively stable economic growth; the benefits of growth had been widely shared, with wages rising along with productivity gains, and income distribution became slightly less unequal (a good deal less unequal as compared to the pre-Great Depression era). There were severe economic problems in the United States, not the least of which were the continued exclusion of African Americans, large gender inequalities, and the woeful inadequacy of social welfare programs. Nonetheless, relatively stable growth, rising wages, and then the advent of the civil rights movement and the War on Poverty gave some important, positive social and economic character to the era—especially in hindsight!

In part, this comparatively favorable experience for the United States had depended on the very dominant position that U.S. firms held in the world economy, a position in which they were relatively unchallenged by international competition. The firms and their owners were not the only beneficiaries of this situation. With less competitive pressure on them from foreign companies, many U.S. firms accepted unionization and did not find it worthwhile to focus on keeping wages down and obstructing the implementation of social supports for the low-income population. Also, having had the recent experience of the Great Depression, many wealthy people and business executives were probably not so averse to a substantial role for government in regulating the economy.

A Power Grab

By about 1970, the situation was changing. Firms in Europe and Japan had long recovered from World War II, OPEC was taking shape, and weaknesses were emerging in the U.S. economy. The weaknesses were in part a consequence of heavy spending for the Vietnam War combined with the government's reluctance to tax for the war because of its unpopularity. The pressures on U.S. firms arising from these changes had two sets of consequences: slower growth and greater instability; and concerted efforts—a power grab, if you will—by firms and the wealthy to shift the costs of economic deterioration onto U.S. workers and the low-income population.

These "concerted efforts" took many forms: greater resistance to unions and unionization, battles to reduce taxes, stronger opposition to social welfare programs, and, above all, a push to reduce or eliminate government regulation of economic activity through a powerful political campaign to gain control of the various branches and levels of government. The 1980s, with Reagan and Bush One in the White House, were the years in which all these efforts were solidified. Unions were greatly weakened, a phenomenon both demonstrated and exacerbated by Reagan's firing of the air traffic controllers in response to their strike in 1981. The tax cuts of the period were also important markers of the change. But the change had begun earlier; the 1978 passage of the tax-cutting Proposition 13 in California was perhaps the first major success of the movement. And the changes continued well after the 1980s, with welfare reform and deregulation of finance during the Clinton era, to say nothing of the tax cuts and other actions during Bush Two.

Ideology Shift

The changes that began in the 1970s, however, were not simply these sorts of concrete alterations in the structure of power affecting the economy and, especially, government's role in the economy. There was a major shift in ideology, the dominant set of ideas that organize an understanding of our social relations and both guide and rationalize policy decisions.

Following the Great Depression and World War II, there was a wide acceptance of the idea that government had a major role to play in economic life. Less than in many other countries but nonetheless to a substantial degree, at all levels of society, it was generally believed that there should be a substantial government safety net and that government should both regulate the economy in various ways and, through fiscal as well as monetary policy, should maintain aggregate demand. This large economic role for government came to be called Keynesianism, after the British economist John Maynard Keynes, who had set out the arguments for an active fiscal policy in time of economic weakness. In the early 1970s, as economic troubles developed, even Richard Nixon declared: "We are all Keynesians now."

The election of Ronald Reagan, however, marked a sharp change in ideology, at least at the top. Actions of the government were blamed for all economic ills: government spending, Keynesianism, was alleged to be the cause of the inflation of the 1970s; government regulation was supposedly crippling industry; high taxes were, it was argued, undermining incentives for workers to work and for businesses to invest; social welfare spending was blamed for making people dependent on the government and was charged with fraud and corruption (the "welfare queens"); and so on and so on.

Alan Greenspan, Symbol of an Era

One significant symbol of the full rise of the conservative ideology that became so dominant in the latter part of the 20th century was Alan Greenspan, who served from 1974 through 1976 as chairman of the President's Council of Economic Advisers under Gerald Ford and in 1987 became chairman of the Federal Reserve Board, a position he held until 2006. While his predecessors had hardly been critics of U.S. capitalism, Greenspan was a close associate of the philosopher Ayn Rand and an adherent of her extreme ideas supporting individualism and *laissez-faire* (keep-the-government-out) capitalism.

When chairman of the Fed, Greenspan was widely credited with maintaining an era of stable economic growth. As things fell apart in 2008, however, Greenspan was seen as having a large share of responsibility for the non-regulation and excessively easy credit (see article) that led into the crisis.

Called before Congress in October of 2008, Greenspan was chastised by Rep. Henry Waxman (D-Calif.), who asked him: "Do you feel that your ideology pushed you to make decisions that you wish you had not made?" To which Greenspan replied: "Yes, I've found a flaw. I don't know how significant or permanent it is. But I've been very distressed by that fact."

And Greenspan told Congress: "Those of us who have looked to the self-interest of lending institutions to protect shareholders' equity, myself included, are in a state of shocked disbelief."

Greenspan's "shock" was reminiscent of the scene in the film *Casablanca* in which Captain Renault (played by Claude Rains) declares: "I'm shocked, shocked to find that gambling is going on in here!" At which point, a croupier hands Renault a pile of money and says, "Your winnings, sir." Renault replies, *sotto voce*, "Thank you very much."

On economic matters, Reagan championed supply-side economics, the principal idea of which was that tax cuts yield an increase in government revenue because the cuts lead to more rapid economic growth through encouraging more work and more investment. Thus, so the argument went, tax cuts would reduce the government deficit. Reagan, with the cooperation of Democrats, got the tax cuts—and, as the loss of revenue combined with a large increase in military spending, the federal budget deficit grew by leaps and bounds, almost doubling as a share of GDP over the course of the 1980s. It was all summed up in the idea of keeping the government out of the economy; let the free market work its magic.

Growing Inequality

The shifts of power and ideology were very much bound up with a major redistribution upwards of income and wealth. The weakening of unions, the increasing access of firms to low-wage foreign (and immigrant) labor, the refusal of government to maintain the buying power of the minimum wage, favorable tax treatment of the wealthy and their corporations, deregulation in a wide range of industries, and lack of enforcement of existing regulation (e.g., the authorities turning a blind eye to offshore tax shelters) all contributed to these shifts.

Many economists, however, explain the rising income inequality as a result of technological change that favored more highly skilled workers; and changing technology has probably been a factor. Yet the most dramatic aspect of the rising inequality has been the rapidly rising share of income obtained by those at the very top (see figures), who get their incomes from the ownership and control of business, not from their skilled labor. For these people the role of new technologies was most important through its impact on providing more options (e.g., international options) for the managers of firms, more thorough means to control labor, and more effective ways—in the absence of regulation—to manipulate fi-

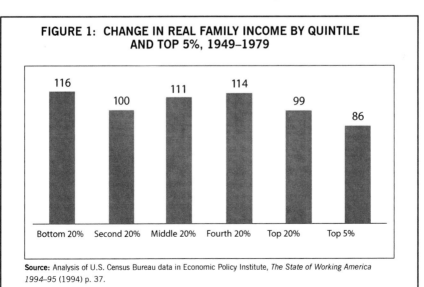

FIGURE 1: CHANGE IN REAL FAMILY INCOME BY QUINTILE AND TOP 5%, 1949–1979

Bottom 20%	Second 20%	Middle 20%	Fourth 20%	Top 20%	Top 5%
116	100	111	114	99	86

Source: Analysis of U.S. Census Bureau data in Economic Policy Institute, *The State of Working America 1994–95* (1994) p. 37.

nance. All of these gains that might be associated with new technology were also gains brought by the way the government handled, or didn't handle (failed to regulate), economic affairs.

Several sets of data demonstrate the sharp changes in the distribution of income that have taken place in the last several decades. Most striking is the changing position of the very highest income segment of the population. In the mid-1920s, the share of all pre-tax income going to the top 1% of households peaked at 23.9%. This elite group's share of income fell dramatically during the Great Depression and World War II to about 12% at the end of the war and then slowly fell further during the next thirty years, reaching a low of 8.9% in the mid-1970s. Since then, the top 1% has regained its exalted position of the earlier era, with 21.8% of income in 2005. Since 1993, more than one-half of all income gains have accrued to this highest 1% of the population.

Figures 1 and 2 show the gains (or losses) of various groups in the 1947 to 1979 period and in the 1979 to 2005 period. The difference is dramatic. For example, in the earlier era, the bottom 20% saw its income in real (inflation-adjusted) terms rise by 116%, and real income of the top 5% grew by only 86%. But in the latter era, the bottom 20% saw a 1% decline in its income, while the top 5% obtained an 81% increase.

The Emergence of Crisis

These changes, especially the dramatic shifts in the distribution of income, set the stage for the increasingly large reliance on credit, especially consumer and mortgage credit, that played a major role in the emergence of the current economic crisis. Other factors were involved, but rising inequality was especially important in effecting the increase in both the demand and supply of credit.

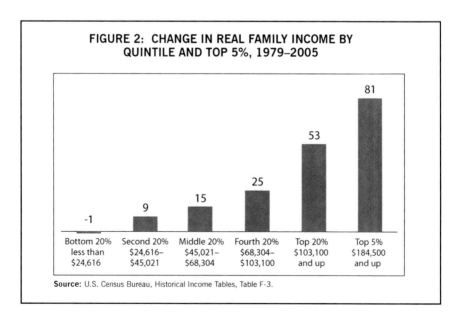

FIGURE 2: CHANGE IN REAL FAMILY INCOME BY QUINTILE AND TOP 5%, 1979–2005

Bottom 20% less than $24,616	Second 20% $24,616– $45,021	Middle 20% $45,021– $68,304	Fourth 20% $68,304– $103,100	Top 20% $103,100 and up	Top 5% $184,500 and up
-1	9	15	25	53	81

Source: U.S. Census Bureau, Historical Income Tables, Table F-3.

Credit Expansion

On the demand side, rising inequality translated into a growing gap between the incomes of most members of society and their needs. For the 2000 to 2007 period, average weekly earnings in the private sector were 12% below their average for the 1970s (in inflation-adjusted terms). From 1980 to 2005 the share of income going to the bottom 60% of families fell from 35% to 29%. Under these circumstances, more and more people relied more and more heavily on credit to meet their needs—everything from food to fuel, from education to entertainment, and especially housing.

While the increasing reliance of consumers on credit has been going on for a long time, it has been especially marked in recent decades. Consumer debt as a share of after-tax personal income averaged 20% in the 1990s, and then jumped up to an average of 25% in the first seven years of the new millennium. But the debt expansion was most marked in housing, where mortgage debt as a percent of after-tax personal income rose from 89% to 94% over the 1990s, and then ballooned to 140% by 2006 as housing prices skyrocketed.

On the supply side, especially in the last few years, the government seems to have relied on making credit readily available as a means to bolster aggregate demand and maintain at least a modicum of economic growth. During the 1990s, the federal funds interest rate averaged 5.1%, but fell to an average of 3.4% in the 2000 to 2007 period—and averaged only 1.4% in 2002 to 2004 period. (The federal funds interest rate is the rate that banks charge one another for overnight loans and is a rate directly affected by the Federal Reserve.) Corresponding to the low interest rates, the money supply grew twice as fast in the new millennium as it had in the 1990s. (And see the box on the connection of the Fed's actions to the Iraq War.)

The increasing reliance of U.S. consumers on credit has often been presented as a moral weakness, as an infatuation with consumerism, and as a failure to look beyond the present. Whatever moral judgments one may make, however, the expansion of the credit economy has been a response to real economic forces—inequality and government policies, in particular.

The Failure to Regulate

The credit expansion by itself, however, did not precipitate the current crisis. Deregulation—or, more generally, the failure to regulate—is also an important part of the story. The government's role in regulation of financial markets has been a central feature in the development of this crisis, but the situation in financial markets has been part of a more general process—affecting airlines and trucking, telecommunications, food processing, broadcasting, and of course international trade and investment. The process has been driven by a combination of power (of large firms and wealthy individuals) and ideology (leave it to the market, get the government out).

The failure to regulate financial markets that transformed the credit expansion into a financial crisis shows up well in three examples:

The 1999 repeal of the Glass-Steagall Act. Glass-Steagall had been enacted in the midst of the Great Depression, as a response to the financial implosion following the

---

Joseph Stiglitz on the War and the Economy

On October 2, 2008, on the Pacifica radio program *Democracy Now!*, Amy Goodman and Juan Gonzalez interviewed Joseph Stiglitz about the economic situation. Stiglitz was the 2001 winner of the Nobel Prize in Economics, former chief economist at the World Bank, and former chair of President Clinton's Council of Economic Advisers. He is a professor at Columbia University. Following is an excerpt from that interview:

AMY GOODMAN: Joseph Stiglitz, you're co-author of *The Three Trillion Dollar War: The True Cost of the Iraq Conflict*. How does the bailout [of the financial sector] connect to war?

JOSEPH STIGLITZ: Very much. Let me first explain a little bit how the current crisis connects with the war. One of the reasons that we have this crisis is that the Fed flooded the economy with liquidity and had lax regulations. Part of that was this ideology of "regulations are bad," but part of the reason was that the economy was weak. And one of the reasons the economy was weak was oil prices were soaring, and part of the reason oil prices were soaring is the Iraq war. When we went to war in 2003, before we went, prices were $23 a barrel. Futures markets thought they would remain at that level. They anticipated the increase in demand, but they thought there would be a concomitant increase in supply from the low-cost providers, mainly in the Middle East. The war changed that equation, and we know what happened to the oil prices.

Well, why is that important? Well, we were spending—Americans were spending hundreds of millions—billions of dollars to buy—more, to buy imported oil. Normally, that would have had a very negative effect on our economy; we would have had a slowdown. Some people have said, you know, it's a mystery why we aren't having that slowdown; we repealed the laws of economics. Whenever anybody says that, you ought to be suspect.

It was actually very simple. The Fed engineered a bubble, a housing bubble to replace the tech bubble that it had engineered in the '90s. The housing bubble facilitated people taking money out of their . . . houses; in one year, there were more than $900 billion of mortgage equity withdrawals. And so, we had a consumption boom that was so strong that even though we were spending so much money abroad, we could keep the economy going. But it was so shortsighted. And it was so clear that we were living on borrowed money and borrowed time. And it was just a matter of time before, you know, the whole thing would start to unravel.

---

stock market crash of 1929. Among other things, it required that different kinds of financial firms—commercial banks, investment banks, insurance companies—be separate. This separation both limited the spread of financial problems and reduced conflicts of interest that could arise were the different functions of these firms combined into a single firm. As perhaps the most important legislation regulating the financial sector, the repeal of Glass-Steagall was not only a substantive change but was an important symbol of the whole process of deregulation.

The failure to regulate mortgage lending. Existing laws and regulations require lending institutions to follow prudent practices in making loans, assuring that borrowers have the capacity to be able to pay back the loans. And of course fraud—lying about the provisions of loans—is prohibited. Yet in an atmosphere where regulation was "out," regulators were simply not doing their jobs. The consequences are illustrated in a December 28, 2008, *New York Times* story on the failed Washington Mutual Bank. The article describes a supervisor at a mortgage processing center as having been "accustomed to seeing babysitters claiming salaries worthy of college presidents, and schoolteachers with incomes rivaling stockbrokers'. He rarely questioned them. A real estate frenzy was under way and WaMu, as his bank was known, was all about saying yes."

One may wonder why banks—or other lending institutions, mortgage firms, in particular—would make loans to people who were unlikely to be able to pay them back. The reason is that the lending institutions quickly combined such loans into packages (i.e., a security made up of several borrowers' obligations to pay) and sold them to other investors in a practice called "securitization."

Credit-default swaps. Perhaps the most egregious failure to regulate in recent years has been the emergence of credit-default swaps, which are connected to securitization. Because they were made up of obligations by a diverse set of borrowers, the packages of loans were supposedly low-risk investments. Yet those who purchased them still sought insurance against default. Insurance sellers, however, are regulated—required, for example, to keep a certain amount of capital on hand to cover possible claims. So the sellers of these insurance policies on packages of loans called the policies "credit-default swaps" and thus were allowed to avoid regulation. Further, these credit-default swaps, these insurance policies, themselves were bought and sold again and again in unregulated markets in a continuing process of speculation.

The credit-default swaps are a form of derivative, a financial asset the value of which is derived from some other asset—in this case the value of packages of mortgages for which they were the insurance policies. When the housing bubble began to collapse and people started to default on their mortgages, the value of credit-default swaps plummeted and their future value was impossible to determine. No one would buy them, and several banks that had speculated in these derivatives were left holding huge amounts of these "toxic assets."

Bubble and Bust

The combination of easy credit and the failure to regulate together fueled the housing bubble. People could buy expensive houses but make relatively low monthly payments. Without effective regulation of mortgage lending, they could get the loans even when they were unlikely to be able to make payments over the long run. Moreover, as these pressures pushed up housing prices, many people bought houses simply to resell them quickly at a higher price, in a process called "flipping." And such speculation pushed the prices up further. Between 2000 and 2006, housing prices rose by 90% (as consumer prices generally rose by only 17%).

While the housing boom was in full swing, both successful housing speculators and lots of people involved in the shenanigans of credit markets made a lot of money. However, as the housing bubble burst—as all bubbles do—things fell apart. The packages of loans lost value, and the insurance policies on them, the credit-default swaps, lost value. These then became "toxic" assets for those who held them, assets not only with reduced value but with unknown value. Not only did large financial firms—for example, Lehman Brothers and AIG—have billions of dollars in losses, but no one knew the worth of their remaining assets. The assets were called "toxic" because they poisoned the operations of the financial system. Under these circumstances, financial institutions stopped lending to one another—that is, the credit markets "froze up." The financial crisis was here.

The financial crisis, not surprisingly, very quickly shifted to a general economic crisis. Firms in the "real" economy rely heavily on a well-functioning financial system to supply them with the funds they need for their regular operations—loans to car buyers, loans to finance inventory, loans for construction of new facilities, loans for new equipment, and, of course, mortgage loans. Without those loans (or with the loans much more difficult to obtain), there has been a general cut-back in economic activity, what is becoming a serious and probably prolonged recession.

What Is to Be Done?

So here we are. The shifts in power, ideology, and income distribution have placed us in a rather nasty situation. There are some steps that will be taken that have a reasonable probability of yielding short-run improvement. In particular, a large increase in government spending—deficit spending—will probably reduce the depth and shorten the length of the recession. And the actions of the Federal Reserve and Treasury to inject funds into the financial system are likely, along with the deficit spending, to "un-freeze" credit markets (the mismanagement and, it seems, outright corruption of the bailout notwithstanding). Also, there is likely to be some re-regulation of the financial industry. These steps, however, at best will restore things to where they were before the crisis. They do not treat the underlying causes of the crisis—the vicious circle of power, ideology, and inequality.

Opportunity for Change

Fortunately, the crisis itself has weakened some aspects of this circle. The cry of "leave it to the market" is still heard, but is now more a basis for derision than a guide to policy. The ideology and, to a degree, the power behind the ideology, have been severely weakened as the role of "keeping the government out" has shown to be a major cause of the financial mess and our current hardships. There is now widespread support among the general populace and some support in Washington for greater regulation of the financial industry.

Whether or not the coming period will see this support translated into effective policy is of course an open question. Also an open question is how much the turn away from "leaving it to the market" can be extended to other sectors of the economy. With regard to the environment, there is already general acceptance of the principle that the government (indeed, many governments) must take an active role in regulating economic activity. Similar principles need to be recognized with regard to health care, education, housing, child care, and other support programs for low-income families.

The discrediting of "keep the government out" ideology provides an opening to develop new programs in these areas and to expand old programs. Furthermore, as the federal government revs up its "stimulus" program in the coming months, opportunities will exist for expanding support for these sorts of programs. This support is important, first of all, because these programs serve real, pressing needs—needs that have long existed and are becoming acute and more extensive in the current crisis.

Breaking the Circle

Support for these social programs, however, may also serve to break into the vicious power-ideology-inequality circle and begin transforming it into a virtuous circle. Social programs are inherently equalizing in two ways: they provide their benefits to low-income people and they provide some options for those people in their efforts to demand better work and higher pay. Also, the further these programs develop, the more they establish the legitimacy of a larger role for public control of—government involvement in—the economy; they tend to bring about an ideological shift. By affecting a positive distributional shift and by shifting ideology, the emergence of stronger social programs can have a wider impact on power. In other words, efforts to promote social programs are one place to start, an entry point to shift the vicious circle to a virtuous circle.

There are other entry points. Perhaps the most obvious ones are actions to strengthen the role of unions. The Employee Free Choice Act may be a useful first step, and it will be helpful to establish a more union-friendly Department of Labor and National Labor Relations Board. Raising the minimum wage—ideally indexing it to inflation—would also be highly desirable. While conditions have changed since the heyday of unions in the middle of the 20th century, and we cannot expect to restore the conditions of that era, a greater role for unions would seem essential in righting the structural conditions at the foundation of the current crisis.

Shifting Class Power

None of this is assured, of course. Simply starting social programs will not necessarily mean that they have the wider impacts that I am suggesting are possible. No one should think that by setting up some new programs and strengthening some existing ones we will be on a smooth road to economic and social change. Likewise, rebuilding the strength of unions will involve extensive struggle and will not be accomplished by a few legislative or executive actions.

Also, all efforts to involve the government in economic activity—whether in finance or environmental affairs, in health care or education, in work support or job training programs—will be met with the worn-out claims that government involvement generates bureaucracy, stifles initiative, and places an excessive burden on private firms and individuals. We are already hearing warnings that in dealing with the financial crisis the government must avoid "over-regulation." Likewise, efforts to strengthen unions will suffer the traditional attacks, as unions are portrayed as corrupt and their members privileged. The unfolding situation with regard to the auto firms' troubles has demonstrated the attack, as conservatives have blamed the United Auto Workers for the industry's woes and have demanded extensive concessions by the union.

Certainly not all regulation is good regulation. Aside from excessive bureaucratic controls, there is the phenomenon by which regulating agencies are often captives of the industries that they are supposed to regulate. And there are corrupt unions. These are real issues, but they should not be allowed to derail change.

The current economic crisis emerged in large part as a shift in the balance of class power in the United States, a shift that began in the early 1970s and continued into the new millennium. Perhaps the present moment offers an opportunity to shift things back in the other direction. Recognition of the complex nexus of causes of the current economic crisis provides some guidance where people might start. Rebuilding and extending social programs, strengthening unions, and other actions that contribute to a more egalitarian power shift will not solve all the problems of U.S. capitalism. They can, however, begin to move us in the right direction.

Article 7.5

BEYOND KEYNESIANISM

Irving Fisher's Depression-era debt-deflation theory, then and now.

BY JAMES M. CYPHER
January/February 2011

According to dominant economic ideas, massive government interventions beginning in 2007—by way of Keynesian fiscal stimulus programs of the Bush and Obama administrations, the TARP program (the Wall Street bailout), and unprecedented interventions by the Federal Reserve—should have reset the economy. But because these interventions have not addressed the economy's huge structural issues, the economy continues to stall. Structural changes have brought an end to the era when wage increases were tightly linked to productivity increases from the end of World War II through the early 1970s. Since then, in a new era of deregulation, globalization, and de-unionization, labor productivity has nearly doubled, but real hourly wages for non-supervisory workers—over 80% of the workforce—have stagnated or fallen slightly for over 30 years. This has left the working class without any viable strategy as jobs were offshored and outsourced. Instead, women flooded into the workforce, workers sought second jobs, money was pumped into 401(k)s in the hope that stock market plays could make up for declining labor opportunities, household debt reached record levels, and the dream of windfall gains from house-flipping became a major focus for millions of working-class and middle-class families. From 2007 onward, the unprecedented interventions of the Bush and Obama administrations were designed to meet the immediate needs of elite financial institutions, leaving largely unaddressed the sorry plight of the dwindling middle and working classes, now marginalized in the new era of neoliberalism.

The stimulus and rescue programs did prevent an even greater avalanche of interlocking bankruptcies from reverberating via Wall Street to Main Street and back again—as occurred for years during the Great Depression of the 1930s. Yet as of the end of 2010, the general state of the U.S. economy looks bleak. With the economy losing over 443,000 jobs from June through September and unemployment rising again in November to an official rate of 9.8%, attention shifted toward further stimulus. By September, with most of his original $787 billion stimulus plan now spent, President Obama at first urged $50 billion for new infrastructure projects. There is a bit of buzz about a "manufacturing strategy"—a belated attempt to address the long-term collapse of the manufacturing sector from nearly 30% of the economy in 1953 to only 11% in 2009. Here, Obama has offered only increased funding for the Export-Import Bank in order to meet his goal of doubling U.S. exports by 2015. And then, in December 2010 came a "second stimulus" package largely limited to extensions of existing tax breaks—nearly 25% of which will go to the richest 1% of income recipients. Additional stimulus will come only from a $110 billion one-year drop in Social Security taxes and—according to White House estimates—roughly $50 billion in new investments due a variety of tax breaks for corporations and small business. But, the same legislation eliminated the "Make Work Pay" provision, which had been worth roughly $55 billion in tax cuts. Thus, for all the fanfare, the net new stimulus from this bill will be no more than $105 billion. In short, the administration proffers small and unimaginative policies as the economy stagnates and weakens.

Still, the interventions have served the purpose of putting a squishy floor underneath the collapsing edifice. All available evidence tends to support the Obama administration's claim that its fiscal interventions have saved or created some 2.7 million jobs. But these numbers constitute a counterfactual that is hard to demonstrate to the general public: the job growth owing to the stimulus has taken place in a broader context of massive job cuts—roughly 8 million jobs lost—since the downturn began. Economists Alan Blinder and Marc Zandi estimate that had it not been for a range of extremely active monetary and fiscal interventions beginning in the closing months of 2008, GDP in 2010 would have been 10.5% lower and an additional 8.5 million Americans would be out of work. Nonetheless, the public mostly rejects the assertions of Obama's economic spokespersons, either because most Americans have never learned of Keynesian economics or because they have been stampeded by a well-greased juggernaut financed by people like Pete Peterson, the Koch brothers, and the many others who would like to return the U.S. political economy to the good old days of 19th-century Social Darwinism.

Neoclassical to Neoliberal:
Economic Theory in a Circular Process

The new era of neoliberalism, which has reigned since the late 1970s, has been anchored in an attempt to sweep away the New Deal policies that had guided the economy during the Keynesian interlude (1933-1978). Prior to the Great Depression economists strongly embraced the neoclassical doctrine of self-adjusting markets seamlessly functioning to bring about a full employment "equilibrium." Any time the economy tended to slow down—causing unemployment to rise as profit, production, and general business activity declined—wages would decline, raw material prices would drop, wholesale prices would plummet, etc. According to received neoclassical dogma, cheap wages, cheap raw materials, readily available credit and under-priced machinery and equipment would all constitute a seductive combination for business interests who would then jump back into the market—hiring workers, building new plants, buying up raw materials, taking on bank loans in order to enjoy an unbeatable profit-making situation. Other things remaining the same, went the argument, the deflation of the economy would create its own recovery momentum as sharp traders availed themselves of a once-in-a-lifetime opportunity.

This approach assumed the economic system functioned as if it were a mechanical apparatus that was somehow "invested with a tendency to an equilibrium." Equilibrium was noted in the fall of 1929, shortly before the great stock market crash, by the most acclaimed economist of the day, Dr. Irving Fisher. Fisher stated that stock prices had reached a "permanently high plateau," adding in September of 1929, as stocks began to crater, that there could not be "anything in the nature of a crash." In the same month President Hoover's powerful Treasury Secretary Andrew Mellon—scion of the robber baron financiers who ran the Pittsburgh-based "House of Mellon"—proclaimed that the "high tide of prosperity will continue." So ended what was, until then, the longest continuous expansion in U.S. history. Prior to the crash the era was dubbed the "New Economy," wherein recession and downturns were understood as things of the past. So, too, the information technology boom of the 1990s was dubbed a "New Economy." In the 1990s, across the United States, congenitally blind economics departments scrapped almost all of their few remaining courses on business cycles.

When the depression of 1929-1939 began, Treasury Secretary Mellon—known as a financial prodigy—ecstatically championed the neoclassical theory of downwardly flexible prices: "liquidate labor, liquidate stocks, liquidate farmers, liquidate real estate … Values will adjust … "! In other words, after a brief bought of deflation, the economy would, in machine-like fashion, quickly restore its balance; the inevitable forces of the New Economy would spring back into motion and the U.S. economic ascent would resume.

Indeed, as the real value of the GDP dropped like a stone from late 1929 through 1933, wages and prices did fall. Autoworkers' money wages fell by 64%, miners' wages plummeted by 74%, steelworkers wages dropped by 62%, and the wages of agricultural workers—one-quarter of the economy was engaged in this sector—fell by 50%. Meanwhile prices in general fell by about 25%. (However, wage and salary income—crucially including managerial and executive incomes—apparently fell by less than the price level. For a few privileged employees with outsized salaries the standard of living rose.)

According to neoclassical theory, the dramatic drop in real wage income—spread throughout the vast manufacturing sector—should have been an inducement for businesses to invest. Along with cheap money, cheap machinery, and cheap commodities, lower wages should have been more than sufficient inducement to restore the economy to high levels of employment at lower price levels. The New York Federal Reserve Bank—the most important in the system—dropped its interest rate from 6% in 1929 to a record low of 1.5% in May 1931. But business cut and cut its investment level: while investment accounted for only 19.3% of GDP in 1929, 56% of the total drop in GDP from 1929 through 1933 was due to the decline in investment! The leading sector of the New Economy of the 1920s had been the auto industry. By 1933 real auto production had fallen by 65%—hardly a situation that would encourage the expansion of plants and equipment, the low cost of labor, machinery, materials, and loans notwithstanding. Left to its own devices and the tepid interventions of the Hoover administration, the economic system became ever more dysfunctional—no mechanical apparatus was at work to bring the system back to any semblance of equilibrium.

Surprisingly, by 1933 Fisher had reflected deeply on the idea that the economy would quickly spring back to full employment. In a 180-degree turn, he now argued that the Depression had unleashed forces that were sending the economy ever downward. The U.S. economy of the 1920s had been built on mountains of business, farm, mortgage, and personal debt. Now deflation was creating its own momentum. The burden of that debt was growing greater and greater as incomes shrank under the relentless pressures of deflation. As farm and business income fell, an ever-larger portion of income was shifted to the financial sector to pay debts that had been contracted when prices were much higher. In short, the growing debt burden was driving farmers and businesses into bankruptcy, thereby leading to further layoffs and more unemployment. Those households that had accumulated mortgage debt or consumer debt were in the same boat. As wages fell, families could not possibly pay an ever-growing share of their shrinking income to make debt payments that did not deflate with the rest of the economy. This was Fisher's all-important debt-deflation theory; it explained how a situation of over-indebtedness would lead to declining overall demand as the economy now favored creditors over debtors.

In neoclassical theory the fact that more of the total income was now shifting to creditors should not have impeded the economy's recovery. What debtors no longer spent, went the argument, creditors would now spend. This symmetrical model, however, just did not apply in the real and non-mechanical world of economic institutions. Banks and other creditors found that their income from debt repayments gave them greater power as money increased in value while wages and all other components of the economy declined in value. But the banks did not then lend out more money because they were fearful of the endless chain of bankruptcies the Depression had unleashed. They wanted to hold lots of funds in reserve against future losses. And to the degree that the income from the creditor institutions was passed through to managers, owners, and shareholders, these well-off groups were less likely to spend the additional income than were the workers, farmers, and owners of small- and medium-sized businesses who suffered growing losses. In sum, shifting a greater share of total income into the hands of wealthy creditors served only to push the economy further downward because (1) banks hoarded funds against future losses, (2) businesses seeing low and falling sales refused to take on any more debt, and (3) the rich did not put much of their new, more powerful, dollars back into the spending stream. Deflation had a supercharger effect—downward movement in the macro-economy unleashed powerful forces that led to further, perhaps accelerating, downward movement.

Today, Fisher is far less well known than another economist who took on neoclassical economics orthodoxy in the 1930s, John Maynard Keynes. Keynes challenged the neoclassicals with his interpretation of how total final demand determined the level of production and employment. He sought to show that the macro-economy could be caught up in a "special case" wherein equilibrium was established at very high levels of unemployment. In this situation, economic forces were aligned and balanced in a way that—whatever the rate of unemployment and excess capacity—the economy could do no more than simply reproduce itself year after year. Monetary policy would not revive the economy. Keynes famously urged massive government intervention to "prime the pump," thereby inducing the economic system to return to its normal state.

Yet Fisher's model of a debt-deflation disequilibrium is much more compelling than Keynes' idea of a high-unemployment equilibrium. Inflation-adjusted GDP fell by 9.5% from 1929 to 1930, and then fell by 7%, 15%, and 2.7% in the following three years. This was a downward spiral, not an equilibrium process.

The Structural Problem

The Great Depression signaled a moment when the U.S. economic system had met with structural barriers to its own expanding reproduction. The period from the 1870s to the 1920s saw the birth and consolidation of the giant corporation and the end of competitive capitalism based on small units of production, as economist Richard DuBoff has documented. By the 1920s, competitive capitalism could be found only in the minds of economists and in the texts and lectures they fed to generations of misinformed students. Along with the consolidation of a new structure of monopoly capitalism, the dynamic engine of the system had shifted from the production of producers' goods to the production of consumer durables such as washing machines and radios. The 1920s were fueled above all by exploding consumer demand for autos and their backward linkages to the oil industry, the auto parts companies, machine-tool firms, mining corporations, and producers of other raw materials such as rubber.

But growing income inequality, of a magnitude precisely equal to that which occurred in the run-up to the financial meltdown of 2007, undermined the future growth of the U.S. auto industry. (The top 1% in the household income distribution received an incredible 24% of all income in both 1928 and 2007.) Investment in the auto industry peaked in 1926, after which stagnating demand forestalled the building of more auto plants. Weak-to-nonexistent union power was a major reason why the economy began to totter both in 1927 (and again in 2006) when the housing boom peaked—a crucial matter ignored by both Fisher and Keynes.

Deeply embedded in the popular consciousness is the idea that the stock-market crash of 1929 caused the depression of the 1930s. The same was true of the most severe 19th century downturn: conventional accounts of the Panic of 1873 claimed that the depression was due to the collapse of the largest financier of the time, Jay Cooke & Company, causing losses to reverberate through the financial centers, particularly New York. Similarly, many of today's commentators pin the current economic crisis on financialization—the growing weight of the finance, insurance and real estate sector—which, the story goes, led to Ponzi finance, excessive leverage and the collapse of Bear Stearns, Lehman Brothers, and (effectively) A.I.G.

In short, the depressions of 1873 and 1929, and the borderline depression that began in 2007, are all widely assumed to have been caused by the alchemy of financial wizards. Those who take this view generally restrict their focus to the complex world of finance, without giving due attention or weight to underlying structural changes that have resulted in unsustainable tensions among the non-financial foundational components of the economy.

In recent years, the pace of structural change has been determined by (1) the realignment of capital-labor relations resulting in the effective de-unionization of the U.S. economy; (2) the outsourcing and offshoring of millions of jobs coupled with the threat of such actions, which has caused a dramatic tilt in the distribution of national income toward capital (partly buried as the greater part of the "salary" portion of the largest national income category, "wages and salaries"); (3) the subsequent delinking of productivity increases from wages, leaving a growing mass of profits to be redirected both to conspicuous consumption on a scale never before imagined and to predatory financial gamesmanship. In brief, a profound process of capital restructuring has taken place, giving rise to a new system of globally integrated production that has left the U.S. working class puzzled, powerless, and leaderless.

A Fisher Forecast?

According to the general perspective of the economics profession, depressions are a thing of the past: clever monetary policy and/or dynamic fiscal policy can reverse any downturn. Through massive injections of cheap credit and/or some combination of tax cuts, automatic countercyclical outlays (such as unemployment benefits), and discretionary expenditures (including especially those that boost the income of military contractors), federal policymakers can induce a recovery. Since 2007 the United States has followed exactly this prescription, and federal deficits will average approximately 10% of GDP in 2009, 2010, and 2011—more than double President Roosevelt's peak New Deal deficits in 1935 and 1936.

We can credit these massive interventions with curbing the forces unleashed as a result of the overcapacity problems, but they have not addressed the Keynesians' prime focus: employment. The U-6 unemployment rate—the best measure of the health of the labor market—includes the officially registered unemployed and also those who are working part-time but are seeking full-time employment and those "discouraged" workers who are not actively seeking employment but would if they thought jobs were available. The U-6 rate started to climb in late 2007 and had already hit 10.6% in 2008. It then soared on to 16.3% in 2009 and 16.7% in the first six months of 2010. If we take these data at face value, the U.S. economy is in a borderline depression, and one that is deepening.

Of course, unemployment is not the only factor. GDP has grown at an anemic annual rate of 3.2% in the past four quarters. Recoveries entail at first merely the reestablishment of previous levels of output, yet third quarter 2010 GDP (constant dollar) was still $86 billion below the last peak, in the fourth quarter of 2007. In the most recent nine-month period (fourth quarter 2009 through second quarter 2010) much of the growth has been in inventories, not in final demand. In fact, in the second quarter of 2010 final demand grew at an annual rate of only 1.3%.

The $64 question is this: what will happen in 2011 when the Obama administration's fiscal stimulus will rapidly drop off? Even though federal fiscal stimulus in 2011 (which began October 1, 2010) will be large, it will be partially counteracted by declining spending on the part of most state and local governments. The total effect of massive cuts at the state and local level in 2011 will be to withdraw funds in relatively labor-intensive areas such as education and health care. An estimated 500,000 local government employees are scheduled to be terminated in 2010 and 2011. To this group should be added another 900,000 public and private sector jobs currently sustained by the 34 states that will face the need to trim their budgets to accommodate falling tax revenues in fiscal years 2011 and 2012. The roughly 1.4 million threatened state and local layoffs could eventually have a much larger impact, potentially forcing twice that number or even more into unemployment. Even with the $26 billion in emergency one-year funding that passed the Congress in 2010, sizeable state and local layoffs and wage cuts will occur in fiscal year 2011. In September local government layoffs hit their highest rate in over 30 years.

In addition, a large amount of the federal deficit in 2011 (including the net $55 billion of new stimulus due to the drop in Social Security taxes in December 2010) will, once again, bleed away as imports. That is, a significant portion of government stimulus funds received by households via unemployment insurance payments, food stamps, tax cuts, jobs saved in construction, etc., will be sent abroad to pay for imported consumer goods, oil, machinery and equipment. Further, the major share of the federal debt (54% of marketable treasury bonds in December 2009) is now owned by foreigners—so most tax payments for interest must be shipped abroad to service the debt accumulated in past years.

Major corporations have continued to avidly restructure their production processes, laying off workers right and left. For example, Ford's North American division posted a huge second-quarter 2010 profit of $1.9 billion—this after cutting its labor force by 50% and seeing its revenue drop by $20 billion since 2005. Even the touted expansion of the Louisville Ford plant in 2011 will generate only a few hundred net new hires making only $14 per hour—half of the average pay of previously hired workers. The new corporate formula is higher profits from lower sales and little investment. Real Gross Investment (new capital spending plus replacement spending for worn-out equipment, adjusted for inflation) fell by 30% from the third quarter of 2007 to the first quarter of 2009. In the second quarter of 2010 overall investment was still 17.4% below the level achieved in late 2007.

Investment, then, is weak, while profits in the third quarter of 2010 reached a 60-year record high of $1.66 *trillion*. This profit rate rose by almost 30% from its recent low in the first quarter of 2008 through the first quarter of 2010. Indeed, the profit rate is now so high—thanks to the great squeeze on workers—that it exceeds the level achieved in the third quarter of 2007 by about 13%. If these bloated profits were channeled back into investment, then the economy would have a tendency to recover. But they are not. Corporations are taking their profits and sitting on them—cash holdings are at their highest levels since the early 1960s.

Across the United States, wage cuts have become a front-line strategy. A 2010 survey of U.S. cities found that 51% were either cutting or freezing existing wages. At General Motors, all new hires make one-half the rate of senior production workers. Even worse, this two-tier wage system is rapidly becoming a three-tier system where jumps in demand are being met by a new cadre of "permanent" temporary workers—known as "casuals"—non-unionized workers with no benefits. In some cases casuals make up more than 25% of the peak workforce, and they are paid only 75% of the second-tier wage. As federal government spending stalls out in late 2010, as the rich pull back from their recent spending binge, as corporations pocket much of their fat profits instead of plowing them back into expanded capacity, as wages stagnate or fall, as most state and local governments retrench further, as the new Republican-dominated congress contemplates federal program cuts in 2011, and as the meager additional net stimulus from the December 2010 Social Security tax cut is considerably shrunk by household debt repayments and the purchase of imported consumer goods, it is very difficult to foresee a continuation of what is convention-ally called a "recovery".

Keynesians assume that massive federal stimulus will somehow cause the for-ward gears of the capitalist system to mesh—but they do not explain how or why. So far, Keynesianism has gained no forward traction, although it has prevented a back-ward slide. This stalemate is not unprecedented. The New Deal was largely stuck in place after 1936 because of the political resistance of the captains of industry and finance to further and larger deficits. Likewise, political opposition to further huge deficits likely explains some of the current situation of stagnation and slippage. But when World War II spending ended the Depression, more was involved that just spending. The war industries created a new industrial base that generated a host of major technological changes, for example in petrochemicals, aircraft engineering, and plastics. The war broke a power logjam and financed the industrial restructur-ing of the U.S. economy.

Since 2008 the government has prioritized policies to push the profit rate up, thereby benefiting the top 5 million (3.7%) of all households, those with incomes above $250,000, while shrugging off the plight of the working and middle classes and the structural problems that have created the current impasse. Millions in these classes are now caught in a Fisher-style debt trap, with their incomes flat or falling and their debt-to-income ratios remaining extremely high. For most fami-lies, wealth continues to shrink: housing values lost an additional $1.7 *trillion* in 2010, with the largest proportional declines being felt in working-class neigh-borhoods. Aside from some largely symbolic gestures, neither the Bush nor the Obama administration's stimulus efforts have addressed the drag effect that Fisher highlighted. This has stalemated the stimulus programs and the easy-money ef-forts of the Fed, leaving the majority in the United States in a condition of crush-ing economic precariousness.

Sources: Alan Blinder and Marc Zandi, "How the Great Recession was Brought to an End" (July 27, 2010); Bureau of Labor Statistics, BLS Data Series: Labor Force Statistics, Table A-15, "Alternative Measures of Labor Underutilization" ; Susan Carter et al., *Historical Statistics of the United States*, Cambridge University Press, Tables Aa9-14, Ba4218 and Ca208-212 (2006); Lester Chandler, *America's Greatest Depression*, New York: Harper & Row (1970); Richard DuBoff, *Accumulation and Power: An Economic History of the United States*, Armonk, New York: M.E. Sharpe (1989); Rendig Fels, "American Business Cycles 1865-1879," *American Economic Review* v. 41 no. 3 (June 1951); Irving Fisher, "The Debt-Deflation Theory of Great Depression," *Econometrica* v.1, no. 4 (October 1933); John K. Galbraith, *The Great Crash*, Houghton Mifflin (1954); Steven Greenhouse, "More Workers Face Pay Cuts, not Furloughs," *New York Times* (August 8, 2010); Nicholas Johnson et al., "An Update on State Budget Cuts," Center on Budget and Policy Priorities (August 4, 2010); J. M. Keynes, *Economic Consequences of the Peace*, New York: Harcourt, Brace & Howe (1920); J. M. Keynes, *The General Theory of Employment, Interest and Money*, New York: Harcourt, Brace & World (1936); David Leonhardt, "Biggest Local Cuts in 30 Years," *New York Times* Economix blog (October 8, 2010); Cathrine Rampell, "Recovery Slows; Outlook on Jobs Grows Dimmer," *New York Times* (July 31, 2010); Cathrine Rampell, "Third Quarter Was Record for Profits," *New York Times* (November 24, 2010); Motoko Rich, "Wealthy Sector of Buying Public is Cutting Back," *New York Times* (July

17, 2010); Emanuel Saez, "Striking it Rich," (August 5, 2010); William Selway, "US Cities and Counties Poised to Cut 500,000 Jobs," (July 27, 2010); Nelson Schwartz, "Industries Find Surging Profits in Deeper Cuts," *New York Times* (July 26, 2010); Louis Uchitelle, "A White House Campaign for Factories," *New York Times* (September 10, 2010); Louis Uchitelle, "Unions Yield on Pay Scales to Keep Jobs" *New York Times* (November 20, 2010); Hui-yong Yu and John Gittelsohn, U.S. Home Values to Drop by $1.7 Trillion This Year, (December 9, 2010); U.S. Department of Commerce, Bureau of Economic Analysis, National Income and Product Accounts, Table 3-b (2010); U.S. Treasury, "The Case for Temporary 100 Percent Expensing: Encouraging Business To Expand Now by Lowering the Cost of Investment" (October 29, 2010); Thorstein Veblen, "Why is Economics not an Evolutionary Science?" in *The Portable Veblen*, Max Lerner, ed., New York: Viking (1948), reprinted from the Quarterly Journal of Economics, (July 1898); Francis Warnock, "How Dangerous Is U.S. Government Debt?" *Capital Flows Quarterly* (Council on Foreign Relations, 2010).

Article 7.6

OPENING PANDORA'S BOX
The basics of Marxist economics.

BY ALEJANDRO REUSS
February 2000

In most universities, what is taught as "economics" is a particular brand of orthodox economic theory. The hallmark of this school is a belief in the optimal efficiency (and, it goes without saying, the equity) of "free markets."

The orthodox macroeconomists—who had denied the possibility of general economic slumps—were thrown for a loop by the Great Depression of the 1930s, and by the challenge to their system of thought by John Maynard Keynes and others. Even so, the orthodox system retains at its heart a view of capitalist society in which individuals, each equal to all others, undertake mutually beneficial transactions tending to a socially optimal equilibrium. There is no power and no conflict. The model is a perfectly bloodless abstraction, without all the clash and clamor of real life.

Karl Marx and the Critique of Capitalist Society

One way to pry open and criticize the orthodox model of economics is by returning to the idiosyncrasies of the real world. That's the approach of most of the articles in this book, which describe real-world phenomena that the orthodox model ignores or excludes. These efforts may explain particular facts better than the orthodoxy, while not necessarily offering an alternative general system of analysis. They punch holes in the orthodox lines but, ultimately, leave the orthodox model in possession of the field.

This suggests the need for a different conceptual system that can supplant orthodox economics as a whole. Starting in the 1850s and continuing until his death in 1883, the German philosopher and revolutionary Karl Marx dedicated himself to developing a conceptual system for explaining the workings of capitalism. The system which Marx developed and which bears his name emerged from his criticism of the classical political economy developed by Adam Smith and David Ricardo. While Marx admired Smith and Ricardo, and borrowed many of their concepts, he approached economics (or "political economy") from a very different standpoint. He had developed a powerful criticism of capitalist society before undertaking his study of the economy. This criticism was inspired by French socialist ideas and focused on the oppression of the working class. Marx argued that wage workers—those working for a paycheck—were "free" only in the sense that they were not beholden to a single lord or master, as serfs had been under feudalism. But they did not own property, nor were they craftspeople working for themselves, so they were compelled to sell themselves for a wage to one capitalist or another. Having surrendered their freedom to the employer's authority, they were forced to work in the way the employer told them while the latter pocketed the profit produced by their labor.

Marx believed, however, that by creating this oppressed and exploited class of workers, capitalism was creating the seeds of its own destruction. Conflict between the workers and the owners was an essential part of capitalism. But in Marx's view of history, the workers could eventually overthrow the capitalist class, just as the capitalist class, or "bourgeoisie," had grown strong under feudalism, only to supplant the feudal aristocracy. The workers, however, would not simply substitute a new form of private property and class exploitation, as the bourgeoisie had done. Rather, they would bring about the organization of production on a cooperative basis, and an end to the domination of one class over another.

This line of thinking was strongly influenced by the ideas of the day in German philosophy, which held that any new order grows in the womb of the old, and eventually bursts forth to replace it. Marx believed that the creation of the working class, or proletariat, in the heart of capitalism was one of the system's main contradictions. Marx studied capitalist economics in order to explain the conditions under which it would be possible for the proletariat to overthrow capitalism and create a classless society. The orthodox view depicts capitalism as tending towards equilibrium (without dynamism or crises), serving everyone's best interests, and lasting forever. Marx saw capitalism as crisis-ridden, full of conflict, operating to the advantage of some but not others, and far from eternal.

Class and Exploitation

Marx studied history closely. Looked at historically, he saw capitalism as only the latest in a succession of societies based on exploitation. When people are only able to produce the bare minimum needed to live, he wrote, there is no room for a class of people to take a portion of society's production without contributing to it. But as soon as productivity exceeds this subsistence level, it becomes possible for a class of people who do not contribute to production to live by appropriating the surplus for themselves. These are the masters in slave societies, the lords in feudal societies, and the property owners in capitalist society.

Marx believed that the owners of businesses and property—the capitalists— take part of the wealth produced by the workers, but that this appropriation is hidden by the appearance of an equal exchange, or "a fair day's work for a fair day's pay."

Those who live from the ownership of property—businesses, stocks, land, etc— were then a small minority and now are less than 5% of the population in countries like the United States (Marx wrote before the rise of massive corporations and bureaucracies, and did not classify managers and administrators who don't own their own businesses as part of the bourgeoisie.) The exploited class, meanwhile, is the vast majority who lived by earning a wage or salary—not just the "blue collar" or industrial workers but other workers as well.

Marx's view of how exploitation happened in capitalist society depended on an idea, which he borrowed from Smith and Ricardo, called the Labor Theory of Value. The premise of this theory, which is neither easily proved nor easily rejected, is that labor alone creates the value which is embodied in commodities and which creates profit for owners who sell the goods. The workers do not receive the full value created by their labor and so they are exploited.

Students are likely to hear in economics classes that profits are a reward for the "abstinence" or "risk" of a businessperson—implying that profits are their just desserts. Marx would argue that profits are a reward obtained through the exercise of power—the power owners have over those who own little but their ability to work and so must sell this ability for a wage. That power, and the tribute it allows owners of capital to extract from workers, is no more legitimate in Marx's analysis than the power of a slaveowner over a slave. A slaveowner may exhibit thrift and take risks, after all, but is the wealth of the slaveowner the just reward for these virtues, or a pure and simple theft from the slave?

As Joan Robinson, an important 20th-century critic and admirer of Marx, argues, "What is important is that owning capital is not a productive activity. The academic economists, by treating capital as productive, used to insinuate the suggestion that capitalists deserve well by society and are fully justified in drawing income from their property."

The Falling Rate of Profit

Marx believed that his theory had major implications for the crises that engulf capitalist economies. In Marx's system, the value of the raw materials and machinery used in the manufacture of a product does not create the extra value that allows the businessman to profit from its production. That additional value is created by labor alone.

Marx recognized that owners could directly extract more value out of workers in three ways: cutting their wages, lengthening their working day, or increasing the intensity of their labor. This need not be done by a direct assault on the workers. Capitalists can achieve the same goal by employing more easily exploited groups or by moving their operations where labor is not as powerful. Both of these trends can be seen in capitalism today, and can be understood as part of capital's intrinsic thirst for more value and increased exploitation.

With the mechanization of large-scale production under capitalism, machines and other inanimate elements of production form a larger and larger share of the inputs to production. Marx believed this would result in a long-term trend of the rate of profit to fall as less of production depended on the enriching contribution of human labor. This, he believed, would make capitalism increasingly vulnerable to economic crises.

This chain of reasoning, of course, depends on the Labor Theory of Value (seeing workers as the source of the surplus value created in the production process) and can be avoided by rejecting this theory outright. Orthodox economics has not only rejected the Labor Theory of Value, but abandoned the issue of "value" altogether. After lying fallow for many years, value analysis was revived during the 1960s by a number of unorthodox economists including the Italian economist Piero Sraffa. Marx was not the last word on the subject.

Unemployment, Part I: The "Reserve Army of the Unemployed"

Marx is often raked over the coals for arguing that workers, under capitalism, were destined to be ground into ever more desperate poverty. That living standards improved in rich capitalist countries is offered as proof that his system is fatally flawed. While Marx was not optimistic about the prospect of workers raising their standard of living very far under capitalism, he was critical of proponents of the "iron law of wages," such as Malthus, who held that any increase in wages above the minimum necessary for survival would simply provoke population growth and a decline in wages back to subsistence level.

Marx emphasized that political and historical factors influencing the relative power of the major social classes, rather than simple demographics, determined the distribution of income.

One economic factor to which Marx attributed great importance in the class struggle was the size of the "reserve army of the unemployed." Marx identified unemployment as the major factor pushing wages down—the larger the "reserve" of unemployed workers clamoring for jobs, the greater the downward pressure on wages. This was an influence, Marx believed, that the workers would never be able to fully escape under capitalism. If the workers' bargaining power rose enough to raise wages and eat into profits, he argued, capitalists would merely substitute labor-saving technology for living labor, recreating the "reserve army" and reasserting the downward pressure on wages.

Though this has not, perhaps, retarded long-term wage growth to the degree that Marx expected, his basic analysis was visionary at a time when the Malthusian (population) theory of wages was the prevailing view. Anyone reading the business press these days—which is constantly worrying that workers might gain some bargaining power in a "tight" (low unemployment) labor market, and that their wage demands will provoke inflation—will recognize its basic insight.

Unemployment, Part II: The Crisis of Overproduction

Marx never developed one definitive version of his theory of economic crises (recessions) under capitalism. Nonetheless, his thinking on this issue is some of his most visionary. Marx was the first major economic thinker to break with the orthodoxy of "Say's Law." Named after the French philosopher Jean-Baptiste Say, this theory held that each industry generated income equal to the output it created. In other words, "supply creates its own demand." Say's conclusion, in which he was followed by Smith, Ricardo, and orthodox economists up through the Great Depression, was that while a particular industry such as the car industry could overproduce, no generalized overproduction was possible. In this respect, orthodox economics flew in the face of all the evidence. In his analysis of overproduction, Marx focused on what he considered the basic contradiction of capitalism—and, in microcosm, of the commodity itself—the contradiction between "use value" and "exchange value." The idea is that a commodity both satisfies a specific need (it has "use value") and can be exchanged for other articles (it has "exchange value"). This distinction was not invented by Marx; it can be found in the work of Smith. Unlike Smith, however, Marx emphasized the way exchange value—what something is worth in the market—overwhelms the use value of a commodity. Unless a commodity can be sold, the portion of society's useful labor embodied in it is wasted (and the product is useless to those in need). Vast real needs remain unsatisfied for the majority of people, doubly so when—during crises of overproduction—vast quantities of goods remain unsold because there is not enough "effective demand."

It is during these crises that capitalism's unlimited drive to develop society's productive capacity clashes most sharply with the constraints it places on the real incomes of the majority to buy the goods they need. Marx developed this notion of a demand crisis over 75 years before the so-called "Keynesian revolution" in economic thought (whose key insights were actually developed before Keynes by the Polish economist Michal Kalecki on the foundations of Marx's analysis).

Marx expected that these crises of overproduction and demand would worsen as capitalism developed, and that the crises would slow down more and more the development of society's productive capacities (what Marx called the "forces of production"). Ultimately, he believed, these crises would be capitalism's undoing. He also pointed to them as evidence of the basic depravity of capitalism. "In these crises," Marx writes in the *Communist Manifesto*,

> there breaks out an epidemic that, in all earlier epochs would have seemed an absurdity, the epidemic of overproduction. Society suddenly finds itself put back into a state of momentary barbarism; it appears as if a famine, a universal war of devastation had cut off the supply of every means of subsistence; industry and commerce seem to be destroyed; and why? Because there is too much civilization, too much means of subsistence, too much industry, too much commerce …

And how does the bourgeoisie get over these crises? On the one hand by enforced destruction of productive force; on the other hand, by the conquest of new markets, and by the more thorough exploitation of old ones.

This kind of crisis came so close to bringing down capitalism during the Great Depression that preventing them became a central aim of government policy. While government intervention has managed to smooth out the business cycle, especially in the wealthiest countries, capitalism has hardly become crisis-free.

While the reigning complacency about a new, crisis-free capitalism is much easier to sustain here than in, say, East Asia, capitalism clearly has not yet run up against any absolute barrier to its development. In fact, Marx's discussions (in the *Communist Manifesto* and elsewhere) of capitalism's irresistible expansive impulse—capital breaking down all barriers, expanding into every crevice, always "thirsting for surplus value" and new fields of exploitation—seem as apt today as they did 150 years ago.

Marx as Prophet

Marx got a great deal about capitalism just right—its incessant, shark-like forward movement; its internal chaos, bursting forth periodically in crisis; its concentration of economic power in ever fewer hands. Judged on these core insights, the Marxist system can easily stand toe-to-toe with the orthodox model. Which comes closer to reality? The capitalism that incessantly bursts forth over new horizons, or the one that constantly gravitates towards comfortable equilibrium? The one where crisis is impossible, or the one that lurches from boom to bust to boom again? The one where perfect competition reigns, or the one where a handful of giants towers over every industry?

In all these respects, Marx's system captures the thundering dynamics of capitalism much better than the orthodox system does. As aesthetically appealing as the clockwork harmony of the orthodox model may be, this is precisely its failing. Capitalism is anything but harmonious.

There was also a lot that Marx, like any other complex thinker, predicted incorrectly, or did not foresee. In this respect, he was not a prophet. His work should be read critically, and not, as it has been by some, as divine revelation. Marx, rather, was the prophet of a radical approach to reality. In an age when the "free market" rides high, and its apologists claim smugly that "there is no alternative," Joan Robinson's praise of Marx is apt: "[T]he nightmare quality of Marx's thought gives it … an air of greater reality than the gentle complacency of the orthodox academics. Yet he, at the same time, is more encouraging than they, for he releases hope as well as terror from Pandora's box, while they preach only the gloomy doctrine that all is for the best in the best of all *possible* worlds."

Resources: Joan Robinson, *An Essay on Marxian Economics* (Macmillan, 1952); "Manifesto of the Community Party," and "Crisis Theory (from Theories of Surplus Value)," in Robert C. Tucker, ed., *The Marx-Engels Reader* (W.W. Norton, 1978); Roman Rosdolsky, *The Making of Marx's 'Capital'* (Pluto Press, 1989); Ernest Mandel, "Karl Heinrich Marx"; Luigi L. Pasinetti, "Joan Violet Robinson"; and John Eatwell and Carlo Panico, "Piero Sraffa"; in John Eatwell, Murray Milgate, and Peter Newman, eds., *The New Palgrave: A Dictionary of Economics* (Macmillan, 1987).

Article 7.7

UNDER THE MARGINS
Feminist economists look at gender and poverty

BY RANDY ALBELDA
September/October 2002

For all the hype about welfare-to-work, most former welfare recipients are still living in poverty. It is true that, since the advent of 1990s-style "welfare reform," families no longer on welfare are earning more, on average, than those still on welfare. But more often than not, the jobs that former welfare mothers find don't provide employer-sponsored health insurance, vacation time, sick leave, or wages sufficient to support their families. In fact, the percentage of families who are "desperately" poor (with incomes at or below 50% of the official poverty line) has gone up since the mid-1990s, and so has the percentage of former welfare recipients who report hardships such as difficulty feeding their families or paying bills. And remember: All of this occurred during a so-called economic boom.

So why does the emphasis on work (and now marriage) continue to dominate the welfare debate? In large part, this is because the poverty "story" of the last 20 years—created and perpetuated by conservative ideologues and politicians—blames poor people for their own poverty. Women supposedly have too many children without husbands, poor black urban dwellers exhibit pathological behaviors, and liberal welfare policies—by expanding government spending and providing an attractive alternative to jobs and marriage—have made matters worse.

At least one group of theorists—feminist economists—says it isn't so. It is women's particular economic role in capitalism—as caregiver—that shapes their relationship to the labor market, men, and the state. Feminist economists have shown how having and caring for children affects the economic status of women—including women who are not mothers but are still relegated to poorly paid care-giving jobs. While their voices are largely ignored in research and policy circles, feminist economists' analyses provide the best understanding of the obstacles low-income families face and the range of policy options that might work.

Women and Poverty

Almost everywhere, women are the majority of poor adults. Recently, a group of sociologists from several U.S. universities looked at poverty in eight industrialized nations. Using a relative poverty measure (half of median family income), they found that, in the 1990s, women's poverty rates exceeded men's in all countries but Sweden. Further, they found that single-mother poverty rates—even in countries with deep social welfare systems—are exceptionally high. (See Figure 1.)

In the United States in 2000, women comprised just over half of the adult population but constituted 61% of all poor adults. (The U.S. poverty income threshold is based on an absolute dollar figure determined in the 1960s and since indexed for inflation.) Toss in children, and the data are even grimmer; 16.2% of all children were poor, while over one-third of all single-mother families were poor. Together, women and children comprised 76% of the poor in the United States, far surpassing their 62% representation in the population as a whole.

Since the late 1950s (when the data were first collected), single-mother families in the United States have never constituted more than 13% of all families; however, they form just under half of all poor families. Figure 2 depicts the proportion of all families—and all poor families—that are single-mother families. The steepest increase occurred in the late 1960s on the heels of the War on Poverty, as poverty rates for everyone were falling.

Economic Theory and Poverty

From Adam Smith onward, most economists have understood poverty by looking at labor markets, labor-market inequality, and economic growth. According to this approach, it is underemployment or the lack of employment—and the resulting lack of income—that causes poverty. A brief summary of the dominant economic theories in the last half of the 20th century illustrates the point.

Keynesian economic theory argues that the lack of demand in the economy as a whole leads to unemployment. When investors and consumers can't jumpstart the economy, we need fiscal or monetary economic stimuli to induce demand. It was this wisdom that has guided economists to promote economic growth as a way to

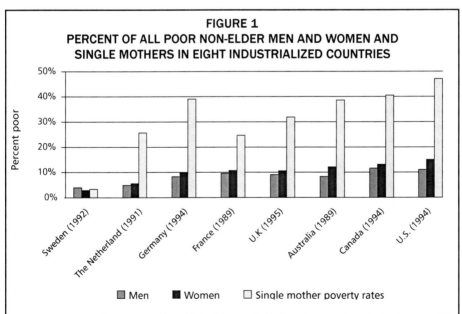

FIGURE 1
PERCENT OF ALL POOR NON-ELDER MEN AND WOMEN AND SINGLE MOTHERS IN EIGHT INDUSTRIALIZED COUNTRIES

Note: Poverty rates are the proportion of non-elderly adults ages 25-54 whose after-tax and transfer family incomes fall below 50% of the median family income.

Source: Table 1, in Karen Christopher et al., "Gender Inequality in Poverty in Affluent Nations: The Role of Single Motherhood and the State," in Karen Vleminckx and Timothy Smeeding, eds., *Child Well-Being, Child Poverty and Child Policy in Modern Nations* (London: Policy Press, 2001).

reduce poverty, arguing that "a rising tide lifts all boats"—as, for example, during the Kennedy and Johnson administrations.

Marxian theorists say that, under capitalism, unemployment cannot be totally eliminated because it is a necessary component of capitalist production that serves to "discipline" workers. Unless we make radical changes to the economic system, there will always be families that are without employment and therefore poor.

Like Marxian economists, *institutional* economists also believe that economic outcomes aren't simply the result of pure market forces; cultural, social, and political forces also come into play. In the 1970s, economists Peter Doeringer and Michael Piore identified distinct labor-market segments. Younger workers, workers of color, and women tend to end up in what they call the "secondary labor market"—characterized by low wages, few promotional opportunities, and easy-to-acquire skills—more than other workers. These workers are particularly vulnerable to unemployment and hence more likely to be poor. The way to relieve poverty is to help these workers move into better jobs, or to create policies that make their jobs better.

These understandings of poverty offer little or no gender analysis—presumably what ails men is equally applicable to women. Analyses of insufficient (aggregate) demand, unemployment, and labor-market inequality rarely mention women or discuss how and why gender matters—unless feminist scholars provide them.

Neoclassical (mainstream) economists also argue that poverty is caused by lack of employment and low wages—but they consider workers responsible for their own

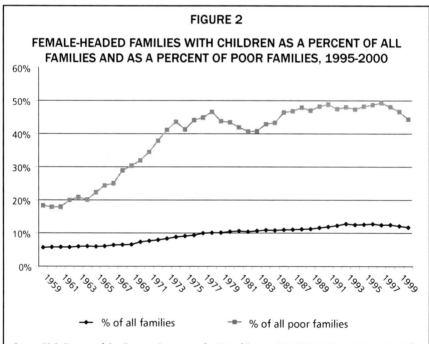

FIGURE 2

FEMALE-HEADED FAMILIES WITH CHILDREN AS A PERCENT OF ALL FAMILIES AND AS A PERCENT OF POOR FAMILIES, 1995-2000

▬●▬ % of all families   ▬■▬ % of all poor families

Source: U.S. Bureau of the Census, *Poverty in the United States: 1999* (P60-210), pp. B-11-12 and for 2000: <www.census.gov/hhes/poverty histpov/hstpov4.html>.

wage levels. Workers who choose not to pursue education, training, or on-the-job experience will participate in the labor force less often than more highly trained and skilled workers, be less productive, and receive lower wages. Unlike the political economy theorists just discussed, many non-feminist economists—the most well known being Nobel Prize winner Gary Becker—have tackled the topic of women's lower wages. But they consistently conclude that women's lack of employment, or employment at low wages, results from rational individual choice. Only policies that boost incentives for individuals to invest in themselves (like tax credits for education) will alleviate poverty.

Gender Matters

It is true that one reason women are poor is that they are not in the labor force or are underemployed. But while employment is an important underpinning to understanding poverty, it is not the same for women as for men.

Most economists who study labor markets assume that workers in capitalist economies are "unencumbered"—that they don't have significant constraints on their time outside of paid work. Encumbered workers are treated as a "special case"—worthy of examination, but understood and analyzed as an exception rather than the rule.

Since the beginnings of capitalism, however, female workers have almost always been "encumbered." And women's role as caregivers—their main encumbrance—has shaped their participation in the economy, as feminist historians and economic historians have shown. Historically, women's economic opportunities have been severely constricted, with race, age, and marital status sending important market "signals" about where women could or should be employed. For example, until the 1960s, many professional and some clerical jobs had "marriage bars," i.e., employers refused to hire married women on the assumption that they did not need the salaries these jobs paid, and would not stick around once they had children. Similarly, before anti-discrimination laws were enacted, many workers of color could not get jobs as managers in many professions, or even as sales clerks if the business catered to a white clientele.

For more than a century, this labor market "ordering" has given rise to employment, income, and wage policies that reinforce and reproduce women's political and economic dependence on men (and non-whites' inferior status in relation to whites). These policies assume that the standard family is a heterosexual married couple with a lone male breadwinner employed in industrial production. For example, in order to collect unemployment insurance benefits, workers must work a minimum number of hours and receive a minimum amount of earnings. Because many women work part-time and earn low wages, they are much less likely to qualify for benefits than men. Similarly, Social Security benefits are based on previous earnings over a sustained period of employment. Women who have spent most of their adult lives as caregivers are thus ineligible for benefits on their own, and must rely on their husbands' contributions instead.

Men's and women's employment patterns are very different. Women's labor force participation rates are lower than men's, and women's employment experiences in economic downturns often differ from men's. Women's job options and choices are also highly influenced by care-giving responsibilities; mothers are more likely than fathers to trade higher-paying jobs for jobs that are closer to childcare, have more flexible schedules, or require fewer hours.

In addition to shaping women's paid labor-market activities, care work has been economically, socially, and politically undervalued, as feminist economists point out. This is true both when that work is done in the home for free and when others do it for low pay. Among the few jobs immigrant women and women of color can almost always find are low-paying care-work jobs, and they are disproportionately represented in those jobs. For example, in 2001, women were 47% of all workers but 97% of child care workers, 93% of registered nurses, 90% of health aides, and 72% of social workers. Black workers comprised 11% of the workforce but were 33% of health aides, 23% of licensed practical nurses, and 20% of cleaning service workers. This type of occupational "stereotyping" reinforces the care-giving roles that women and people of color fill, and the low pay (relative to jobs with similar skill requirements) reinforces women's dependence on men and racial inequality. Economist Nancy Folbre, in her 2001 book *The Invisible Heart: Economics and Family Values*, calls this the "care penalty."

It is because of their low-paid and unpaid care work, then, that women are particularly economically vulnerable and much more likely to be poor than are men. The role of care giving—as distinct from other factors like employment, economic growth, and labor-market inequality—helps to explain not only women's employment patterns but also women's poverty. So theories of poverty that rely on analyses of employment that assume all people are men—or that women are a special case of men—are not only incomplete, they are wrong.

Feminist Analyses of Poverty

It is no coincidence that, when there has been a viable women's movement—in the early part of the 20th century and in the late 1960s—feminists and women researchers have paid particular attention to poor women.

Documenting poor families: early efforts

In the early 20th century, there was a good deal of concern about how women fit into the capitalist economy. Social scientists living in or near poor communities—often in settlement houses established by women reformers—conducted surveys of women workers, mostly through government-sponsored research. Many of the surveys found that the biggest problems faced by two-parent families were a lack of employment and insufficient wages. Researchers readily recognized that families headed by women were constrained by women's role as caregiver and women's low wages. Instead of advocating more employment for women, they promoted relatively meager levels of public assistance.

In the 1910s and 1920s, women reformers were key players not only in doing research but also in creating policies directed toward poor women and children. These women imposed white middle-class values about child-rearing, hygiene, and education; their construction of "deservingness" replicated and reinforced the ways in which women and men, immigrants and non-immigrants, were supposed to act. At the same time, they successfully implemented income supplement programs for single-mother families at the state level, and they were instrumental in incorporating AFDC (Aid to Families with Dependent Children) into the Social Security Act of 1935. Feminist poverty researchers and reformers did not emerge again until the late 1960s.

Sisterhood may be powerful, but motherhood is not: recent efforts

The women's movement of the late 1960s and 1970s laid some important foundations for understanding women's poverty, even though its main economic strategies were aimed at improving the wages of women who were employed. Feminists fought for affirmative action, which was most successful in creating opportunities for college-educated women. Today, women hold 46% of executive and professional jobs—exactly their representation in all jobs—and comprise just under 30% of all doctors and lawyers. Feminists also organized for comparable worth, which was intended to lift wages for low-income women by recognizing and rewarding the skill level and effort needed to perform low-paying women's jobs (including care-giving ones).

At the same time, feminist scholars called attention to women's "double day" (now called "work/family conflict") and theorized about the role of care work and reproduction in capitalist economies. From the outset, feminist analysts understood that "housework" was work and a vital component of capitalist production. This intellectual work paralleled "wages for housework" campaigns that were launched in Italy, Canada, Great Britain, and the United States.

Using these tools to reinterpret poverty was not hard. Among the first to apply a feminist analysis to women's poverty was sociologist Diana Pearce, in an 1978 article entitled "The Feminization of Poverty: Women, Work, and Welfare." Pearce called attention to the fact that women were disproportionately represented among the poor. Her phrase—"the feminization of poverty"—became very popular in feminist circles as well as in the mainstream press.

Economist Nancy Folbre followed up with a theoretical framework directly linking women's care work as mothers to their poverty. In her 1985 article, "The Pauperization of Motherhood: Patriarchy and Social Policy in the U.S.," she argued that, when the costs of raising children are shifted onto women, women (and children) become dependent on men. Then, when fathers abandon their families, women and children are consigned to poverty. Folbre also argues that public policies around divorce, child support, unemployment insurance, and welfare reinforce this relationship. For example, welfare policies—even before the 1990s reforms—never provided enough income for women to support their families without working "under the table" or getting unreported income, paying a big price for not being married.

Single mothers especially bear the burden of these policies in the form of incredibly high poverty rates. But, Folbre points out, the benefits of care labor—healthy, productive children who become tax-paying adults—are enjoyed by all of society, not merely the mothers who provided the care. If society recognized the value of women's care work and compensated them for it, then fewer women would be poor.

Current trends

Currently, some feminist scholars are addressing the ways that gender influences government allocation of income supports (like pensions, unemployment insurance, and welfare) and non-cash assistance (e.g., education and child care). Sociologist Ann Orloff and political scientists Diane Sainsbury and Jane Lewis argue that state welfare policies (construed broadly) embody deeply gendered notions of citizenship and need. Much of this work is theoretical and does not explicitly address poverty. However, it helps to explain the lack of policies that would correct women's poverty.

Other researchers are focusing on how people's capacity—access to health and education, living conditions, how they are treated in a society—affects their potential to generate income and causes poverty. Building on the work of economist Amartya Sen, feminist economists in the United States have shown that it is unreasonable and unlikely to expect single mothers to "work" their way out of poverty—because women earn lower wages than men, because they have care-giving responsibilities, and because the additional costs associated with caring for children restrict their capacity to be employed even while family needs remain high. For example, Barbara Bergmann and Trudi Renwick developed budgets for low-income families in the 1990s. Chris Tilly and I have demonstrated that the income needs of single-mother families far exceed their earnings possibilities—even with full-time employment. This work refutes the claims of liberals who supported welfare reform in the naïve belief that welfare recipients could easily substitute earnings for public assistance.

Finally, feminist economists are documenting how low-income women—especially single-mother families in which the same adult is both caregiver and breadwinner—relate to the labor market, fathers, and the state. Using longitudinal data, feminist social scientists Roberta Spalter-Roth and Heidi Hartmann found that many poor single-mother families either combine government assistance with wages (under or above the table) or cycle between the two. This research is confirmed and extended by feminist sociologists like Kathryn Edin and Laura Lein, who, through extensive interviews with poor single mothers, documented the particular ways and times that poorly paying jobs as well as men and their incomes drift in and out of women's lives. These studies make it clear that women's employment is not family-sustaining, and that, to survive, single-mother families need a sane combination of earnings, child support, *and* government assistance. In contrast to the narrowly focused, incentive-based literature that characterizes poor women's behavior as pathological, these approaches demonstrate that poor women's lives are dynamic yet fragile, and that the decisions they make are creative, adaptive, and almost always child-centered.

Who Cares?

Despite their efforts, feminist scholars have not had much impact on the poverty literature—at least not in economics—nor have they influenced policies intended to alleviate poverty. Much (though not all) poverty research is grant-funded, and it tends to focus narrowly on evaluating the individual impact of welfare reform, mostly by looking at welfare "leavers." These factors discourage the use of feminist analysis, since most funding goes either to conservative think tanks with a specific ideological aversion to feminism or to "liberal" think tanks that have made their fortunes in mainstream analysis fitted to their main consumer—the federal government.

Further, these conventional studies often preclude the larger political economy approach taken by feminists. Welfare reform is a mechanism of social control over poor single women—especially women of color—that is part of a larger conservative agenda to justify if not exacerbate economic inequality, assure a large pool of low-wage labor, and silence important political movements. Feminist analysis suggests the need for policies that would not only reduce poverty but also change women's (and people of color's) relationship to the labor market, (white) men, and the state, thus loosening the grip of economic dependence. This isn't in line with the right-wing agenda at all.

However, feminist economic analysis has been very useful to activists who are trying to help poor women. For example, in the mid-1990s, Wider Opportunity for Women (WOW), a feminist group based in Washington, D.C., started conducting family economic self-sufficiency standard projects. Currently, WOW operates projects in 40 states and D.C. The studies demonstrate how much income a single-mother family needs to survive, and are being used as organizing tools in the states.

During the mid-1990s welfare reform debates and now in discussions about reauthorization of Temporary Assistance for Needy Families (TANF), feminist scholars—connected informally through the "Women's Committee of 100"—have argued that raising children is work and that responsible legislation should recognize unpaid work as work. The Committee has called for a caregiver's allowances (see "Wages for Housework," article 1.5, and <www. welfare2002.org>). And while Congress has not embraced these ideas, a TANF reauthorization bill sponsored by Representative Patsy Mink (D-Hawaii) in the spring of 2002 garnered support from close to 90 members of the House.

Feminist economists argue that the role of economists is to understand how societies do or do not provide for people's needs. Through their research and skills, they provide the tools for activists to argue that women's employment status and care-giving responsibilities place many at the bottom of the economic pecking order. At the same time, feminist economists are connecting their work directly to social movements, lending their expertise—and their own voices—to living wage campaigns, efforts to improve compensation for child care workers and home health aides, and efforts to eliminate poverty, not welfare.

Resources: Kathryn Edin and Laura Lein, *Making Ends Meet: How Single Mothers Survive Welfare and Low Wage Work* (Russell Sage Foundation, 1997); Nancy Folbre, "The Pauperization of Motherhood: Patriarchy and Social Policy in the U.S.," *Review of Radical Political Economics*, vol. 16, no. 4 (1984): 72-88; Nancy Folbre, *The Invisible Heart: Economics and Family Values* (New York: The New Press, 2001); Jane Lewis, "Gender and the Development of Welfare Regimes," *Journal of European Social Policy* 3 (1992): 159-73; Alice O'Connor, *Poverty Knowledge: Social Science, Social Policy, and the Poor in Twentieth Century U.S. History* (Princeton, N.J.: Princeton

University Press, 2001); Ann Orloff, "Gender and the Social Rights of Citizenship: The Comparative Analysis of Gender Relations and Welfare States," *American Sociological Review* 58 (1993): 303-28; Diana Pearce, "The Feminization of Poverty: Women, Work, and Welfare," *Urban and Social Change Review* (February 1978); Trudi Renwick and Barbara Bergmann, "A Budget-based Definition of Poverty with an Application to Single-parent Families," *Journal of Human Resources* 28, no. 1 (1993): 1-24; Diane Sainsbury, *Gender, Equality, and Welfare States* (Cambridge: Cambridge University Press, 1996); Amartya K. Sen, *Development as Freedom* (New York: Alfred A. Knopf, 1999); Roberta SpalterRoth et al., *Welfare That Works: The Working Lives of AFDC Recipients* (Washington, D.C.: Institute for Women's Policy Research, 1995); Chris Tilly and Randy Albelda, "Family Structure and Family Earnings: The Determinants of Earnings Differences among Family Types," *Industrial Relations* 33, no. 2 (1994): 151-167; U.S. Census, *Current Population Surveys* <www.census. gov/hhes/income/histinc/histpovtb.html>; Bureau of Labor Statistics, *Employment and Earnings*, Table 11 *<www.bls.gov/cps/home.htm#charemp.§§>*

Chapter 8

INTERNATIONAL TRADE
AND FINANCE

INTRODUCTION

When it comes to the global economy, most textbooks line up behind the "Washington Consensus"—a package of free trade and financial liberalization policies that the U.S. Treasury Department, the International Monetary Fund (IMF), and the World Bank have spun into the prevailing prescriptions for the world's developing economies. Mainstream textbook discussions of exchange rates, international trade, and economic development policies almost always promote a market-dictated integration into the world economy. Outside the classroom, however, popular discontent with the Washington Consensus has spawned a worldwide movement calling into question the myth of self-regulating markets on which these policies rest.

While the doctrines of free trade and financial liberalization are seldom questioned in mainstream economics textbooks, both are scrutinized here. Arthur MacEwan gives an overview of the process of globalization today, what is new and what continues long-established patterns, and the difficulties opposition groups face coming to grips with the power and the complexity of these forces (Article 8.1). MacEwan's second article shows how industrialized economies developed by protecting their own manufacturing sectors—never preaching the "gospel of free trade" until they were highly developed. Today, he argues, these countries prescribe free trade not because it's the best way for others to develop, but because it gives U.S. corporations free access to the world's markets and resources, which in turn strengthens the power of businesses against workers (Article 8.2).

Ramaa Vasudevan takes a critical look at the doctrine of comparative advantage, the backbone of free trade theory, and shows that it comes up short as a guide for economic development (Article 8.3). John Miller debunks the Economic Freedom Index that the Heritage Foundation and other backers of neoliberal globalization use to argue that economic freedom and prosperity go hand-in-hand. Miller argues that the Index measures neither prosperity nor freedom, but rather corporate freedom from accountability (Article 8.4). What has happened to world income inequality is another matter of intense debate. Many analysts claim that globally, incomes have converged, leading to a sharp reduction in world inequality in the second half of the twentieth century. Many others report that the gaps between the poorest and the richest people and between countries have continued to widen over the last two decades. In a *Dollars & Sense* interview, economist Bob Sutcliffe reports that "the wide range of different results of respected studies of world inequality in the last two decades casts doubt on the idea that world inequality has sharply and unambiguously declined or increased during the epoch of neoliberalism" (Article 8.7).

Smriti Rao assesses the impact of the recent global economic crisis and traces how the crisis, which largely began in the United States, was transmitted to the developing world (Article 8.6). Economist Katherine Sciacchitano traces the evolution of the regimes that have governed global trade since World War II based on the U.S. dollar. She asks whether the large U.S. trade deficit threatens the dollar's status as global reserve currency (Article 8.5). And Dariush Sokolov reports on the efforts of some South American countries to establish a regional development fund that would allow them to escape the clutches of the world creditors' cartel controlled by the IMF and the World Bank (Article 8.8).

The relationship of the United States and China does much to shape the global economy. Exports are the engine of China's recent rapid growth, and the Chinese policy of actively pushing down the value of its currency, the yuan, to keep its exports cheaper is the subject of another article by MacEwan. By examining why the United States, which has lost manufacturing jobs, does not protest more strenuously against this policy, MacEwan exposes the mutual dependence of the Chinese and U.S. economies (Article 8.9). Low wages in China keep the cost of Chinese exports low as well. But the combination of tighter labor markets and labor militancy has been pushing up wages in China since 2009. Miller reports on the labor unrest in China's export factories and argues that improving conditions for workers in China is good news for factory workers across the global economy (Article 8.10).

Labor standards are another casualty of neoliberal globalization. In his last article, Arthur MacEwan argues that using trade agreements to pressure governments to allow unhindered union organizing is always a good thing. But when it comes to including other labor standards in trade agreements, from child labor restrictions to health and safety standards, MacEwan counsels first-world activists to take their lead from the workers in the developing world affected by those agreements (Article 8.12). John Miller replies to *New York Times* columnist Nicholas Kristof, who steadfastly maintains that more sweatshops, not fewer, are the key to lifting young men and women in sub-Saharan Africa out of poverty. Miller then offers an alternative set of policies to bring development to the region (Article 8.13). Martha Ojeda, executive director of the Coalition for Justice in the Maquiladoras, paints a devastating picture of the effects of the North American Free Trade Agreement (NAFTA) on workers in *maquiladoras*, or border factories, over the last twenty years. In her article, she recounts how women played a central role in the struggle to establish a democratic union at a Sony plant in the Mexican border city of Nuevo Laredo (Article 8.11).

Discussion Questions

1. (Article 8.1) According to MacEwan, what aspects of today's globalization are new and what continues earlier trends? How might opposition forces best push for a more democratic and equitable globalization process?

2. (Article 8.2) MacEwan claims that the "infant industry" argument for trade protection is much more widely applicable than standard theory suggests. To what countries and industries might it apply in today's world economy? Explain your answer.

3. (Article 8.2) Free trade, MacEwan argues, gives business greater power relative to labor. Why is this so? Is it a good reason to oppose free trade?

4. (Article 8.3) What is the doctrine of comparative advantage? And why, according to Vasudevan, is it not a good guide to successful economic development?

5. (Article 8.4) According to Miller, how is the Economic Freedom Index misleading about the relationship between "free market policies," economic growth, and vulnerability to economic crises?

6. (Article 8.5) How does the denomination of oil prices in dollars affect the U.S. trade deficit and sustain the value of the dollar? Why is this dollar-denominated trading system under threat in today's global economy?

7. (Article 8.6) How was the economic crisis that originated in the developed world transmitted to the developing world? How might its devastating effects be remedied?

8. (Article 8.7) If Sutcliffe is correct and world inequality has neither declined nor increased sharply during the epoch of neoliberalism, what does his reading of the world inequality data suggest about the convergence hypothesis—the hypothesis that per capita income in countries with similar institutional structures will converge to the higher level?

9. (Article 8.8) What advantages might a regional development fund offer South American countries over IMF funding? And how are these and other countries trying to change the way the IMF operates?

10. (Article 8.9) How does China's government keep down the prices of its exports? And what are the reasons the U.S. government does not protest more strenuously against this policy?

11. (Article 8.10) What explains rising wages in Chinese export factories? How do Miller's and the *Wall Street Journal*'s definition of the virtuous cycle of development differ?

12. (Article 8.11) What was the role of women workers in organizing Sony's Nuevo Laredo factory? How has NAFTA affected the rights of Mexican workers in the *maquiladora* plants?

13. (Article 8.12) What are the pros and cons of including labor standards in trade agreements? Why does MacEwan consider the right to organize unions a special case? Do you agree with MacEwan that first-world activists pressing for more stringent labor standards across the global economy should take their cues from workers in the developing world?

14. (Article 8.13) What is the basis of journalist Nicholas Kristof's claim that young men on the streets of Namibia's capital city need the opportunity to work in sweatshops? Why does Miller find Kristof's claim unconvincing? Who do you think is right? Why?

Article 8.1

WHAT IS GLOBALIZATION?

BY ARTHUR MacEWAN

Reprinted with permission from Radical Teacher, Issue 61, 2001

Ever since Adam and Eve left the garden, people have been expanding the geographic realm of their economic, political, social and cultural contacts. In this sense of extending connections to other peoples around the world, globalization is nothing new. Also, as a process of change that can embody both great opportunities for wealth and progress and great trauma and suffering, globalization at the beginning of the 21st century is following a well established historical path. Yet the current period of change in the international system does have its own distinctive features, not the least important of which is the particular sort of political conflict it is generating.

"Greatest Events" and "Dreadful Misfortunes"

We are fond of viewing our own period as one in which great transformations are taking place, and it is easy to recite a list of technological and social changes that have dramatically altered the way we live and the way we connect to peoples elsewhere in the world. Yet, other surges of globalization in the modern era have been similarly disruptive to established practices. The first surge by which we might mark the beginning of modern globalization came with the invasion of the Western Hemisphere by European powers and with their extension of ocean trade around Africa to Asia. Adam Smith, writing *The Wealth of Nations* in 1776, did not miss the significance of these developments:

> The discovery of America, and that of a passage to the East Indies by the Cape of Good Hope, are the two greatest and most important events recorded in the history of mankind... By uniting, in some measure, the most distant parts of the world, by enabling them to relieve one another's wants, to increase one another's enjoyments, and to encourage one another's industry, their general tendency would seem to be beneficial.

Alongside of what Adam Smith saw as the great gains of globalization (not his term!), were the slaughter, by battle and disease, of millions of Native Americans, the enslavement and associated deaths of millions of Africans, and the subjugation of peoples in Asia. Smith did recognize the "dreadful misfortunes" that fell upon the peoples of the East and West Indies as a result of these "greatest events" (though he does not mention Africans in this expression of concern). He saw these misfortunes, however, as arising "rather from accident than from any thing in the nature of the events themselves."

The first stage of modern globalization illustrates not only the combined great gains and "dreadful misfortunes" that have characterized globalization but also the vast scope of the process. The political and economic changes that followed from the

European conquest of the Americas and forays into Asia are relatively well known. Equally momentous were the huge cultural transformations that were tied to the great expansion of economic contacts among the continents. Peoples moved, or they were moved by force. As they came to new locations and in contact with other peoples, almost every aspect of their lives was altered—from what people eat ("Italian" spaghetti with tomato sauce comes from Asia, the spaghetti, and America, the tomatoes) to their music (jazz is now the best known example, blending the backgrounds of different continents to emerge in America) to religion (the cross accompanied the sword in the era of colonial conquest).

The second great surge of modern globalization came in the 19th century, both as product and cause of the Industrial Revolution. On the one hand, the expansion of industry generated large reductions in transport costs that brought huge increases in international commerce. On the other hand, for the emerging commercial centers of Europe and North America, the opening of foreign markets and access to foreign sources of raw materials fueled (sometimes literally) the expansion of industry. Great Britain, as the "workshop of the world," was at the center of these changes and over the course of the century saw its foreign trade increase three times as rapidly as national income.

Britain during the 19th century provided a foreshadowing of current-day globalization as it officially touted "free trade" as the proper mode of organization for commerce—not just for itself, but for the entire world. The gospel of "free trade" was then carried around the globe by the British navy, and heroic ideological gymnastics allowed a growing colonial empire to be included under this same rubric. As the British historian E. J. Hobsbawm has commented, "British industry could grow up, by and large, in a protected home market until strong enough to demand free entry into other people's markets, that is 'Free Trade'." In today's globalization it is the United States, a country that also attained its economic power on the foundation of protectionism, that preaches the gospel of "free trade" to the rest of the world.

Current-day globalization is, by and large, a continuation of the process that began in the 19th century (which in turn had its roots in the great transformation that began along with the 16th century). Two world wars and the Great Depression disrupted the progress of globalization for some sixty years and shifted its center from Britain to the United States, but it is now back on track. By the 1980s, the extent of economic connections that had been established among the world's national economies by 1913 had been reattained, and in subsequent years international trade and investment have continued to expand their roles in the economies of most nations.

Homogenization and Competition

Change in the world economy today, however, is not simply an extension of what went on in earlier periods, not simply a quantitative extension of well established trends. What distinguishes the current era from earlier phases of globalization is that now capitalism is ubiquitous. Virtually everywhere, production takes place for profit and is based on wage labor. In the 19th century, capitalism may have provided the leading dynamic of the international economy, but in many parts of the world—

most everywhere outside of Europe and North America—a great deal of economic activity was organized through families (peasant farms or shops), under semi-feudal conditions, or through slavery. These activities were all connected to markets and to a world capitalist system, but they were not capitalist in themselves. Certainly there are important aspects of life and work today which take place outside of markets and are not directly capitalist—for example, work in the home, interactions within governments, volunteer activity, and some other forms of production. Yet capitalism holds sway, dominating and defining economic relationships in almost all parts of the world.

The ubiquity of capitalism gives a new character to the economic connections among peoples in distant parts of the world. There has, in particular, been a grand homogenization, both of consumer markets and of production activity. Wal-Mart and McDonald's establish themselves in Mexico to sell the same sorts of products in the same way as in the United States. At the same time, Mexican workers at the Ford plant in Hermosillo produce the same cars that are produced in U.S. factories and they do so with equipment and procedures that are among the most "modern" in the world. Also on the production side, plants in Mexico and the United States are sometimes integrated with one another in a "global assembly line," with Mexican workers engaged in the labor intensive aspects of the operation and U.S. workers engaged in the more highly skilled activities; for example, in clothing production, design and cutting is done in the United States while the pieces are stitched together on the Mexican side of the border.

Mexico, because of its proximity to the United States and the reduction of trade restrictions between the two countries, presents an extreme example of the cross-border integration of production. Yet in broad terms, we are presented today with a new international organization of production, as people on different corners of the globe produce the same sorts of products with the same technologies and often for the same employers—though the ultimate employers often operate through local subcontractors.

The homogenization of the world economy creates a new set of relationships, a direct competition, among workers in different parts of the world. Although such competition always existed, it is much more extensive and intense than in the past and, most important, it takes place between workers whose wages are dramatically different from each other. It is one thing when U.S. and Canadian workers, who have very similar wages and standards of living, are in competition with each other. It is quite another thing when the U.S. and Canadian workers are in competition with Mexican workers.

This new relationship among workers in different countries presents obvious problems for the workers in the rich countries: they simply cannot compete with workers who, using the same equipment and methods of production (i.e., the same technology), are paid far, far lower wages. Yet similar, though perhaps less obvious, problems exist for the low-wage workers as well. With wage labor markets existing throughout most of the world, virtually all workers are placed in competition with one another. While workers in Bangladesh may be willing to accept very low wages to assemble clothing for the European market, they are always faced with the prospect that Vietnamese workers may accept even lower wages. Or Indonesian workers, who assemble sports shoes for the U.S.

market, may face the prospect of production innovations that will substitute machinery and skilled workers for unskilled workers on an assembly line, making it profitable for the firms to move their production back to the United States.

In a capitalist world, where many different sites around the world provide firms with the labor markets they need, those firms can have a great advantage over workers. That advantage, however, depends upon "free trade," the elimination of government barriers to the movement of goods and funds across national boundaries. Free trade has given firms the option of either moving themselves or moving their sources of supply in response to cost differences (wage differences, but also other cost differences). Free trade, however, does not include the reduction—let alone the elimination—of barriers to the movement of workers. So labor does not enjoy the same freedom in the globalized economy as does capital. Since "freedom" means having alternatives, and having alternatives means having power, a system that enhances the freedom of firms relative to the freedom of labor means giving businesses more power relative to labor. (Even were barriers to migration to be reduced, there are still substantial costs to labor movement compared to capital movement; and capital's advantage, while reduced, would not be eliminated.)

The drive for free trade existed, as pointed out above, in the British-led globalization of the 19th century, but the United States has been able to push the concept to a whole new level. In part, free trade is important for the power it confers on business, but it is also important as ideology. The ideology of free trade has provided the defining rationale for the North American Free Trade Agreement (NAFTA), the Free Trade Agreement of the Americas (FTAA), the World Trade Organization (WTO), and the programs pushed on low income countries by the International Monetary Fund (IMF) and the World Bank. The opening of markets, the opening of sources of supply, the spread of private economic activity—all of this is supposed to provide a new era of rapid economic growth for the world and serve the needs of the poor as well as the rich.

Not So Fast

The concept of free trade has a certain intuitive appeal. After all, if the firms and people of a nation are free to buy their supplies from the lowest-cost source of supply, then they will be able to buy more and satisfy their needs more thoroughly than if their government limits the sources from which they can buy those supplies (bans imports) or imposes extra costs (tariffs) on supplies from abroad. For low income countries, desperate for economic growth, it would seem absurd for their governments to place restrictions on imports, forcing firms and people to waste resources on expensive domestic goods. Moreover, it only takes a moment's reflection to note the huge gains we attain from international commerce: not only the banana I eat for breakfast and a good portion of the oil that fuels my car and heats my home, but also the ideas and culture from elsewhere in the world—to say nothing of the competitive pressures from abroad that help drive economic advances in my own country. For a small country, the gains from foreign commerce are a virtual necessity.

Another moment's reflection, however, reveals that things are not so simple. Free trade is not the only way to engage extensively in international commerce. In fact, none of the countries we now denote as "developed" attained their development through free trade, though all engaged extensively in international commerce. There are, it seems, some substantial advantages to having the production of certain kinds of goods take place within a country, as compared to obtaining those same goods from abroad. The US textile industry in the 19th century, the U.S. auto industry through most of the 20th century, the Japanese computer industry in the mid-20th century, the South Korean steel and ship building industries later in the 20th century—all generated broad economic gains in terms of the transformation of technology and the formation of a skilled work force that far surpassed the costs that arose from the government protection they received in their early stages of expansion. None of this provides a justification for protectionism in general; continuing protection of sugar and steel production in the United States imposes costs with no off-setting benefits (except to those directly engaged in the industries). Yet the experience of two centuries of capitalist development does demonstrate the fallacy of the free trade argument. Efforts by the U.S. government to push free trade on low income countries today may make sense from the perspective of the interests of U.S. firms, but it is hardly a prescription for economic advancement in low income countries.

But there is more. Globalization as it is being organized under the banner of free trade is doing nothing to reduce the "development gap," the huge difference in material well-being between the peoples of the rich nations and the peoples of most of the rest of the world. In fact, there is some evidence that under the regime of increasingly open world markets, the "development gap" is increasing. Worse yet: there is a good deal of evidence that free trade globalization is contributing to increasing inequality within nations, not only within the low income countries of the "South" but also within the United States and the other high income countries of the "North."

As the international economy is increasingly organized in a way that enhances the power of firms and tends to undermine the power of labor, it is certainly likely that greater inequality would be the outcome. Unfortunately, available data do not allow us to draw strong conclusions about what has been happening to world income inequality in recent decades. What we do know is that income distribution in today's world is already grossly unequal, with hundreds of millions of people living at the edge of subsistence, while the elites in all countries live in obscene luxury. We also know that, although some low income countries have made substantial gains (South Korea and some other countries of East Asia), the current surge of globalization has provided no general relief for the world's poor. Furthermore, we know that globalization—new patterns of international trade and investment—has disrupted people's lives, pushed people out of their traditional lines of work, shifted the location of economic activity, and forced people to adopt new patterns of consumption. All of this makes many people's lives very unpleasant, regardless of what can be uncovered with the aggregate statistics regarding income distribution and economic growth.

What Else Is New?

One might well absorb this summary of change in the world economy and respond with the comment: So, what else is new? It does seem that periods of great change in the world economy, whatever immediate benefits they may generate for the elite and whatever their long run benefits for society in general, are accompanied by severe disruptions, hardships and inequalities. Current-day experience seems to fit well with the pattern established in the 16th and 19th centuries, to say nothing of earlier eras of imperial expansion. (Many commentators quite reasonably reject the term "globalization" in favor of "imperialism" precisely because the latter term underscores the great inequalities of power and income that are always so important in international affairs.)

Yet perhaps there is something new in the current era in the particular type of political response to globalization that has been generated in recent years. The "dreadful misfortunes" of earlier eras have also generated political responses—sometimes in the form of spontaneous rebellion, sometimes as more organized resistance and revolution, and sometimes as waves of new oppositional organizations and alliances. The political response to globalization at the beginning of the 21st century, however, has some distinguishing characteristics that are worth emphasizing.

Most important, parts of the response to globalization are themselves global. The coming out "party" for the anti-globalization movement in Seattle in the fall of 1999 involved people and organizations from all over the world. As a coordinated effort by groups from many rich countries and many poor countries, the action in Seattle—and the ones that have followed in Washington, Quebec, Prague, Puerto Allegre, and elsewhere—suggest something is different about the nature of political action. Many times, opposition movements based on national identities have, at least implicitly, been in conflict with one another; at other times, organizations in rich countries have opted to "support" groups in poor countries, but not as a joint and coordinated effort. While progressive movements have always talked about their internationalism, this time around the talk may translate more effectively into practice.

Also, the globalization of political opposition to globalization has included steps by labor unions, which have long adhered to highly nationalist positions. So far, more of the new internationalism of the US labor movement has been in the realm of rhetoric rather than practice, but US unions have made some important efforts at cross border organizing—in the form, for example, of supporting efforts of Mexican workers to organize firms in their country that supply the US market. (NAFTA, while allowing corporations, the organizations of capital, to operate in both the United States and Mexico, as well as Canada, makes no parallel provision for unions, the organizations of labor.) The rhetoric of internationalism, too, is important, especially because it marks such a departure from the past practices of the US labor movement. Some critics complain that the new-found interest of the US labor movement in conditions abroad arises from its own immediate concerns, the competition from low-cost imports, instead from a concern for workers elsewhere in the world. But that is just the point. If globalization forces US unions to secure the interests of their own members by pursuing a new internationalism, then that is certainly a change of significance.

The organized opposition to globalization goes far beyond the labor movement, however, involving a wide spectrum of social movements. Environmental and women's organizations, peasant groupings, student-based action committees, and others have all been a part of the actions. In addition, well established non-governmental organizations such as Oxfam, while not engaged in the protest actions in Seattle and elsewhere, have been a part of the general opposition to globalization. Not only is this opposition based on a wide range of social movements, but these different movements have at least begun to work in alliance with one another. Some aspects of this alliance, particularly that between environmental groups and labor unions, suggest a major shift from past conflicts.

Opposition actions have taken place in a wide spectrum of countries. On the one hand, there have been the much publicized actions led by young, often middle-class activists in the United States, focused on meetings of the principal international economic agencies such as the IMF, World Bank, and WTO. On the other hand, there have been actions in India, where peasant organizations have demonstrated against the international pharmaceutical and seed companies that are trying to use the internationalization of patent regulations to secure their control of world markets. While these geographically disparate actions are not coordinated through any cohesive international organization, they are part of an interconnected movement.

The opposition that has developed to globalization is not a cohesive movement, and it is not so well developed that we can have confidence in its lasting impact. Furthermore, it has many problems. Opposition to globalization sometimes is expressed as an opposition to connections with other peoples rather than as an opposition to the way those connections are exacerbating inequalities of power and income. Thus xenophobic protectionism is sometimes just below the surface of protest actions. By and large, however, the opposition to globalization appears to be based on an internationalism that may provide a basis for a progressive, and perhaps lasting, movement.

The more serious problems of this opposition arise from the difficulties in coming to grips with the power and complexity of the globalization process itself. A small example is provided by efforts in the rich countries to respond to the proliferation of imports of goods produced in "sweat shop" conditions in low income countries. Protests against the companies that utilize these shops—firms such as Nike and Gap—are met with the response that workers in these "sweat shops" are eager to obtain their jobs because these jobs are significantly better in terms of pay and working conditions than other available jobs. What's more, the response is often true. A sophisticated movement can come to terms with this reality by emphasizing the need to alter the context that impoverishes workers in low income countries and by stressing that such a context is most effectively transformed through political struggle. Also, by focusing on workers' right to political freedom—in particular, the right to organize unions—rather than on particular aspects of workers' conditions, anti-sweat shop activists can have a positive impact.

The "sweat shop" example helps clarify that globalization is not simply a collection of practices, not simply a peculiar set of connections among peoples around the globe. It is part of the long historical development and spread of capitalism. Within the framework of capitalism, it is difficult to solve problems that are based on the inequality of income and power, because those problems are generated by the system itself. Nonetheless, capitalism is not an immutable system, and it is probably not a permanent system. The oppositional struggles are not only responses to globalization, but they are part of the process of globalization itself. They will play a role in shaping events and in shaping the entire nature of the process. And they will contribute to answering the question: What is globalization?

Article 8.2

THE GOSPEL OF FREE TRADE: THE NEW EVANGELISTS

BY ARTHUR MacEWAN
November 1991, updated July 2009

Free trade! With the zeal of Christian missionaries, for decades the U.S. government has been preaching, advocating, pushing, and coercing around the globe for "free trade."

As the economic crisis emerged in 2007 and 2008 and rapidly became a global crisis, it was apparent that something was very wrong with the way the world economy was organized. Not surprisingly, as unemployment rose sharply in the United States, there were calls for protecting jobs by limiting imports and for the government to "buy American" in its economic stimulus program. Similarly, in many other countries, as unemployment jumped upwards, pressure emerged for protection—and some actual steps were taken. Yet, free trade missionaries did not retreat; they continued to preach the same gospel.

The free-traders were probably correct in claiming that protectionist policies would do more harm than good as a means to stem the rising unemployment generated by the economic crisis. Significant acts of protectionism in one country would lead to retaliation—or at least copying—by other countries, reducing world trade. The resulting loss of jobs from reduced trade would most likely outweigh any gains from protection.

Yet the argument over international economic policies should not be confined simply to what should be done in a crisis. Nor should it simply deal with trade in goods and services. The free-traders have advocated their program as one for long-run economic growth and development, yet the evidence suggests that free trade is not a good economic development strategy. Furthermore, the free-traders preach the virtue of unrestricted global movement of finance as well as of goods and services. As it turns out, the free flow of finance has been a major factor in bringing about and spreading the economic crisis that began to appear in 2007—as well as earlier crises.

The Push

While the U.S. push for free trade goes back several decades, it has become more intense in recent years. In the 1990s, the U.S. government signed on to the North American Free Trade Agreement (NAFTA) and in 2005 established the Central American Free Trade Agreement (CAFTA). Both Republican and Democratic presidents, however, have pushed hard for a *global* free trade agenda. After the demise of the Soviet Union, U.S. advisers prescribed unfettered capitalism for Eastern and Central Europe, and ridiculed as unworkable any move toward a "third way." In low-income countries from Mexico to Malaysia, the prescription has been the same: open markets, deregulate business, don't restrict international investment, and let the free market flourish.

In the push for worldwide free trade, the World Trade Organization (WTO) has been the principal vehicle of change, establishing rules for commerce that assure markets are open and resources are available to those who can pay. And the International Monetary Fund (IMF) and World Bank, which provide loans to many governments, use their financial power to pressure countries around the world to accept the gospel and open their markets. In each of these international organizations, the United States—generally through the U.S. Treasury—plays a dominant role.

Of course, as with any gospel, the preachers often ignore their own sermons. While telling other countries to open their markets, the U.S. government continued, for instance, to limit imports of steel, cotton, sugar, textiles, and many other goods. But publicly at least, free-trade boosters insist that the path to true salvation—or economic expansion, which, in this day and age, seems to be the same thing—lies in opening our market to foreign goods. Get rid of trade barriers at home and abroad, allow business to go where it wants and do what it wants. We will all get rich.

Yet the history of the United States and other rich countries does not fit well with the free-trade gospel. Virtually all advanced capitalist countries found economic success through heavy government regulation of their international commerce, not in free trade. Likewise, a large role for government intervention has characterized those cases of rapid and sustained economic growth in recent decades—for example, Japan after World War II, South Korea in the 1970s through the 1990s, and China most recently.

Free trade does, however, have its uses. Highly developed nations can use free trade to extend their power and control of the world's wealth, and business can use it as a weapon against labor. Most important, free trade can limit efforts to redistribute income more equally, undermine social programs, and keep people from democratically controlling their economic lives.

A Day in the Park

At the beginning of the 19th century, Lowell, Massachusetts, became the premier site of the U.S. textile industry. Today, thanks to the Lowell National Historical Park, you can tour the huge mills, ride through the canals that redirected the Merrimack River's power to those mills, and learn the story of the textile workers, from the Yankee "mill girls" of the 1820s through the various waves of immigrant laborers who poured into the city over the next century.

During a day in the park, visitors get a graphic picture of the importance of 19th-century industry to the economic growth and prosperity of the United States. Lowell and the other mill towns of the era were centers of growth. They not only created a demand for Southern cotton, they also created a demand for new machinery, maintenance of old machinery, parts, dyes, *skills*, construction materials, construction machinery, *more skills*, equipment to move the raw materials and products, parts maintenance for that equipment, *and still more skills*. The mill towns also created markets—concentrated groups of wage earners who needed to buy products to sustain themselves. As centers of economic activity, Lowell and similar mill towns contributed to U.S. economic growth far beyond the value of the textiles they produced.

The U.S. textile industry emerged decades after the industrial revolution had spawned Britain's powerful textile industry. Nonetheless, it survived and prospered. British linens inundated markets throughout the world in the early 19th century, as the British navy nurtured free trade and kept ports open for commerce. In the United States, however, hostilities leading up to the War of 1812 and then a substantial tariff made British textiles relatively expensive. These limitations on trade allowed the Lowell mills to prosper, acting as a catalyst for other industries and helping to create the skilled work force at the center of U.S. economic expansion.

Beyond textiles, however, tariffs did not play a great role in the United States during the early 19th century. Southern planters had considerable power, and while they were willing to make some compromises, they opposed protecting manufacturing in general because that protection forced up the prices of the goods they purchased with their cotton revenues. The Civil War wiped out the planters' power to oppose protectionism, and from the 1860s through World War I, U.S. industry prospered behind considerable tariff barriers.

Different Countries, Similar Experiences

The story of the importance of protectionism in bringing economic growth has been repeated, with local variations, in other advanced capitalist countries. During the late 19th century, Germany entered the major league of international economic powers with substantial protection and government support for its industries. Likewise, in 19th-century France and Italy, national consolidation behind protectionist barriers was a key to economic development.

Britain—which entered the industrial era first—is often touted as the prime example of successful development without tariff protection. Yet, Britain embraced free trade only after its industrial base was well established; as in the U.S., the early and important textile industry was erected on a foundation of protectionism. In addition, Britain built its industry through the British navy and the expansion of empire, hardly prime ingredients in any recipe for free trade.

Japan provides an especially important case of successful government protection and support for industrial development. In the post-World War II era, when the Japanese established the foundations for their economic "miracle," the government rejected free trade and extensive foreign investment and instead promoted its national firms.

In the 1950s, for example, the government protected the country's fledgling auto firms from foreign competition. At first, quotas limited imports to $500,000 (in current dollars) each year; in the 1960s, prohibitively high tariffs replaced the quotas. Furthermore, the Japanese allowed foreign investment only insofar as it contributed to developing domestic industry. The government encouraged Japanese companies to import foreign technology, but required them to produce 90% of parts domestically within five years.

The Japanese also protected their computer industry. In the early 1970s, as the industry was developing, companies and individuals could only purchase a foreign machine if a suitable Japanese model was not available. IBM was allowed to produce within the country, but only when it licensed basic patents to Japanese firms. And IBM computers produced in Japan were treated as foreign-made machines.

In the 20th century, no other country matched Japan's economic success, as it moved in a few decades from a relative low-income country, through the devastation of war, to emerge as one of the world's economic leaders. Yet one looks back in vain to find a role for free trade in this success. The Japanese government provided an effective framework, support, and protection for the country's capitalist development.

Likewise, in many countries that have been late-comers to economic development, capitalism has generated high rates of economic growth where government involvement, and not free trade, played the central role. South Korea is a striking case. "Korea is an example of a country that grew very fast and yet violated the canons of conventional economic wisdom," writes Alice Amsden in *Asia's Next Giant: South Korea and Late Industrialization,* widely acclaimed as perhaps the most important analysis of the South Korean economic success. "In Korea, instead of the market mechanism allocating resources and guiding private entrepreneurship, the government made most of the pivotal investment decisions. Instead of firms operating in a competitive market structure, they each operated with an extraordinary degree of market control, protected from foreign competition."

Free trade, however, has had its impact in South Korea. In the 1990s, South Korea and other East Asian governments came under pressure from the U.S. government and the IMF to open their markets, including their financial markets. When they did so, the results were a veritable disaster. The East Asian financial crisis that began in 1997 was a major setback for the whole region, a major disruption of economic growth. After extremely rapid economic growth for three decades, with output expanding at 7% to 10% a year, South Korea's economy plummeted by 6.3% between 1997 and 1998.

Mexico and Its NAFTA Experience

While free trade in goods and services has its problems, which can be very serious, it is the free movement of capital, the opening of financial markets that has sharp, sudden impacts, sometimes wrecking havoc on national economies. Thus, virtually as soon as Mexico, the United States and Canada formed NAFTA at the beginning of 1994, Mexico was hit with a severe financial crisis. As the economy turned downward at the beginning of that year, capital rapidly left the country, greatly reducing the value of the Mexican peso. With this diminished value of the peso, the cost of servicing international debts and the costs of imports skyrocketed—and the downturn worsened.

Still, during the 1990s, before and after the financial crisis, free-traders extolled short periods of moderate economic growth in Mexico —3% to 4% per year—as evidence of success. Yet, compared to earlier years, Mexico's growth under free trade has been poor. From 1940 to 1990 (including the no-growth decade of the 1980s), when Mexico's market was highly protected and the state actively regulated economic affairs, output grew at an average annual rate of 5%.

Most important, Mexico's experience discredits the notion that free-market policies will improve living conditions for the masses of people in low-income countries. The Mexican government paved the way for free trade policies by reducing or eliminating social welfare programs, and for many Mexican workers wages declined sharply during the free trade era. The number of households living in poverty rose dramatically, with some 75% of Mexico's population below the poverty line at the beginning of the 21st century.

China and Its Impact

Part of Mexico's problem and its economy's relatively weak performance from the 1990s onward has been the full-scale entrance of China into the international economy. While the Mexican authorities thought they saw great possibilities in NAFTA with the full opening of the U.S. market to goods produced with low-wage Mexican labor, China (and other Asian countries) had even cheaper labor. As China also gained access to the U.S. market, Mexican expectations were dashed.

The Chinese economy has surely gained in terms of economic growth as it has engaged more and more with the world market, and the absolute levels of incomes of millions of people have risen a great deal. However, China's rapid economic growth has come with a high degree of income inequality. Before its era of rapid growth, China was viewed as a country with a relatively equal distribution of income. By the beginning of the new millennium, however, it was much more unequal than any of the other most populace Asian countries (India, Indonesia, Bangladesh, Pakistan), and more in line with the high-inequality countries of Latin America. Furthermore, with the inequality has come a great deal of social conflict. Tens of thousands of "incidents" of conflict involving violence are reported each year, and most recently there have been the major conflicts involving Tibetans and Ouigers.

In any case, the Chinese trade and growth success should not be confused with "free trade." Foundations for China's surge of economic growth were established through state-sponsored infrastructure development and the vast expansion of the country's educational system. Even today, while private business, including foreign business, appears to have been given free rein in China, the government still plays a controlling role—including a central role in affecting foreign economic relations.

A central aspect of the government's role in the county's foreign commerce has been in the realm of finance. As Chinese-produced goods have virtually flooded international markets, the government has controlled the uses of the earnings from these exports. Instead of simply allowing those earnings to be used by Chinese firms and citizens to buy imports, the government has to a large extent held those earnings as reserves. Using those reserves, China's central bank has been the largest purchaser of U.S. government bonds, in effect becoming a major financer of the U.S. government's budget deficit of recent years.

China's reserves have been one large element in creating a giant pool of financial assets in the world economy. This "pool" has also been built up as the doubling of oil prices following the U.S. invasion of Iraq put huge amounts of funds in the pockets of oil-exporting countries and firms and individuals connected to the oil industry. Yet slow growth of the U.S. economy and extremely low interest rates, resulting from the Federal Reserve Bank's efforts to encourage more growth, limited the returns that could be obtained on these funds. One of the consequences—through a complex set of connections—was the development of the U.S. housing bubble, as financial firms, searching for higher returns, pushed funds into more and more risky mortgage loans.

It was not simply free trade and the unrestricted flow of international finance that generated the housing bubble and subsequent crisis in the U.S. economy. However, the generally unstable global economy—both in terms of trade and finance—that has emerged in the free trade era was certainly a factor bringing about the crisis. Moreover, as is widely recognized, it was not only the U.S. economy and U.S. financial institutions that were affected. The free international flow of finance has meant that banking has become more and more a global industry. So as the U.S. banks got in trouble in 2007 and 2008, their maladies spread to many other parts of the world.

The Uses of Free Trade

While free trade is not the best economic growth or development policy and, especially through the free flow of finance, can precipitate financial crises, the largest and most powerful firms in many countries find it highly profitable. As Britain preached the loudest sermons for free trade in the early 19th century, when its own industry was already firmly established, so the United States—or at least many firms based in the United States—find it a profitable policy at the beginning of the 21st century. The Mexican experience provides an instructive illustration.

For U.S. firms, access to foreign markets is a high priority. Mexico may be relatively poor, but with a population of 105 million it provides a substantial market. Furthermore, Mexican labor is cheap relative to U.S. labor; and using modern production techniques, Mexican workers can be as productive as workers in the United States. For U.S. firms to obtain full access to the Mexican market, the United States has to open its borders to Mexican goods. Also, if U.S. firms are to take full advantage of cheap foreign labor and sell the goods produced abroad to U.S. consumers, the United States has to be open to imports.

On the other side of the border, wealthy Mexicans face a choice between advancing their interests through national development or advancing their interests through ties to U.S. firms and access to U.S. markets. For many years, they chose the former route. This led to some development of the Mexican economy but also—due to corruption and the massive power of the ruling party, the PRI—huge concentrations of wealth in the hands of a few small groups of firms and individuals. Eventually, these groups came into conflict with their own government over regulation and taxation. Having benefited from government largesse, they came to see their fortunes in greater freedom from government control and, particularly, in greater access to foreign markets and partnerships with large foreign companies. National development was a secondary concern when more involvement with international commerce would produce greater riches more quickly.

In addition, the old program of state-led development in Mexico ran into severe problems. These problems came to the surface in the 1980s with the international debt crisis. Owing huge amounts of money to foreign banks, the Mexican government was forced to respond to pressure from the IMF, the U.S. government, and large international banks which sought to deregulate Mexico's trade and investment. That pressure meshed with the pressure from Mexico's own richest elites, and the result was the move toward free trade and a greater opening of the Mexican economy to foreign investment.

Since the early 1990s, these changes for Mexico and the United States (as well as Canada) have been institutionalized in NAFTA. The U.S. government's agenda since then has been to spread free trade policies to all of the Americas through more regional agreements like CAFTA and ultimately through a Free Trade Area of the Americas. On a broader scale, the U.S. government works through the WTO, the IMF, and the World Bank to open markets and gain access to resources beyond the Western Hemisphere. In fact, while markets remain important everywhere, low-wage manufacturing is increasingly concentrated in Asia—especially China—instead of Mexico or Latin America.

The Chinese experience involves many of the same advantages for U.S. business as does the Mexican—a vast market, low wages, and an increasingly productive labor force. However, the Chinese government, although it has liberalized the economy a great deal compared to the pre-1985 era, has not abdicated its major role in the economy. For better (growth) and for worse (inequality and repression), the Chinese government has not embraced free trade.

Who Gains, Who Loses?

Of course, in the United States, Mexico, China and elsewhere, advocates of free trade claim that their policies are in everyone's interest. Free trade, they point out, will mean cheaper products for all. Consumers in the United States, who are mostly workers, will be richer because their wages will buy more. In Mexico and China, on the one hand, and in the United States, on the other hand, they argue that rising trade will create more jobs. If some workers lose their jobs because cheaper imported goods are available, export industries will produce new jobs.

In recent years this argument has taken on a new dimension with the larger entrance of India into the world economy and with the burgeoning there of jobs based in information technology—programming and call centers, for example. This "outsourcing" of service jobs has received a great deal of attention and concern in the United States. Yet free-traders have defended this development as good for the U.S. economy as well as for the Indian economy.

Such arguments obscure many of the most important issues in the free trade debate. Stated, as they usually are, as universal truths, these arguments are just plain silly. No one, for example, touring the Lowell National Historical Park could seriously argue that people in the United States would have been better off had there been no tariff on textiles. Yes, in 1820, they could have purchased textile goods more cheaply, but in the long run the result would have been less industrial advancement and a less wealthy nation. One could make the same point with the Japanese auto and computer industries, or indeed with numerous other examples from the last two centuries of capitalist development.

In the modern era, even though the United States already has a relatively developed economy with highly skilled workers, a freely open international economy does not serve the interests of most U.S. workers, though it will benefit large firms.

U.S. workers today are in competition with workers around the globe. Many different workers in many different places can produce the same goods and services. Thus, an international economy governed by the free trade agenda will tend to bring down wages for many U.S. workers. This phenomenon has certainly been one of the factors leading to the substantial rise of income inequality in the United States during recent decades.

The problem is not simply that of workers in a few industries—such as auto and steel, or call-centers and computer programming—where import competition is an obvious and immediate issue. A country's openness to the international economy affects the entire structure of earnings in that country. Free trade forces down the general level of wages across the board, even of those workers not directly affected by imports. The simple fact is that when companies can produce the same products in several different places, it is owners who gain because they can move their factories and funds around much more easily than workers can move themselves around. Capital is mobile; labor is much less mobile. Businesses, more than workers, gain from having a larger territory in which to roam.

Control Over Our Economic Lives

But the difficulties with free trade do not end with wages. In both low-income and high-income parts of the world, free trade is a weapon in the hands of business when it opposes any progressive social programs. Efforts to place environmental restrictions on firms are met with the threat of moving production abroad. Higher taxes to improve the schools? Business threatens to go elsewhere. Better health and safety regulations? The same response.

Some might argue that the losses from free trade for people in the United States will be balanced by gains for most people in poor countries—lower wages in the United States, but higher wages in Mexico and China. Free trade, then, would bring about international equality. Not likely. In fact, as pointed out above, free trade reforms in Mexico have helped force down wages and reduce social welfare programs, processes rationalized by efforts to make Mexican goods competitive on international markets. China, while not embracing free trade, has seen its full-scale entrance into global commerce accompanied by increasing inequality.

Gains for Mexican or Chinese workers, like those for U.S. workers, depend on their power in relation to business. Free trade or simply the imperative of international "competitiveness" are just as much weapons in the hands of firms operating in Mexico and China as they are for firms operating in the United States. The great mobility of capital is business's best trump card in dealing with labor and popular demands for social change—in the United States, Mexico, China and elsewhere.

None of this means that people should demand that their economies operate as fortresses, protected from all foreign economic incursions. There are great gains that can be obtained from international economic relations—when a nation manages those relations in the interests of the great majority of the people. Protectionism often simply supports narrow vested interests, corrupt officials, and wealthy industrialists. In rejecting free trade, we should move beyond traditional protectionism.

Yet, at this time, rejecting free trade is an essential first step. Free trade places the cards in the hands of business. More than ever, free trade would subject us to the "bottom line," or at least the bottom line as calculated by those who own and run large companies.

Article 8.3

COMPARATIVE ADVANTAGE

BY RAMAA VASUDEVAN
July/August 2007

> Dear Dr. Dollar:
> *When economists argue that the outsourcing of jobs might be a plus for the U.S.*
> *economy, they often mention the idea of comparative advantage. So free trade*
> *would allow the United States to specialize in higher-end service-sector business-*
> *es, creating higher-paying jobs than the ones that would be outsourced. But is it*
> *really true that free trade leads to universal benefits?*
> —David Goodman, Boston, Mass.

You're right: The purveyors of the free trade gospel do invoke the doctrine of comparative advantage to dismiss widespread concerns about the export of jobs. Attributed to 19th-century British political-economist David Ricardo, the doctrine says that a nation always stands to gain if it exports the goods it produces *relatively* more cheaply in exchange for goods that it can get *comparatively* more cheaply from abroad. Free trade would lead to each country specializing in the products it can produce at *relatively* lower costs. Such specialization allows both trading partners to gain from trade, the theory goes, even if in one of the countries production of *both* goods costs more in absolute terms.

For instance, suppose that in the United States the cost to produce one car equals the cost to produce 10 bags of cotton, while in the Philippines the cost to produce one car equals the cost to produce 100 bags of cotton. The Philippines would then have a comparative advantage in the production of cotton, producing one bag at a cost equal to the production cost of 1/100 of a car, versus 1/10 of a car in the United States; likewise, the United States would hold a comparative advantage in the production of cars. Whatever the prices of cars and cotton in the global market, the theory goes, the Philippines would be better off producing only cotton and importing all its cars from the United States, and the United States would be better off producing only cars and importing all of its cotton from the Philippines. If the international terms of trade—the relative price—is one car for 50 bags, then the United States will take in 50 bags of cotton for each car it exports, 40 more than the 10 bags it forgoes by putting its productive resources into making the car rather than growing cotton. The Philippines is also better off: it can import a car in exchange for the export of 50 bags of cotton, whereas it would have had to forgo the production of 100 bags of cotton in order to produce that car domestically. If the price of cars goes up in the global marketplace, the Philippines will lose out in relative terms—but will still be better off than if it tried to produce its own cars.

The real world, unfortunately, does not always conform to the assumptions underlying comparative-advantage theory. One assumption is that trade is balanced. But many countries are running persistent deficits, notably the United States, whose trade deficit is now at nearly 7% of its GDP. A second premise, that there is full employment within the trading nations, is also patently unrealistic. As global trade intensifies, jobs created in the export sector do not necessarily compensate for the jobs lost in the sectors wiped out by foreign competition.

The comparative advantage story faces more direct empirical challenges as well. Nearly 70% of U.S. trade is trade in similar goods, known as *intra-industry trade*: for example, exporting Fords and importing BMWs. And about one third of U.S. trade as of the late 1990s was trade between branches of a single corporation located in different countries (*intra-firm trade*). Comparative advantage cannot explain these patterns.

Comparative advantage is a static concept that identifies immediate gains from trade but is a poor guide to economic development, a process of structural change over time which is by definition dynamic. Thus the comparative advantage tale is particularly pernicious when preached to developing countries, consigning many to "specialize" in agricultural goods or be forced into a race to the bottom where cheap sweatshop labor is their sole source of competitiveness.

The irony, of course, is that none of the rich countries got that way by following the maxim that they now preach. These countries historically relied on tariff walls and other forms of protectionism to build their industrial base. And even now, they continue to protect sectors like agriculture with subsidies. The countries now touted as new models of the benefits of free trade—South Korea and the other "Asian tigers," for instance—actually flouted this economic wisdom, nurturing their technological capabilities in specific manufacturing sectors and taking advantage of their lower wage costs to *gradually* become effective competitors of the United States and Europe in manufacturing.

The fundamental point is this: contrary to the comparative-advantage claim that trade is universally beneficial, nations as a whole do not prosper from free trade. Free trade creates winners and losers, both within and between countries. In today's context it is the global corporate giants that are propelling and profiting from "free trade": not only outsourcing white-collar jobs, but creating global commodity chains linking sweatshop labor in the developing countries of Latin America and Asia (Africa being largely left out of the game aside from the export of natural resources such as oil) with ever-more insecure consumers in the developed world. Promoting "free trade" as a political cause enables this process to continue.

It is a process with real human costs in terms of both wages and work. People in developing countries across the globe continue to face these costs as trade liberalization measures are enforced; and the working class in the United States is also being forced to bear the brunt of the relentless logic of competition.

Sources: Arthur MacEwan, "The Gospel of Free Trade: The New Evangelists," *Dollars & Sense*, July/August 2002; Ha-Joon Chang, *Kicking away the Ladder: The Real History of Fair Trade*, Foreign Policy in Focus, 2003; Anwar Shaikh, "Globalization and the Myths of Free Trade," in *Globalization and the Myths of Free Trade: History, Theory, and Empirical Evidence*, ed. Anwar Shaikh, Routledge 2007.

Article 8.4

(ECONOMIC) FREEDOM'S JUST ANOTHER WORD FOR ... CRISIS-PRONE

BY JOHN MILLER
September/October 2009

In "Capitalism in Crisis," his May op-ed in the *Wall Street Journal*, U.S. Court of Appeals judge and archconservative legal scholar Richard Posner argued that "a capitalist economy, while immensely dynamic and productive, is not inherently stable." Posner, the long-time cheerleader for deregulation, added, quite sensibly, "we may need more regulation of banking to reduce its inherent riskiness."

That may seem like a no-brainer to you and me, right there in the middle of the road with yellow-lines and dead armadillos, as Jim Hightower is fond of saying. But *Journal* readers were having none of it. They wrote in to set Judge Posner straight. "It is not free markets that fail, but government-controlled ones," protested one reader.

And why wouldn't they protest? The *Journal* has repeatedly told readers that "economic freedom" is "the real key to development." And each January for 15 years now the *Journal* tries to elevate that claim to a scientific truth by publishing a summary of the Heritage Foundation Index of Economic Freedom, which they assure readers proves the veracity of the claim. But in the hands of the editors of the *Wall Street Journal* and the researchers from the Heritage Foundation, Washington's foremost right-wing think tank, the Index of Economic Freedom is a barometer of corporate and entrepreneurial freedom from accountability rather than a guide to which countries are giving people more control over their economic lives and over the institutions that govern them.

This January was no different. "The 2009 Index provides strong evidence that the countries that maintain the freest economies do the best job promoting prosperity for all citizens," proclaimed this year's editorial, "Freedom is Still the Winning Formula." But with economies across the globe in recession, the virtues of free markets are a harder sell this year. That is not lost on *Wall Street Journal* editor Paul Gigot, who wrote the foreword to this year's report. Gigot allows that, "ostensibly free-market policymakers in the U.S. lost their monetary policy discipline, and we are now paying a terrible price." Still Gigot maintains that, "the *Index of Economic Freedom* exists to chronicle how steep that price will be and to point the way back to policy wisdom."

What the Heritage report fails to mention is this: while the global economy is in recession, many of the star performers in the Economic Freedom Index are tanking. Fully one half of the ten hardest-hit economies in the world are among the 30 "free" and "mostly free" economies at the top of the Economic Freedom Index rankings of 179 countries.

Here's the damage, according to the IMF. Singapore, the Southeast Asian trading center and perennial number two in the Index, will suffer a 10.0% drop in output this year. Slotting in at number four, Ireland, the so-called Celtic tiger, has seen its rapid export-led growth give way to an 8.0% drop in output. Number 13 and number 30, the foreign-direct-investment-favored Baltic states, Estonia and Lithuania, will each endure a 10.0% loss of output this year. Finally, the economy of Iceland, the loosely regulated European banking center that sits at number 14 on the Index, will contract 10.6% in 2009.

As a group, the Index's 30 most "free" economies will contract 4.1% in 2009. All of the other groups in the Index ("moderately free," "mostly unfree," and "repressed" economies) will muddle through 2009 with a much smaller loss of output or with moderate growth. The 67 "mostly unfree" countries in the Index will post the fastest growth rate for the year, 2.3%.

So it seems that if the Index of Economic Freedom can be trusted, then Judge Posner was not so far off the mark when he described capitalism as dynamic but "not inherently stable." That wouldn't be so bad, one *Journal* reader pointed out in a letter: "Economic recessions are the cost we pay for our economic freedom and economic prosperity is the benefit. We've had many more years of the latter than the former."

Not to Be Trusted

But the Index of Economic Freedom cannot and should not be trusted. How free or unfree an economy is according to the Index seems to have little do with how quickly it grows. For instance, economist Jeffrey Sachs found "no correlation" between a country's ranking in the Index and its per capita growth rates from 1995 to 2003. Also, in this year's report North America is the "freest" of its six regions of the world, but logged the slowest average rate over the last five years, 2.7% per annum. The Asia-Pacific region, which is "less free" than every other region except Sub-Saharan Africa according to the Index, posted the fastest average growth over the last five years, 7.8% per annum. That region includes several of the fastest growing of the world's economies, India, China, and Vietnam, which ranked 123, 132, and 145 respectively in the Index and were classified as "mostly unfree." And there are plenty of relatively slow growers among the countries high up in the Index, including Switzerland (which ranks ninth).

The Heritage Foundation folks who edited the Index objected to Sachs' criticisms, pointing out that they claimed "a close relationship" between *changes* in eco-

ECONOMIC FREEDOM AND ECONOMIC GROWTH IN 2009	
Degree of Economic Freedom	IMF Projected Growth Rate for 2009
"Free" (7 Countries)	-4.54%
"Mostly Free" (23 Counties)	-3.99%
"Moderately Free" (53 Counties)	-0.92%
"Mostly Unfree" (67 Countries)	+2.31%
"Repressed" (69 Counties)	+1.65%
Sources: International Monetary Fund, *World Economic Outlook: Crisis and Recovery*, April 2009, Tables A1, A2, A3; Terry Miller and Kim R. Holmes, eds., *2009 Index of Economic Freedom*, heritage.org/Index/, Executive Summary.	

nomic freedom, not the *level* of economic freedom, and growth. But even that claim is fraught with problems. Statistically it doesn't hold up. Economic journalist Doug Henwood found that improvements in the index and GDP growth from 1997 to 2003 could explain no more than 10% of GDP growth. In addition, even a tight correlation would not resolve the problem that many of the fastest growing economies are "mostly unfree" according to the Index.

But even more fundamental flaws with the Index render any claim about the relationship between prosperity and economic freedom, as measured by the Heritage Foundation, questionable. Consider just two of the ten components the Economic Freedom Index uses to rank countries: fiscal freedom and government size.

Fiscal freedom (what we might call the "hell-if-I'm-going-to-pay-for-government" index) relies on the top income tax and corporate income tax brackets as two of its three measures of the tax burden. These are decidedly flawed measures even if all that concerned you was the tax burden of the rich and owners of corporations (or the super-rich). Besides ignoring the burden of other taxes, singling out these two top tax rates doesn't get at effective corporate and income tax rates, or how much of a taxpayer's total income goes to paying these taxes. For example, on paper U.S. corporate tax rates are higher than those in Europe. But nearly one half of U.S. corporate profits go untaxed. The effective rate of taxation on U.S. corporate profits currently stands at 15%, far below the top corporate tax rate of 35%. And relative to GDP, U.S. corporate income taxes are no more than half those of other OECD countries.

Even their third measure of fiscal freedom, government tax revenues relative to GDP, bears little relationship to economic growth. After an exhaustive review, economist Joel Slemrod, former member of the Reagan Treasury Department, concludes that the literature reveals "no consensus" about the relationship between the level of taxation and economic growth.

The Index's treatment of government size, which relies exclusively on the level of government spending relative to GDP, is just as flawed as the fiscal freedom index. First, "richer countries do not tax and spend less" than poorer countries, reports economist Peter Lindhert. Beyond that, this measure does not take into account how the government uses its money. Social spending programs—public education, child-care and parental support, and public health programs—can make people more productive and promote economic growth. That lesson is not lost on Hong Kong and Singapore, number one and number two in the index. They both provide universal access to health care, despite the small size of their governments.

The size-of-government index also misses the mark because it fails to account for industrial policy. This is a serious mistake, because it overestimates the degree to which some of the fastest growing economies of the last few decades, such as Taiwan and South Korea, relied on the market and underestimates the positive role that government played in directing economic development in those countries by guiding investment and protecting infant industries.

This flaw is thrown into sharp relief by the recent report of the World Bank's Commission on Growth and Development. That group studied 13 economies that grew at least 7% a year for at least 25 years since 1950. Three of the Index's "free" and "mostly free" countries made the list (Singapore, Hong Kong, and Japan) but so did three of the index's "mostly unfree" countries (China, Brazil, and Indonesia). While these rapid growers were all export-oriented, their governments "were not free-market purists," according the Commission's report. "They tried a variety of policies to help diversify exports or sustain competitiveness. These included industrial policies to promote new investments."

Still More

Beyond all that, the Index says nothing about political freedom. Consider once again the two city-states, Hong Kong and Singapore, which top their list of free countries. Both are only "partially free" according to Freedom House, which the editors have called "the Michelin Guide to democracy's development." Hong Kong is still without direct elections for its legislatures or its chief executive and proposed internal security laws threaten press and academic freedom as well as political dissent. In Singapore, freedom of the press and rights to demonstrate are limited, films, TV, and the like are censored, and preventive detention is legal.

So it seems that the Index of Economic Freedom in practice tells us little about the cost of abandoning free market policies and offers little proof that government intervention into the economy would either retard economic growth or contract political freedom. In actuality, this rather objective-looking index is a slipshod measure that would seem to have no other purpose than to sell the neoliberal policies that brought on the current crisis, and to stand in the way of policies that might correct the crisis.

Sources: "Capitalism in Crisis," by Richard A Posner, *Wall Street Journal*, 5/07/09; "Letters: Recessions are the Price We Pay for Economic Freedom," *Wall Street Journal*, 5/19/09/; "Freedom is Still the Winning Formula," by Terry Miller, *Wall Street Journal*, 1/13/09 ; "The Real Key to Development," by Mary Anastasia O'Grady, *Wall Street Journal*, 1/15/08; Terry Miller and Kim R. Holmes, eds., *2009 Index of Economic Freedom*, heritage.org/Index/; Freedom House, "Freedom in the World 2009 Survey," freedomhouse.org; Joel Slemrod and Jon Bakija, *Taxing Ourselves: A Citizen's Guide to the Debate over Taxes*, MIT Press, 2008; International Monetary Fund, *World Economic Outlook,: Crisis and Recovery*, April 2009; Peter H. Lindert, *Growing Public*, Cambridge University Press, 2004; Doug Henwood, "*Laissez-faire* Olympics: An LBO Special Report," leftbusinessobserver.com, March 26, 2005; Jeffrey Sachs, *The End of Poverty: Economic Possibilities for Our Time*, Penguin, 2005.

Article 8.5

W(H)ITHER THE DOLLAR?

The U.S. trade deficit, the global economic crisis, and the dollar's status as the world's reserve currency.

BY KATHERINE SCIACCHITANO

For more than half a century, the dollar was both a symbol and an instrument of U.S. economic and military power. At the height of the financial crisis in the fall of 2008, the dollar served as a safe haven for investors, and demand for U.S. Treasury bonds ("Treasuries") spiked. More recently, the United States has faced a vacillating dollar, calls to replace the greenback as the global reserve currency, and an international consensus that it should save more and spend less.

At first glance, circumstances seem to give reason for concern. The U.S. budget deficit is over 10% of GDP. China has begun a long-anticipated move away from Treasuries, threatening to make U.S. government borrowing more expensive. And the adoption of austerity measures in Greece—with a budget deficit barely 3% higher relative to GDP than the United States—hovers as a reminder that the bond market can enforce wage cuts and pension freezes on developed as well as developing countries.

These pressures on the dollar and for fiscal cut-backs and austerity come at an awkward time given the level of public outlays required to deal with the crisis and the need to attract international capital to pay for them. But the pressures also highlight the central role of the dollar in the crisis. Understanding that role is critical to grasping the link between the financial recklessness we've been told is to blame for the crisis and the deeper causes of the crisis in the real economy: that link is the outsize U.S. trade deficit.

Trade deficits are a form of debt. For mainstream economists, the cure for the U.S. deficit is thus increased "savings": spend less and the bottom line will improve. But the U.S. trade deficit didn't balloon because U.S. households or the government went on a spending spree. It ballooned because, from the 1980s on, successive U.S. administrations pursued a high-dollar policy that sacrificed U.S. manufacturing for finance, and that combined low-wage, export-led growth in the Global South with low-wage, debt-driven consumption at home. From the late nineties, U.S. dollars that went out to pay for imports increasingly came back not as demand for U.S. goods, but as demand for investments that fueled U.S. housing and stock market bubbles. Understanding the history of how the dollar helped create these imbalances, and how these imbalances in turn led to the housing bubble and sub-prime crash, sheds important light on how labor and the left should respond to pressures for austerity and "saving" as the solution to the crisis.

Gold, Deficits, and Austerity

A good place to start is with the charge that the Federal Reserve triggered the housing bubble by lowering interest rates after the dot-com bubble burst and plunged the country into recession in 2001.

In 2001, manufacturing was too weak to lead a recovery, and the Bush administration was ideologically opposed to fiscal stimulus other than tax cuts for the wealthy. So the real question isn't why the Fed lowered rates; it's why it was able to. In 2000, the U.S. trade deficit stood at 3.7% of GDP. Any other country with this size deficit would have had to tighten its belt and jump-start exports, not embark on stimulating domestic demand that could deepen the deficit even more.

The Fed's ability to lower interest rates despite the U.S. trade deficit stemmed from the dollar's role as the world's currency, which was established during the Bretton Woods negotiations for a new international monetary system at the end of World War II.

A key purpose of an international monetary system—Bretton Woods or any other—is to keep international trade and debt in balance. Trade has to be mutual. One country can't do all the selling while other does all the buying; both must be able to buy and sell. If one or more countries develop trade deficits that persist, they won't be able to continue to import without borrowing and going into debt. At the same time, some other country or countries will have corresponding trade surpluses. The result is a global trade imbalance. To get back "in balance," the deficit country has to import less, export more, or both. The surplus country has to do the reverse.

In practice, economic pressure is stronger on deficit countries to adjust their trade balances by importing less, since it's deficit countries that could run out of money to pay for imports. Importing less can be accomplished with import quotas (which block imports over a set level) or tariffs (which decrease demand for imports by imposing a tax on them). It can also be accomplished with "austerity"—squeezing demand by lowering wages.

Under the gold standard, this squeezing took place automatically. Gold was shipped out of a country to pay for a trade deficit. Since money had to be backed by gold, having less gold meant less money in domestic circulation. So prices and wages fell. Falling wages in turn lowered demand for imports and boosted exports. The deficit was corrected, but at the cost of recession, austerity, and hardship for workers. In other words, the gold standard was deflationary.

Bretton Woods

The gold standard lasted until the Great Depression, and in fact helped to cause it. Beyond the high levels of unemployment, one of the most vivid lessons from the global catastrophe that ensued was the collapse of world trade, as country after country tried to deal with falling exports by limiting imports. After World War II, the industrialized countries wanted an international monetary system that could correct trade imbalances without imposing austerity and risking another depression. This was particularly important given the post-war levels of global debt and deficits, which could have suppressed demand and blocked trade again. Countries pursued these aims at the Bretton Woods negotiations in 1944, in Bretton Woods, New Hampshire.

John Maynard Keynes headed the British delegation. Keynes was already famous for his advocacy of government spending to bolster demand and maintain employment during recessions and depressions. England also owed large war debts to the United States and had suffered from high unemployment for over two decades. Keynes therefore had a keen interest in creating a system that prevented the build-up of global debt and avoided placing the full pressure of correcting trade imbalances on debtor countries.

His proposed solution was an international clearing union—a system of accounts kept in a fictitious unit called the "bancor." Accounts would be tallied each year to see which countries were in deficit and which were in surplus. Countries with trade deficits would have to work to import less and export more. In the meantime, they would have the unconditional right—for a period—to an "overdraft" of bancors, the size of the overdraft to be based on the size of previous surpluses. These overdrafts would both support continued imports of necessities and guarantee uninterrupted global trade. At the same time, countries running trade surpluses would be expected to get back in balance too by importing more, and would be fined if their surpluses persisted.

Keynes was also adamant that capital controls be part of the new system. Capital controls are restrictions on the movement of capital across borders. Keynes wanted countries to be able to resort to macroeconomic tools such as deficit spending, lowering interest rates, and expanding money supplies to bolster employment and wages when needed. He worried that without capital controls, capital flight—investors taking their money and running—could veto economic policies and force countries to raise interest rates, cut spending, and lower wages instead, putting downward pressure on global demand as the gold standard had.

Keynes's system wouldn't have solved the problems of capitalism—in his terms, the problem of insufficient demand, and in Marx's terms the problems of overproduction and under-consumption. But by creating incentives for surplus countries to import more, it would have supported global demand and job growth and made the kind of trade imbalances that exist today—including the U.S. trade deficit—much less likely. It would also have taken the pressure off deficit countries to adopt austerity measures. And it would have prevented surplus countries from using the power of debt to dictate economic policy to deficit countries.

At the end of World War II, the United States was, however, the largest surplus country in the world, and it intended to remain so for the foreseeable future. The New Deal had lowered unemployment during the Depression. But political opposition to deficit spending had prevented full recovery until arms production for the war restored manufacturing. Many feared that without continued large U.S. trade surpluses and expanded export markets, unemployment would return to Depression-era levels.

The United States therefore blocked Keynes' proposal. Capital controls were permitted for the time being, largely because of the danger that capital would flee war-torn Europe. But penalties for surplus countries were abandoned; pressures remained primarily on deficit countries to correct. Instead of an international clearing union with automatic rights to overdrafts, the International Monetary Fund (IMF) was established to make short-term loans to deficit countries. And instead of the neutral bancor, the dollar—backed by the U.S. pledge to redeem dollars with gold at $35 an ounce—would be the world currency.

Limits of the System

The system worked for just over twenty-five years, not because trade was balanced, but because the United States was able and willing to recycle its huge trade surpluses. U.S. military spending stayed high because of the U.S. cold-war role as "global cop." And massive aid was given to Europe to rebuild. Dollars went out as foreign aid and military spending (both closely coordinated). They came back as demand for U.S. goods.

At the same time, memory of the Depression created a kind of Keynesian consensus in the advanced industrial democracies to use fiscal and monetary policy to maintain full employment. Labor movements, strengthened by both the war and the post-war boom, pushed wage settlements and welfare spending higher. Global demand was high.

Two problems doomed the system. First, the IMF retained the power to impose conditions on debtor countries, and the United States retained the power to control the IMF.

Second, the United States stood outside the rules of the game: The larger the world economy grew, the more dollars would be needed in circulation; U.S. trade deficits would eventually have to provide them. Other countries would have to correct their trade deficits by tightening their belts to import less, exporting more by devaluing their currencies to push down prices, or relying on savings from trade surpluses denominated in dollars (known as "reserves") to pay for their excess of imports over exports. But precisely because countries needed dollar reserves to pay for international transactions and to provide cushions against periods of deficits, other countries would need to hold the U.S. dollars they earned by investing them in U.S. assets. This meant that U.S. dollars that went out for imports would come back and be reinvested in the United States. Once there, these dollars could be used to finance continued spending on imports—and a larger U.S. trade deficit. At that point, sustaining world trade would depend not on recycling U.S. surpluses, but on recycling U.S. deficits. The ultimate result would be large, destabilizing global capital flows.

The Crisis of the Seventies

The turning point came in the early 1970s. Europe and Japan had rebuilt from the war and were now export powers in their own right. The U.S. trade surplus was turning into a deficit. And the global rate of profit in manufacturing was falling. The United States had also embarked on its "War on Poverty" just as it increased spending on its real war in Vietnam, and this "guns and butter" strategy—an attempt to quell domestic opposition from the civil right and anti-war movements while maintaining global military dominance—led to high inflation.

The result was global economic crisis: the purchasing power of the dollar fell, just as more and more dollars were flowing out of the United States and being held by foreigners.

What had kept the United States from overspending up to this point was its Bretton Woods commitment to exchange dollars for gold at the rate of $35 an ounce. Now countries and investors that didn't want to stand by and watch as the purchasing power of their dollar holdings fell—as well as countries that objected to the Vietnam War—held the United States to its pledge.

There wasn't enough gold in Ft. Knox. The United States would have to re-trench its global military role, reign in domestic spending, or change the rules of the game. It changed the rules of the game. In August 1971, Nixon closed the gold window; the United States would no longer redeem dollars for gold. Countries and individuals would have to hold dollars, or dump them and find another currency that was more certain to hold its value. There was none.

The result was that the dollar remained the global reserve currency. But the world moved from a system where the United States could spend only if could back its spending by gold, to a system where its spending was limited only by the quantity of dollars the rest of the world was willing to hold. The value of the dollar would fluctuate with the level of global demand for U.S. products and investment. The value of other currencies would fluctuate with the dollar.

Trading Manufacturing for Finance

The result of this newfound freedom to spend was a decade of global inflation and crises of the dollar. As inflation grew, each dollar purchased less. As each dollar pur-chased less, the global demand to hold dollars dropped—and with it the dollar's exchange rate. As the exchange rate fell, imports became even more expensive, and inflation ratcheted up again. The cycle intensified when OPEC—which priced its oil in dollars—raised its prices to compensate for the falling dollar.

Owners of finance capital were unhappy because inflation was eroding the value of dollar assets. Owners of manufacturing capital were unhappy because the global rate of profit in manufacturing was dropping. And both U.S. politicians and elites were unhappy because the falling dollar was eroding U.S. military power by making it more expensive.

The response of the Reagan administration was to unleash neoliberalism on both the national and global levels—the so-called Reagan revolution. On the do-mestic front, inflation was quelled, and the labor movement was put in its place, with high interest rates and the worst recession since the Depression. Corporate profits were boosted directly through deregulation, privatization, and tax cuts, and indirectly by attacks on unions, unemployment insurance, and social spending.

When it was over, profits were up, inflation and wages were down, and the dollar had changed direction. High interest rates attracted a stream of investment capital into the United States, pushing up demand for the currency, and with it the exchange rate. The inflows paid for the growing trade and budget deficits—Reagan had cut domestic spending, but increased military spending. And they provided abundant capital for finance and overseas investment. But the high dollar also made U.S. exports more expensive for the rest of the world. The United States had effec-tively traded manufacturing for finance and debt.

Simultaneously, debt was used as a hammer to impose neoliberalism on the Third World. As the price of oil rose in the seventies, OPEC countries deposited their grow-ing trade surpluses—so-called petro-dollars—in U.S. banks, which in turn loaned them to poor countries to pay for the soaring price of oil. Initially set at very low interest rates, loan payments skyrocketed when the United States jacked up its rates to deal with inflation. Third World countries began defaulting, starting with Mexico in 1981. In response, and in exchange for more loans, the U.S.-controlled IMF imposed austerity programs, also known as "structural adjustment programs."

The programs were similar to the policies in the United States, but much more severe, and they operated in reverse. Instead of pushing up exchange rates to attract finance capital as the United States had done, Third World countries were told to devalue their currencies to attract foreign direct investment and export their way out of debt. Capital controls were dismantled to enable transnational corporations to enter and exit at will. Governments were forced to slash spending on social programs and infrastructure to push down wages and demand for imports. Services were privatized to create opportunities for private capital, and finance was deregulated.

Policies dovetailed perfectly. As the high dollar hollowed out U.S. manufacturing, countries in the Global South were turned into low-wage export platforms. As U.S. wages stagnated or fell, imports became cheaper, masking the pain. Meanwhile, the high dollar lowered the cost of overseas production. Interest payments on third world debt—which continued to grow—swelled the already large capital flows into the United States and provided even more funds for overseas investment.

The view from the heights of finance looked promising. But Latin America was entering what became known as "the lost decade." And the United State was shifting from exporting goods to exporting demand, and from recycling its trade surplus to recycling its deficit. The world was becoming dependent on the United States as the "consumer of last resort." The United States was becoming dependent on finance and debt.

Consolidating Neoliberalism

The growth of finance in the eighties magnified its political clout in the nineties. With the bond market threatening to charge higher rates for government debt, Clinton abandoned campaign pledges to invest in U.S. infrastructure, education, and industry. Instead, he balanced the budget; he adopted his own high-dollar policy, based on the theory that global competition would keep imports cheap, inflation low, and the living standard high—regardless of sluggish wage growth; and he continued deregulation of the finance industry—repealing Glass-Steagall and refusing to regulate derivatives. By the end of Clinton's second term, the U.S. trade deficit had hit a record 3.7% of GDP; household debt had soared to nearly 69% of GDP and financial profits had risen to 30% of GDP, almost twice as high as they had been at any time up to the mid 1980s.

Internationally, Clinton consolidated IMF-style structural adjustment policies under the rubric of "the Washington Consensus," initiated a new era of trade agreements modeled on the North American Free Trade Agreement, and led the charge to consolidate the elimination of capital controls.

The elimination of capital controls deepened global economic instability in several ways.

First, eliminating restrictions on capital mobility made it easier for capital to go in search of the lowest wages. This expanded the globalization of production, intensifying downward pressure on wages and global demand.

Second, removing capital controls increased the political power of capital by enabling it to "vote with its feet." This accelerated the deregulation of global finance and—as Keynes predicted—limited countries' abilities to run full-employment policies. Regulation of business was punished, as was deficit spending, regardless of its purpose. Low inflation and deregulation of labor markets—weakening unions and making wages more "flexible"—were rewarded.

Finally, capital mobility fed asset bubbles and increased financial speculation and exchange rate volatility. As speculative capital rushed into countries, exchange rates rose; as it fled, they fell. Speculators began betting more and more on currencies themselves, further magnifying rate swings. Rising exchange rates made exports uncompetitive, hurting employment and wages. Falling exchange rates increased the competitiveness of exports, but made imports and foreign borrowing more expensive, except for the United States, which borrows in its own currency. Countries could try to prevent capital flight by raising interest rates, but only at the cost of dampening growth and lost of jobs. Lacking capital controls, there was little countries could do to prevent excessive inflows and bubbles.

Prelude to a Crash

This increased capital mobility, deregulation, and speculation weakened the real economy, further depressed global demand, and greatly magnified economic instability. From the eighties onward, international financial crises broke out approximately every five years, in countries ranging from Mexico to the former Soviet Union.

By far the largest crisis prior to the sub-prime meltdown took place in East Asia in the mid-nineties. Speculative capital began flowing into East Asia in the mid nineties. In 1997, the bubble burst. By the summer of 1998, stock markets around the world were crashing from the ripple effects. The IMF stepped in with $40 billion in loans, bailing out investors but imposing harsh conditions on workers and governments. Millions were left unemployed as Asia plunged into depression.

When the dust settled, Asian countries said "never again." Their solution was to build up large dollar reserves—savings cushions—so they would never have to turn to the IMF for another loan. To build up reserves, countries had to run large trade surpluses. This meant selling even more to the United States, the only market in the world able and willing to run ever-larger trade deficits to absorb their exports.

In addition to further weakening U.S. manufacturing, the Asia crisis set the stage for the sub-prime crisis in several ways.

First, as capital initially fled Asia, it sought out the United States as a "safe haven," igniting the U.S. stock market and nascent housing bubbles.

Second, the longer-term recycling of burgeoning Asian surpluses ensured an abundant and ongoing source of capital to finance not only the mounting trade deficit, but also the billowing U.S. consumer debt more generally.

Third, preventing their exchange rates from rising with their trade surpluses and making their exports uncompetitive required Asian central banks to print money, swelling global capital flows even more.

Between 1998 and 2007, when the U.S. housing bubble burst, many policy makers and mainstream economists came to believe this inflow of dollars and debt would never stop. It simply seemed too mutually beneficial to end. By financing the U.S. trade deficit, Asian countries guaranteed U.S. consumers would continue to purchase their goods. The United States in turn got cheap imports, cheap money for consumer finance, and inflated stock and real estate markets that appeared to be self-financing and to compensate for stagnating wages. At the same time, foreign holders of dollars bought increasing quantities of U.S. Treasuries, saving the U.S. government from having to raise interest rates to attract purchasers, and giving the United States cheap financing for its budget deficit as well.

It was this ability to keep interest rates low—in particular, the Fed's ability to lower rates after the stock market bubble collapsed in 2000—that set off the last and most destructive stage of the housing bubble. Lower interest rates simultaneously increased the demand for housing (since lower interest rates made mortgages cheaper) and decreased the returns to foreign holders of U.S. Treasuries. These lower returns forced investors to look for other "safe" investments with higher yields. Investors believed they found what they needed in U.S. mortgage securities.

As Wall Street realized what a lucrative international market they had, the big banks purposefully set out to increase the number of mortgages that could be repackaged and sold to investors by lowering lending standards. They also entered into complicated systems of private bets, known as credit default swaps, to insure against the risk of defaults. These credit default swaps created a chain of debt that exponentially magnified risk. When the bubble finally burst, only massive stimulus spending and infusions of capital by the industrialized countries into their banking systems kept the world from falling into another depression.

Deficit Politics

The political establishment—right and center—is now licking its chops, attacking fiscal deficits as if ending them were a solution to the crisis. The underlying theory harks back to the deflationary operation of the gold standard and the conditions imposed by the IMF: Government spending causes trade deficits and inflation by increasing demand. Cutting spending will cut deficits by diminishing demand.

Like Clinton before him, Obama is now caving in to the bond market, fearful that international lenders will raise interest rates on U.S. borrowing. He has created a bi-partisan debt commission to focus on long-term fiscal balance—read: cutting Social Security and Medicare—and revived "PAYGO," which requires either cuts or increases in revenue to pay for all new outlays, even as unemployment hovers just under 10%.

By acquiescing, the U.S. public is implicitly blaming itself for the crisis and offering to pay for it twice: first with the millions of jobs lost to the recession, and again by weakening the safety net. But the recent growth of the U.S. budget deficit principally reflects the cost of cleaning up the crisis and of the wars in Iraq and Afghanistan. Assumptions of future deficits are rooted in projected health-care costs in the absence of meaningful reform. And the U.S. trade deficit is driven mainly by the continued high dollar.

The economic crisis won't be resolved by increasing personal savings or enforcing fiscal discipline, because its origins aren't greedy consumers or profligate governments. The real origins of the crisis are the neoliberal response to the crisis of the

1970s—the shift from manufacturing to finance in the United States, and the transformation of the Global South into a low-wage export platform for transnational capital to bolster sagging profit rate. The U.S. trade and budget deficits may symbolize this transformation. But the systemic problem is a global economic model that separates consumption from production and that has balanced world demand—not just the U.S. economy—on debt and speculation.

Forging an alternative will be the work of generations. As for the present, premature tightening of fiscal policy as countries try to "exit" from the crisis will simply drain global demand and endanger recovery. Demonizing government spending will erode the social wage and undermine democratic debate about the public investment needed for a transition to an environmentally sustainable global economy.

In the United States, where labor market and financial deregulation have garnered the most attention in popular critiques of neoliberalism, painting a bulls-eye on government spending also obscures the role of the dollar and U.S. policy in the crisis. For several decades after World War II, U.S. workers benefited materially as the special status of the dollar helped expand export markets for U.S. goods. But as other labor movements throughout the world know from bitter experience, it's the dollar as the world's currency, together with U.S. control of the IMF, that ultimately provided leverage for the United States to create the low-wage export model of growth and financial deregulation that has so unbalanced the global economy and hurt "first" and "third" world workers alike.

Looking Ahead

At the end of World War II, John Maynard Keynes proposed an international monetary system with the bancor at its core; the system would have helped balance trade and avoid the debt and deflation in inherent in the gold standard that preceded the Great Depression. Instead, Bretton Woods was negotiated, with the dollar as the world's currency. What's left of that system has now come full circle and created the very problems it was intended to avoid: large trade imbalances and deflationary economic conditions.

For the past two and a half decades, the dollar enabled the United States to run increasing trade deficits while systematically draining capital from some of the poorest countries in the world. This money could have been used for development in the Global South, to replace aging infrastructure in the United States, or to prepare for and prevent climate change. Instead, it paid for U.S. military interventions, outsourcing, tax cuts for the wealthy, and massive stock market and housing bubbles.

This mismanagement of the dollar hasn't served the long-term interests of workers the United States any more than it has those in of the developing world. In domestic terms, it has been particularly damaging over the last three decades to U.S. manufacturing, and state budgets and workers are being hit hard by the crisis. Yet even manufacturing workers in the United States cling to the high dollar as if it were a life raft. Many public sector workers advocate cutting back on government spending. And most people in the United States would blame bankers' compensation packages for the subprime mess before pointing to the dismantling of capital controls.

After suffering through the worst unemployment since the Depression and paying for the bailout of finance, U.S. unions and the left are right to be angry. On the global scale, there is increased space for activism. Since the summer of 2007, at least 17 countries have imposed or tightened capital controls. Greek workers have been in the streets protesting pension cuts and pay freezes for months now. And a global campaign has been launched for a financial transactions tax that would slow down speculation and provide needed revenue for governments. Together, global labor and the left are actively rethinking and advocating reform of the global financial system, the neoliberal trade agreements, and the role and governance of the International Monetary Fund. And there is increasing discussion of a replacement for the dollar that won't breed deficits, suck capital out of the developing world, impose austerity on deficit countries—or blow bubbles.

All these reforms are critical. All will require more grassroots education. None will come without a struggle.

Sources: C. Fred Bergsten, "The Dollar and the Deficits: How Washington Can Prevent the Next Crisis," Peterson Institute for International Economics, *Foreign Affairs*, Volume 88 No. 6, November 2009; Dean Baker, "The Budget, the Deficit, and the Dollar," Center for Economic Policy and Research, www.cepr.net; Martin Wolf, "Give us fiscal austerity, but not quite yet," *Financial Times* blogs, November 24, 2009; Tom Palley, "Domestic Demand-led Growth: A New Paradigm for Development," paper presented at the Alterantives to Neoliberalism Conference sponsored by the New Rules for Global Finance Coalition, May 21-24, 2002, www. economicswebinstitute.org; Sarah Anderson, "Policy Handcuffs in the Financial Crisis: How U.S. Government And Trade Policy Limit Government Power To Control Capital Flows, " Institute for Policy Studies, February 2009; Susan George, "The World Trade Organisation We Could Have Had," *Le Monde Diplomatique*, January 2007.

Article 8.6

PUTTING THE "GLOBAL" IN THE GLOBAL ECONOMIC CRISIS

BY SMRITI RAO

November/December 2009

There is no question that the current economic crisis originated in the developed world, and primarily in the United States. Much of the analysis of the crisis has thus focused on institutional failures within the United States and there is, rightly, tremendous concern here about high rates of domestic unemployment and under-employment. But after three decades of globalization, what happens in the United States does not stay in the United States; the actions of traders in New York City will mean hunger for children in Nairobi. We now know what crisis looks like in the age of globalization and it is not pretty.

This crisis is uniquely a child of the neoliberal global order. For developing countries the key elements of neoliberalism have consisted of trade liberalization and an emphasis on exports; reductions in government social welfare spending; a greater reliance on the market for determining the price of everything from the currency exchange rate to water from the tap; and, last but not least, economy-wide privatization and deregulation. In each case, the aim was also to promote cross-border flows of goods, services, and capital—and, to a far lesser degree, of people.

Despite Thomas Friedman's assertions of a "flat" world, this age of globalization did not in fact eliminate global inequality. Indeed if we exclude China and India, inequality between countries actually increased during this period. The globalization of the last 30 years was predicated upon the extraction by the developed world of the natural resources, cheap labor, and, in particular, capital of the developing world, the latter via financial markets that siphoned the world's savings to pay for U.S. middle-class consumption. What could be more ironic than the billions of dollars in capital flowing every year from developing countries with unfunded domestic needs to developed countries, which then failed to meet even their minimum obligations with respect to foreign aid? Africa, for example, has actually been a net creditor to the United States for some time, suggesting that the underlying dynamic of the world economy today is not that different from the colonialism of past centuries.

These "reverse flows" are partly the result of attempts by developing countries to ward off balance-of-payment crises by holding large foreign exchange reserves. Within the United States, this capital helped sustain massive borrowing by households, corporations, and governments, exacerbating the debt bubble of the last eight years. Meanwhile, the global "race to the bottom" among developing-county exporters ensured that the prices of most manufactured goods and services remained low, taking the threat of inflation off the table and enabling the U.S. Federal Reserve to keep interest rates low and facilitate the housing bubble.

Now that this debt bubble has finally burst, it is no surprise that the crisis has been transmitted back to the global South at record speed.

Measuring the Impact

A country-by-country comparison of the growth in real (i.e., inflation-adjusted) GDP from 2007 to 2008 against the average annual growth of the preceding three years (2005-2007) gives us a picture of the differential impact of the economic crisis—at least in its early stages—on various countries. Consistent data are available for 178 developed and developing countries.

Overall, GDP growth for these 178 countries was down by 1.3 percentage points in 2008 compared to the average for 2005-2007. Of course, the financial crisis only hit in full force in September 2008, so the 2009 data will give us a more complete picture of the impact of the crisis. The International Monetary Fund (IMF) estimates that global GDP will decline in 2009 for the first time since World War II. Currently, the IMF is expecting a 1.4% contraction this year. According to the International Labor Organization, global unemployment increased by 10.7 million in 2008, with a further increase of 19 million expected in 2009 by relatively conservative estimates. As a result, the number of people living in poverty will increase by an estimated 46 million this year according to the World Bank.

The initial impact in 2008 was greatest in Eastern Europe and Central Asia: six of the ten countries with the steepest declines in real GDP growth were from the Eastern Europe/Central Asia region (see Table 1). Joined by Ireland, this is a list of global high-fliers—countries with very high rates of growth (before 2008, that is) that had globalized rapidly and enthusiastically in the last decade and a half. Singapore of course was an early adopter of globalization, touted by the IMF as a model for other small countries, while Seychelles has depended heavily on international tourism. Myanmar would seem to be the exception to this pattern of intensive globalization, given its political isolation. From an economic perspective, however, this was a country whose economic growth depended heavily on the rising prices of its commodity exports (natural gas and gems).

Indeed, if we rank these 178 countries by the share of their GDP represented by exports before the crisis, we find a correlation between dependence on exports and steeper declines in GDP growth. The 50 most export-dependent countries actually saw larger declines in GDP in 2008 than those less dependent on exports (see Table 2). Likewise with certain other key markers of neoliberal globalization.

That globalizers appear to be most affected by the crisis is no accident. It turns out that each of the three primary channels through which the crisis has been transmitted from the United States to other countries is a direct outcome of the policy choices that developing countries were urged and sometimes coerced into making—with assurances that this particular form of globalization was the best way to build a healthy and prosperous economy.

Transmission Channels of the Crisis

Lowered exports and remittances. The recession in the United States and Europe has hit exports from the developing world hard. Globally, trade in goods and services did rise by 3% in 2008, but that was compared to 10% and 7% in the previous two years. Trade is expected to decline by a sharp 12% in 2009. The United States, the world's most important importer, has seen imports drop by an unprecedented 30% since July 2008. For countries ranging from Pakistan to Cameroon, this has meant lower foreign exchange earnings, slower economic growth, and higher unemployment.

Meanwhile, for many developing countries, the emphasis on export promotion meant the increasing export not of goods and services but of people, who sought work in richer countries and sent part of their earnings back home. Remittance flows from temporary and permanent migrants accounted for 25% of net inflows of private capital to the global South in 2007. These flows are also affected by the crisis, although they have proved more resilient than other sources of private capital.

Migrant workers in construction, in particular, find that they are no longer able to find work and send money back home, and countries in Latin America have seen sharp declines in remittance inflows. However, as Indian economist Jayati Ghosh points out, women migrants working as maids, nurses, and nannies in the West have not been as hard hit by the recession. This has meant that remittance flows to countries with primarily female migrants, such as Sri Lanka and the Philippines, are not as badly affected. The Middle Eastern countries that are important host countries for many Asian migrants have also been relatively shielded from the crisis. As a result, for the developing world as a whole, remittances actually rose in 2008. Because other private capital flows declined sharply post-crisis, remittances accounted for 46% of net private capital inflows to the developing world in 2008.

Outflows of portfolio capital. In the boom years up to 2007, developing countries were encouraged to liberalize their financial sectors. This meant removing regulatory barriers to the inflow (and outflow) of foreign investors and their money. While

TABLE 1: STEEPEST DECLINES IN ECONOMIC GROWTH		
TOP TEN COUNTRIES BY DECLINE IN 2008 REAL GDP GROWTH VS. 2005-07 ANNUAL AVERAGE		
	Country	**Change in 2008 real GDP growth compared to 2005-07 average (in percentage points)**
1	Latvia	–15.56
2	Azerbaijan	–14.44
3	Estonia	–12.26
4	Georgia	–8.42
5	Myanmar	–8.32
6	Ireland	–8.30
7	Seychelles	–7.62
8	Armenia	–6.85
9	Singapore	–6.66
10	Kazakhstan	–6.57

Source: Author's calculations based on data from World Development Indicators online, World Bank, June 2009.

some foreign investors did buy factories and other actual physical assets in the developing world, a substantial portion of foreign capital came in the form of portfolio capital—short-term investments in stock and real estate markets. Portfolio capital is called "hot money" for a reason: it tends to be incredibly mobile, and its mobility has been enhanced by the systematic dismantling of various government restrictions ("capital controls") that formerly prevented this money from entering or leaving countries at the volume and speed it can today.

Around the time of the collapse of Bear Stearns in the United States in early 2008, various global financial powerhouses began pulling their money out of developing-country markets. The pace of the pullout only accelerated after the crash that September. One consequence for developing countries was a fall in their stock market indices, which in turn depressed growth. Another was that as foreign investors converted their krona, rupees, or rubles into dollars in order to leave, the value of the local currency got pushed down.

The IMF has long touted the virtues of allowing freely floating exchange rates, where market forces determine the value of each currency. In the aftermath of the

TABLE 2: EXPORTS AND FOREIGN INVESTMENT		
CHANGE IN 2008 REAL GDP GROWTH COMPARED TO 2005-07 ANNUAL AVERAGE (IN PERCENTAGE POINTS) FOR COUNTRIES RANKED BY:		
	Export share of GDP	FDI share of GDP
Average for top 50 countries	–2.25	–1.85
Average for countries ranked 51-100	–1.50	–1.70
Average for the remaining countries	–0.88	–1.07
Total number of countries	167	171

TABLE 3: EXCHANGE RATE AND FISCAL POLICY			
AVERAGE CHANGE IN 2008 REAL GDP GROWTH COMPARED TO ANNUAL 2005-07 AVERAGE (IN PERCENTAGE POINTS) FOR COUNTRY GROUPINGS:			
Exchange Rate Policy		Fiscal Policy	
Countries with fixed exchange rate	–1.19	Countries with no inflation targeting	–1.18
Countries with managed float or other mixed policy	–1.19	Countries with inflation targeting	–2.35
Countries with freely floating exchange rate	–2.04		
Total number of countries	178		171

Sources: Author's calculations based on data from World Development Indicators online, World Bank, June 2009 and De Facto Classification of Exchange Rate Regimes and Monetary Policy Frameworks as of April 31, 2008, IMF.

financial crisis, this meant a sharp depreciation in the value of many local currencies relative to the dollar. This in turn meant that every gallon of oil priced in dollars would cost that many more, say, rupees. Similarly, any dollar-denominated debt a country held became harder to repay. The dollar cost of imports and debt servicing went up, just as exports and remittances—the ability to earn those dollars—were falling. Predictably, countries with floating (i.e., market-determined) exchange rates were harder hit in 2008 (see Table 3).

Falling flows of FDI and development aid. Meanwhile, one other source of foreign exchange, foreign investment in actual physical assets such as factories (known as foreign direct investment, or FDI), is stagnant and likely to fall as companies across the world shelve expansion plans. The signs of vulnerability are evident in the fact that countries most dependent upon FDI inflows (as a percentage of GDP) between 2005 and 2007 suffered greater relative GDP declines in 2008 (see Table 2).

Developed countries are also cutting back on foreign aid budgets, citing the cost of domestic stimulus programs and reduced tax revenues. Such cuts particularly affect the poorest countries. With the economic slowdown their governments are losing domestic tax and other revenues, so falling aid flows are likely to hurt even more. The importance of continued aid flows can be seen in the fact that higher levels of aid per capita from 2005 to 2007 were actually associated with more mild drops in GDP growth in 2008 (see Table 2). This may be partly due to the fact that these countries already had low or negative rates of GDP growth so that 2008 declines appear smaller relative to that baseline. Nevertheless, aid flows appear to have protected the most vulnerable countries from even greater economic disaster. In fact the so-called HIPC group (highly indebted poor countries) actually saw an increase of one percentage point in GDP growth rates when compared to the 2005-2007 average.

Both FDI and aid work their way into and out of economies more slowly, so we may have to wait for 2009 data to estimate the full impact of the crisis via this channel.

The simultaneous transmission of the crisis through these three channels has left developing countries reeling. What makes the situation even worse is that unlike developed countries, developing countries are unlikely to be able to afford generous stimulus packages (China is an important exception). Meanwhile, the IMF and its allies, rather than supporting developing-country governments in their quest to stimulate domestic demand and investment, are hindering the process by insisting on the same old policy mix of deficit reductions and interest rate hikes. In an illustration of how ruinous this policy mix can be, countries that had followed IMF advice and adopted "inflation targeting" before the crisis suffered greater relative GDP declines once the crisis hit (see Table 3).

The tragedy of course is that while the remnants of the welfare state still protect citizens of the developed world from the very worst effects of the crisis, developing countries have been urged for two decades to abandon the food and fuel subsidies and public sector provision of essential services that are the only things that come close to resembling a floor for living standards. They were told they didn't need that safety net, that it only got in the way; now, of course, they are free to fall.

For those unwilling to let this tragedy unfold, this is the time to apply pressure on developed-country governments to maintain aid flows. Even more importantly, this is the time to apply pressure on the IMF and the other multilateral development banks, and on their supporters in the halls of power, so that they offer developing countries a genuine chance to survive this crisis and begin to rebuild for the future.

It is worth recalling that the end of the previous "age of globalization," signaled by the Great Depression, led to a renewed role for the public sector the world over and an attempt to achieve growth alongside self-reliance. In the years after World War II, led by Latin America, newly independent developing countries attempted to prioritize building a domestic producer and consumer base. In the long run, perhaps this crisis will result in a similar rethinking of the currently dominant model of development. In the short run, however, the world seems ready to stand by and watch while the poor and vulnerable in developing countries, truly innocent bystanders, suffer.

Sources: Dilip Ratha, Sanket Mohapatra, and Ani Silwal, "Migration and Development Brief 10," Migration and Remittances Team, Development Prospects Group, World Bank, July 13, 2009; Atish R. Ghosh et al. 2009, "Coping with the Crisis: Policy Options for Emerging Market Countries," IMF Staff Position Note, SPN/09/08, April 23, 2009; World Bank, "Swimming Against the Tide: How Developing Countries Are Coping with the Global Crisis," Background Paper prepared by World Bank Staff for the G20 Finance Ministers and Central Bank Governors Meeting, Horsham, United Kingdom on March 13-14, 2009; Jayati Ghosh, "Current Global Financial Crisis: Curse or Blessing in Disguise for Developing Countries?" Presentation prepared for the IWG-GEM Workshop, Levy Economics Institute, New York, June 29-July 10, 2009.

Article 8.7

RICH AND POOR IN THE GLOBAL ECONOMY

Interview with Bob Sutcliffe

March/April 2005

Whether economic inequality is rising or falling globally is a matter of intense debate, a key question in the larger dispute over how three decades of intensified economic global- ization have affected the world's poor. Bob Sutcliffe is an economist at the University of the Basque Country in Bilbao, Spain, and the author of 100 Ways of Seeing an Un- equal World. *He has been analyzing both the statistical details and the broader politi- cal-economic import of the debate and shared some of his insights in a recent interview with* Dollars & Sense.

DOLLARS & SENSE: If someone asked you whether global inequality has grown over the past 25 years, I assume you'd say, "It depends—on how inequality is defined, on what data is used, on how that data is analyzed." Is that fair?

BOB SUTCLIFFE: Yes, it's fair, but it's not enough. First, the most basic fact about world inequality is that it is monstrously large; that result is inescapable, whatever the method or definition. As to its direction of change in the last 25 years, to some extent there are different answers. But also there are different questions. Inequality is not a simple one-dimensional concept that can be reduced to a single number. Single overall measures of world inequality (where all incomes are taken into ac- count) give a different result from measures of the relation of the extremes (the rich- est compared with the poorest). Over the last 25 years, you find that the bottom half of world income earners seems to have gained something in relation to the top half (so, in this sense, there is less inequality), but the bottom 10% have lost seriously in comparison with the top 10% (thus, more inequality), and the bottom 1% have lost enormously in relation to the top 1% (much more inequality). None of these mea- sures is a single true measure of inequality; they are all part of a complex structure of inequalities, some of which can lessen as part of the same overall process in which others increase.

We do have to be clear about one data-related question that has caused huge confusion. To look at the distribution of income in the world, you have to reduce incomes of different countries to one standard. Traditionally it has been done by using exchange rates; this makes inequality appear to change when exchange rates change, which is misleading. But now we have data based on "purchasing power par- ity" (the comparative buying power, or real equivalence, of currencies). Using PPP values achieves for comparisons over space what inflation-adjusted index numbers have achieved for comparisons over time. Although many problems remain with PPP values, they are the only way to make coherent comparisons of incomes between countries. But they produce estimates that are astonishingly different from exchange rate-based calculations. For instance, U.S. income per head is 34 times Chinese in- come per head using exchange rates, but only 8 times as great using PPP values.

(And, incidentally, on PPP estimates the total size of the U.S. economy is now only 1.7 times that of China, and is likely to be overtaken by it by 2011.) So when you make this apparently technical choice between two methods of converting one currency to another, you come up not only with different figures on income distribution but also with two totally different world economic, and thus political, perspectives.

D&S: So even if some consensus were reached on the choices of definition, data, and method, you're urging a complex, nuanced portrait of what is happening to global inequality, rather than a yes or no answer. Could you give a brief outline of what you think that portrait looks like?

BS: Most integral measures—integral meaning including the entire population rather than comparing the extremes—that use PPP figures suggest that overall income distribution at the global level during the last 25 years has shown a slight decline in inequality, though there is some dissent on this. In any event this conclusion is tremendously affected by China, a country with a fifth of world population which has been growing economically at an unprecedented rate. Second, there seems to me little room for debate over the fact that the relative difference between the very rich and the very poor has gotten worse. And the smaller the extreme proportions you compare, the greater the gap. So the immensely rich have done especially well in the last 25 years, while the extremely poor have done very badly. The top one-tenth of U.S. citizens now receive a total income equal to that of the poorest 2.2 billion people in the rest of the world.

There have also been clear trends within some countries. Some of the fastest growing countries have become considerably more unequal. China is an example, along with some other industrializing countries like Thailand. The most economically liberal of the developed countries have also become much more unequal—for instance, the United States, the United Kingdom, and Australia—and so have the post-communist countries. The most extreme figures for inequality are found in a group of poor countries including Namibia and Botswana in southern Africa and Paraguay and Panama in Latin America.

Finally, the overall index of world inequality (measured by the Gini coefficient, a measure of income distribution) is about the same as that for two infamously unequal countries, South Africa and Brazil. And in the last few years it has shown no signs of improvement whatsoever.

D&S: People use the terms "unimodal" and "bimodal" to describe the global distribution of income. Can you explain what these mean? Also, you have referred elsewhere to a possible trimodal distribution—what does that refer to?

BS: The mode of a distribution is its most common value. In many countries there is one level of income around which a large proportion of the population clusters; at higher or lower levels of income there are progressively fewer people, so the distribution curve rises to a peak and then falls off. That is a unimodal distribution. But in South Africa, for example, due to the continued existence of entrenched ethnic division and economic inequality, the curve of distribution has two peaks—a low one, the most common income received by black citizens, and another, higher one, the the most common received by whites. This is a bimodal distribution because there are two values that are relatively more common than those above or below them. Because of its origins you could call it the "Apartheid distribution." The world distribution is in many respects uncannily like that of South Africa. It could be becoming trimodal in the sense that the frequency distribution of income has three peaks— one including those in very poor countries which have not been growing economically (e.g., parts of Africa), one in those developing countries which really have been developing (e.g., in South and East Asia), and one in the high-income industrialized countries. It's a kind of "apartheid plus" form of distribution.

D&S: In 2002, you wrote that many institutions, like the United Nations and the World Bank, were not being exactly honest in this debate—for example, emphasizing results based on data or methods that they elsewhere acknowledged to be poor. Has this changed over the past few years? Has the quality of the debate over trends in global income inequality improved?

BS: The most egregious pieces of statistical opportunism have declined. But I think there is a strong tendency in general for institutions to seize on optimistic conclusions regarding distribution in order to placate critics of the present world order. This increasingly takes the form of putting too much weight on measures of welfare other than income, for instance, life expectancy, for which there has been more international convergence than in the case of income. But there has been very little discussion of the philosophical basis for using life expectancy instead of or combined with income to measure inequality. If poor people live longer but in income terms remain as relatively poor as ever, has the world become less unequal?

The problem of statistical opportunism is not confined to those who are defending the world economic order; it also exists on the left. So, on the question of inequality, there is a tendency to accept whatever numerical estimate shows greatest inequality on the false assumption that this confirms the wickedness of capitalism. But capitalist inequality is so great that the willful exaggeration of it is not needed as the basis of anti-capitalist propaganda. It is more important for the left to look at the best indicators of the changing state of capitalism, including indicators of inequality, in order to intervene more effectively.

Finally, the quality of the debate, regardless of the intentions of the participants, is still greatly restricted by the shortage of available statistics about inequalities. That has improved somewhat in recent years although there are many things about past and present inequalities which we shall probably never know.

D&S: Do you see any contexts in which it's more important to focus on absolute poverty levels and trends in those levels rather than on inequality?

BS: The short answer is no, I do not. Plans for minimum income guarantees or for reducing the number of people lacking basic necessities can be important. But poverty always has a relative as well as an absolute component. It is a major weakness of the Millenium Development Goals, for example, that they talk about halving the number of people in absolute extreme poverty without a single mention of inequality. [The Millenium Development Goals is a U.N. program aimed at eliminating extreme poverty and achieving certain other development goals worldwide by 2015. —*Eds.*] And there is now a very active campaign on the part of anti-egalitarian, pro-capitalist ideologues in favor of the complete separation of the two. That is wrong not only because inequality is what partly defines poverty but more importantly because inequality and poverty reduction are inseparable. To separate them is to say that redistribution should not form part of the solution to poverty. Everyone is prepared in some sense to regard poverty as undesirable. But egalitarians see riches as pathological too. The objective of reducing poverty is integrally linked to the objective of greater equality and social justice.

D&S: Can you explain the paradox that China's economic liberalization since the late 1970s has increased inequality within China and at the same time reduced global inequality? Some researchers and policymakers interpret China's experience over this period as teaching us that it may be necessary for poor countries to sacrifice some equality in order to fight poverty. Do you agree with this—if not, how would you respond?

BS: When you measure *global* inequality, you are not just totalling the levels of inequality in individual countries. In theory all individual countries could become more unequal and yet the world as a whole become more equal, or vice versa. In China, a very poor country in 1980, average incomes have risen much faster than the world average and this has reduced world inequality. But different sections of the population have done much better than others so that inequality within China has grown. If and when China becomes on average a richer country than it is now, further unequal growth there may contribute to increasing rather than decreasing world inequality.

China's growth has been very inegalitarian, but it has been very fast. And the proportion of the population in poverty seems to have been reduced. But it is possible to envisage a more egalitarian growth path which would have been slower in aggregate but which would have reduced the number of poor people at least as much if not more than China's actual record. So I do not think it is right to say that higher inequality is the cause of reduced poverty, though it may for a time be a feature of the rapid growth which in turn creates employment and reduces poverty.

This does not mean that all increases in inequality are necessarily pathological. The famous Kuznets curve sees inequality first rising and then falling during economic growth as an initially poor population moves by stages from low-income, low-productivity work into high-income, high-productivity work, until at the end of the process 100% of the population is in the second group. If you measure inequality during such a process, it does in fact rise and then fall again to its original level—in this example at the start everyone is equally poor, at the end everyone is equally richer. That might be called transitional inequality; many growth processes may include an element of it. In that case equality is not really being "sacrificed" to reduce poverty—poverty is reduced by a process which increases inequality and then eliminates it again. But at the same time inequality may be growing for many other reasons which are not, like the Kuznets effect, self-eliminating, but rather cumulative. When inequality grows, this malign variety tends to be more important than the self-eliminating variety. But many economists are far too ready to see growing inequality as the more benign, self-eliminating variety.

D&S: Where do you think the question of what is happening to global income inequality fits into the broader debate over neoliberalism and globalization?

BS: Many people say that since some measures of inequality started to improve in about 1980 and that is also when neoliberalism and globalization accelerated, it is those processes which have produced greater equality. There are many problems with this argument, among them the fact that at least on some measures global inequality has grown since 1980. In any case, measures which show global inequality falling in this period are, as we have seen, very strongly influenced by China. China's extraordinary growth has, of course, in part been expressed in and permitted by greater globalization (its internationalization has grown faster than its production), and it is also clear that liberalization of economic policy has played a role, though China hardly has a neoliberal economy. But to permit is not to cause. The real cause is surely to be found not so much in economic policy as in a profound social movement in which a new and highly dynamic capitalist class (combined with a supportive authoritarian state) has once again become an agent of massive capitalist accumulation, as seen before in Japan, the United States, and Western Europe. So, an important part of what we are observing in figures which show declining world inequality is not any growth of egalitarianism, but the dynamic ascent of Chinese and other Asian capitalisms.

This interview also appears on the website of the Political Economy Research Institute at the University of Massachusetts-Amherst, along with Bob Sutcliffe's working paper "A More or Less Unequal World? World Income Distribution in the 20th Century." See <www.umass.edu/peri>.

Article 8.8

BEYOND THE WORLD CREDITORS' CARTEL

In Latin America and elsewhere, the IMF may be re-emerging—but in a changed landscape.

BY DARIUSH SOKOLOV
September/October 2009

One group of financiers seems to be doing nicely out of the global recession: the International Monetary Fund and other international financial institutions (IFIs) are enjoying a return to relevance and lining up for increased funding.

The London G20 Summit in April was the IMF's big comeback gig. In 2007 the fund's loan book was down to just $20 billion; now its capital is set to triple to $750 billion, plus permission to issue $250 billion in "special drawing rights" (the fund's quasi-currency which allows member countries to borrow from each others' reserves). Since September 2008 a range of East European and ex-Soviet states have taken out new loans. So too have Pakistan, El Salvador, and Iceland—the fund's first Western European client since Britain in 1976.

The World Bank and regional development banks are also getting in on the party. In Latin America, the World Bank's regional vice president Pamela Cox says she expects lending to triple in 2009 to $14 billion. The Inter-American Development Bank (IDB), the most active IFI in the region, expects to lend $18 billion—its typical loan portfolio is under $8 billion. And the development banks are queuing up behind the IMF with their caps out for capital increases: the Asian Development Bank wants to triple its capital to $165 billion; the IDB is asking for an extra $50 to $80 billion on top of its current $101 billion.

Why now? The IFIs, says Vince McElhinny of the Bank Information Center, a group that monitors them, are opportunists at heart. Just like any private bank or corporation they fight for market share, and as the world economy and global capital markets grow they need to increase their lending apace or lose relevance. The freezing of world capital markets, particularly severe in emerging markets, has created a need which they can seize as opportunity. The Institute of International Finance predicts private net capital flows to emerging markets of $141 billion in 2009, down from $392 billion in 2008, after a record $890 billion in 2007. The IFIs see themselves helping to fill this gap.

But the issues at stake here go beyond the IFIs' own agendas. On the one hand, their revival implies a reassertion of U.S. and global North dominance. They aren't called "Washington-based" just as a matter of real estate: the United States has a 17% voting share on the IMF and World Bank, enough to give it a veto on some major changes; Europe and the United States control the top management positions.

On the other hand, the story underscores how parts of the global South are gaining in economic power. In the crises of the 1990s, or so the neoliberal story went, the IMF stepped in to clean up the messes made when fragile Third World economies exploded. This time around things are very different: the mess is in the North, and the likelihood is that the emerging economies of Asia and Latin America will emerge from it stronger and more independent. (It's important to note, though, that large areas in the South, notably Africa, are not part of this story—nor is Eastern Europe.) The so-called BRIC nations in particular (Brazil, Russia, India, China) are getting the bargaining power to back up their claims on the global financial system. Will these claims be met within the existing institutions, or by creating a new financial architecture that bypasses Washington altogether? The future of the IFIs is a key arena in which global rebalancing of economic power is playing out.

New Financial Architecture?

In May 2007 finance ministers from Brazil, Argentina, Venezuela, Bolivia, and Ecuador signed the "Quito declaration" in the Ecuadorian capital. The plan includes a regional monetary fund and moves toward a South American single currency, but the first step is the creation of the Banco del Sur, a new regional development bank. While the bank's launch is behind schedule, this March its constitution was agreed to, with an initial capitalization of $7 billion. Besides the original five, Paraguay and Uruguay are also members. (Even Colombia had announced its support before its late-2007 row with Venezuela over hostages.)

The aim of Banco del Sur is to replace the Washington-based lenders altogether with institutions run by and for South America. Maria Jose Romero, who researches the IFIs at the Third World Institute in Montevideo, encapsulates this spirit. "In responding to the crisis Latin American countries have two options," she says. "We can return to the old institutions and the failed recipes of the 1990s, or we can move forward with alternatives."

For many Latin American countries a return to the IMF is politically out of the question. According to Mark Weisbrot, co-director of the Center for Economic and Policy Research in Washington, the decline of the IMF started with the Asian financial crisis over a decade ago. After the fund's failure to act as emergency lender of last resort to Asian banking systems in 1997, those states moved to build up sizeable currency reserves, determined not to be dependent on the fund again; others followed suit.

This turning away has been more dramatic in Latin America, where IMF policies are blamed for precipitating the 1998 crisis in Argentina which led to the collapse of its banking system and eventually to its 2002 default. Argentina and Bolivia both paid off the last of their debts to the fund in 2006; in April 2007 Ecuador announced it had paid off its IMF loans and requested the fund withdraw its country manager; the same month Venezuela announced itself debt-free, and a few weeks later said it would withdraw from fund membership altogether. When Daniel Ortega won the Nicaraguan presidential election in May 2007 he promised the country would be "free from the fund" within five years.

How has this freedom-from-Washington line held in the current crisis? U.S.-friendly Mexico was the first to sign up for the new Flexible Credit Lines the IMF is granting without conditions to "pre-approved" governments, followed by Colombia—though neither has yet drawn on them. So far only El Salvador and Costa Rica have taken out new loans. In sharp contrast to Eastern Europe, most Latin American states had healthy reserve cushions coming into the crunch. And with commodity prices now rising again, it may be that the region's anti-IMF resolve is not going to face the test many had anticipated.

As for Banco del Sur, the arrival of crisis no doubt slowed the process: domestic firefighting comes before regional cooperation. But, according to Romero, in the medium term it will help push change:

"The crisis has focused attention to the failings of the existing financial system," she says. "It is helping build the impetus for Banco del Sur, as well as for moves to settle bilateral trade in local currencies [rather than dollars], which is the first step towards monetary union, and for broader South-South cooperation initiatives."

To be fair, Banco del Sur may not live up to proponents' hopes. With just $7 billion in capital, the bank won't be in the same league as the Washington-based IFIs. Nor is there any immediate plan to create an emergency monetary fund—an Ecuadorian proposal to that effect has been dropped. And the principle of one country one vote, perhaps the biggest rallying point of all, has been modified: equal votes will apply only on loans under $70m, above which approval is required from members with two-thirds of the capital contributions.

Finally, there is still no clarity on the focus of lending. Campaigners hope for a true emphasis on poverty reduction and projects to build regional cooperation, and have scored the provision of a socially focused "audit board." But some fear that more conservative members (read: Brazil) could push Banco del Sur toward being just one more development bank.

Across Asia, there are parallel developments. A proposal by Japan to set up an Asian Monetary Fund met the same fate as an earlier Malaysian-backed scheme called the East Asian Economic Caucus—both were dropped after expressions of disapproval from the IMF and U.S. officials. But now the Chiang Mai Initiative, a longstanding plan for a system of swap arrangements between the central banks of the southeast Asian countries plus China, Japan, and South Korea is expected to come on line this year, and the proposed size of the scheme was upped to $120 billion in February. Chiang Mai is linked to the IMF (members need IMF agreements in place to withdraw more than 20% of the total), but some see it leading towards an eventual independent regional fund. For now, though, at least officially, the talk is usually of "complementing," not supplanting, the IMF.

Rise of the BRICs

If the Quito project is the idealistic side of the regionalization movement, the BRIC bloc is global power shift as realpolitik. The BRICs together now account for 22% of world production (by purchasing power parity), up from 16% ten years ago and rising.

Even as they move ahead with building regional institutions independent of the IFIs, the BRICs are pushing for more power within the Washington-based institutions. Increased say at the IMF is one of the four governments' main demands. In March 2008 China's vote share was raised all the way up to 3.7%—putting the world's most populous country on a par with Belgium plus the Netherlands, combined population 27 million. The BRICs jointly muster a 9.82% quota.

According to Vince McElhinny, the BRICs' contributions to the fund's current capital boost are aimed at bolstering their demands for more say in IFI governance.

When, a week before the BRIC summit, Brazil's President Lula announced a $10 billion contribution, he talked of thereby gaining "moral authority to keep pushing for changes needed at the IMF."

The IMF's desire to placate emerging powers such as the BRICs may explain the makeover it has displayed in its current comeback—dubbed "IMF 2.0" by *Time* magazine. Managing director Dominique Strauss-Kahn has called for the fund to spend against recession: less structural adjustment, more counter-cyclical stimulus. But the changes may be largely cosmetic. According to a study by the Third World Network, the actual conditions of recent IMF loans to Pakistan, Hungary, Ukraine, and other countries are familiar: the borrowers must reduce their fiscal deficits through public spending cuts, wage freezes, higher fuel tariffs, and interest rate hikes.

What real changes are the BRICs really likely to get? There's plenty of gossip flying around: some are touting Lula as the next World Bank president; perhaps China will get to pick Strauss-Kahn's successor.

Mark Weisbrot, however, does not see the U.S. government giving any ground on voting shares. "The U.S. would rather walk away from the IMF than give up control," he says.

Beyond the Cartel

Weisbrot describes the IMF as "the most important instrument of influence the U.S. government has in developing countries—beyond the military, beyond the CIA. Or, at least, that's the role it's played for most of the last 30 years. A good part of that influence has been lost recently; now they're trying to get it back."

The IMF's power has never really been about its own lending, however. Its influence over countries' economic policies is far greater than would be suggested by its share in overall capital flows. The real issue is the fund's role as "gatekeeper" of a global "creditors' cartel."

Multilateral loans from the World Bank and regional development banks and bilateral loans from the wealthy countries typically come with some form of "cross-conditionality" clause. You only get your loan if you first have an IMF agreement in place; installments only keep flowing so long as you stick to it. Similar conditions can also apply in private capital transactions. For instance, Venezuela's 2007 threat to give up its IMF membership triggered a market sell-off because under covenants written into its sovereign bonds, a break with the fund would count as a "technical default."

Now, though, recent shifts in Latin America have dealt what Weisbrot says could be "a final blow to the IMF creditors' cartel in middle-income countries."

This is a continental tale, but Argentina is a good place to begin. The country cut itself off from international capital markets with its 2002 default, and is still being chased by "hold-out" bond investors in the New York courts. Yet Argentina grew at almost 9% a year from 2003 through 2007—the country's most rapid growth in 50 years, and some of the fastest growth rates on the continent. This expansion has been funded largely by selling bonds to another emerging regional power, Venezuela. These bond transfers are no subsidies—Argentina pays commercial interest rates—but they do come free of Washington conditions. For Weisbrot,

"Venezuela's offers of credit, without policy conditions, to Argentina, Bolivia, Ecuador, Nicaragua, and other countries has changed the equation."

It's true that easy Venezuelan credit dried up early on in the crisis as oil prices plummeted. It's also true that Argentina is now allowing IMF staff in to monitor its economy and taking out new loans from the World Bank and the IDB. But it's telling that Argentina got these loans without any IMF agreement in place: the cartel, at least in its old form, appears to be broken. And then there's the other plank in Argentina's current crisis management strategy: a $10.2 billion swap line direct with China.

In short, the IMF and allied institutions have regained some lost ground in the crisis, but forms of "South-South cooperation" that stand to weaken the Washington-based creditors' cartel have kept on building too.

According to one very plausible interpretation, this crisis has been about the consequences of the rich countries' capital piling into the financial services sphere to compensate for the loss of manufacturing production to the Third World. Control of the world's financial capital flows was one last highly profitable channel where Northern capital still ruled unopposed. Increasingly, though, global-South states and corporations are cutting out the middle man to trade directly with each other. It's against the background of these new possibilities that the next chapter in the story of the IFIs will play out.

Article 8.9

IS CHINA'S CURRENCY MANIPULATION HURTING THE U.S.?

BY ARTHUR MacEWAN
November/December 2010

> Dear Dr. Dollar:
> *Is it true that China has been harming the U.S. economy by keeping its currency "undervalued"? Shouldn't the U.S. government do something about this situation?*
> —Jenny Boyd, Edmond, W.Va.

The Chinese government, operating through the Chinese central bank, does keep its currency unit—the yuan—cheap relative to the dollar. This means that goods imported *from* China cost less (in terms of dollars) than they would otherwise, while U.S. exports *to* China cost more (in terms of yuan). So we in the United States buy a lot of Chinese-made goods and the Chinese don't buy much from us. In the 2007 to 2009 period, the United States purchased $253 billion more in goods annually from China than it sold to China.

This looks bad for U.S workers. For example, when money gets spent in the United States, much of it is spent on Chinese-made goods, and fewer jobs are then created in the United States. So the Chinese government's currency policy is at least partly to blame for our employment woes. Reacting to this situation, many people are calling for the U.S. government to do something to get the Chinese government to change its policy.

But things are not so simple.

First of all, there is an additional reason for the low cost of Chinese goods—low Chinese wages. The Chinese government's policy of repressing labor probably accounts for the low cost of Chinese goods at least as much as does its currency policy. Moreover, there is a lot more going on in the global economy. Both currency problems and job losses involve much more than Chinese government actions—though China provides a convenient target for ire.

And the currency story itself is complex. In order to keep the value of its currency low relative to the dollar, the Chinese government increases the supply of yuan, uses these yuan to buy dollars, then uses the dollars to buy U.S. securities, largely government bonds but also private securities. In early 2009, China held $764 billion in U.S. Treasury securities, making it the largest foreign holder of U.S. government debt. By buying U.S. government bonds, the Chinese have been financing the federal deficit. More generally, by supplying funds to the United States, the Chinese government has been keeping interest rates low in this country.

If the Chinese were to act differently, allowing the value of their currency to rise relative to the dollar, both the cost of capital and the prices of the many goods imported from China would rise. The rising cost of capital would probably not be a serious problem, as the Federal Reserve could take counteraction to keep interest rates low. So, an increase in the value of the yuan would net the United States some jobs, but also raise some prices for U.S. consumers.

It is pretty clear that right now what the United States needs is jobs. Moreover, low-cost Chinese goods have contributed to the declining role of manufacturing in the United States, a phenomenon that both weakens important segments of organized labor and threatens to inhibit technological progress, which has often been centered in manufacturing or based on applications in manufacturing (e.g., robotics).

So why doesn't the U.S. government place more pressure on China to raise the value of the yuan? Part of the reason may lie in concern about losing Chinese financing of the U.S. federal deficit. For several years the two governments have been co-dependent: The U.S. government gets financing for its deficits, and the Chinese government gains by maintaining an undervalued currency. Not an easy relationship to change.

Probably more important, however, many large and politically powerful U.S.-based firms depend directly on the low-cost goods imported from China. Wal-mart and Target, as any shopper knows, are filled with Chinese-made goods. Then there are the less visible products from China, including a power device that goes into the Microsoft Xbox, computer keyboards for Dell, and many other goods for many other U.S. corporations. If the yuan's value rose and these firms had to pay more dollars to buy these items, they could probably not pass all the increase on to consumers and their profits would suffer.

Still, in spite of the interests of these firms, the U.S. government may take some action, either by pressing harder for China to let the value of the yuan rise relative to the dollar or by placing some restrictions on imports from China. But don't expect too big a change. ❑

Article 8.10

CHINESE WORKERS STAND UP
What is the real cause of increasing wages in China?

BY JOHN MILLER
September/October 2010

> THE RISE OF CHINESE LABOR:
> WAGE HIKES ARE PART OF A VIRTUOUS CYCLE OF DEVELOPMENT
>
> The recent strikes at Honda factories in southern China represent another data point in an emerging trend: Cheap labor won't be the source of the Chinese economy's competitive advantage much longer.
>
> The auto maker has caved and given workers a 24% pay increase to re-start one assembly line. Foxconn, the electronics producer that has experienced a string of worker suicides, has also announced big raises. This is all part of the virtuous cycle of development: Productivity increases, which drive wages higher, forcing businesses to adjust, leading to more productivity growth.
> —*Wall Street Journal* op-ed, June 9, 2010

Wages in China are in fact rising. But that hardly constitutes a "virtuous cycle of development" that is the inevitable result of market-led economic growth, as the *Wall Street Journal* editors contend.

Rather, higher wages in China are the hard-fought gains of militant workers who have used tightening labor markets as a lever to pry wage gains out of employers whose coffers have long been brimming with cash.

Labor unrest taking advantage of tightening labor markets is the story in China today—not abstract economic forces lifting wages, the tale the *Journal*'s editors want to pass off as a paean to free-market economics.

A Changing Labor Outlook

In recent years rapid economic growth has indeed tightened the Chinese labor market, drying up the seemingly bottomless pool of jobseekers from the countryside. As of May 2010, job vacancies in China outnumbered the number of job applicants, according to the Chinese Labor Market Information Center.

And wages are rising for many. Pay for China's 150 million or so internal-migrant workers increased 16% in 2009 despite the global financial crisis, according to Cai Fang, head of the Institute of Population and Labor Economics at the Chinese Academy of Social Sciences.

Higher wages aren't about to break the corporate piggybank. In recent years the biggest increase in China's extraordinarily high national savings (which includes household and business savings) has come from retained earnings—the undistributed profits of Chinese corporations. Retained earnings did so much to boost the country's savings because low wages kept corporate profits high. For more than a decade, labor's share of national income has been on the decline in China as the corporate share has increased dramatically. On top of that, the strong productivity growth that the *Journal* editors laud has offset wage increases, keeping labor costs per unit of output in check. At the beginning of 2010 Chinese unit labor costs were no higher than in 2004.

Wage increases notwithstanding, working conditions in China remain oppressive, as even the *Journal* editors seem to recognize. In May 2010 a thirteenth worker attempted to commit suicide at a Foxconn factory in southern China. The world's largest maker of computer components, Foxconn supplies Apple, Dell, and Hewlett-Packard, among others. While working conditions at this Taiwanese-owned company are far from the worst in China, the hours are long, the assembly line moves too fast, and managers enforce military-style discipline.

Foxconn's string of suicides is just the tip of the iceberg. Early in 2008, the *New York Times* reported that worker abuse is still commonplace in many of the Chinese factories that supply Western companies. The *Times* quoted labor activists who reported unfair labor practices—child labor, enforced 16-hour days, and sub-minimum wages, among others—in factories supplying several U.S. firms including WalMart, Disney, and Dell. The activists also reported that factories routinely withhold health benefits, employ dangerous machinery, and expose workers to lead, mercury, and other hazardous chemicals. According to government statistics, an average of 187 Chinese workers die each day in industrial accidents; the equivalent U.S. figure is three.

The Real Virtuous Cycle

Rapid economic growth and rising productivity undoubtedly laid the groundwork for higher wages. But it is labor militancy that has exploited workers' improved bargaining position. The number of labor disputes in China doubled from 2006 to 2009. Workers have won wage increases in excess of 20% at several large export factories, including Foshan Fengfu Autoparts, the company that supplies exhaust pipes to Japanese automaker Honda, and Hon Hai Precision Industry Co., the Taiwan-based electronics manufacturer that supplies iPads and iPhones for Apple and a range of gadgets for Hewlett-Packard and Nintendo.

Predictably, the editors misrepresent how social improvement comes about with economic development. Not just in China but in the developed economies as well, improvements in working conditions have come about not due to market-led forces alone, but when economic growth was combined with social action and worker militancy.

The history of sweatshops in the United States makes that clear. The shirtwaist strike of 1909, the tragedy of the Triangle Shirtwaist fire two years later, and the hardships of the Great Depression inspired garment workers to unionize and led to the imposition of government regulations on the garment industry and other industries, beginning with the New York Factory Acts and extending to the Fair Labor

Standards Act of 1938. The power of those reforms along with the postwar boom nearly eradicated sweatshops in the United States.

Since then, sweatshops have returned with a vengeance to the U.S. garment industry. Why? Declining economic opportunity is part of the answer. But severe cutbacks in the number of inspectors and a drop-off in union density paved the way as well. The U.S. experience confirms the take-away message from rising Chinese wages: Economic development by itself will not eliminate inhuman working conditions. Improve-ments in working conditions are neither inevitable nor irreversible.

Not only is labor organizing crucial for improving working conditions, but those organizing efforts need to be international if workers are to succeed in reaping durable gains from economic development.

China's case makes that clear. Rising wages in China have prompted footwear and apparel firms to shift their manufacturing elsewhere—to Indonesia, Bangladesh, and Vietnam, for example. Jim Sciabarrasi, head of sourcing and procurement at U.S.-based sneaker company New Balance, was clear about the reason for the firm's move. "Indonesia has a ready supply of workers and their wages are not going up as fast as in China," he told the *Boston Globe*.

Chinese workers attempting to organize and improve their situation always face the threat that their employer will simply pack up and depart for even lower-cost countries. This kind of threat, which helps employers resist demands for better wages and working conditions not just in China but elsewhere in global South and in the developed economies as well, has been increasingly effective as globalization has weakened limits on the mobility of corporations. It throws into sharp relief the common interests of workers in all countries in improving conditions at the bottom, in robust full-employment programs that raise their incomes and enhance their bargaining power.

In that way, the rise of China's workers and the bold labor unrest there should benefit manufacturing workers across the globe, a virtuous cycle the *Wall Street Journal* editors would not only be loathe to recognize but have gone out of their way to obscure.

Sources: David Barboza, "In Chinese Factories, Lost Fingers and Low Pay," *New York Times*, Jan. 5, 2008; William Foreman, "13th worker attempts suicide at Foxconn tech factory in southern China, report says," *Los Angeles Times*, May 27, 2010; Jenn Abelson, "Local sneaker firms are making it in Indonesia," *Boston Globe*, May 29, 2010; Norihiko Shirouzo, "Chinese Workers Challenge Beijing's Authority," *WSJ*, June 13, 2010; Elizabeth Holmes, "U.S. Apparel Retailers Turn Their Gaze beyond China," *WSJ*, June 15, 2010; "NW: Wage disputes in China put world on notice," NIKKEI, June 14, 2010; Aileen Wang and Simon Rabinovitch, "Why labor unrest is good for China and the world," Reuters, June 2, 2010; World Bank, China Quarterly Update, June 2010; James Areddy, "Accidents Plague China's Workplaces," *WSJ*, July 28, 2010.

Article 8.11

WOMEN OF NAFTA

BY MARTHA OJEDA, FELICITAS CONTRERAS, AND YOLANDA TREVIÑO
September/October 2007

The outstanding collection *NAFTA From Below: Maquiladora Workers, Farm- ers, and Indigenous Communities Speak Out on the Impact of Free Trade in Mex- ico*, combines worker testimony with analytical and historical essays to provide a devastating picture of the effects of neoliberal international trade policies—cul- minating in the North American Free Trade Agreement (NAFTA)—on workers throughout Mexico. The book, available in both English and Spanish, also offers inspiring accounts of resistance to those policies.

The book's early chapters focus on *maquiladora* workers in the north of the country, addressing key labor issues such as health and safety, environmental con- cerns, and freedom of association. Later chapters take up organizing by agricultur- al workers in the south, especially in the state of Chiapas, in response to neoliberal "reforms." That the Zapatista uprising in Chiapas began on January 1, 1994, the very day that NAFTA went into effect, was no accident.

One of the book's achievements is to show how the struggles of industrial workers in the north of Mexico are related to those of agricultural workers in the south. Knitting these struggles together is one of the central aims of the Coalition for Justice in the Maquiladoras, which produced *NAFTA From Below*. The coali- tion has helped bring *maquila* workers and organizers from the north together with members of grassroots *campesino* and indigenous groups in the south to help strengthen cooperative projects in both regions and to share information about the history of organized struggle in the workplace. Women's strong leadership roles in workplace struggles in the north have been of particular interest to organizers in the south, especially as former agricultural workers from the south migrate to work in *maquiladoras* near the northern border.

Women played a central role in the struggle of workers at a Sony plant in Nuevo Laredo for a democratic union, described in the selections that follow. The events at Sony vividly illustrate the frequent conflicts between Mexico's corrupt official unions and rival independent unions that Chris Tilly and Marie Kennedy describe (pp. 26-30). The Sony workers' struggle was also a key early test of NAFTA's labor side-agreement, the North American Agreement on Labor Cooperation, and the bodies it established, known as National Administrative Offices (NAOs), to investigate violations.

These excerpts include testimony from Martha Ojeda (co-editor of *NAFTA From Below*, with Rosemary Hennessy), a *maquila* worker from 1973 to 1994 who is now executive director of the Coalition for Justice in the Maquiladoras; from Fe- licitas (Fela) Contreras, an activist with CETRAC (Center for Workers and Com- munities) in Nuevo Laredo who worked at the Sony plant from 1985 through 1998; and from Yolanda Treviño, a former Sony worker who testified before the NAO as part of the Sony workers' NAFTA complaint.

MARTHA A. OJEDA: Official history is always written so that the reality people were living is hidden. If everyone told the part they lived or knew, the truth would be in their collective word.

In 1979 Sony arrived in my town [Nuevo Laredo].... Sony manually assembled audiocassettes and Beta videocassettes. In 1982, after the first devaluation of the peso, there were more than 1,000 workers working three shifts in five plants, and by then the workers were also producing the VHS videocassette and the 3.5 inch diskette.

They began to bring machines for semiautomatic and automatic assembly of the cassettes. The plastic molding injection plant was providing the plastic cases and the components for the audio and video plants. It was the boom of assembly line production.

In this era children with birth defects began to be born, but the company doctor said that this happened because the parents were alcoholics or because they had genetic problems. By 1993 there were 2,000 employees in seven plants in three shifts. There was a lot of overtime, but still it wasn't enough to meet production quotas.

The molding ingestion plants never stopped working; they were going three shifts seven days a week. For the first time the company proposed 12 hour shifts for four and three days a week. This implied that Sony got their production, because the machines were running around the clock, but they avoided paying overtime. This twelve-hour shift was unknown to workers because it didn't exist in the Federal Labor Law.

It was in this labor and political context that in October 1993 we visited Fidel Velázquez, the CTM national leader, in Mexico City and solicited union elections within the framework of the CTM. All of the *maquilas* were affiliated with this union because it was the only one; if you didn't belong to them there was no other alternative for workers anywhere. But the leaders negotiated the contract with the company even before it was established in the locality.

Fidel told us that he agreed with the elections (but he never said when they would be). We trusted his word and began the process that the Federal Labor Law sets down for forming the union sections.

On January 1, 1994, we were informed of the Zapatista uprising, but equally surprising to us was to find out in the newspaper on January 4 that Chema Morales had declared that on the order of Fidel Velázquez he would be the new Secretary General of the *maquilas*—without sectionals—and, worst of all, he was already named to the Labor Board at the state level because of his position as Secretary General, not only of the Maquila Union but also of the Workers Federation of Nuevo Laredo.

Shocked, we tried to communicate with Fidel Velázquez, but our efforts were in vain. Then we learned that he was coming to Ciudad Victoria, the capital of Tamaulipas, on January 12. We traveled all night. But when we arrived it was obvious that they would not let us enter. We guessed that Fidel would come in by the side door and we waited there until he arrived with the media.

I demanded publicly that he retract his authorization of Chema Morales as Secretary General. Then I asked for a public debate with him and with Chema. I don't know if I was the only woman from the provinces who had publicly challenged him, but what I do know is that so much corruption repulsed me and gave me the courage to make sure that the two of them, both Chema and Fidel, would be exposed even to the President of the Labor Board of the state who was present. He had authorized naming Chema to be Secretary General even though he had never worked in the *maquilas*, and according to the union by-laws that was one of the requirements.

In the face of the media and all of the evidence, Fidel looked ridiculous and he had no alternative but to accept that there would be union elections. So he declared that he would send a national representative to hold them. When I went to say good-bye to him at the podium he told me, "You are going to eat fire." And I told him, "I'm ready." But I never imagined what he was referring to.

FELICITAS ("FELA") CONTRERAS: In 1993 they began to change the delegates in all of the *maquiladoras* who were not agreed with the CTM. I heard that there were going to be elections in all the *maquilas*, not only in Sony, and we were asking when Sony's turn would be. But before the elections they were changing the delegates. They fired the ones we wanted and after work we had meetings to change the delegates so that they would really be for us. We met in one house and another with Martha because we wanted to change the delegates who were imposed by the CTM. I would get home at 4:00 or 5:00 in the morning. We always were hiding here and there, and that is how we put together a slate, even though they fired our candidates.

Those union delegates who were with Chema Morales (of the CTM) developed their slates with the old delegates from Sony… They preferred Chema instead of our democratic union. In April of 1994 the day arrived for the elections, and Chema's representative from the union and a representative of Fidel Velázquez were set up in the parking lot of Plant #7. We had our slate, but they didn't give us a chance to let our other co-workers know that the voting was taking place.

Representatives of Fidel Velázquez and of the company were there. They told the people to go to the parking lot and they arranged to meet the other shift and take them out to vote. They said on this side go all those in favor of the blue slate, on the other side those in favor of the CTM slate. Our slate won because everyone came to our side. But Fidel's representative said that the other delegates from the CTM won. And so we said, "How is that possible if we are all here, voting for our slate? We were the majority. What are we going to do?" We were really mad! Those who were working came out and we took to the streets to protest that they were doing this fraudulent election, and we made signs that said, "We want democratic elections!!"

YOLANDA TREVIÑO: On Saturday April 16, which was my day off, I went to plant #3 to see what resolution Mayor Horacio Garza had been able to make as to when we would have new elections. The *compañeras* who had spoken with him told us that he wasn't going to help us. That's when we started to hold our protest on the sidewalk in front of the plants, showing our frustration, but in a peaceful manner. We didn't stop anyone who wanted to from going into work and we didn't commit any act of violence.

We continued protesting in this way until Horacio Garza and Maricela López arrived. We had a meeting there with Horacio and he told us to stop the protest and that afterwards he would help us. We answered that the only thing we wanted was

Señor Avila's word that they would hold new elections. But he said no. So Horacio Garza left and soon afterward the police and the firemen arrived. The girls were afraid when they saw the police and some of them asked if the were going to take us away, but we told them if we didn't act violently then they shouldn't either.

But that wasn't the case. Francisco Xavier Rios [Vice President of Human Resources at Sony] signaled to the police with a motion of his hand to enter through a side door, and they positioned themselves on the inside lot of the company. Then without any warning the police began to push us with their Plexiglas shields and their billy clubs. They beat us badly; they knocked a *compañera* unconscious, a woman named Alicia Soto, and they pushed the rest of us down with their shields, insulting us all the while, calling us names like "goddamn bitches."

I have been told that the company claims that the police didn't commit any acts of violence and that they only person who acted violently was Alicia who attacked the police with a magazine. I ask you: how is it possible that a 24 year old woman can harm a group of 35 well-armed police agents carrying Plexiglas shields and billy clubs? How is it possible to say they didn't commit acts of violence when my friend Alicia was knocked out by a blow to the head and has had problems ever since? I have here the newspaper *El Mañana*, dated 17 April, which shows very clearly a picture of Alicia unconscious. If they don't want to read the newspapers they should just look at their own videos because they were filming the entire attack.

FELICITAS ("FELA") CONTRERAS: They had pressed charges against us—Martha Ojeda and various others—because Sony had lost millions with the work stoppage. They issued a summons for us to appear at the police department and told us that our lives were not even worth enough to pay for the company's losses.

They wanted us to say that Martha was responsible, and they pitted us against each other. They told Lupe that I had confessed that Martha was doing it all, and they told me that Lupe confessed that Martha told us to stop working. But of the 40 they called to testify all of us said, "We are all responsible, and so you will have to arrest all of us not just Martha." All of our *compañeras* were outside the police department yelling that they would have to arrest everyone. But since there were more than a thousand and we didn't all fit in the cells, after hours of interrogations and threats they let us go.

On the fifth day, in the early morning, around 5:00 am the governor –Manuel Cavazos Lerma- ordered that they state police from Reynosa, Matamoros and Cd. Victoria be brought in. The police arrived and the soldiers with machine guns and rifles. And they said to you, "Get out of here or I'll kill you." According to them they came to restore order, and with blows and kicks. They awakened us and ran after those who were sleeping on the sidewalk. You were waking up with a gun pointing in your face and they were yelling, "Get out or we will kill you."

We withdrew, and we were like this for five days and nights. In those days the trucks tried to mow us down because they wanted to take out the production, but we were all sleeping in the main gate so they couldn't cross and take it out.

Unfortunately, we didn't get it. We didn't get our union, and they fired a lot of people without giving them any severance payment because they said that they were leaders of the movement. We stayed there because we wanted an independent union.

In 1994 NAFTA was signed, and they said that the rights of workers would not be violated. But they beat us up and violated our rights. With the help of CJM and the lawyers from ANAD a demand was presented to the NAO. In 1995 we had a hearing and we all went to San Antonio to testify. Sony brought lawyers from New York and they said that our testimony was a lie, but we took the newspapers and the evidence, the videos. We won this trial, but we didn't really win anything because they didn't punish or fine Sony and we never had the elections or anything. They just put in these offices [the NAO] just to prop us NAFTA.

For me NAFTA was no good. The workers are still just as poor. The only difference is that now there are many settlements, *colonias*, many squatters, a lot of insecurity and a contaminated river. Before I used to drink water from the river and now you cant, and you cant go into it either. Our air is contaminated. There is a lot of sickness. There is a lot of illiteracy. The only one NAFTA helped were the businessmen because they are the ones that have gotten rich. And now they say, "I am going to China; I screwed the Mexicans so now I'm going to screw the Chinese." That is what says with me about NAFTA. We are poor and screwed.

MARTHA A. OJEDA: Each one of my *compañeras* risked her life, her children, and her family. They kidnapped Yolanda and threatened her. They persecuted the others, calling them on the phone and intimidating them. Wherever any of them are, because there were many and I will never forget one, to each of them I render homage and a special tribute to their "*coraje*"—their courage and bravery—for trying to reclaim workers' right to freedom of association. For resisting and never giving up.

That is what NAFTA left me after 20 years in the *maquilas*: it gave me the opportunity to denounce at a global level the failure of this agreement and of the side agreements and to share the rebellion and resistance of my *compañeras*. It taught me that there is a world of solidarity. It clarified the horizon we are looking for, and above all the hope to reach it with a team like this team of women, united until the end.

To order NAFTA From Below *or for more information, visit www.coalitionforjustice.net, write to the Coalition for Justice in the Maquiladoras, 4207 Willowbrook Dr., San Antonio, TX 78228, or call 210-732-8324.*

Article 8.12

INTERNATIONAL LABOR STANDARDS

BY ARTHUR MacEWAN
September/October 2008

> Dear Dr. Dollar:
> *U.S. activists have pushed to get foreign trade agreements to include higher labor standards. But then you hear that developing countries don't want that because cheaper labor without a lot of rules and regulations is what's helping them to bring industries in and build their economies. Is there a way to reconcile these views? Or are the activists just blind to the real needs of the countries they supposedly want to help?*
> —Philip Bereaud, Swampscott, Mass.

In 1971, General Emilio Medici, the then-military dictator of Brazil, commented on economic conditions in his country with the infamous line: "The economy is doing fine, but the people aren't."

Like General Medici, the government officials of many low-income countries today see the well-being of their economies in terms of overall output and the profits of firms—those profits that keep bringing in new investment, new industries that "build their economies." It is these officials who typically get to speak for their countries. When someone says that these countries "want" this or that— or "don't want" this or that—it is usually because the countries' officials have expressed this position.

Do we know what the people in these countries want? The people who work in the new, rapidly growing industries, in the mines and fields, and in the small shops and market stalls of low-income countries? Certainly they want better conditions— more to eat, better housing, security for their children, improved health and safety. The officials claim that to obtain these better conditions, they must "build their economies." But just because "the economy is doing fine" does not mean that the people are doing fine.

In fact, in many low-income countries, economic expansion comes along with severe inequality. The people who do the work are not getting a reasonable share of the rising national income (and are sometimes worse off even in absolute terms). Brazil in the early 1970s was a prime example and, in spite of major political change, remains a highly unequal country. Today, in both India and China, as in several other countries, economic growth is coming with increasingly severe inequality.

Workers in these countries struggle to improve their positions. They form—or try to form—independent unions. They demand higher wages and better working conditions. They struggle for political rights. It seems obvious that we should support those struggles, just as we support parallel struggles of workers in our own country. The first principle in supporting workers' struggles, here or anywhere else, is supporting their right to struggle—the right, in particular, to form independent unions without fear of reprisal. Indeed, in the ongoing controversy over the U.S.-Colombia Free Trade Agreement, the assassination of trade union leaders has rightly been a major issue.

Just how we offer our support—in particular, how we incorporate that support into trade agreements—is a complicated question. Pressure from abroad can help, but applying it is a complex process. A ban on goods produced with child labor, for example, could harm the most impoverished families that depend on children's earnings, or could force some children into worse forms of work (e.g., prostitution). On the other hand, using trade agreements to pressure governments to allow unhindered union organizing efforts by workers seems perfectly legitimate. When workers are denied the right to organize, their work is just one step up from slavery. Trade agreements can also be used to support a set of basic health and safety rights for workers. (Indeed, it might be useful if a few countries refused to enter into trade agreements with the United States until we improve workers' basic organizing rights and health and safety conditions in our own country!)

There is no doubt that the pressures that come through trade sanctions (restricting or banning commerce with another country) or simply from denying free access to the U.S. market can do immediate harm to workers and the general populace of low-income countries. Any struggle for change can generate short-run costs, but the long-run gains—even the hope of those gains—can make those costs acceptable. Consider, for example, the Apartheid-era trade sanctions against South Africa. To the extent that those sanctions were effective, some South African workers were deprived of employment. Nonetheless, the sanctions were widely supported by mass organizations in South Africa. Or note that when workers in this country strike or advocate a boycott of their company in an effort to obtain better conditions, they both lose income and run the risk that their employer will close up shop.

Efforts by people in this country to use trade agreements to raise labor standards in other countries should, whenever possible, take their lead from workers in those countries. It is up to them to decide what costs are acceptable. There are times, however, when popular forces are denied even basic rights to struggle. The best thing we can do, then, is to push for those rights—particularly the right to organize independent unions—that help create the opportunity for workers in poor countries to choose what to fight for.

Article 8.13

NIKE TO THE RESCUE?
Africa needs better jobs, not sweatshops.

BY JOHN MILLER
September/October 2006

IN PRAISE OF THE MALIGNED SWEATSHOP

WINDHOEK, Namibia—Africa desperately needs Western help in the form of schools, clinics and sweatshops.

On a street here in the capital of Namibia, in the southwestern corner of Africa, I spoke to a group of young men who were trying to get hired as day laborers on construction sites.

"I come here every day," said Naftal Shaanika, a 20-year-old. "I actually find work only about once a week."

Mr. Shaanika and the other young men noted that the construction jobs were dangerous and arduous, and that they would vastly prefer steady jobs in, yes, sweatshops. Sure, sweatshop work is tedious, grueling and sometimes dangerous. But over all, sewing clothes is considerably less dangerous or arduous—or sweaty—than most alternatives in poor countries.

Well-meaning American university students regularly campaign against sweatshops. But instead, anyone who cares about fighting poverty should campaign in favor of sweatshops, demanding that companies set up factories in Africa.

The problem is that it's still costly to manufacture in Africa. The headaches across much of the continent include red tape, corruption, political instability, unreliable electricity and ports, and an inexperienced labor force that leads to low productivity and quality. The anti-sweatshop movement isn't a prime obstacle, but it's one more reason not to manufacture in Africa.

Imagine that a Nike vice president proposed manufacturing cheap T-shirts in Ethiopia. The boss would reply: "You're crazy! We'd be boycotted on every campus in the country."

Some of those who campaign against sweatshops respond to my arguments by noting that they aren't against factories in Africa, but only demand a "living wage" in them. After all, if labor costs amount to only $1 per shirt, then doubling wages would barely make a difference in the final cost.

One problem ... is that it already isn't profitable to pay respectable salaries, and so any pressure to raise them becomes one more reason to avoid Africa altogether.

One of the best U.S. initiatives in Africa has been the African Growth and Opportunity Act, which allows duty-free imports from Africa—and thus has stimulated manufacturing there.

—Op-ed by Nicholas Kristof, *New York Times*, June 6, 2006

Nicholas Kristof has been beating the pro-sweatshop drum for quite a while. Shortly after the East Asian financial crisis of the late 1990s, Kristof, the Pulitzer Prize-winning journalist and now columnist for the *New York Times*, reported the story of an Indonesian recycler who, picking through the metal scraps of a garbage dump, dreamed that her son would grow up to be a sweatshop worker. Then, in 2000, Kristof and his wife, *Times* reporter Sheryl WuDunn, published "Two Cheers for Sweatshops" in the *Times Magazine*. In 2002, Kristof's column advised G-8 leaders to "start an international campaign to promote imports from sweatshops, perhaps with bold labels depicting an unrecognizable flag and the words 'Proudly Made in a Third World Sweatshop.'"

Now Kristof laments that too few poor, young African men have the opportunity to enter the satanic mill of sweatshop employment. Like his earlier efforts, Kristof's latest pro-sweatshop ditty synthesizes plenty of half-truths. Let's take a closer look and see why there is still no reason to give it up for sweatshops.

A Better Alternative?

It is hardly surprising that young men on the streets of Namibia's capital might find sweatshop jobs more appealing than irregular work as day laborers on construction sites.

The alternative jobs available to sweatshop workers are often worse and, as Kristof loves to point out, usually involve more sweating than those in world export factories. Most poor people in the developing world eke out their livelihoods from subsistence agriculture or by plying petty trades. Others on the edge of urban centers work as street-hawkers or hold other jobs in the informal sector. As economist Arthur MacEwan wrote a few years back in *Dollars & Sense*, in a poor country like Indonesia, where women working in manufacturing earn five times as much as those in agriculture, sweatshops have no trouble finding workers.

But let's be clear about a few things. First, export factory jobs, especially in labor-intensive industries, often are just "a ticket to slightly less impoverishment," as even economist and sweatshop defender Jagdish Bhagwati allows.

Beyond that, these jobs seldom go to those without work or to the poorest of the poor. One study by sociologist Kurt Ver Beek showed that 60% of first-time Honduran maquila workers were previously employed. Typically they were not destitute, and they were better educated than most Hondurans.

Sweatshops don't just fail to rescue people from poverty. Setting up export factories where workers have few job alternatives has actually been a recipe for serious worker abuse. In *Beyond Sweatshops*, a book arguing for the benefits of direct foreign investment in the developing world, Brookings Institution economist Theodore Moran recounts the disastrous decision of the Philippine government to build the Bataan Export Processing Zone in an isolated mountainous area to lure foreign investors with the prospect of cheap labor. With few alternatives, Filipinos took jobs in the garment factories that sprung up in the zone. The manufacturers typically paid less than the minimum wage and forced employees to work overtime in factories filled with dust and fumes. Fed up, the workers eventually mounted a series of crippling strikes. Many factories shut down and occupancy rates in the zone plummeted, as did the value of exports, which declined by more than half between 1980 and 1986.

Kristof's argument is no excuse for sweatshop abuse: that conditions are worse elsewhere does nothing to alleviate the suffering of workers in export factories. They are often denied the right to organize, subjected to unsafe working conditions and to verbal, physical, and sexual abuse, forced to work overtime, coerced into pregnancy tests and even abortions, and paid less than a living wage. It remains useful and important to combat these conditions even if alternative jobs are worse yet.

The fact that young men in Namibia find sweatshop jobs appealing testifies to how harsh conditions are for workers in Africa, not the desirability of export factory employment.

Oddly, Kristof's desire to introduce new sweatshops to sub-Saharan Africa finds no support in the African Growth and Opportunity Act (AGOA) that he praises. The Act grants sub-Saharan apparel manufacturers preferential access to U.S. markets. But shortly after its passage, U.S. Trade Representative Robert Zoellick assured the press that the AGOA would not create sweatshops in Africa because it requires protective standards for workers consistent with those set by the International Labor Organization.

Anti-Sweatshop Activism and Jobs

Kristof is convinced that the anti-sweatshop movement hurts the very workers it intends to help. His position has a certain seductive logic to it. As anyone who has suffered through introductory economics will tell you, holding everything else the same, a labor standard that forces multinational corporations and their subcontractors to boost wages should result in their hiring fewer workers.

But in practice does it? The only evidence Kristof produces is an imaginary conversation in which a boss incredulously refuses a Nike vice president's proposal to open a factory in Ethiopia paying wages of 25 cents a hour: "You're crazy! We'd be boycotted on every campus in the country."

While Kristof has an active imagination, there are some things wrong with this conversation.

First off, the anti-sweatshop movement seldom initiates boycotts. An organizer with United Students Against Sweatshops (USAS) responded on Kristof's blog: "We never call for apparel boycotts unless we are explicitly asked to by workers at a particular factory. This is, of course, exceedingly rare, because, as you so persuasively argued, people generally want to be employed." The National Labor Committee, the largest anti-sweatshop organization in the United States, takes the same position.

Moreover, when economists Ann Harrison and Jason Scorse conducted a systematic study of the effects of the anti-sweatshop movement on factory employment, they found no negative employment effect. Harrison and Scorse looked at Indonesia, where Nike was one of the targets of an energetic campaign calling for better wages and working conditions among the country's subcontractors. Their statistical analysis found that the anti-sweatshop campaign was responsible for 20% of the increase in the real wages of unskilled workers in factories exporting textiles, footwear, and apparel from 1991 to 1996. Harrison and Scorse also found that "anti-sweatshop activism did not have significant adverse effects on employment" in these sectors.

Campaigns for higher wages are unlikely to destroy jobs because, for multinationals and their subcontractors, wages make up a small portion of their overall costs. Even Kristof accepts this point, well documented by economists opposed to sweatshop labor. In Mexico's apparel industry, for instance, economists Robert Pollin, James Heintz, and Justine Burns from the Political Economy Research Institute found that doubling the pay of nonsupervisory workers would add just $1.80 to the production cost of a $100 men's sports jacket. A recent survey by the National Bureau of Economic Research found that U.S. consumers would be willing to pay $115 for the same jacket if they knew that it had not been made under sweatshop conditions.

Globalization in Sub-Saharan Africa

Kristof is right that Africa, especially sub-Saharan Africa, has lost out in the globalization process. Sub-Saharan Africa suffers from slower growth, less direct foreign investment, lower education levels, and higher poverty rates than most every other part of the world. A stunning 37 of the region's 47 countries are classified as "low-income" by the World Bank, each with a gross national income less than $825 per person. Many countries in the region bear the burdens of high external debt and a crippling HIV crisis that Kristof has made heroic efforts to bring to the world's attention.

But have multinational corporations avoided investing in sub-Saharan Africa because labor costs are too high? While labor costs in South Africa and Mauritius are high, those in the other countries of the region are modest by international standards, and quite low in some cases. Take Lesotho, the largest exporter of apparel from sub-Saharan Africa to the United States. In the country's factories that subcontract with Wal-Mart, the predominantly female workforce earns an average of just $54 a month. That's below the United Nations poverty line of $2 per day, and it includes regular forced overtime. In Madagascar, the region's third largest exporter of clothes to the United States, wages in the apparel industry are just 33 cents per hour, lower than those in China and among the lowest in the world. And at Ramatex Textile, the large Malaysian-owned textile factory in Namibia, workers only earn about $100 per month according to the Labour Resource and Research Institute in Windhoek. Most workers share their limited incomes with extended families and children, and they walk long distances to work because they can't afford better transportation.

On the other hand, recent experience shows that sub-Saharan countries with decent labor standards *can* develop strong manufacturing export sectors. In the late 1990s, Francis Teal of Oxford's Centre for the Study of African Economies compared Mauritius's successful export industries with Ghana's unsuccessful ones. Teal found that workers in Mauritius earned ten times as much as those in Ghana— $384 a month in Mauritius as opposed to $36 in Ghana. Mauritius's textile and garment industry remained competitive because its workforce was better educated and far more productive than Ghana's. Despite paying poverty wages, the Ghanaian factories floundered.

Kristof knows full well the real reason garment factories in the region are shutting down: the expiration of the Multifiber Agreement last January. The agreement, which set national export quotas for clothing and textiles, protected the garment industries in smaller countries around the world from direct competition with China. Now China and, to a lesser degree, India, are increasingly displacing other garment producers. In this new context, lower wages alone are unlikely to sustain the sub-Saharan garment industry. Industry sources report that sub-Saharan Africa suffers from several other drawbacks as an apparel producer, including relatively high utility and transportation costs and long shipping times to the United States. The region also has lower productivity and less skilled labor than Asia, and it has fewer sources of cotton yarn and higher-priced fabrics than China and India.

If Kristof is hell-bent on expanding the sub-Saharan apparel industry, he would do better to call for sub-Saharan economies to gain unrestricted access to the Quad markets—the United States, Canada, Japan, and Europe. Economists Stephen N. Karingi, Romain Perez, and Hakim Ben Hammouda estimate that the welfare gains associated with unrestricted market access could amount to $1.2 billion in sub-Saharan Africa, favoring primarily unskilled workers.

But why insist on apparel production in the first place? Namibia has sources of wealth besides a cheap labor pool for Nike's sewing machines. The *Economist* reports that Namibia is a world-class producer of two mineral products: diamonds (the country ranks seventh by value) and uranium (it ranks fifth by volume). The mining industry is the heart of Namibia's export economy and accounts for about 20% of the country's GDP. But turning the mining sector into a vehicle for national economic development would mean confronting the foreign corporations that control the diamond industry, such as the South African De Beers Corporation. That is a tougher assignment than scapegoating anti-sweatshop activists.

More and Better African Jobs

So why have multinational corporations avoided investing in sub-Saharan Africa? The answer, according to international trade economist Dani Rodrik, is "entirely due to the slow growth" of the sub-Saharan economies. Rodrik estimates that the region participates in international trade as much as can be expected given its economies' income levels, country size, and geography.

Rodrik's analysis suggests that the best thing to do for poor workers in Africa would be to lift the debt burdens on their governments and support their efforts to build functional economies. That means investing in human resources and physical infrastructure, and implementing credible macroeconomic policies that put job creation first. But these investments, as Rodrik points out, take time.

In the meantime, international policies establishing a floor for wages and safeguards for workers across the globe would do more for the young men on Windhoek's street corners than subjecting them to sweatshop abuse, because grinding poverty leaves people willing to enter into any number of desperate exchanges. And if Namibia is closing its garment factories because Chinese imports are cheaper, isn't that an argument for trying to improve labor standards in China, not lower them in sub-Saharan Africa? Abusive labor practices are rife in China's export factories, as the National Labor Committee and *BusinessWeek* have documented. Workers put in 13- to 16-hour days, seven days a week. They enjoy little to no health and safety enforcement, and their take-home pay falls below the minimum wage after the fines and deductions their employers sometimes withhold.

Spreading these abuses in sub-Saharan Africa will not empower workers there. Instead it will take advantage of the fact that they are among the most marginalized workers in the world. Debt relief, international labor standards, and public investments in education and infrastructure are surely better ways to fight African poverty than Kristof's sweatshop proposal.

Sources: Arthur MacEwan, "Ask Dr. Dollar," *Dollars & Sense*, Sept–Oct 1998; John Miller, "Why Economists Are Wrong About Sweatshops and the Antisweatshop Movement," *Challenge*, Jan–Feb 2003; R. Pollin, J. Burns, and J. Heintz, "Global Apparel Production and Sweatshop Labor: Can Raising Retail Prices Finance Living Wages?" Political Economy Research Institute, Working Paper 19, 2004; N. Kristof, "In Praise of the Maligned Sweatshop," *New York Times*, June 6, 2006; N. Kristof, "Let Them Sweat," *New York Times*, June 25, 2002; N. Kristof, "Two Cheers for Sweatshops," *New York Times*, Sept 24, 2000; N. Kristof, "Asia's Crisis Upsets Rising Effort to Confront Blight of Sweatshops," *New York Times*, June 15, 1998; A. Harrison and J. Scorse, "Improving the Conditions of Workers? Minimum Wage Legislation and Anti-Sweatshop Activism," *Calif. Management Review*, Oct 2005; Herbert Jauch, "Africa's Clothing and Textile Industry: The Case of Ramatex in Namibia," in *The Future of the Textile and Clothing Industry in Sub-Saharan Africa*, ed. H. Jauch and R. Traub-Merz (Friedrich-Ebert-Stiftung, 2006); Kurt Alan Ver Beek, "Maquiladoras: Exploitation or Emancipation? An Overview of the Situation of Maquiladora Workers in Honduras," *World Development*, 29(9), 2001; Theodore Moran, *Beyond Sweatshops: Foreign Direct Investment and Globalization in Developing Countries* (Brookings Institution Press, 2002); "Comparative Assessment of the Competitiveness of the Textile and Apparel Sector in Selected Countries," in *Textiles and Apparel: Assessment of the Competitiveness of Certain Foreign Suppliers to the United States Market*, Vol. 1, U.S. International Trade Commission, Jan 2004; S. N. Karingi, R. Perez, and H. Ben Hammouda, "Could Extended Preferences Reward Sub-Saharan Africa's Participation in the Doha Round Negotiations?," *World Economy*, 2006; Francis Teal, "Why Can Mauritius Export Manufactures and Ghana Can Not?," *The World Economy*, 22 (7), 1999; Dani Rodrik, "Trade Policy and Economic Performance in Sub-Saharan Africa," Paper prepared for the Swedish Ministry for Foreign Affairs, Nov 1997.

CONTRIBUTORS

Randy Albelda, a *Dollars & Sense* Associate, teaches economics at the University of Massachusetts-Boston.

Sylvia Allegretto is an economist at the Institute for Research on Labor and Employment at the University of California, Berkeley.

William K. Black is an associate professor of economics and law at the University of Missouri-Kansas City.

Heather Boushey is a senior economist at the Center for American Progress.

Ben Collins is a member of the *Dollars & Sense* collective and a research analyst at a socially responsible investment research firm.

Felicitas Contreras is a former Sony *maquiladora* worker and an activist with the Center for Workers and Communities (CETRAC) in Nuevo Laredo, Mexico.

James M. Cypher is professor of economics at California State University, Fresno and in the Programa de Doctorado en Estudios del Desarrollo, Universidad Autónoma de Zacatecas, Mexico. He is a *Dollars & Sense* Associate.

Ryan Dodd is a Ph.D. student in economics and a research associate at the Center for Full Employment and Price Stability, both at the University of Missouri-Kansas City.

Marie Duggan is an associate professor of economics at Keene State College in New Hampshire.

Katherine Faherty is a former *Dollars & Sense* intern.

Ellen Frank teaches economics at the University of Massachusetts-Boston and is a *Dollars & Sense* Associate.

Gerald Friedman is a professor of economics at the University of Massachusetts-Amherst.

Heidi Garrett-Peltier is a research fellow at the Political Economy Research Institute at the University of Massachusetts-Amherst.

Amy Gluckman is co-editor of *Dollars & Sense.*

Elise Gould is a staff economist at the Economic Policy Institute.

Lena Graber is a former *Dollars & Sense* intern.

William Greider is the author of many books, including Secrets of the Temple: How the Federal Reserve Runs the Country. A political journalist for 40 years, he is currently the national affairs correspondent for *The Nation* magazine.

Joel Harrison, PhD, MPH, is a consultant in epidemiology and research design. He has worked in the areas of preventive medicine, infectious diseases, medical outcomes research, and evidence-based clinical practice guidelines.

Marianne Hill, PhD, is a frequent contributor to economics journals. She also writes for the American Forum and the Mississippi Forum.

Joshua Holland is a senior writer and editor with AlterNet.org.

Paul Krugman, 2008 Nobel Prize winner, teaches economics at Princeton and is a columnist for the *New York Times.*

Arthur MacEwan, a *Dollars & Sense* Associate, is professor emeritus of economics at the University of Massachusetts-Boston.

Gretchen McClain, a former member of the *Dollars & Sense* collective, is an economic consultant.

John Miller, a *Dollars & Sense* collective member, is a professor of economics at Wheaton College.

Fred Moseley is a professor of economics at Mt. Holyoke College.

Gina Neff is the associate director of Economists Allied for Arms Reduction.

Martha A. Ojeda is the executive director of the Texas-based Coalition for Justice in the Maquiladoras.

Doug Orr teaches economics at Eastern Washington University.

Robert Pollin teaches economics and is co-director of the Political Economy Research Institute at the University of Massachusetts-Amherst. He is also a *Dollars & Sense* Associate.

Smriti Rao teaches economics at Assumption College in Worcester, Mass., and is a *Dollars & Sense* collective member.

Alejandro Reuss is an economist and historian, and a member of the *Dollars & Sense* collective.

Jonathan Rowe was a fellow at the Tomales Bay Institute and a former contributing editor at the *Washington Monthly*. He died in March 2011.

Katherine Sciacchitano is a former labor lawyer and organizer. She teaches political economy at the National Labor College.

Orlando Segura, Jr. has worked for an Atlanta-based global management consulting company that consults for private equity firms, and for a private equity firm based in Boston.

Bryan Snyder is a senior lecturer in economics at Bentley University.

Dariush Sokolov is an activist and independent journalist based in Argentina.

Bob Sutcliffe is an economist at the University of the Basque Country in Bilbao, Spain.

Alissa Thuotte is a former *Dollars & Sense* intern.

Chris Tilly, a *Dollars & Sense* Associate, is director of the Institute for Research on Labor and Employment and professor of urban planning, both at UCLA.

Yolanda Treviño is a former worker at a Sony *maquiladora* in Nuevo Laredo, Mexico.

Ramaa Vasudevan is assistant professor of economics at Colorado State University and a member of the *Dollars & Sense* collective.

Jeannette Wicks-Lim is an assistant research professor at the Political Economy Research Institute at the University of Massachusetts-Amherst.

Marty Wolfson teaches economics at the University of Notre Dame and is a former economist with the Federal Reserve Board in Washington, D.C.

9 781878 585868